The Online Teaching Survival Guide

The Online Teaching Survival Guide

Simple and Practical Pedagogical Tips

Judith V. Boettcher
Rita-Marie Conrad

Second Edition

Foreword by Pam McQuesten

JB JOSSEY-BASS™
A Wiley Brand

Published by Jossey-Bass
A Wiley Brand
One Montgomery Street, Suite 1000, San Francisco, CA 94104-4594—www.josseybass.com

Library of Congress Cataloging-in-Publication Data

Names: Boettcher, Judith V., author. | Conrad, Rita-Marie, author.
Title: The online teaching survival guide : simple and practical pedagogical
  tips / Judith V. Boettcher, Rita-Marie Conrad.
Description: Second edition. | San Francisco, CA : Jossey-Bass, 2016. |
  Includes bibliographical references and index.
Identifiers: LCCN 2016022347 (print) | LCCN 2016025298 (ebook) | ISBN
  9781119147688 (pbk.) | ISBN 9781119147695 (ePDF) | ISBN 9781119147701 (ePub)
Subjects: LCSH: Web-based instruction. | Computer-assisted instruction. |
  Distance education. | Education, Higher—Computer-assisted instruction.
Classification: LCC LB1044.87 .B64 2016 (print) | LCC LB1044.87 (ebook) | DDC
  371.33/44678—dc23
LC record available at https://lccn.loc.gov/2016022347

Cover image: ©I_Mac/iStockphoto
Cover design: Wiley

Printed in the United States of America
SECOND EDITION
PB Printing   V10010325_051619

To our families for their constant support and patience
To all faculty striving to do a great job at teaching and learning
wherever they may be

Contents

List of Tables, Figures, and Exhibits

Chapter 6

Chapter 7

Chapter 8

Chapter 9

Chapter 10

Foreword

IN THE PAST five to ten years, we've seen online modalities become the default in our daily lives, for communication, commerce, entertainment, and our interactions in many other sectors. Data on popular technologies is mind-boggling: On average, 300 hours of video are uploaded to YouTube every minute. Over 1 billion people login to Facebook each day. An estimated 73 percent of the world's population is now connected by cell phone. The world is already online.

For the most part, however, education is late to rethinking where students already are in this larger picture. Perhaps most importantly, too many education institutions—and teachers themselves—have continued to treat online learning as an afterthought, rather than devising new approaches to student learning.

Overwhelmingly, most students today are actively engaged online in many areas of their daily lives. Mobile apps and messaging, social media, and tools for deep engagement on the Internet are embedded in their routines. User-generated content has exploded across many platforms they use. All of that participation provides massive amounts of data for analytics that can, at least potentially, shape behavior and support the user experience. How can we as educators use relevant online technologies to create the same level of involvement with learning as our students have in so many other areas of their lives?

In this, the second edition of *The Online Teaching Survival Guide: Simple and Practical Pedagogical Tips*, Boettcher and Conrad have responded to the rapid expansion in online tools, technologies, and practices, with an insightful update to the original 2010 publication. This updated edition provides the support and inspiration that can situate the efforts of teachers as they define and redefine their roles and behaviors in the education of students in current online or blended environments.

The opportunity to teach online presents those special teachable moments that all good teachers should recognize. It is a chance for mindfulness, a theoretical frame that the authors note hinges on discerning the difference between one environment and another. While teaching online can be informed by the same theories of learning as face-to-face instruction, the enactment of the online experience, for both teachers and students, will—and should—differ significantly from the physical classroom.

The authors identify ten core principles and 14 best practices grounded in learning theory and brain science that empower teachers to create quality learning experiences whether in traditional face-to-face settings or anywhere along the continuum from blended to a completely online course. By grounding what they will do in the philosophies of learning as well as in light of updated best practices, those who teach online or in a blended environment will be better prepared to reimagine their work in consideration of both the affordances of technology and principles of effective learning.

The extensive overlay of practical tips throughout this book also serves much like that all-important phrase book that lets you function immediately in a foreign country until you become a more acculturated participant in the new culture, its behaviors, and its language.

As faculty consult the guide, whether they are new to online learning or seasoned veterans, and no matter the type and size of their institution, they develop a mindset for applying the core learning principles, best practices, and tips effectively to create highly relevant teaching and learning that meets the challenges of today's dynamic and shifting education landscape.

How will faculty create the best online learning designs and practices? Faculty are experts in their disciplines, but we need to help them develop a deep understanding of online pedagogy. We're still in early days on how to do this well: The evolution of our technologies and our processes for online instruction is really just beginning.

Happily, we're constantly discovering advantages to online instruction and blended models. Consider a faculty member's responsibility to prepare students to do a collaborative project. Most students have done collaborative work face-to-face, but there is still a good chance they have not had this experience in an online setting. Yet in the online model, the faculty member doesn't have to be directly "on tap" for everything the student will need, because the instructional team can more easily expand to offer additional support from other staff on the instructional side. That, along with an array of new tools—like computer-generated planning calendars, syllabi accessible through a shared database, and online course resources— creates room for the role of faculty to change. They may be inclined now to take on more work as mentor/guide/director, as well as maintaining their traditional role as the expert voice students want to hear.

Vast changes are in store for students as well, as new options for online learning help us focus on learner needs and success. Students are individuals, and we want to support that. Now we can align educational experiences with the student's goals and individual traits, and build on their desires and choices. At the same time we are growing transferable skills like problem solving along with the ability to explore, research, and take charge of one's own learning. These are the outcomes we truly want. The flexibility of online instructional programs that may incorporate elements like multiple starts, recommendation engines, and competency-based assessment strategies will allow us to promote personalization and customize the student's educational experience so that we can achieve our higher learning goals both for the student and for society. Faculty insight and invention will take all this even further. There are myriad examples: At the heart of a liberal education is gaining the ability to connect disparate concepts and insights. What if we could expand the instructional team based on what the recommendation engine learns about the student, and assist the student in building research skills to support her interests relative to the institution's overall program context?

You can return to this book again and again to discover more choices and inspiration. Be willing to innovate, and if your experiments don't work, draw again on the many ideas presented here to modify your strategies.

I'm very happy to see the 2016 revision of this valuable guide. It is much needed, given the recent, rapid evolution of online technologies and teaching practices, and it will come at just the right time for so many. If you aren't already teaching online, more likely than not you will be in the very near future. And if you do it well, it will be a new, differentiated, and rewarding educational experience for you and your students.

Pam McQuesten, Ph.D.
Vice President & CIO
Southwestern University

Preface

EVERY BOOK HAS a beginning, and the seeds of this one were planted in 2006 with a request from the leadership at Duquesne University in Pittsburgh, Pennsylvania. The administration wanted to provide more active and ongoing support to online faculty to ensure the quality of the online teaching and learning experience. The path they chose was to request coaching services tailored to the online faculty. Thus began the creation of a set of tips to guide faculty practices in online learning. Between 2006 and 2009 the library of tips grew to over 70 and feedback on the usefulness of the tips also increased. Then the idea of organizing these course delivery tips and adding tips on developing online courses in a more permanent and easily referenced format took hold. The library of tips continued to grow after the first edition and by 2015 and over 100 tips, it seemed time for a second edition of the guide.

We have been colleagues for over twenty years now, and by the time we launched this edition, we had already completed two editions of the *Faculty Guide for Moving Teaching and Learning to the Web* and the first edition of this book, *The Online Teaching Survival Guide*. We have been active participants in higher education organizations while helping faculty integrate classic and emerging research and pedagogical theory with the developing digital environments. We are well versed in the challenges that higher education faces in providing continued professional and teaching support for faculty. A book focusing on the life of a course and the tips for each phase of it seems a natural choice as a way to continue supporting the higher education community and building quality learning experiences.

Acknowledgments

It is never possible to acknowledge everyone who contributed to the ideas, structure, and book creation. But we must try. First and foremost, thanks go to past and current leadership at Duquesne University in Pittsburgh for their innovative thinking in launching coaching services for online faculty. This includes Benjamin Hodes, Boris Vilic, Dorothy Basset, and Michael Forlenza; and director of technology David McGeehan, leader of the leadership faculty Jim Wolford-Ulrich, and faculty consultant Mark Prestopnik. We also want to thank dean William Riffee and Diane Beck of the University of Florida for their support of faculty development efforts that suggested some of the tip topics.

We also want to thank the many faculty and students whose questions inspired many of the tips and who contributed their ideas and suggestions for making the tips practical, simple, and pedagogically sound. Although the tips were originally written for the faculty at Duquesne, faculty from institutions large and small, public and private, graduate and undergraduate, and degree and certificate programs alike inspired the questions. Thanks also go to our colleagues who provided feedback on early drafts of the chapters and to the reviewers for their suggestions and feedback that resulted in an improved guide overall.

Special thanks to our editors Erin Null and Alison Knowles for their encouragement and support during the sometimes arduous but always satisfying task of completing this book and keeping it focused. A special thanks also goes to friends and colleagues Pam McQuesten, vice president and CIO of Southwestern College and Mary Grush, campus technology editor extraordinaire. To Pam for her captivating Foreword to this edition and to Mary for her energizing and thoughtful help in the process of preparing this Foreword.

About the Authors

JUDITH V. BOETTCHER is a nationally known consultant and author on online and distance learning. In addition to reaching hundreds of faculty through workshops, columns, articles, and conferences, she has worked closely with faculty at Penn State University, Florida State University, the University of Florida and Duquesne University. Currently, she is founder and principal of Designing for Learning. Judith is a frequent keynoter at teaching and learning conferences, conducts faculty workshops on best practices in online learning, and consults on program and course designs for online and distance learning. Judith is the coauthor with Rita-Marie Conrad of two editions of the *Faculty Guide for Moving Teaching and Learning to the Web* (1999, 2004), published by the League for Innovation as well as the first edition of *The Online Teaching Survival Guide: Simple and Practical Pedagogical Tips* (Jossey-Bass, 2010).

Rita-Marie Conrad is an experienced online educator, award-winning author, and digital learning strategist. She is currently a senior consultant with the Center for Teaching and Learning at the University of California, Berkeley. Prior to Berkeley, Rita-Marie also served as the instructional strategist and technologist for Duke University's Institute for Educational Excellence in the School of Nursing. She has also taught online for nearly two decades. In addition to the books co-authored with Judith Boettcher, Rita-Marie wrote *Engaging the Online Learner* (Jossey-Bass, 2004 and 2011) with J. Ana Donaldson, as well as *Continuing to Engage the Online Learner* (Jossey-Bass, 2012) and *Assessing Learners Online* (Pearson, 2008) with Albert Oosterhof and Donald Ely.

Introduction

THIS BOOK IS a practical resource for faculty who want to develop expertise in teaching quality online and blended courses. Moving from a campus face-to-face environment to a rich mobile technology environment can be intimidating and challenging. Adapting lifelong teaching habits to a new environment takes time, energy, patience, and a willingness to try different teaching strategies using digital tools. While instructors who are new to online and blended teaching need many kinds of support, from technology to course design to simple encouragement, faculty often appreciate help in the form of simple, practical tips and best practices.

This book meets the needs of many online and blended faculty by providing tips for effective pedagogy and practices for technology-enriched environments. It particularly meets the needs of faculty with limited access to support for designing and teaching in technology-enabled, mobile environments. It is not unusual for faculty to be assigned to take one of their existing courses and teach it in an online or blended environment with only a few weeks' notice. They may be expected to redesign the course without any additional time, resources, or support. What happens next is often a frustrating and unsatisfactory teaching experience for faculty and a frustrating and unsatisfactory learning experience for students. This book details not only what faculty must do to offer excellent courses that are effective and satisfying for learners, but also how to do this with ease and confidence.

The set of simple, practical, theory-based instructional strategies and practices in this guide are mapped to the four phases of a course: Course Beginnings, the Early Middle, the Late Middle, and Closing Weeks. This organizational approach not only helps new faculty to survive their first teaching experience but also lays a foundation for many future successful and rewarding experiences. This guide also provides answers to all-important questions such as, "What is absolutely critical to getting ready to teach an online or blended course?" "What should I—and my learners—be doing now?" and "What should I—and my learners—be planning on doing next?"

Many resources for assisting faculty in teaching in digitally enhanced environments address the need to learn the new technologies. This book combines theory-based and practice-based pedagogy needed to achieve the effective and enjoyable teaching and learning experiences using technologies. When learning principles inform teaching practices, faculty design learning experiences that integrate rich mentor-learner relationships, encourage developing personal competencies, and create a richness of community among the learners.

Intended Audiences and Uses for This Book

This book can help faculty wherever they might be, on campuses large or small or in areas remote from their home campuses. It can be most helpful for instructors with limited access to faculty support services and for faculty with little or no experience in online instructional environments and, likely, little time to prepare for online teaching. This is a useful resource as well for faculty who are planning a gradual transition from the face-to-face-only environment to blended or fully online environments. Even faculty already experienced in technology-rich environments will find practical tips for developing more expertise in effective teaching practices. For institutions requiring online faculty to complete a course or program prior to teaching online, this guide can be used as a resource for a faculty development program and as an ongoing resource after the initial training.

Research about teaching practices for online and blended courses has been proceeding concurrently with development of voice, video, and mobile technologies and digital resources for many decades now. Online courses as we now recognize them first started being available in the early 1980s. A brief timeline is available at https://docs.moodle.org/23/en/Online_Learning_History. A review of the various and inconsistent use of terminologies in this field (Moore, Dickson-Deane, & Galyen, 2011) provides useful perspective on how to use research results and practice recommendations.

Given the relatively recent history of designing and teaching in the online and blended environments, it is not surprising that structures and processes for supporting faculty for teaching online are still evolving (Sorcinelli, Austin, Eddy, & Beach, 2006). In addition, more faculty development is critically important, as the use of adjuncts, graduate students, and other less experienced personnel as members of instructional teams is increasing and is projected to increase even more (Bennett, 2009). For example, a 2012–2013 report (Curtis & Thorton, 2013) reported that 41 percent of American university faculty are now adjunct professors. A report from EDUCAUSE offers many recommendations for faculty development, including the need for flexibility depending on faculty needs and interests and the need for modeling "best practices in assessment, active learning, new instructional delivery modes, and/or deeper learning" (Diaz et al., 2009). This book provides a means for meeting many of the faculty needs where they are.

Book Overview

Part One provides an overview of the essential online teaching and learning concepts and practices. Chapter One provides the big picture of the organization of a course, from the course beginnings to the early middle, the late middle, and closing weeks of a course. This chapter also describes how faculty and learner roles change over the term of a course as a community develops and learners assume increasing responsibility for directing their learning. Very importantly, this chapter describes a few of the more significant theories and theorists that inspired the integrated view of constructivism and social (situated) learning that inspired the tips.

Chapter Two focuses on the description of a learning experiences framework composed of the four elements of learner, mentor, knowledge, and environment. This framework is useful for guiding the design and implementation of any learning experience and simplifies the design and development process of online teaching and learning experiences. This chapter then examines each of these elements and their pedagogical role in learning experiences. This learning experiences framework encourages an analysis of learner characteristics, faculty characteristics, the knowledge and skill structures and competencies desired, and the environment—the *where, when, with whom,* and *with what resources* that determine how a learning experience happens. This chapter is organized around a set of ten core learning principles, many following from the framework. The principles draw on the disciplines of instructional design, constructivist teaching and learning theory, and practical uses of technology tools. These ten principles serve as the foundational thinking for all the tips in this book.

Chapter Three provides a set of effective online teaching practices that describe the core best practices of an effective online or blended instructor. This set of best practices was expanded from ten to fourteen for this book and is the best chapter to use to introduce faculty to the digital teaching and learning experience. Chapter Four focuses on the technologies. This is always challenging, given the pace of change, but essential to address how and when and for what purposes technology use makes sense. Almost all institutions now rely on the use of learning management systems of some type; these are now large, complex systems that combine administrative uses as well as teaching uses. This chapter describes three sets of tools for teaching in technology-enriched environments: a basic set, a basic enhanced set, and a set for contextual practice and emerging possibilities.

Chapter Five provides an overview of the themes and happenings of the four phases of a course. This is very helpful for developing a sense of the cyclical nature of any structured instructional experiences. We first describe the guiding themes for each phase, followed by the key happenings and goals for each phase. We conclude with a description of the recommended behaviors for achieving the goals.

Part Two is the core of the book: five chapters of practical theory-based tips mapped to the four stages of a course plus tips on teaching intensive accelerated courses.

Chapter Six addresses the first phase of a course, the course beginnings. This chapter provides tips for course design and getting a course site ready for students, the essential elements of an effective syllabus for the digital environment, launching the social dimensions of community, getting to know the initial cognitive states of the learners, and creating, designing, and managing discussion forums. Chapter Seven addresses the early middle phase. It provides strategies and hints for nurturing the growth of the learning community and engaging learners with the core content concepts. Chapter Eight turns to the late middle phase of the course. It focuses on hints for supporting project work and supporting learners' move to independence. Chapter Nine addresses the last phase of a course, the closing weeks. It discusses hints and strategies for projects, presentations, and ideas and practices for closing out course experiences. Chapter Ten provides tips on teaching intensive accelerated courses, describing the strategies and practices that work best with compressed and focused learning times.

Part Three looks ahead to how faculty might want to proceed after completing their initial online teaching and learning experiences. Chapter Eleven reviews some of the recommended ways for reflecting on, analyzing, and then making changes and plans for the next offering of a course. The Appendix sets out resources for continued development as a professional online instructor.

In summary, this book provides support for a four-stage structure of courses within a design framework based on traditional pedagogical principles integrated with current memory and brain research, instructional design, and online learning research. In addition, these tips describe pedagogical uses of collaborative and synchronous applications such as live classrooms, wikis, blogs, podcasts, and social media apps. The current and emerging sets of tools now make possible deeper and more lasting collaboration, communication, and synchronicity for developing learning and relationships than we have ever had before. We are indeed fortunate to have these tools and resources to support teaching and learning experiences.

How to Use This Guide

Each faculty teaching an online or blended course will find his or her own particular way of using this book. The basic design of the book is a step-by-step guide describing the tasks of preparing and teaching a course and following through the four phases of a course. It can also be used as a resource for adapting existing courses for more integration of mobile tools and as a reference resource for practical, pedagogically effective tips.

The initial chapters lay the foundation for thinking about pedagogy; the chapters with the tips provide answers to questions that make a difference in the effectiveness and satisfaction of online teaching and learning experiences. These tips help instructors survive and enjoy the challenges of teaching in what is, for many, a strange and even intimidating environment. Many faculty will find this book a useful resource as they develop expertise in teaching online, which takes time, energy, and patience.

A faculty member new to teaching online may have time only for scanning the initial chapters and then focusing on building assessment plans and creating the posts for the initial set of discussion forums. During the second cycle of a course, a faculty member may be ready to apply many more of the tips. Subsequent to those initial experiences, the faculty member should find the deeper analysis tips and issues of great interest. Most innovative practices take root over a period of these three cycles. The first cycle is survival, the second cycle is a feeling of competency, and the third integrates exploration and innovation.

This is a book that will grow in value as the instructor grows in online experience. The phased nature of the book can be a lifesaver for both faculty and the students they teach.

Part One

Core Principles and Best Practices of Online Teaching and Learning

Chapter 1

Teaching Online: The Big Picture

WHY DOESN'T THIS book jump right into the tips for effective online and blended learning? Because using the tips depends on an understanding of how people learn, or pedagogy. Pedagogy is the science of how to design and teach so that students experience lasting and significant learning. The most important missing element in the preparation of many higher education faculty is a foundation in teaching and learning principles and practices. This chapter attempts to help you build that foundation, one that will have long-lasting impact as you journey toward becoming an expert in online and blended teaching and learning.

The first part of the chapter focuses briefly on a big-picture perspective of higher education and its near-term future. This perspective will be valuable for understanding the context within which to interpret and possibly adapt the new gadgets and movements that often promise silver bullet solutions. Some of the new emerging ideas are grounded in solid pedagogical theories, holding great promise. Other ideas are simply variations of traditional practices that still need a great deal of refinement and work. Unfortunately, some of these emerging new trends are truly ineffective strategies, grounded in outmoded and ineffective teaching practices.

Secondly, this chapter provides a quick look at the most influential and meaningful learning theorists. The learning theories of these giants can truly help guide you into designing and teaching courses well. We know that most faculty have little patience or tolerance for spending time learning practices and principles not of their own professional discipline, but knowing just a little about these theorists will help build a long-lasting, effective personal philosophy of teaching. The brief sketches of the key constructivist learning theories and theorists illustrate the thinking that have shaped and inspired many of the tips, principles, and practices in this book.

Additionally, to encourage thinking about the future of digital learning environments, one of the sections highlights the major differences between a mostly digital course and a mostly face-to-face course. We then provide an overview of the four phases of a course—course beginnings, the early middle, the late middle, and the closing weeks—and the happenings, themes, and behaviors that normally occur in those course stages.

In summary, this chapter serves as one of the foundation chapters to Chapters Six through Nine, where you will find tips, suggestions, and guidelines on how to create and deliver an efficient, effective, and satisfying course.

Preparing to Teach in the Online and Blended Environments

As the demand for online programs has increased over the past several decades, deans and department chairs have often turned to their faculty and simply assigned them to online courses without much support or training. The expectation is that faculty will use whatever resources are available on campus from technology centers or teaching centers and learn to use online tools: course management systems, synchronous collaborative "live" classrooms, and working with and assessing media of all types, including audio, video, and images. Many institutions do acknowledge the need for time and for assistance, but as the tools are becoming easier to use and more widely dispersed generally, getting time and assistance to learn how to teach online—and to redesign a course for the new online environment—is increasingly difficult. These expectations reflect a belief that teaching online is not much different from teaching in a face-to-face environment. This is not the case. Teachers who are effective in the face-to-face environment can be effective as online teachers, but it is not automatic, and it does not happen overnight.

Uh-Oh. What Did I Say I Would Do?

We've all done it at one time or another: agreed to do something and then found ourselves wondering how we were going to do it. Many faculty find themselves in this state of concern and trepidation when they agree to teach a course listed as either an online or blended course. Just minutes later, they often wonder what they have agreed to do. Minutes after that, they experience confusion and even fear, feeling clueless about what the first step might be. Even experienced campus faculty feel a little nervous about teaching with the new digital tool set for the first time. Faculty may feel alone, thinking that everyone else knows exactly how to prepare and teach online, while they can't even begin to know what questions to ask or of whom.

Well, how hard can it be? A common practice for teaching in the face-to-face environment is to use the syllabus and notes from someone who has taught the course before. This often happens when a mentor hands a new instructor a large binder with his notes and says, "Go forth and teach." For a new course, the strategy is a bit more complex. The instructor must determine the goals and learning outcomes for the course learners, explicitly define the content of the course, review textbooks or resources that map to the learning outcomes, order the resources (probably a textbook), and plan the assessments and assignments and experiences so that students achieve the learning outcomes. Do the steps in preparing a course for the digital environment map to these steps, or is there more to do? This chapter answers these questions.

Is This You?

The current cadre of faculty teaching online includes the following major categories of faculty: a tenured faculty member with decades of teaching experience; an assistant professor facing the need to teach, do research, and meet tenure requirements; an untenured faculty member with a heavy teaching load; and a part-time adjunct with content expertise and a touch of teaching experience.

You have been teaching for five, ten, or even twenty to thirty years. You are an expert in your subject area, but not in technology or in the pedagogy of how to ensure learning in different environments. You wish you had someone who could walk you through the steps in preparing a course for online students. You wish you knew which of your face-to-face teaching strategies and behaviors will work well in the online environment and what new behaviors and strategies you need to learn.

Or you may be a tenure-track faculty member who must focus on meeting tenure requirements. You do not have the time or the energy to develop all the new skills associated with teaching online. You wish there was a way to reduce the amount of time and energy spent teaching, but you also would like the learners in your online courses to enjoy learning with you.

You have been assigned to teach your course online as part of a larger program degree online offering. Are there ways to teach online but within defined time and technology knowledge parameters?

Or are you an adjunct faculty member who will be teaching an occasional course online? In a weak moment, you volunteered. You are excited about the opportunity to teach a course online because you enjoy teaching; you enjoy the dialogue and relationships you build with students, but you don't enjoy the hassles of getting to campus and parking late at night. How can you—with limited time and expertise—create and develop an online course that students will love?

This book can help you achieve your goals. But to get us started—just what is a course, anyway?

The Definition of a Course

We often assume that as faculty, we know what a course is and what pedagogy, the study of teaching, is. But do we? Sometimes it is helpful to review the origins of the terms that we use every day. Particularly as we move to new learning environments, assumptions as to how we structure teaching and learning, the purposes of learning, and the resources and time for learning are worth a new look.

For example, the following definition of *pedagogy* by Basil Bernstein, a British sociologist and linguist, captures the key elements of the teaching and learning experience. It also suggests some interesting possibilities as to the means of instruction other than the faculty member, particularly in our world of learning objects, tutorials, simulations, and mobile everything. The italics are to highlight the key elements to consider.

> Pedagogy is a sustained process whereby *somebody(s) acquires new forms or develops existing forms of conduct, knowledge, practice and criteria* from *somebody(s) or something* deemed to be an appropriate provider and evaluator. Appropriate either from the point of view of the acquirer or by some other body(s) or both [Bernstein, in Daniels, 2007, p. 308].

This definition highlights the three essential elements of teaching and learning: (1) a learner, (2) someone or something appropriate who is guiding or directing the learner, and (3) the acquisition of attitude, knowledge, or practice by the learner. The element of "someone or something" leaves open the possibility of learning being guided by a "something," which might include resources such as texts, tutorials, simulations, virtual worlds, or even robots. This will be very common in our future world. It is also worth noting that pedagogy, as defined here, requires a *sustained process*, which needs a context or an environment; that is, a place of learning. In higher education, a course provides that context, and the sustained process is a series of learning experiences in a course. This leads us to the following operational definition of a course that captures the elements of learners and their experiences, mentoring and assessment by an instructor, time, and earned credit or record of some type.

> *A course is a set of learning experiences within a specified time frame, often between six and fifteen weeks, in which learners, mentored by an instructor, expect to develop a specific set of knowledge, skills, and attitudes. Learners are then assessed as to whether they achieve these goals and are assigned a grade for academic credit.*

This description of a course provides the backdrop for a course design that focuses on a learner and his or her learning outcomes.

The definition of a course varies depending on your role either as a student or instructor. From a student perspective, a course is a set of requirements and expectations, often including meetings, that results in learning new knowledge, skills, or attitudes and counts toward a degree or certificate that certifies a certain level of competency or skill. Students often get stressed regarding the time needed to complete course requirements and develop the level of competencies required to earn appropriate credit.

From an instructor's viewpoint, teaching a course requires time and expertise over a specific span of time. A common faculty concern is a question of workload: "How much time does it take to design, develop, and deliver a three-credit online course, and will I have time for my other responsibilities?" Generally a three-credit campus course represents from 20 to 25 percent of a full-time faculty's workload, or about eight to ten hours a week. Thus, after an initial investment of time, developing new habits, resourcing of tools and materials, and completing course redesign, the goal is that an online course will not require more than eight to ten hours a week of a faculty's time. Is this possible? Yes.

Some of the preparation required and the tool learning is dependent on the percentage of a course that is online and the percentage that uses the traditional face-to-face model with a digital component; that is, a blended course. The definition of whether a course is an online or blended course is addressed in the section on "Types of Online and Blended Courses." Preparation effort and time is also dependent on the teaching and assessment strategies used in achieving student outcomes in updated courses.

How Do Online and Blended Courses Differ from Traditional Courses?

The differences between traditional courses and online and blended courses are getter smaller and smaller for two reasons. First of all, technology advances have made synchronous meetings and gatherings much easier. This means that faculty and students can interact in real time, close to the interactions in a traditional classroom. Secondly, understanding about how we learn from brain and cognitive research has resulted in more active teaching and learning strategies, no matter which environment is being used.

There still are differences, and designing a fully online or blended digital environment is easier if you approach the design task with the characteristics that follow in mind. Notice that this list is organized according to the four key elements of teaching experiences—learner, faculty mentor, content, and environment, plus the assessment element.

1. **The faculty role shifts to more coaching, guiding, and mentoring.** In the newer digital, twenty-first-century environments, there is much less "telling" on the part of the instructor. Rather than preparing fifty-minute lectures, instructors prepare short concept introductions and challenging, concept-focused discussions, monitor discussions, manage student interactions, and support students' creative work. This means that an instructor assumes a predominately coaching, mentoring, guiding, and directing learning role. Constructivist theory posits—and research supports—that learners must construct their own knowledge base. It is more effective for students to follow their own lines of thinking and inquiry by talking to peers and immersing themselves in resources, rather than listening to the delivery of content from an instructor for long periods. Research is supporting this pedagogical theory, indicating that lecturing alone, without periodic questioning or discussion, is an ineffective way of learning. In most lectures, learners are too passive for much higher-level learning to occur (McKeachie, Pintrich, Lin, & Smith, 1986; Wieman, 2008; Svinicki & McKeachie, 2011). This shift means that you as an instructor do not have to invest time preparing for live lectures. Your teaching time shifts to preparing recorded or written mini-lectures and resource introductions, preparing facilitation and community building experiences, and monitoring and guiding students in their learning experiences.

2. **Learners are more active and direct more of their own learning experiences.** While course design is the major influencer of how actively

students direct their own learning, online course designs tend to place more emphasis on student choice and personal learning decisions. Learners' dialogue and activity are often higher in online courses. Learners must do more thinking, writing, doing, sharing, reflecting, collaborating, and peer reviewing as part of a community of learners. Students often come to a campus class without completing the reading assignment and expect that the instructor will enlighten them, saving them time. Learners in an online course cannot similarly hide passively. If they have not prepared and processed the content prior to posting their discussion responses, that shortcoming is evident to everyone. Learners are therefore motivated to complete the readings to interact well with the others. This change means that faculty must design discussion forums with effective catalyst discussion questions before the course begins.

have students come up with ideas for each topic / field

3. **Content resources are flexible and virtually infinite.** This content characteristic is now the same for any type of course; the main distinction for online and blended courses tends to be that students in online and blended courses likely use a greater variety and sourcing of content resources. This is probably linked to the greater self-direction described earlier. This characteristic has pros and cons for all students. Self-directed students have more freedom, although not necessarily more time, to search out and use content resources that support effective building of their own knowledge base. At the same time, the greater abundance and diversity of content media of all types probably means that students focus less and process content less deeply. Also, as content resources are now increasingly mobile, resources are accessible on smartphones, iPods, tablets, and other small, mobile devices. This means that learners have many more options than in the past as to when, where, and with whom they work on course goals. Too much flexibility can be overwhelming, so establishing a weekly rhythm with regular, rigorous milestones is essential. In addition to the usual mix of required, highly recommended, and other resources, students will be suggesting and contributing and creating additional content resources. The core learning principle on content in Chapter Two discusses this in more detail.

4. **Learning environments for gathering and dialogue are primarily asynchronous with occasional synchronous meetings.** Online and blended class discussions are primarily asynchronous—available at different times depending on the learner's physical location, rather

than synchronous in real time at the instructor's location of choice. Since online discussions are asynchronous and require learners' comments and statements, there is an expectation that learners reflect on what they have learned from the resource assignments before they come to class (online) to participate in the course activities, such as posting their reflections in the discussion areas. Online classrooms now provide opportunities for synchronous gatherings, but good online practice uses these gatherings for consensus-building discussions, question-and-answer sessions, peer critiques, collaborative project work, and presentations—anything that is less reflective work.

5. **Assessment is continuous.** Assessment in online courses should be continuous, multiphased with community input rather than episodic, concentrated, and focused on the individual-faculty dialogue (Moallem, 2005). This is pedagogically beneficial and makes cheating and other forms of fraud more difficult. Assessment in any course improves when instructors get to know learners as individuals and invest time in coaching and mentoring. In online and blended course designs students also get to know themselves as learners and also benefit from other students' learning work. Most online course assessments are not closed-book tests and thus do not require proctoring, which eliminates a whole range of potential challenges. Rather, assessment in online and blended courses generally uses a combination of low-stakes automated quizzes; frequent, regular postings in discussion forums; short papers; case study practices and analyses; and customized projects.

Although these are the primary differences in online and blended courses, all courses are still more similar than different. Also, with the growing popularity of blended courses combining online and traditional elements, all courses are actually becoming even more similar. This means that a good way of beginning your own personal growth toward being an expert online instructor is to shift your campus course to a blended environment that combines online, technology-rich activities and resources with active learning strategies that involve the class community.

Types of Online and Blended Courses

Table 1.1 describes four general types of courses. The first type of course listed is the traditional face-to-face course that still meets regularly in some shared physical space. In the first edition of this book, this type of course had virtually no digital components. We are now rapidly approaching a

TABLE 1.1

Types of Courses

Proportion of Content Delivered Online	Type of Course	Typical Description
None to 14 percent	Traditional face-to-face campus course	Course with little or no content delivered online; regular and frequent weekly synchronous gatherings; content delivered orally, with assigned meetings and readings, and assessed with proctored tests, papers, or projects. The course may use a course site for handouts and emergency communications. This type of course offering is decreasing as all courses become blended or hybrid offerings.
15 to 39 percent	Lightly blended or hybrid course; might also be called a flipped course	Course that uses technology to facilitate what is essentially a face-to-face course. Uses a course management system to post the syllabus and assignments and lectures, for example. Similar to face-to-face courses.
40 to 79 percent	Blended or hybrid	Course that blends online and face-to-face delivery. A substantial proportion of the content is delivered online; typically uses online discussions and has some, but fewer face-to face or synchronous meetings.
80 percent or more	Online/MOOCs	A course where most or all of the content is delivered online. These courses are shifting to regularly include synchronous online meetings.

Source: Adapted from Boettcher and Conrad (2004) and Allen and Seaman (2008)
Note: Percentages were changed in this edition to reflect changing practices in blended, flipped, and MOOC courses and trends.

time in which there are no traditional face-to-face courses; all courses will use some digital gathering and communications tools and spaces such as those offered by course management systems. The traditional face-to-face course now frequently uses digital communications for distributing digital course documents, such as syllabi, readings, and managing 24/7 communications. Many traditional courses now also use technology when normal campus operations need to be suspended due to severe weather or other emergencies.

The next type of course is described as "lightly blended or hybrid courses." We wish we had a better term for these courses, but this term tries to capture the fact that the percentage of time for face-to-face meetings is decreasing and that more teaching and learning experiences are designed and offered using digital tools and resources. These courses might also be described as "flipped" courses when lectures are digital and available asynchronously 24/7 and face-to-face gatherings are used for discussion and collaborative problem-solving.

The third type of course is one firmly planted in the blended or hybrid mode. In blended courses, the times that teaching and learning experiences are synchronous using shared physical spaces might be a two- to three-hour session every two or three weeks. All other teaching and learning discussion, brainstorming, and engagement are digital, often using the tools and spaces of a course management system.

The fourth category of online courses includes those courses in which most or all of the content is delivered online and that rely very heavily on asynchronous (at different times) discussions and occasional synchronous meetings.

Note that the description of the four types of courses has been shifting over the last fifteen to twenty years. We are rapidly approaching a time in which there are no traditional face-to-face courses; all courses will use some digital gathering and communications tools and spaces such as those offered by course management systems.

The table is intended to serve only as a way of talking about the type of course you will be designing. For example, the table defines an online course as having few face-to-face or synchronous meetings, but many programs are designed with frequent synchronous digital gatherings and occasional face-to-face gatherings for introductory, assessment, or celebratory meetings. Some research (Means et al., 2010) suggests that the preferred and most effective model, if possible, is a course that is a blend of asynchronous, synchronous, and face-to-face gatherings.

Given the variables of gathering times, places, and asynchronous and synchronous tools and resources that are available to support teaching and learning strategies, it might be best to categorize courses within a continuum of digital instruction featuring flipped courses, blended/hybrid courses, online courses, MOOCs (massive open online courses). As can be deduced from Table 1.1, all of the types of courses we offer contain some or all of the characteristics of digital instruction: (1) online availability of content, (2) online quizzes and assessments, (3) video and audio resources, (4) online forums, and (5) peer and self-assessment. Glance, Forsey, and Riley (2013) provide more descriptions of these elements in their article on the pedagogical foundations of MOOCs.

And speaking of MOOCs, a word is probably in order. What exactly are MOOCs, and what educational need will they be meeting in the higher education landscape? Very briefly, MOOCs accommodate large numbers of students that generally cannot be managed or accommodated in the traditional campus course model. Here are some of the major characteristics of MOOCs: they are open to anyone who registers (usually at no cost); the primary content resource is videos of professors delivering lectures; forums for students to discuss ideas with others are available; little or no self-assessment or certification. If there is a certification badge of some sort, there are usually costs associated with that assessment process. It is very early in the evolution of MOOCs, and just how they will evolve is uncertain, but it is likely they will successfully play a twofold role in higher education. First, they may help to satisfy the need for continuing lifelong professional development. Second, they may provide a path to higher learning for those who cannot afford to pay and who may be able to prove competency without certification. Another potential benefit may be that innovations discovered for MOOCs might inform traditional campus models.

The tips offered later in this book can be applied or adapted to any type of online or blended course, including MOOCs.

The Four Stages of a Course

Now that we have discussed how courses differ, let's consider how they are the same. Each course has a minimum of four distinct stages: Course Beginnings, Early Middle, Late Middle, and Wrap Up. This is reflected in how the four elements of learner, faculty-mentor, content, and environment interact and flow within teaching and learning experiences. Chapter Five describes in detail what is happening in each of these stages and delves more deeply into the themes, behaviors, and tools for accomplishing the goals of each of these stages.

Learning Theories and Theorists

The principles, practices, and tips in this book are grounded in learning theory, principles, and research. More specifically, the tips in this book build extensively on constructivism, the philosophy that learners actively construct and create their personalized knowledge structures from the interaction of three inputs: what they already know; what they pay attention to in their environment, including language, people, and images; and what they process deeply. The constructivism philosophy is the foundation of how we view learning and how our minds work. Closely related to constructivism is the social theory of learning, which emphasizes the role of the context or environment of learning.

Figure 1.1 presents a few of the more significant theories and theorists that inspired this integrated view of constructivism and social (situated) learning. These sketches of key learning theorists are in no particular order other than generally chronological. We have also attempted to show relative relationships and linkages among these theorists who are so important to the tips. There are many other truly significant theorists and theories, but all cannot be profiled in this chapter. However, many of these others will be mentioned in the principles, practices, and tips.

For more information on the learning theorists mentioned here and any others that are not, the Theories into Practice database developed by Greg Kearsley and now integrated into www.instructionaldesign.org is an excellent resource. This database contains descriptions of over 50 theories relevant to human learning and instruction, descriptions of learning concepts, and important domains of learning.

Lev Vygotsky (1896–1934): Theory of Social Development

Vygotsky is a twentieth-century Russian psychologist, linguist, and philosopher whose work became accessible in the mid-1960s when it was translated into English. His theory is usually referred to as a social development theory because a major theme in his theoretical framework is that social interaction plays an essential role in the development of cognition. His work also included significant investigations into the processes of concept acquisition that led to a study of problem-solving strategies. Perhaps his best-known concept is the zone of proximal development (ZPD), which defines for each individual the state of readiness for learning. The formal definition of the zone is "the distance between the actual development level as determined by independent problem solving and the level of potential development as determined through problem solving under adult guidance or in collaboration with more capable peers" (Vygotsky, 1978, p. 86). It is always interesting to think about the similarities of Vygotsky's thinking with his contemporaries, the Swiss psychologist Jean Piaget and John Dewey, the giant of American psychological thought (whose profiles follow). The writings of van der Veer (1996) suggest that Vygotsky and Piaget definitely were in contact with each other, but that language and geography barriers prevented regular contact to resolve differing perspectives. What is worth focusing on, we believe, are their shared core concepts of the staging of learning and the importance of context in learning.

FIGURE 1.1

Influential Learning Theorists

LEV VYGOTSKY (1896–1934)
1. Theory of Social Development – encourages small teams and groups.
2. Zone of Proximal Development – Small window of readiness and opportunity suggests choices and personalization, and close monitoring.

JOHN DEWEY (1859–1952)
1. Experiential Learning – characterized by interaction and continuity. Encourages hands-on collaborative activities and projects.
2. Development of reflective, creative, responsible thought as primary aim of education.

JEAN PIAGET (1896–1980)
1. Stage theory of child development – how reasoning abilities develop.
2. Learning occurs with two processes: assimilation and accommodation – requires active use of content and time for processing.

WHAT THEY SHARE
1. Emphasis on developing critical reasoning skills
2. Focus on engaging with content and influence of context

JOHN SEELY BROWN (1940 -)
1. Theory of cognitive apprenticeship – promotes hands-on doing and problem-solving.
2. Concept of collective social mind – promotes community and collaborative work.

JEROME BRUNER (1915 -)
1. Learning as an active process, adding to learner's existing knowledge – promotes discovery and problem-solving.
2. Concept of scaffolding, designing experiences to match learner's state of readiness – encourages options and personalization, relationship with learners.

WHAT THEY SHARE
1. Emphasis on learner discovery, active engagement with content and others

ALBERT BANDURA (1925 -)
1. Social learning theory – we learn by observing others. Suggests use of models, case studies, examples.
2. Self-efficacy – belief in oneself to take appropriate actions. Suggests learning as attitudinal as well as cognitive growth.

JEAN LAVE (1939 -)
1. Social learning theory – Learning is a *cognitive* process that takes place in a social context. Learning includes elements of observation, extraction of ideas, and decision-making. Suggests need for observation, reflection, and decision-making.

ROGER SCHANK (1946 -)
1. Schema Theory – scripts, plans, mental models to describe knowledge structure. Suggests use of context, patterns, relationships.
2. Curriculum Design – Promotes combining learning by doing experiences with mentoring.

K. ANDERS ERICSSON (1947 -)
1. Need for deliberate practice to acquire expertise. Argues for monitored practice in varied and multiple contexts to develop expertise. Suggests use of examples with evaluative activities.

WHAT THEY SHARE
1. Learning is cognitive activity within a social context observing modeling behaviors

DANIEL GOLEMAN (1947 -)
1. Theory of emotional intelligence. Emotional intelligence can mean ability to perceive and regulate emotions in self and others. Argues to include dimensions of feeling and attitude in learning situations.

ELLEN LANGER (1947 -)
1. Mindful Learning – Learning requires mindful engagement with content. Noticing distinctions, the novel within the familiar, and the familiar within the novel. Argues for thoughtful reflections.

John Dewey (1859–1952): Experiential Learning

John Dewey, an American philosopher, psychologist, and educational reformer, was a major proponent of experiential learning in the first half of the twentieth century. He foresaw an active and collaborative student experience that, almost a hundred years later, we finally have the tools and shared collective acceptance to implement. Dewey emphasized the unique and individualized nature of interaction in the learning experience. He believed, as do many constructivist theorists, that learners construct new knowledge based on previous knowledge and that experiences are unique to each learner. Dewey promoted the active participation of the learner in the learning environment, and he championed the role of an instructor as a facilitator or mentor.

Dewey focused his ideas on developing what he believed to be the aims of education: the development of reflective, creative, responsible thought. In his 1933 treatise, *How We Think*, Dewey said, "We state emphatically that, upon its intellectual side, education consists of the formation of wide-awake, careful, thorough habits of thinking" (p. 78). This single sentence, which captures the essence of Dewey's thinking, sets forth one of the ultimate goals of education. Another key concept in Dewey's work is that interaction and continuity are the two primary characteristics of effective teaching and learning experiences. The characteristic of interaction reinforces the importance of dialogue and communication and engagement in learning; the characteristic of continuity reinforces the perspective that the individual learner must be viewed as the key design element.

Jean Piaget (1896–1980): Theory of Genetic Epistemology or Origins of Thinking

A twentieth-century Swiss psychologist and natural scientist, Piaget is best known for his stage theory of child development, beginning with the sensorimotor stage (0 to 2 years), preoperational thinking (3 to 7 years), concrete operations (8 to 11 years), culminating in abstract thinking in the formal operations stage (ages 12 to 15 years). Piaget called his general theoretical framework "genetic epistemology" because he was primarily interested in how cognitive knowledge, including moral reasoning, develops in humans. In his view, cognitive development consists of a constant effort to adapt to the environment in terms of the processes of assimilation (adding information to existing knowledge structure) and accommodation (modifying a knowledge structure to accommodate new information). In this sense, Piaget's theory is similar in nature to the constructivist perspectives of Vygotsky and Jerome Bruner (whose profile follows), including an emphasis on context and environment. Another concept central to Piaget's theory is cognitive structures, which he defined as patterns of physical or mental action that underlie specific acts of intelligence and correspond to stages of child development. These cognitive structures are similar to the schemas of Roger Schank and the concepts of mental models (Schank & Abelson, 1977). Piaget's theories have been used extensively in the development of logic and math programs, providing a planned sequence or spiraling of instruction, from simple to more complex. Seymour Papert, the MIT mathematician who developed the Logo programming language for children, worked with Piaget in the 1950s and 1960s. Papert expanded on Piaget's thinking with a focus on how children build knowledge structures through a progressive internalization of actions, or making things.

Jerome Bruner (1915–): Constructivism

Jerome Bruner is an American educational psychologist who is a senior research fellow at the New York University School of Law. As a constructivist, Bruner's work incorporates strong support for discovery learning. He believes that mastery of the fundamental ideas of a field involves not only the grasping of general principles, but also the development of an attitude toward learning and inquiry, toward guessing and hunches, toward the possibility of solving problems on one's own (Bruner, 1963). As a constructivist, Bruner emphasizes the active process of discovery and trial and error through which a student can uncover the interrelationships of concepts and ideas (Clabaugh, 2009).

One of Bruner's best-known statements and one of my favorites is that any subject can be taught to any child at any stage of development if it is presented in the proper manner (Bruner, 1963).

Another oft-used quote is about the usefulness of knowledge. Bruner (1963) stated, "The first object of any act of learning, over and beyond the pleasure it may give, is that it should serve us in the future. Learning should not only take us somewhere; it should allow us later to go further more easily" (p. 17). The focus of this thought is twofold. First, Bruner emphasizes that learning should be purposeful; for example, developing skills to serve us in the future. Second, every time we learn something, we add links or nodes to a cognitive structure on which we can build and link to later; as we grow these connections and nodes, we are able to learn more and to learn faster. In this view, the more one knows, the more one can know, and know quickly. Also attributed to Bruner is the concept of scaffolding. He observes that it takes a very skilled teacher to structure a learning experience so that the learner discovers new knowledge on his own. This means "scaffolding the task in such a way that assures that only those parts of the task within the child's reach are left unresolved, and knowing what elements of a solution the child will recognize though he cannot yet perform them" (p. xiv of 1977 edition of *The Process of Education*). This statement reiterates the importance of design for successful learning experiences.

Bruner's belief can be summarized as follows: "Learning is an active process in which learners construct new ideas or concepts based on current/past knowledge." http://www.instructionaldesign.org/theories/constructivist.html

John Seely Brown (1940–): Cognitive Apprenticeship

John Seely Brown is best known as the chief scientist at the Xerox Corporation; he directed the company's Palo Alto Research Center, known as PARC, for twelve years, up to 2000. He is now a visiting scholar and advisor to the provost at the University of Southern California and independent cochairman of Deloitte Center for the Edge. As early as 1991, in a *Harvard Business Review* article, Brown envisioned how "advanced multimedia information systems" would make it possible to plug into a "collective social mind" (Brown, 1997), laying the groundwork for our thinking about communities in online learning. Brown explored similar ideas about "learning communities capable of generating, sharing, and deploying highly esoteric knowledge" (p. 127) in *The Social Life of Information*, the book he coauthored with University of California, Berkeley researcher Paul Duguid in 2000. His work on cognitive apprenticeships (Brown, Collins, & Duguid, 1989; Collins, Brown, & Holum, 1991) and learning environments (Brown, 2006) examine how technologies can support problem solving and hands-on learning. A recent article explores how activities within virtual worlds create a "sense of shared space and co-presence which make real-time coordination and interaction not only possible, but a necessary part of the world" (Thomas & Brown, 2009, p. 37). Brown's latest initiative focuses on the maker movement, which leverages technology and the world economy for making anything and everything. What is a maker? "Broadly, a maker is someone who derives identity and meaning from the act of creation" (Hagel, Brown, & Kulasooriya, 2014, p. 3).

Our students are maturing in the midst of this wave of making; if we can find ways to incorporate "making" into our courses, students will engage with energy and enthusiasm.

Roger Schank (1946–): Schema Theory

Roger Schank was one of the influential early contributors to artificial intelligence and cognitive psychology in the 1970s and 1980s and continues as a major contributor to learning theory and the building of virtual learning environments. His concepts of case-based reasoning and dynamic memory were significant contributions to these fields. The central focus of Schank's work has been the structure of knowledge, especially in the context of language understanding. He is well known for his work on schema theory—the concepts of scripts, plans, and themes to handle story-level understanding (Schank & Abelson, 1977). Schema theory is similar to the concept of mental models; it is another way of describing knowledge structures and a way of predicting and inferring information from incomplete information. His work in this area extended into developing programs to enable computers to understand and predict what might be coming next.

Schank is now working to design and implement learning-by-doing, story-centered curricula in schools, universities, and corporations. Why is Schank's work important to learning tips? His work encourages categorizing content knowledge into patterns, relationships, and dependencies. If we identify patterns and relationships, our knowledge structures will be more useful and memorable, and we will be able to see more quickly and clearly the application of knowledge in new situations.

Albert Bandura (1925–): Social Learning Theory

Albert Bandura is best known as the psychologist responsible for learning theories that transition behaviorism and observational learning, also referred to as social learning theory. While behaviorism depends on learning theories of reward and punishment, Bandura researched the power of observational learning, that children could learn from simple observation of others. He is also known for the construct of self-efficacy, the belief in oneself to be able to take appropriate actions.

What does his work contribute to learning design? Observational learning theory suggests the use of models, case studies, examples, and videos of behaviors and actions. The concept of self-efficacy suggests that learning is multidimensional—not just cognitive, but also attitudinal—foreshadowing the emotional intelligence focus of Daniel Goleman (see later profile).

Jean Lave (1939–): Situated Learning Theory

Jean Lave, University of California, Berkeley, is a social anthropologist whose learning theories emphasize the role of the context in which learning occurs. Her situated learning theory suggests that classroom activities that are abstract and lack context are not effective. Situated learning theory is similar to social learning theory, which describes learning as a cognitive process that takes place in a social context. Her theories may go to the extreme of the emphasis on social learning, as she says, "participation in everyday life may be thought of as the process of changing understanding in practice, that is, as learning" (Lave, 2009, p. 201).

What does her work contribute to learning design? Situated learning theory includes elements of observation, extraction of ideas, decision-making, and reflection. This view of learning sees social interaction as a critical component encouraging learners to become a community of learners espousing certain beliefs and behaviors.

K. Anders Ericsson (1946–): Expert Performance Theory

K. Anders Ericsson is a Swedish psychologist widely recognized for his theoretical and experimental research on expertise. One of his most well-known contributions is the framework for development of expertise and the need for "deliberate practice" (Ericsson, 2000). Deliberate practice is more than simply practicing a skill over and over. In Ericsson's words, deliberate practice "entails considerable, specific, and sustained efforts to do something you can't do well—or even at all. Deliberate practice involves two kinds of learning: improving the skills you already have and extending the reach and range of your skills. This type of practice usually requires a well-informed coach not only to guide you through deliberate practice, but also to help you learn to coach yourself" (Ericsson, Prietula, & Cokely, 2007, p. 2).

What does this mean for designing learning? It suggests the need for designing monitored practice into varied and multiple contexts to develop expertise. It also suggests the use of many examples across and within a discipline to provide a range of experiences with evaluative activities.

Ellen Langer (1947–): Theory of Mindful Learning

Ellen Langer, a professor of psychology at Harvard, has applied the concept of mindfulness to any situation requiring decision-making. She defines mindfulness as having three characteristics: continually creating new categories, openness to new information, and an implicit awareness of more than one perspective (Langer, 1997, p. 4). Mindfulness might be a close relation to critical thinking, encouraging teaching skills and facts set within multiple different contexts.

What does this mean for designing learning? Mindful learning means engaging thoughtfully with the content and questioning positions, values, and decisions. One strategy to use is to encourage noticing the novel within the familiar, and the familiar within the novel. The value of mindfulness also argues for making time for thoughtful and questioning reflections.

Daniel Goleman (1947–): Theory of Emotional Intelligence

Daniel Goleman is the author of a 1995 book, *Emotional Intelligence: Why It Can Matter More Than IQ*, that caused a rethinking of the skills and traits needed for effective leadership and management. Goleman's research found that the qualities usually associated with effective leadership—such as intelligence, toughness, determination, and vision—were insufficient. Emotional intelligence, which includes self-awareness, self-regulation, motivation, empathy, and social skill, is also needed.

What does this mean for designing learning? It suggests that we include dimensions of feeling and attitude in learning experiences. The buzz around this "new" topic encourages a look back to the 1973 affective domain work of Krathwohl, Bloom, and Masia, corresponding to the much more familiar Bloom's cognitive taxonomy.

Other Theorists and Influencers

As previously mentioned, many other significant researchers, theorists, and thinkers have influenced the theory and practices behind the tips in this book. You will come to know many of them in the context of the tips. Before leaving the topic of key influencers, however, we want to call attention to the 2000 work of Bransford, Brown, and Cocking and the Committee on Developments in the Science of Learning that resulted in the book, *How People Learn: Brain, Mind, Experience, and School*.

This committee reviewed decades of learning research and identified five themes that are changing our views on the theory of learning:

- Memory and the structure of knowledge
- Problem solving and reasoning
- Early foundations of learning, attempting to answer, "Who knows what, and when?"
- Metacognitive processes and self-regulatory learning processes
- Cultural experience and community participation

These five topics are active research areas that will continue to influence teaching and learning in all environments in the future, and they echo throughout this book.

Summary—and What's Next

This chapter introduced the key concepts in getting started with online and blended teaching and learning. The big picture of the four stages of a course—course beginnings, early middle, late middle, and closing weeks—helps you envision your course as a series of learning experiences that provide the context for you and your learners to develop a community for learning and developing skills.

With the constructivist landscape in place, the next two chapters describe ten core learning principles and ten—plus four—best practices to guide you as you develop new mental models, habits, and skills for teaching in online and blended environments.

Chapter Two discusses a set of ten core learning principles that capture most of the key principles suggested by constructivist theories and related instructional design approaches. Chapter Three is a summary of a set of best practices for teaching online. The first edition had only ten best practices. It has been expanded to ten plus four to address key recommended practices in design and assessment.

Self-Directed Exercise—Application

Which one to three of the top theorists or theories resonate with you?

Chapter 2

Pedagogical Principles for Effective Teaching and Learning: Ten Core Learning Principles

THE GOAL OF this chapter is for you to develop a mindset based on the science and theory of teaching and learning principles. This mindset means you will continually be asking questions such as these:

- What are some truths about learning that I want to acknowledge and build into the design of my course?

- What kinds of activities make a difference in my students' learning?

- How should I structure learning activities so that my learners acquire certain skills and behaviors and develop expertise?

- What types of learning experiences encourage students to work together so they can learn the content in the course, experience the value of multiple perspectives, and develop lasting relationships?

While we have an abundance of research on how people learn, distilling that research into a usable and ready set of learning principles has proven challenging. In recent years various sets of learning principles have been proposed, and they have been very helpful. We'll have more on these later in the book.

Working with faculty in the emerging online, blended and hybrid environments, we wanted a set of learning principles that more specifically addressed these environments and their digital tools. The set of learning principles in this chapter is our response, enriched through many conversations with colleagues. This particular set of learning principles strives to integrate these three threads of teaching and learning knowledge: (1) instructional design, (2) learning theory, and (3) learning research. The faculty we have worked with over the years have generally regarded these principles as clear, concise, and usable. Various versions have also been widely distributed among faculty centers.

To achieve this mindset, this chapter provides an overview of the theoretical foundations of pedagogy—the science of teaching and learning. While it is common to be impatient with theory, this knowledge base informs all the design practices and practical tips for teaching in this book. You will also want theory and science to guide the teaching designs you create to fit your discipline and course needs.

It is generally assumed that faculty know the fundamentals of teaching and learning theory. Unfortunately, this is not necessarily so. An instructor's preparation for teaching generally focuses on becoming an expert in a discipline's content and practices, not in communicating and developing that expertise in others. The theory and practice of teaching and learning is often an afterthought and learned somewhat haphazardly through years of practice. As Derek Bok, a former president of Harvard University, has noted, faculty are "rarely exposed to research on teaching during graduate school" (2005).

This cultural practice is starting to change due in large part to the Scholarship of Teaching and Learning (SoTL) movement (2004 to present) that encourages scholarly inquiry into learning. As a discipline, we have centuries of research on how people learn, but there remains a significant gap between what we know from the research and theory and our general teaching design and practices.

The net result is that most of us gravitate to teach the way we have been taught. This has not been a serious problem in the past, but the proliferation of new technologies, environments, devices, and students whose attentions are focused on digital screens are creating new challenges. In many cases, faculty today have not experienced learning in hybrid, blended, or online courses and therefore have few examples on which to model their own technology-enhanced teaching. Rather than listening passively to lectures, students want to be doing and creating. Fortunately, doing and creating are exactly the kinds of learning activities that support lasting growth and learning. So we may be on a good path.

Supporting learning growth means we need to design more active learning strategies into course designs and experiences. The challenge is how to transition to these new active learning strategies. A related challenge is how to support instructors to become knowledgeable in the principles of effective teaching and learning designs and practices. We hope this book can help in meeting this challenge.

Studying the science of teaching and learning processes is best done as a lifelong pursuit. For instructors who have the time and inclination to pursue the study of pedagogy, this chapter provides a good foundation and useful starting point for designing effective and efficient learning experiences. For instructors who have the time for only a simple set of basic learning principles, this chapter provides a solid foundation and vocabulary for a deeper understanding of the best practices and tips in this book.

Background of the Ten Core Learning Principles

Research programs launched with the Decade of the Brain initiative (1990–2000) have greatly enriched our understanding of the brain, mind, and consciousness. In work at a lab at the University of California, San Francisco (UCSF) and other labs, neuroscientists are working on tools that let us see how our brains work in real time responding to visual and motor stimuli (Gazzaley, 2014).

A key finding from this brain research is that our brains keep growing and changing throughout our lives, creating new physical neurons and new connections, in response to changing conditions and stimuli. Some research suggests that the actual structure of the brain is changed by meditation practice. This characteristic of the brain to adapt is called neuroplasticity and is defined as the "ability of the brain to respond to stimuli and stresses by remodeling its structure, function and connections" (Brain and Behavior Research Foundation, 2013, p. 28). In other words, research has affirmed that, given the right conditions, our brains are able to create new physical structures and connections.

The abundance of new understandings of the brain combined with the ready availability of wearable, mobile communication devices is stimulating a rethinking of our traditional approaches to teaching and learning experiences. Insights into how the brain works (Bransford, Brown, & Cocking, 2000; Damasio, 1999; Kandel, 2006; Ramachandran, 2011; Schacter, 2001) are deepening our appreciation and interpretation of core learning principles. These understandings provide new insights as to how we design and manage modern learning experiences and develop learning communities (Bransford, Brown, & Cocking, 2000; Brown, 2006; Clark & Meyer, 2011; Garrison & Vaughan, 2008; Swan & Ice, 2010; Vaughan, Cleveland-Innes, & Garrison, 2013).

That's the good news. The flip side of all this research is that, while the avalanche of research findings is exciting and breathtaking, deriving a simple, workable set of principles from the research can be daunting. It is our hope that this chapter provides a simple, practical starting set of core learning principles that you can use to design and teach your course.

The principles in this chapter have been particularly inspired by the work of leading educational theorists of the twentieth century as described in Chapter One. This set of principles is obviously not the last word on core learning principles, but we have found them useful in our many years of work with faculty. We believe these principles capture the core of constructivist learning theories and serve as a guide to designing, creating, and managing effective teaching and learning experiences. Each principle is defined, its source identified, and examples provided showing how the principle can guide the design of teaching and learning processes in online environments.

Ten Core Learning Principles

Table 2.1 lists a set of ten core learning principles that can guide you in the design, creation, and teaching of any structured learning experience.

TABLE 2.1

Ten Core Learning Principles

Principle	Description
Principle 1	Every structured learning experience has four elements, with the learner at the center.
Principle 2	Learners bring their own personalized and customized knowledge, skills, and attitudes to the experience.
Principle 3	Faculty mentors are the directors of the learning experience.
Principle 4	All learners do not need to learn all course content; all learners do need to learn the core concepts.
Principle 5	Every learning experience includes the environment or context in which the learner interacts.
Principle 6	Every learner has a zone of proximal development that defines the space that a learner is ready to develop into useful knowledge.
Principle 7	Concepts are not words but organized and interconnected knowledge clusters.
Principle 8	Different instruction is required for different learning outcomes.
Principle 9	Everything else being equal, more time on task equals more learning.
Principle 10	We shape our tools, and our tools shape us.

Principle 1: Every Structured Learning Experience Has Four Elements, with the Learner at the Center

The first core learning principle asserts that all structured learning experiences are created by the presence and interaction of four elements:

- The learner who is at the center of the teaching and learning process

- The faculty mentor who directs, supports, and assesses the learner

- The content knowledge, skills, and perspectives that the learner is to develop and acquire

- The environment or context within which the learner is experiencing the learning event

This principle is illustrated in the learning experiences framework shown in Figure 2.1. Learning experiences designed with this framework feature the *learner* "on stage" actively doing and creating under the direction of the *mentor* using learning resources guiding the acquisition of *knowledge, skills, and perspective* within an *environment* of a particular time and place.

This framework simplifies the process of designing and managing instructional experiences. Instructors can use the four elements as a checklist. Who is the learner and what are they hoping to learn to do? How can I

FIGURE 2.1

Learning Experience Framework

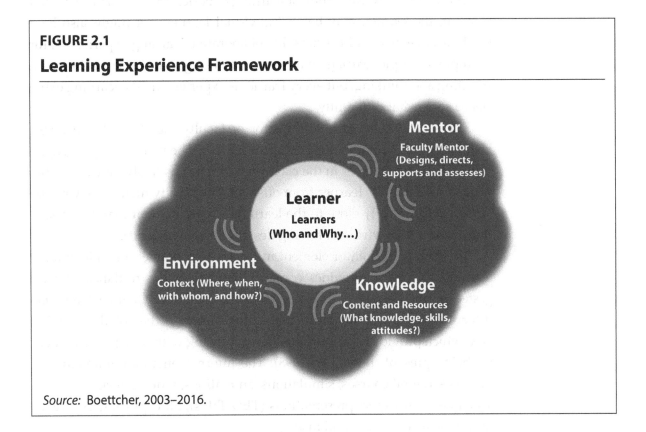

Source: Boettcher, 2003–2016.

as their mentor guide them? What tools or resources can help make this happen? Where and when and possibly with whom will the learner be learning?

This framework captures a complex set of interactions among these four elements and the roles those elements play in a learning experience. Instructional designers and instructors can use this framework to analyze learning experiences, focusing on (1) learner and faculty behaviors and actions; (2) the knowledge, skill, or attitudes being developed; and (3) the where, when, with whom, and with what resources a learning experience is occurring.

We find it helpful to think of a course as comprising a set of 60 to 100 different learning experiences (Boettcher, 2000). To simplify design, instructors often use a set of five to seven templates for different learning experiences. For example, one template might be for a reading or listening assignment followed by a journal entry or forum posting. Another template might be for a discussion forum assignment to analyze a problem and suggest strategies for addressing the problem. Other templates might be for peer review or collaborating experiences, research experiences, or other targeted writing and creating tasks.

There are many variations of learning experiences, of course. The first element, the learner, may be an individual learner, but might also be a small or large group of learners. In collaborative learning experiences, for example, multiple learners may well be "on stage" at the same time contributing and thinking, but every learner is experiencing the learning experience somewhat differently.

The second element is the mentor or faculty member who manages instruction and provides support to the learner. The mentor may be physically present on stage or in the classroom, but just as likely may be "in the wings" directing the learner from offstage. The faculty mentor may not be anywhere physically close to the learning experience but may be present only implicitly by virtue of having designed the experience.

The faculty or mentor element may also be contained in an inanimate learning object that provides content, instructions, or guidance, as suggested by the definition of pedagogy by Bernstein in Chapter One. One futuristic example of an inanimate faculty element is the holodeck on *Star Trek*, which provides an environment for learning without a physical mentor being present (Boettcher, 1998). The Internet offers an abundance of podcasts, digital courses, simulations, animations, video tutorials (such as YouTube), and expert presentations (TED Talks), all capturing experts as they explain, expound, and inspire.

In such cases, the mentor is present by virtue of having selected or created the learning resource and provided instructions for the use of the object. Note that *mentor* is our preferred term for the instructor or faculty member who is directing the students' learning experiences.

The third element in the learning experiences framework is the knowledge, the content, or the skill that is the focus of the learning experience. In instructional design terms, the knowledge component is the answer to the question, "What is the knowledge, what is the skill, and what is the attitude that the learning experience is intended to facilitate in each of the students?" In a physiology course, for example, the knowledge or skill may involve student proficiency in identifying the various parts of our muscular and cardiovascular systems and the mechanisms of actions for the systems. In a psychology course, the knowledge may be understanding how our bodies react to stress and how to regulate those reactions, and the skill might be interpreting an interview with a person under stress. In an engineering design course the knowledge might be thinking holistically about the life cycle of the construction elements of a project.

The fourth element is that of the environment. Mobile and wearable communications devices now make it possible to learn anytime, anywhere, and any while, as learners are exercising, driving, cooking, riding the subway, or even just daydreaming.

The environment element answers the question: "When will the learning experience take place, with whom, where, and with what resources?" Learners taking online courses need to be particularly disciplined about deciding just when and where they are going to be doing their learning.

For example, the desired outcome of an instructional experience in geology might be for a learner to accurately identify the different types of sedimentary rocks, the locations where they might be found, and the processes required to find them. This might be done in a virtual environment where the student can examine a rock in three dimensions or the student may be tasked to collect real specimens in the field, photograph them, and contribute these specimens and photographs to a collection using mobile handheld photography technology. Another example of a desired outcome might be to study the effects of fracking and the potential link to increased earthquake activity. If feasible, learners might be able to visit a fracking site. Another example of the environment element might be more familiar, such as a group of students gathering in a study group, in either the same physical space or a virtual space.

Whatever the scenario, the core of this first principle is that the learner is at the center of his or her individual learning experience. The learner is actively doing something, guided in the experience as designed by the mentor, accessing whatever resources might be needed, and acquiring useful knowledge, skill, or perspectives from the experience within a particular and specific context. Learning happens within our heads as we construct and grow neurons and strengthen connections between neurons, aided by resources, experiences, and active doing. Learning happens as we interact with our environment. This fact echoes Vygotsky's emphasis on learning as a sociocultural activity. This is also the essence of John Seely Brown's theory of situated cognition. It affirms the experiential theories of John Dewey and Jean Piaget, and the constructivist theories of Jerome Bruner, David Ausubel, and Roger Schank.

Principle 2: Learners Bring Their Own Personalized and Customized Knowledge, Skills, and Attitudes to the Learning Experience

This core learning principle focuses on the learner as an individual with a unique and personalized set of knowledge, skills, and attitudes. The goal of any learning experience is for learners to grow from where they are. This means growing the neurons, connections, and structures in their brains. It means developing knowledge representations that can be accessed quickly and meaningfully.

Every course has a set of core concepts and knowledge. If learners and mentors work well together, the learners create and integrate those core concepts into their unique knowledge structures. Each learner's brain is as individualized and singular as his or her fingerprints and DNA. Our learners' knowledge structures thus become even more individualized over time, resulting from the combinations of personal DNA, interactions with life experiences and responses to those experiences. Learners may share learning and life experiences, but how these experiences are encoded, linked, and connected in their individual brains is distinctive. Thus it is impossible to develop standardized brains in our learners. Our goals must be to develop richly differentiated, creative brains with overlapping common human understandings, experiences, and feelings.

When designing learning experiences, instructors are generally working with broad assumptions and expectations of what their students know and what they want to know. Getting to know learners means getting to know the existing knowledge structure and composition of their brains. Some students will come to the course experience with a brain replete with intricate patterns of knowledge about an existing field of study, say, art, biology, electricity, and communications. Call this a "jungle" brain, as it is richly embellished, with almost infinite connections and relationships (Boettcher, 2005, 2007). Other students may come to the course experience with a brain populated by isolated, unrelated bits and pieces of information resembling scraggly weeds, scrawny bushes, or a sparse, bare tundra on this topic (Kandel, 2006; Boettcher, 2007).

The kind of learning experiences we design will depend on how well developed our students' networks of neurons and dendrites are and how detailed and rich are the patterns and images in their brains. Learners who are encountering not just one concept but an overwhelming number of new terms and concepts have to work hard to make sense of this new information by attaching the incoming knowledge to existing nodes and patterns. This requires effort, time, and practice.

A classic educational principle asserts, "Build on what students already know" (Dewey, 1938; Bruner, 1963). Memory research is confirming the biology behind this principle by demonstrating the impact of students' existing mental models on incoming knowledge (Damasio, 1999). Damasio explains that the process of learning might be described as our brain's working to find receptor nodes for bits of new information and then arranging that information into a useful mental model. A simple rule of thumb can follow from this: "The more you know, the more you can know" (Bransford, Brown, & Cocking, 2000; Brown, Roediger, & McDaniel, 2014). The more concepts, the more patterns, and the more linkages within knowledge representations, the more receptor nodes exist. By knowing what students know, instructors can design experiences to ensure an accurate knowledge structure and then support the growth of that structure. Reports from the National Research Council (Donovan, Bransford, & Pellegrino, 1999; Bransford, Brown, & Cocking, 2000) emphasize the importance of two aspects of a student's knowledge: (1) finding out what students know and (2) finding out what information they may have that is inaccurate and using those existing understandings to construct more complete accurate understandings.

How can faculty get to know their students' knowledge structure? The best approach is to increase the number of ways that information flows from the students back to the instructor. At the launch of a new topic or experience, ask students what they know or think they know about the topic. Or provide simple problem-solving challenges, questions, scenarios, and case studies to assess their knowledge and skills they can bring to the learning. Some of the tools that can be used for these kinds of activities are discussion forums, simple inquiries, and stories.

Principle 3: Faculty Mentors Are the Directors of the Learning Experience

The learning experiences framework affirms the importance of learners by placing them at center stage of any learning experience. The framework also affirms the critical role of the faculty mentor, who provides direction and purpose by doing the following:

- Designing and structuring the course experiences
- Directing and supporting learners through the instructional experiences
- Assessing learner outcomes

To continue the theater metaphor, the faculty mentor is the director of the learning experiences, helping students develop and practice their knowledge. The faculty mentor is not a sage on the stage transmitting knowledge or a guide on the side. When the faculty member takes center stage, a learner may retreat and be more passive unless the faculty is encouraging interaction and engagement with the content every few minutes while also providing time for reflection and integration.

An important goal is for students to be engaged with the content at the same level of intensity as the faculty mentor. Strategies that support this shift in responsibilities include assigning students roles in moderating forums; preparing concept explanations, summaries, and examples for other students; conducting peer reviewing activities; and occasionally assuming responsibility for being the forum moderator.

The role of the faculty member in this learning experiences framework is to mentor, monitor, examine, affirm acquired knowledge, and challenge the thinking of students doing these types of teaching and learning activities.

The learning experiences framework assumes that the designing, managing, and assessing functions are the responsibilities of a faculty mentor. This does not mean that all these functions are necessarily embodied in one person. Many education models unbundle these responsibilities, so that an instructor can concentrate on the best use of his or her expertise, or to ensure consistency of instruction across many instructors or environments. For example, the design and development of online courses might be done by an instructional designer collaborating with one or more faculty members. In this case, an instructor who is new to online teaching and learning will be teaching a course that is designed with a significant portion of the teaching facilitation and direction materials prepared. The instructor is then responsible for teaching the course, including the functions of directing, supporting, and assessing the learning of students.

Most courses are still being taught in the bundled mode, with one faculty member responsible for all major tasks of design, teaching, managing, and assessing learners. The need for technical support 24/7 is accelerating a shift away from this "lone ranger" faculty member to the model of learning supported by an instructional team. With a team, the faculty member has more time to mentor the learning processes of students. Less time is spent on addressing technological, administrative, and content access issues and more time on the formation of thought and knowledge.

Mobile and collaborative technologies free a faculty mentor from the need to be physically in any particular place at any particular time. Synchronous collaborative tools are accelerating this flexibility. A faculty mentor can monitor student learning and facilitate discussions from anywhere in the world with a high-bandwidth connection: a home office, a coffee shop, or a hotel or office. Members of the extended instructional team can also support students for the faculty member for selected periods of time as well if schedule or emergencies occur.

Principle 4: All Learners Do Not Need to Learn All Course Content; All Learners Do Need to Learn the Core Concepts

This core learning principle focuses on course content, usually described in the desired learning outcomes. These are the knowledge, skills, and perspectives to be learned, acquired, or developed. The essential idea here is that not all content is equal. Only a portion of the content of any course is core concept knowledge; the bulk of course content is in the application and use of core concepts in simple to complex scenarios.

It helps to imagine course content arrayed as a set of concentric circles similar to a pie (see Figure 2.2). The innermost circle represents the core concepts; the next circle represents the content resources that learners use in initial practice experiences as they apply the core concepts to relatively straightforward problems with known solutions. The third circle represents content resources that learners use to solve more complex problems that may have a variety of solutions. As students move outwards from the core, students apply the core concepts in ever more complex and novel scenarios. By the time students reach the content resources in the fourth layer, the students select and direct much of their own experience and work on applying concepts to complex problems where solutions may or may not be able to be known.

In brief, the goal for each student is to master a slice of the pie, but to be sure that the slice includes the whole of the center with the core concepts

FIGURE 2.2

Customizing Content Resources

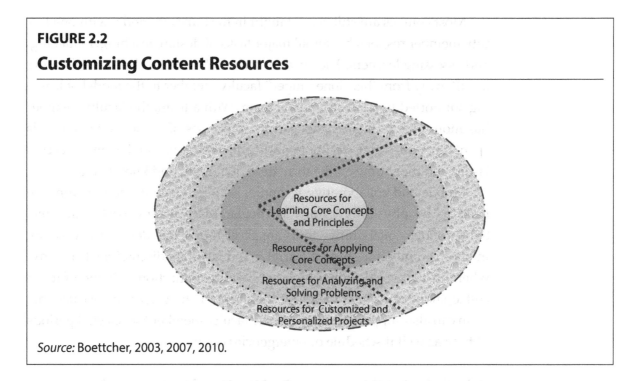

Resources for Learning Core Concepts and Principles

Resources for Applying Core Concepts

Resources for Analyzing and Solving Problems

Resources for Customized and Personalized Projects

Source: Boettcher, 2003, 2007, 2010.

and principles. The slice of the course content that the student masters is illustrated by the dotted lines creating a pie slice. As students develop expertise in the use of content, they increasingly customize their learning according to their own needs, interests, and priorities.

There are many challenges to implementing this model in learning: (1) identifying the core concepts in a course (Roediger et al., 2007), (2) finding and selecting a range of resources to support learners, (3) structuring learning experiences appropriate to learners' knowledge, and (4) managing the time available in a course model so learners can construct the knowledge representations for the concepts and skills. Let's briefly address the task of identifying and finding the content resources.

In this content model, the faculty member is not responsible for defining and making all the content accessible. It is a team effort that includes the campus resource infrastructure—the library team and information technology team—and the student. Designing a learner-centered course means providing access to a rich database of content and experiences to meet students' needs and interests. Instructors will want to select and identify content for each of the categories just described in the content pie. These include core/required content that students will make their own and integrate into their knowledge structures, core-shared content that provides common experiences for community building, content that supports use and application of core concepts, and content that supports customized and personalized learning.

A good rule of thumb for faculty is to select required course content focusing on the core concepts that are available in digital form, as this increases the likelihood that students will use and learn the content.

Principle 5: Every Learning Experience Includes the Environment or Context in Which the Learner Interacts

This core learning principle completes the four elements of any learning experience: the environment in which the learner interacts with the content, knowledge, skill, fellow learners or expert. The environment might be simple, as in a learner using one resource independently, at home, or out and about while jogging or driving, or working in a popular "third place" (Oldenburg, 1999) such as a coffee shop. Alternatively, the environment might be more complex. Several learners may be gathered together working on problems or a project in a face-to-face study group, or several may be on a conference call or in a collaborative virtual setting. Or learners might be gathered at the same time in a virtual meeting place using a collaborative web place, sharing documents on cell phones or laptops. An instructor may or may not be present.

The types of environment questions to be anticipated by a faculty member when designing a set of course experiences include the following:

- Where, when, with whom, and with what resources is this particular instructional experience likely to occur?

- What are the expected learning outcomes or interim points of learning?

- Will this experience be an individual experience where the student is working through a complex and lengthy simulation?

- Will the learning experience be a small team meeting using synchronous tools?

- Will this event be a face-to-face experience, such as one or two learners interviewing restaurant workers about public health regulations, or visiting a museum?

An interesting and effective course balances the three dialogues of faculty to learner, learner to learner, and learner to resources (Moore and Kearsley, 1996) and also includes a variety of individual, small, and large group activities. Different groupings and dialogues bring stimulating and varied interactions with people and with content resources.

Principle 6: Every Learner Has a Zone of Proximal Development That Defines the Space That a Learner Is Ready to Develop into Useful Knowledge

Vygotsky's theory of the zone of proximal development (ZPD) is one of the foundational concepts within the school of constructivist thought. It is a concept that sheds significant light on the characteristics of effective learning experiences. First let's review the definition of the zone. According to Vygotsky (1978), a learner's ZPD is "the distance between the actual developmental level as determined by independent problem solving and the level of potential development as determined through problem solving under the adult guidance or in collaboration with more capable peers" (p. 86).

It is relatively easy to link this definition to the four elements we just discussed. The learner experiences the zone of development during his learning experience; the distance to be traveled refers to the knowledge, skill, or attitude to be developed; the adult guidance or collaboration with more capable peers is the mentor guiding the learning. The fourth element of environment is not specifically included in the definition, but it is safe to say that the learning has to happen somewhere and at some time.

The definition of the ZPD posits the learning or growth that is to happen, echoing the familiar dictum of John Dewey that all learning is growth. The concept of the ZPD emphasizes that all learning experiences need to pull learners forward and "that the 'only good learning' is in advance of development" (p. 89). It means that students should be encountering problems and concepts beyond that which they already know, which is their actual developmental level and helping them to work on their "potential development." So the ZPD is the space between what students can do independently and what they can do successfully with the help or guidance of a person who might be an expert or simply a more capable peer.

The concept of the ZPD is very similar to the concept of learning readiness used in instructional design, positing the probable level of readiness of a set of learners. The ZPD focuses on an individual learner and suggests that a learner's zone of openness to a particular learning experience might be fairly narrow. In other words, the window of learning opportunity may be smaller than we think. When students say they are "totally lost," they are probably expressing the feeling of being outside their effective ZPD. When they sit back and obviously disengage, they have probably lost the link—the relationship of one idea to the other. When this happens in a group situation or a discussion board, the learning community needs to support the student in asking a question and having someone back up to where the student got lost so that he can get linked up again. Otherwise the time will probably be lost to the learner; the learner will disengage and have difficulty catching up to what might be called the "group zone."

The concept of the ZPD is simultaneously comforting and overwhelming. What are the elements of the learning community that support students' comfort levels in asking questions or in the mentor checking in with each learner? How do faculty mentors determine a learner's ZPD, and how do they determine what kinds of problems students can solve now?

This ZPD principle and its companion, readiness for learning, emphasizes the need to be continually alert to students' state of understanding and capabilities. This principle encourages embedding feedback and demonstrations from students earlier and more consistently throughout a course experience. Student questions, comments, participation, and outputs are means of determining more precisely the progress or state of concept development in learners.

Principle 7: Concepts Are Not Words But Organized and Interconnected Knowledge Clusters

This principle, also inspired by Vygotsky's writings, is simple but profound. Concept formation is not a one-time event. Vygotsky, for example, describes concept formation as a series of intellectual operations including the centering of attention, abstracting, synthesizing, and symbolizing (1962). Similarly, neuroscientist Walter Freeman observes that meanings are assimilated as a process of "successive approximations in conversation" (2000, p. 15). Freeman's work focuses on how the brain puts a priority on meaning rather than data and notes that meanings reside only in observers, not in objects. This work affirms the role of interaction and dialogue in the creation of meanings.

What are the implications about concept formation being a "series of intellectual operations" for designing learning experiences and courses? Consider, for example, learners who are encountering a new discipline. These learners often focus, almost in desperation, on learning the vocabulary of that discipline. They struggle, however, as they are often grappling with the vocabulary in isolation from the concepts that give the words meaning. Without the underlying richness of the full concept, words are akin to isolated seeds likely to be blown away by the winds of time, usually mere hours after an exam. Learners can in fact become quite proficient at using vocabulary while not having the ability to really think with the words (Bloom, 2002). They have the words but not the underlying rich concepts.

Activities using discussion forums, blogs, wikis, journals, and small group work are all excellent strategies for engaging learners in clarifying and enriching their mental models and concepts and identifying and establishing meaningful links and relationships. Blogs and forum spaces are particularly helpful in supporting the building of concepts because they provide a public, continuous space in which the cumulative, step-by-step process of concept formation, refinement, application, and revision is fully visible to student peers as well as their mentors. These different communication forms can provide a detailed, comprehensive record of how concepts take form as integrated clusters of knowledge and promote the development of more complex and lasting knowledge and competencies in students.

Principle 8: Different Instruction Is Required for Different Learning Outcomes

Robert Gagné, widely considered the father of instructional design, observed that all instruction is not equal and that different types of instruction are required for different learning outcomes. This is not a groundbreaking concept today, but the idea was quite novel when Gagne wrote *The Conditions of Learning* in 1965. This principle means that *what an instructor or mentor does makes a difference* in what students learn and what concepts and skills students may or may not develop. This principle reinforces the recommended instructional design practice of planning student assessments at the same time that one plans the learning experiences. Designing instruction and assessments simultaneously helps to ensure congruency and to manage expectations as to learning outcomes.

This principle affirms this fundamental instructional design question: "What knowledge, set of skills, and perspectives do you want your students to develop competence in through their participation in the instructional experiences of this course or program?" Once that question is answered, the instructional designer or faculty member's task is to design and develop the teaching and learning events to accomplish those goals. The matching of learning experiences to learning outcomes increases, but obviously does not guarantee, the probability that learning goals will be achieved by the majority of the learners.

A simple and effective example of this principle is the apprenticeship model. If the desired outcome is for students to be great chefs, they need to cook; if the desired set of skills is to become an entrepreneur, learners need to practice entrepreneurial activities or apprentice themselves in an entrepreneurial environment. This principle is also at work with pilots training on simulators and students' practicing of lab techniques in a model environment. The types of learning experiences do affect what is learned and what students feel competent in doing. In short, courses designed to transmit knowledge do just that: courses designed to develop competencies must design experiences in which students will be practicing use of the ✓ knowledge. Knowledge can sometimes be transmitted, but experience and competence must be developed.

Principle 9: Everything Else Being Equal, More Time on Task Equals More Learning

This is one of the best known of all learning principles. It is basically the time-on-task principle: that as learners spend more time interacting with, creating, and using knowledge and skills, the more facile, accomplished, and confident they will be (Carroll, 1963; Bloom, 1964, 1976; Carroll, 1989). Time on task is what is required for learners to make knowledge their own, creating the structures, links, and connections within their own knowledge structures. A key belief promoted by Bloom, an American educational psychologist, is that of mastery learning. Mastery learning posits that time is an important variable in learning; that is, that some students will take more time than others, but that all can learn (1976). Learning and developing new ideas and skills is intrinsically rewarding and enjoyable. Imagine the delight of a one-year-old at repeatedly pushing light switches on and off, or a fifteen-year-old with a driver's permit and her excitement at driving and driving and more driving. On college campuses, students find it exciting to practice and apply skills at creating and making robots, manipulating biology objects, or devising strategies for helping small businesses. These experiences create excitement and a learning zone in which we can lose ourselves and all sense of time. When we design engaging learning experiences, learners spend more time interacting with and developing more complex, better-structured knowledge bases and efficient automatic behaviors.

A corollary of the time-on-task principle is that learning can be more efficient if we chunk information. Chunking, according to psychology, is the process of taking small units of information and grouping or chunking them into larger units so that we can store more information in our short-term memory (Miller, 1956). Miller's work is the classic reference acknowledging limits on short-term memory. It is interesting to note that the term "chunking" has been evolving to include cognitive strategies of any kind that make information easier to remember, such as using the acronym ROYGBIV to remember the names and sequence of the ~~eight~~ seven colors of the rainbow. The traditional chunking example notes that dividing phone numbers into three chunked units reduces the number of units to remember from 10 to 3. Another rule of thumb is to keep bullet lists manageable by not exceeding seven, and ideas are often captured in groups of three. In today's environments, simulations, animations, and "living worlds" such as the *Minecraft*, *Warcraft*, and *SimCity* games are powerful learning chunkers of many discrete facts. Chunking is one reason games and role-playing scenarios are popular and valuable. Other valuable features of games and simulations are their unpredictability and infinite variety. These are the kinds of challenges students enjoy working to master. In contrast, canned, predictable, and static learning resources are less interesting and less engaging and, dare we say, tiring and boring.

Principle 10: We Shape Our Tools, and Our Tools Shape Us

The fact that we are shaped by our tools and that we shape our tools may appear at first to be a strange design and learning principle. The essence of this principle is that learning always occurs within a particular context that influences the learning. Simply put, learning tools make a difference. Where we learn and what we learn with makes a difference. This contextual aspect of learning—that it occurs only through a process of a person interacting with the environment—is a key conceptual element of the theories of Dewey (1933) and Vygotsky (1978), the more recent work of Damasio (1999), the How People Learn work (Bransford et al., 2000), and the situated and embodied cognition theories of Brown, Collins, and Duguid (1989) and Shapiro (2011). The environment as envisioned in these theories includes all the tools, resources, and people who form the context of any particular learning experience.

Learning tools are part of our environment and often dictate how our brains engage with a context and content. An environment in which all learners and instructors have their own personal digital devices makes a difference in the kinds of teaching and learning experiences that are possible. These tools create an environment powered, literally, with personalized psychological learning tools. The current wave of social media, virtually synchronous "friending" applications help you find your buddies and the coffee shop where you may be meeting. These tools have dramatically changed the traditional communication patterns and relationships between learners and faculty, supplanting the traditional two or three weekly meetings.

Many faculty remain daunted by the shift in learning dynamics and relationships created by these tools, and many are still struggling to adapt. In an environment infused with these tools, the faculty member moves from the center of the class communication pattern, as was common in the traditional transmission mode of learning, to the periphery or, in the stage model, to the wings.

A second far-reaching impact of these tools is the ease by which students can customize their own learning experiences because courses no longer have content boundaries. Students now live and move in a community-building state of always being connected. The anywhere, anytime, any while access to communication tools makes it easy for students to go outside the organized course structure.

Communication tools support information access and flow in real time, enabling current events, global perspectives, and far-flung resources to be brought into immediate and fresh relief. Every statement by a faculty member is subject to challenge or confirmation from a student as searching and verification tools are at their fingertips. This means that faculty need to adapt the course and the content to students who bring in ideas and content that might be quite unfamiliar to them, and to defend, support, and expand their own mental models.

Summary—and What's Next?

The research on how we learn illuminates in new and significant ways the processes of teaching and learning. This research, integrated with core learning principles, can help guide our design of learning so that teaching and learning can be efficient and effective. A major insight is the uniqueness of each brain in its structure and its accumulated experiences. We each experience and remember events just a little differently from everyone else. This richness of perspective is a challenge as well as a potent creative force. The combination of the uniqueness of each learner and the richness of perspective argues persuasively for much more emphasis on teaching and experiencing community, culture, and ethics in combination with knowledge, content, and skills.

These ten core learning principles provide the theoretical context and inspiration for the many tips that follow in the next chapters. You may want to refer back to these frequently.

The next chapter is designed as a companion chapter to this chapter in that it describes ten plus four best practices that together apply many of the ten core learning principles from this chapter. Instructors who use these practices can significantly increase the probabilities of an initial satisfactory teaching and learning outcome. However, following these practices without a deep appreciation and use of the core principles and many of the tips in the book is a bit like students knowing the words but not the concepts of new knowledge. So aim for the deep understanding and lifelong learning of teaching and learning. Aim high, dig deep, and enjoy our new world of teaching and learning.

Exercise—Stop, Reflect, Integrate

If you are using this book for a course in **faculty development**, here are two activities to consider using to have faculty think more deeply about these core learning principles and to share their ideas and beliefs with their colleagues.

1. Exercise for design thinking

Refer to Table 2.1, summarizing the ten core learning principles. Which of these principles is the most familiar to you? As you design learning experiences in your course, what question do you like to focus on? Do you refer back to the goal of what skills your students will be working on? What types of assignments or discussions will prepare your students for building a particular skill?

2. Developing a deeper understanding of pedagogy, the science of teaching and learning

Which of the ten core learning principles piques your curiosity about how it might help you design a new learning experience for your course? Is it the principle on content (#4) that pushes you to really identify the core concepts of your course? Is it the principle on the zone of proximal development (#6) that causes you to reflect on how you can increase the richness of resources for your students? Or is it the principle of the role of the environment or context (#10)? Are you wondering how you might increase the power of the tools that can support student's learning? Share your questions, ideas, or possibilities with a colleague or friend.

Chapter 3

Best Practices for Teaching Online: Ten Plus Four

OUR KNOWLEDGE ABOUT best practices in online and blended learning environments continues to grow rapidly. That is the good news. On the other hand, the amount of available knowledge quickly overwhelms anyone teaching in the array of online and blended environments. Where does one begin?

This chapter describes fourteen best teaching and learning practices for online and blended environments. Ten of these best practices, as published in the first edition of this book, were developed to assist faculty who were thrust into online teaching somewhat unexpectedly. Over the years we discovered that we were constantly recommending four additional practices. So now there are ten plus four, depending on your state of readiness and anticipation.

Research and experience suggest that these types of practices contribute to an *effective, efficient*, and *satisfying* teaching and learning experience for both faculty and students. Using these practices can help faculty develop confidence, comfort, and experience in teaching online quickly and easily.

This particular set of best practices originated from a number of sources. We have developed and selected these practices from our experiences working with faculty and colleagues since the early 1990s. Most importantly, these best practices are rooted in the research and educational theories of cognitive and experts such as those discussed in Chapters One and Two. These practices are also rooted in articles by Chickering and Ehrmann (1996), sets of best practices by WCET (Krauth, 1996), and books on moving instruction to the Web (Boettcher & Conrad, 1999, 2004;

Sherron & Boettcher, 1997). Other sets of best practices that affirm and support similar practices are those of the Online Learning Consortium (Swan, 2004; Moore, 2011) and the Quality Matters Rubric, now in its fifth edition (www.qualitymatters.org, 2015).

Many other writers (Garrison, Anderson, & Archer, 2001; Garrison, 2006; Swan, 2004; Swan & Ice, 2010; Palloff & Pratt, 2007, 2011; Lehman & Conceição, 2010; Bain, 2012; Conrad & Donaldson, 2012; Vaughan, Cleveland-Innes, & Garrison, 2013; and Miller, Benke, Chaloux, et. al., 2013) have affirmed and recommended similar practices.

Just as the ten core learning principles in Chapter Two are not necessarily "the" best set of core learning principles, this set of practices is not necessarily "the" best set; rather, it captures much of what we now know about effective and efficient teaching online and, in most cases, teaching in any environment. These practices will likely continue to evolve with ongoing research and practice. Instructors who follow these practices increase the probability of an effective, efficient, and satisfying teaching and learning experience for themselves and their students.

We hope you enjoy getting to know and using these best practices as you work to develop and expand your expertise in online and blended learning.

Best Practices for Online and Blended Teaching and Learning

Table 3.1 lists the ten plus four best practices to guide your online teaching experiences. You may want to keep the list handy and prominent as reminders to your design plans and your interactions with your students.

Best Practice 1: Be Present at Your Course

Being present digitally for your course is the most fundamental and most important of all the practices. Your students want to know you as a person and as an expert. They want to know what you think, based on your expertise and experiences. They want to know that you care about them and that you care they are learning. Since they can't always see you in person, they want to see and hear you through your words and audio and video messages.

Liberal use of communication tools such as announcements, unit introductions, discussion forums, feedback, and generally "being there" frequently communicates to learners that you care about their learning, their questions, and their concerns. Liberal use of these tools means that you are present to your students, to do the guiding, mentoring, and challenging that teaching is all about.

TABLE 3.1

Best Practices for Teaching Online

Best Practice	Description
Best practice 1	Be present at the course site.
Best practice 2	Create a supportive online course community.
Best practice 3	Develop a set of explicit expectations for your learners and yourself as to how you will communicate and how much time students should be working on the course each week.
Best practice 4	Use a variety of large group, small group, and individual work experiences.
Best practice 5	Use synchronous and asynchronous activities.
Best practice 6	Ask for informal feedback early in the term.
Best practice 7	Prepare discussion posts that invite responses, questions, discussions, and reflections.
Best practice 8	Search out and use content resources that are available in digital format.
Best practice 9	Combine core concept learning with customized and personalized learning.
Best practice 10	Plan a good closing and wrap activity for the course.
Best practice 11	Assess as you go by gathering evidences of learning.
Best practice 12	Rigorously connect content to core concepts and learning outcomes.
Best practice 13	Develop and use a content frame for your course.
Best practice 14	Design experiences to help learners make progress on their novice-to-expert journey.

We have begun to quantify just what it means to be present in digital learning for our learners. The best online faculty—according to students—are faculty who are present in some way, every day. The concept of daily presence may be alarming to you, as it might fuel the widely reported perception that online courses take significantly more time than classroom-based courses. One way to create presence without consuming too much of your time is to focus on group discussion areas and avoid one-to-one e-mails. Time-released announcements that remind learners of due dates and audio containing additional content are other ways to let the learners know you are there while conserving your time. Video/audio mini-lectures made on your smart phones also create positive presence and energy.

Of course, there is the danger that too much faculty presence will stunt the discussion as well as delay the development of learner self-direction. So while you may check in on each course daily to see if there are questions, you should by no means feel that you must add significant daily comments to the discussion forums each day. Be sure to communicate this philosophy to learners, as they may wait for you to kick off the discussion and lead it.

Students who feel alone and isolated from faculty or other learners are likely to quietly disappear; others who are more engaged may post questions, such as "Is there anybody out there?" Such statements are clear and unambiguous signals that an instructor is not communicating regularly or well.

If a faculty member has a life or career event that requires their full attention away from a course for more than just one day, it is good practice to alert students about this change in schedule and to encourage the students to be particularly alert to helping each other during this time.

Why is presence so important in online or blended environments? When faculty actively interact and engage students in a face-to-face classroom, the class evolves as a group and develops intellectual and personal bonds. This same group or community bonding happens in an online setting if the faculty presence is felt consistently. Regular, thoughtful, daily presence plays a significant role in learner satisfaction with learning experiences.

Three Types of Presence

Research on presence suggests three types of presence: social presence, teaching presence, and cognitive presence (Garrison, Anderson, & Archer, 2000). Here are brief descriptions:

- **Social presence** creates connections with learners based on who we are as three-dimensional persons with families, lives, and favorite ideas, people, and places. Pictures of ourselves and our hobbies and interests convey these many dimensions of ourselves and help to build connections and trust.

- **Teaching presence** guides students' learning experiences. Teaching presence is the sum of all the behaviors faculty use to direct, guide, and design the learning experiences. Teaching presence is conveyed through, first, the design of courses and materials prior to teaching the course, and second, the mentoring, guiding, and directing during the course.

- **Cognitive presence** supports, mentors, and guides students' intellectual growth, ideas, and challenges. Cognitive presence is conveyed by all the interactions with learners that an instructor has to support the development of skills, knowledge, and understanding in his or her students.

Cultivating these three types of presences supports effective learning and the development of a mutually respectful and intellectual community that often lasts well beyond any learning experience.

Research on presence and its framework model, the Community of Inquiry (CoI), was the focus of a Canadian Social Sciences and Humanities project. The seminal paper (Garrison, Anderson, & Archer, 2000) launched an ongoing research agenda that has produced many prominent papers and books (such as Garrison, Anderson, & Archer, 2004; Garrison & Cleveland-Innes, 2005; Garrison & Vaughan, 2008; Akyol & Garrison, 2008; Swan & Ice, 2010; Lehman and Conceição, 2010; Shea et al., 2012; and many more).

Best Practice 2: Create a Supportive Online Course Community

Nurturing a learning community as part of a course is almost as important as being present for your learners. We often assume that a learning community in a face-to-face environment develops spontaneously, as students generally have opportunities to get to know one another and develop friendships. In digital environments, more explicit nurturing and planning is required.

Community building has been one focus of research in online learning since its inception (Brown, 2001; Rovai, 2002; Shea, 2006; Palloff & Pratt, 2007, 2011). Some of the research seeks to define a community; other research examines the stages of a community and the faculty and student behaviors that facilitate community building at these different stages.

Building a supportive online community requires using a set of diverse and balanced dialogue patterns. The traditional teaching dialogue is that of faculty to student. But that is gradually changing. Building an online community that supports individual and group learning means designing a course that promotes a high proportion of student-to-student dialogue. The time devoted to the three basic dialogue patterns—faculty to student, student to student, and student to resource—should be about equal in any course design (Newman, 1853; Pelikan, 1992; Moore & Kearsley, 1996). So a good question to ask is, "How do I achieve this type of dialogue balance?" Let's look at some examples.

In online and blended courses, the dialogue of faculty to student is often provided with these types of resources:

- Module introductions and mini-lectures in text, video, or audio podcasts

- Announcements that remind, coach, suggest, inspire

- Explanations and interactions with the students via e-mail, forums, and live classroom events

For example, an instructor might use the following three types of communications for the faculty-to-learner dialogue: short mini-concept introductions, thrice-weekly announcements, and interactions with the student postings. In another course, an instructor might use written mini-lectures, audio and video podcasts, and announcements and discussion postings, with a heavier reliance on audio messages and resources. Whatever communication a faculty uses to direct, support, coach, or mentor learners is part of the teaching presence.

Designing for learner-to-learner dialogue requires other types of communication activities. Numerous books are devoted to providing activity examples, such as those by Barkley, Major and Cross (2014); Conrad and Donaldson (2011, 2012); Bonk & Khoo (2014); and Shank (2011). These authors provide descriptions of collaborative learning techniques that include small teams and groups forming for problem-solving, gaming activities, and collaborative writing. Activities that encourage learner-to-learner engagement are detailed in the tip sections.

A note of caution about the need for flexibility regarding expectations of community: Learning collaboratively with fellow learners in the setting of an online and blended course community will work better for some students than for others. Some students may choose not to participate very actively with other students. Other students enjoy the collaboration, feel that it improves their learning, and find it overcomes some of the isolation that learners feel when they don't gather in real time. The learning theories of Vygotsky and John Seely Brown in particular remind us that the social context of learning strengthens connections and meaning. The learning community is part of what makes this happen, and this should be shared with students to maximize their understanding of the purpose of communities.

Best Practice 3: Develop a Set of Explicit Workload and Communication Expectations for Your Learners and for Yourself

This best practice helps your work-life balance and models good habits for your learners as well. Developing and communicating explicit expectations reduces uncertainty and encourages good time and learning management. Post prominently on your course communication spaces a set of expectations for how often students will communicate and dialogue online and how they should communicate with you. For example, many faculty have a rule that they do not answer content-focused e-mails. This is a good practice because content-focused queries belong in the public spaces of the course site. Queries and responses posted in open course spaces benefit all the learners, as students see both the questions and the responses. You can also encourage students to answer each other's questions as appropriate. Of course, e-mail remains a good choice for personal and confidential communications.

What about a policy on response time for questions posted on a course site or to e-mail? Institutions have varying policies on this question. Some institutions have a policy that faculty are expected to respond to learners within twenty-four hours during the week. Expectations for responses during the weekend can vary, but as most working professionals work on their online courses during the weekend, faculty should establish a general rule as to weekend windows of opportunity. It is also good practice to plan and do more frequent communications during the first week or two of a course while everyone is getting started, getting materials, and puzzling out access and tool processes.

Another common effective practice is for faculty to schedule virtual office hours, specifying windows when they will be available for text messaging, chat or live classroom, e-mail, or phone. Learners particularly appreciate almost real-time response times when they are likely to be working on an important assignment.

Many faculty often set these "available times" concurrently when they are likely to be reviewing postings or assignments. In the interests of time and community, it is best to use a communication tool where responses and content can be shared with everyone and archived for flexibility in access and review.

The expectation of a twenty-four-hour response time during the week can be modified, provided this policy is communicated to the students and any change is consistent with an institution's policies. It is important to develop your own policies or rules of thumb if the institution does not have them in place. Think about the students as family for the duration of a course or program. Students are very accepting of a faculty member's time and life requirements IF they know what is going on. And students often step in and help each other even more when they know a faculty member is sick, traveling, or engaged in significant professional or family obligations. Often students can agree to monitor course questions posted in the open forum or in the discussion boards, for example.

Teaching and learning experiences in any environment are demanding of both teachers and students, and the time to do the work needs to be scheduled and planned. Being clear as to how much effort and time will be required on a weekly basis keeps surprises to a minimum (Anderson, 2008; Lehman & Conceição, 2014).

How much time should learners be expected to dedicate weekly to an online course? A good rule of thumb is that a fifteen-week online course will generally require an absolute minimum of six productive hours of learning time each week, and an eight-week course a minimum of twelve hours a week. This includes time for activities such as reading and processing content, as well as participating in online discussions. For many learners, it can take ten scheduled hours to achieve six productive hours, due to dealing with interruptions, and focusing on transitioning tasks and challenges, as in "Oh, yes, I need to warm my coffee, feed my children, get laundry started, or find the support materials for the document I was working on.

Best Practice 4: Use a Variety of Large Group, Small Group, and Individual Work Experiences

A learning community has more ways to develop when learners participate in a variety of learning experiences. Many students enjoy the opportunity to brainstorm concepts and work through assignments with one or two or more fellow students, particularly when they don't gather in a physical space very often. At the same time many students really enjoy working and learning independently. Building in options and opportunities for students to work together and individually is a key characteristic of good learning design. Variety gives students ways of tapping into their own varied skills and abilities.

For example, developing skills and knowledge can be more stimulating when students immerse themselves in course content by working through cases and challenging problems and discussing stimulating ideas with fellow students. Teams are particularly effective when students are working on complex case studies or scenarios for the first time. Research (Light, 2004; Bernard et al., 2009; Abrami et al., 2011; Bain, 2012) confirms that talking through problems with others, as in study groups, and other collaborative work, increases learning. In his book *What the Best College Students Do* (2012), Bain noted stories of students who had studied together, quizzing and probing one another, each person taking a turn at teaching the others (p. 246).

Early in a course, students often respond positively to working with just one or two other students. Later in the course, with more complex projects, groups of three or four can work well. Smaller teams generally offer more time for full participation. It is also invigorating to build in whole-class activities such as the live classroom Q&A sessions or events with invited experts.

Here are some starting points for designing learning experiences using different size groups:

- Individual work: Tools such as journals and personal blogs support individual creation, reflection, and review. Combined with small group work, these tools can also support sharing of ideas and innovative and critical thinking. We like the reminder that "Reflection is a form of retrieval practice" (Brown, Roediger, & McDaniel, 2014, p. 66).

- Small groups: Working in small groups is particularly recommended when working on problem-solving scenarios and more complex case studies.

- Large groups: The now-ubiquitous mobile and synchronous tools allow us to spontaneously plan large group activities such as expert visits and virtual conferences and do real-time project planning, brainstorming, and presentations.

It is tempting to design one type of weekly learning module and then just create a set of similar modules for the other weeks or units of your course. We believe that this can save time and energy in designing and preparing a course. However, student feedback from personal communications suggests that online courses can quickly become too predictable, consisting of reading, posting on discussion boards, and writing papers. Students share that they begin to suffer from a week-to-week sameness factor, as early as after only two or three weeks. Consider including an activity that is based on student feedback or is student-determined, such as using a discussion question they write, to break up the sameness of course activities.

Best Practice 5: Use Synchronous and Asynchronous Activities

Another way of providing variety in your course design is to balance asynchronous activities with synchronous activities. When online courses were initially offered, they were almost totally asynchronous. In many ways, they represented a new generation of the correspondence distance learning courses so widespread in the middle of the twentieth century (Sherron & Boettcher, 1997). Now we have tools supporting entirely new generations of online and blended courses. We have social media tools and the "Internet of things" connecting everyone with everything. We have learning management and course management systems, real-time synchronous classrooms, massive open online courses (MOOCs), spontaneous collaboration tools, and an almost infinite number of web tools, smart phones, and wearables that support synchronous chat, video messaging, and more. These tools make it possible to do almost everything that we have been accustomed to doing in face-to-face classrooms, and discussions and events can be recorded and archived for later and multiple views. In addition, we can engage learners in more extensive collaborative and reflective activities, from anywhere, at any time we choose to be awake and communicating.

Sometimes there is nothing better than a real-time interactive brainstorming and sharing discussion; other times, the requirement to think, plan, write, and reflect is what makes learning most effective for an individual. The variety of activities now possible makes it easy to create many types of effective learning experiences and environments. Many problembased courses, such as financial, statistical, or engineering courses, use live classroom tools for interactive, real-time problem-solving. These same tools can be used for virtually any discipline for real-time Q&A review sessions, project reviews, virtual coaching, or office hours.

While working professionals often choose to complete advanced degrees online so that they can make use of the asynchronous, anytime, anywhere features of a program, these same learners enjoy getting together at a specific time to interact in real time. When getting together synchronously doesn't work for reasons such as multiple time zones or travel requirements, the recording and archiving features make it possible to feel as if one has actually "been there."

Some of the most robust synchronous tools are set up and run by institutions and accommodate small to large groups. Informal tools such as Google Hangout and Skype, as well as the simple telephone service that is essentially free with smart phones, are excellent tools for small group collaboration, team work, role plays, debates, and presentations.

Best Practice 6: Ask for Informal Feedback Early in the Term

Course evaluations have been called "postmortem evaluations" because they are done after the fact. This means nothing can be changed to increase satisfaction or facilitate more learning and engagement. Early feedback surveys or informal discussions are effective in getting students to provide feedback on what is working well in a course and solicit suggestions and ideas on what might help them have a better course experience. Often early feedback can alert you to students having difficulty with something as fixable as access to materials, or some minor technology glitch.

This early feedback is done in about week 2 of a fifteen-week course so time is available to make corrections and modifications while the course is ongoing. For the many popular shorter courses, as six- or eight-week terms, informal feedback can be done as early as midweek of the first week.

Best Practice 7: Prepare Discussion Posts That Invite Responses, Questions, Discussions, and Reflections

One of the primary differences between the online and blended classroom and the classroom of the campus-based course is how students and faculty communicate and the range of tools that they use to do so. After all, we don't see the students as often; rather, we get to know them by what they write and say in the discussion boards and their assignments and, to a lesser degree, in e-mail, phone, and collaborative online classrooms.

The communication space that is the heart and soul of the online course community is the discussion board. This is the primary place where faculty talk to students and students talk to other students. This is also the place where students and faculty get to know one another, and the tool that helps a widely dispersed group of students and faculty become a learning community.

Discussions in an online course are the equivalent of class discussions in a face-to-face class. A key difference, of course, is that these discussions are asynchronous, meaning that students have time for thought and reflection. Another key difference is that discussions, blogs, and other tools require written or audio comments that are captured and become part of a course archive.

Discussions are often designed for one of the following learning purposes (Painter, Coffin, & Hewings, 2003; Goodyear, Jones, Asensio, Hodgson, & Steeples, 2003, cited in Grogan, 2005):

- Provide a place for an open question-and-answer forum
- Encourage critical or creative thinking
- Reinforce domain or procedural processes
- Achieve social interaction and community building so learners get to know each other personally and intellectually
- Validate thinking and experiences
- Support students in their own reflections and inquiries

Here are a few hints for discussion postings culled from many conversations with experienced online faculty:

- Create open-ended questions that learners can explore and apply the concepts that they are learning.
- Model Socratic-type probing and follow-up questions: "Why do you think that?" "What is your reasoning?" "Is there an alternative strategy?"

- Ask clarifying questions that encourage students to think about what they know and don't know.

- Stagger due dates of the responses, and consider a midpoint summary or encouraging comments.

Provide guidelines and instruction on responding to other students. For example, suggest a two-part response: (1) "Say what you liked or agreed with or what resonated with you," and (2) "Conclude with a follow-up question such as what you are wondering about or curious about."

Best Practice 8: Think Digital for All Course Content

If course content is not digital, it is as if it does not exist. If it is not digital, we can't access it from our phones, tablets, and laptops, or the cloud. Students turn first and most frequently to the content and applications that are available with their digital devices.

Learners today want to be learning anywhere, anytime, and often while they are doing other things, such as driving, taking care of children, or exercising. While paper and physical books are still handy and convenient and can be restful for our eyes, most students expect to be able to access course content from wherever they happen to be and whenever they have even five to fifteen minutes to read, think or reflect. Smartphones, tablets, the Internet, and the cloud provide a digital environment that means learners do not have to worry about the physical location or carry-weight of course content.

E-textbooks, replete with animations and study tools, are becoming widely available, so it is now easier to design a course with options for digital content while also providing physical text options. Selecting a textbook available in multiple formats can be a boon to students, particularly working professionals. Another reason for thinking digital is that digital content often includes audio and video resources, adding a dimension above and beyond text that can engage and help learners with core concepts, and provides links to a world of professional examples and tools. Digital resources such as animations and immersive simulations can provide practice in building skills and increase the types of learning outcomes that learners can achieve.

A reference document with instructions on remotely accessing library resources is a must for online courses. In addition, a key member of the instructional team is the library reference person assigned to support online learners. Make friends with your library personnel.

Students enjoy seeing how what they are learning links to current events. Thus building links to current events into discussions, blogs, and announcements supports the exploration stage of early grappling with core course concepts. So this best practice includes encouraging students to make good use of Internet resources.

Another effective practice is to enlist student help in finding and iden- tifying relevant and engaging resources. Students often are better than their instructors at discerning which resources will be of interest and use to themselves and to their peers. Enlisting students in this task also means that students will find resources that illustrate course content in action, helping them make more connections to the content and to their lives.

Best Practice 9: Combine Core Concept Learning with Customized and Personalized Learning

This best practice integrates a number of core learning principles. Briefly, this practice requires faculty, as part of their course design process *prior* to the course, to identify the core concepts, questions, and performance goals for a course. Then *during* the course a faculty's responsibility is to mentor learners through a set of increasingly complex and customized questions, problems, and projects to help learners apply these core concepts and develop their own knowledge structures.

In practical terms for online courses, it means designing options and choices within learning experiences, assignments, and special projects. Supporting learners with their personal and professional goals that are closely linked to the performance goals of a course and even beyond the course parameters benefits the learners individually and as a group. It enhances the meaningfulness of the learning and infuses learner enthusiasm for completing the assignments.

A key principle supporting concept learning comes from psychologist Lev Vygotsky (1962, 1978). He noted that concepts are not words, but rather organized and intricate knowledge clusters. This simple but profound truth means that while we usually teach in a linear fashion, presenting concepts individually and in small clusters, we need to continually reapply core concepts within differing contexts, such as those in case studies, problems, and scenarios. The wealth of research studies on the brain and the mind confirms this practice (Brown, Roediger, and McDaniel, 2014).

Effectively learning concepts, as studies of novice and expert learners demonstrate, requires a knowledge of patterns and relationships. Individual facts and vocabulary are part of a knowledge structure, but they require connections to make them meaningful (Ericsson, Charness, Feltovich & Hoffman, 2006; Chi, 2006).

When faced with a new field or discipline, students initially focus on learning the vocabulary of a discipline, but this activity is often done in isolation from an understanding of the concepts that give the words meaning. Without the underlying concepts, words are akin to isolated weeds and seeds likely to be blown away by the winds of time, usually mere hours after an exam or other learning experience. Learning individual facts and vocabulary is just one of the early steps in learning concepts.

One effective teaching and learning strategy advocates making students' thinking visible (Collins, Brown, & Holum, 1991; Ritchhart, Church & Morrison, 2011; visiblethinking.org). Making our thinking visible requires students to create, talk, write, explain, analyze, judge, report, and inquire. These activities make it clear to students themselves, the faculty, and fellow learners what they know or don't know, what they are puzzled about, and what they might be curious about. Such activities stimulate students' growth from concept awareness to concept acquisition, building in that "series of intellectual operations" that Vygotsky believes is required for concept acquisition. Such a series of activities also maps the development of knowledge as described in Bloom's taxonomy.

Discussion forums, blogging, journals, wikis, and similar social networking type tools provide excellent communication channels for engaging learners in clarifying and enlarging their mental models or concepts and building links and identifying relationships.

This best practice builds flexibility into learning experiences to meet the needs of individual learners while designing to ensure that all students reach competency in the learning outcomes of a course. This practice means that an instructor is continuously referring to and building in relationships of core concepts, as expanded in Best Practice 12, rigorously connecting core concepts to learning outcomes, while also focusing on learners as individuals.

Customizing practices asks students how they plan on using the learning experiences. If they are to talk or share any particular facts, examples, or stories with others, just which ones would they share? We build these questions into forums and assignments, always ensuring that the learners elaborate, apply, relate, and share knowledge with others.

As noted in the content best practice, the best learning experience is a shared learning experience that meets the individual needs of each of the learners.

This practice is a way of implementing three of the core learning principles from Chapter Two: Principle 2, "Learners bring their own personalized and customized knowledge, skills, and attitudes to the experience"; Principle 4, "All learners do not need to learn all the course content"; and Principle 6, "Every learner has a zone of proximal development that defines the space that a learner is ready to develop into useful knowledge."

Best Practice 10: Plan a Good Closing and Wrap Activity for the Course

As a course starts coming to a close and winding down, it is easy to focus on assessing and grading students and forget the value of a good closing experience. In the final weeks of a course, students are likely to be stressed and somewhat overwhelmed by the remaining work. In this state, they often do not pause to make the lists and do the planning that can help reduce stress and provide a calming atmosphere. A useful image for reducing stress is in David Allen's book *Getting Things Done* (2015). Allen notes that making a list helps us to clear the "psychic ram" of our brains so that we feel more relaxed and more in control. Once we have made lists and prepared our schedule, we don't have to continually remind ourselves of what needs to be done and when.

End-of-course experiences often include student presentations, summaries, and analyses. These reports and presentations provide insights into what useful knowledge students are taking away from a course. At the same time, these learning events can provide a final opportunity for faculty to remind students of core concepts and fundamental principles. These end-of-course experiences are a good time to use live classrooms, YouTube, and other synchronous collaborative tools. Chapter Nine is devoted to course wrapping (CW) tips and ideas.

Four More Best Practices for Online and Blended Teaching and Learning

These additional best practices started their lives as tips in the 2010 version of this *Survival Guide*. However, the power of these practices to help ensure meaningful learning suggests that they touch on overarching themes that should have higher visibility as we design learning experiences. In the years since the first edition, these practices kept coming to the fore as we coached faculty.

As noted earlier, the last few years has witnessed a flowering of research on teaching in a multitude of online and blended environments. While the ten best practices are really still the absolute beginner's set of best practices, these four additional best practices go beyond the basics and contribute significantly to the design of experiences that learners savor and enjoy.

Tips on how to implement these practices are expanded significantly in the tip section of the book.

Best Practice 11: Assess as You Go by Gathering Evidences of Learning

This best practice makes sense for everyone—for learners, for instructors, and for administrators. It keeps a focus on what the learner is doing and thinking throughout a course. This practice supports the gathering of evidences of learning throughout the course and also provides additional data for program accountability (Banta & Blaich, 2011; Suskie, 2009). This practice is one of the Principles of Good Practice for Assessing Student Learning, published by AAHE in 1996 and updated over time (Astin, et al., 2012; Hutchings, Ewell, & Banta, 2012).

What does this best practice mean? Rather than pushing all assessment toward papers, exams, and/or a final project, this practice recommends distributing assessment throughout a course. One of the key elements of course design is an assessment plan, showing the relative value and importance of assignments, project milestones, and other course contributions and participation.

One feature of emerging assessment practice that supports "assessing as you go" is expanding the audience for a student's work. In addition to the classic approach of assessment being a one-way street between an individual learner and an instructor, this practice recommends having learners work in small teams that work collaboratively on peer review and peer consulting on assignments such as project proposals. Outside experts can also play a role and participate in review and evaluation of student's work (Moallem, 2005). Public exhibitions, as they are traditionally done in media classes, can lead the way. Also consider providing options for students to create many types of experiences beyond just writing papers. (Boettcher, 2011)

Applying this practice means we gather evidences of learning throughout the course. This relieves the end-of-course stress and burdens. Another stress-reliever is also giving learners more choice in how they demonstrate knowledge.

Best Practice 12: Rigorously Connect Content to Core Concepts and Learning Outcomes

This best practice is rooted in learning principles such as distributed review practices and elaboration of facts and concepts. We know that learning takes time. We know that learning takes practice. We know that deep learning depends on seeing and using concepts in different contexts and scenarios and relationships. This best practice means "always coming back to how knowledge is embodied in the core concepts, patterns, relationships." Repetition and use of knowledge is what helps learners construct a meaningful knowledge representational structure in their minds (Kandel, 2006; Brown, Roediger, & McDaniel, 2014).

We spend a great deal of time developing learning outcomes, but then these outcomes are tucked away in a section of the syllabus that is mostly invisible. A best practice in the first week of the course is to assign your students a task to read the section, review the learning outcomes, and identify the ones that make the most sense to them; then, to customize and personalize some of the learning outcomes, have them answer this question, "How do I want to be different in my person, in my mind after this course?"

Best Practice 13: Develop and Use a Content Frame for the Course

This best practice involves two steps: first, designing a content frame for the course, and second, developing a habit of using and referring to that cognitive map, while teaching the course. The biggest danger generally faced by students is the feeling of being totally overwhelmed by all the content and as a consequence getting lost in the forest of details and not developing confidence in the really important ideas.

What is a content frame? Content frames are also called cognitive maps, visual graphics, and overviews. We like to use the term *content frame* because preparing a frame for a course helps learners get a holistic sense of a course. It presents a clear picture of what is to be learned in a course and what can be learned later as interests develop and time permits. Adventurous, curious students can always delve more deeply into course content, but they know at what point they can stop and still know what they need to know. Providing a clear overview of the core concepts, key knowledge, and types of problems competent learners should be able to handle provides a focus for the term of the course. Additionally, being able to refer back to the content frame regularly and see the content visually helps students to construct their own knowledge representations in their minds.

One of the tips (CB Tip 3 in Chapter Six) focuses on strategies and ideas for creating a syllabus with this type of content frame. Don't miss it. This tip suggests that creating a syllabus that really jump-starts learning is a fantastic investment. Think of the choices our students have before them.

How do we pull them in? How do we make working on our course something that they look forward to? The goal is to create a content frame that causes students to say, "Wow, thanks so much. I can really see what we are going to be doing and how everything all fits together."

Best Practice 14: Design Experiences to Help Learners Make Progress on Their Novice-to-Expert Journey

This best practice views students as learners, working their way along a path from novice to expert. It suggests strategies and approaches that assume the learner wants to develop knowledge, skill, and expertise in a field of inquiry and to do what it takes to help the learners move forward toward that goal.

It is sometimes assumed that motivating students is a problem. But while learning takes time, effort, and energy, the positive feelings that result from developing confidence in using knowledge to solve problems is intrinsically very motivating.

An entire body of research literature examines and describes the various steps and stages on the way from being a novice to becoming an expert. This body of literature includes work by researchers and theorists we have examined earlier: Piaget, Bruner, Brown, and more recently, Ericsson and Chi. The most of t-quoted "fact" about developing expertise is that it takes about 10,000 hours. If that is the case, then what are the steps, and how do we structure and design courses to help students on their preferred expertise journey? As we design the learning experiences, what stage of their journey is each learner on and how can the learning experiences help them move forward?

Briefly, here are the major milestones in a journey to expertise: novice, advanced novice (initiate), apprentice, journeyman, expert, and master (Chi, 2006). Each of these milestones represents from 1,500 to 2,500 hours of knowledge, skill, and acquisition investment. To be useful at the course level, it will be important for an instructor to identify core concepts and set specific competency goals that link the learning outcomes to the development of expertise. The research on deliberate practice initiated by Ericsson and Charness (1994) is particularly useful for graduate-level professional studies.

Conclusion

Course designs have traditionally focused on content questions, such as what content to present, in what order and what depth. Then in response, instructors have focused on covering the material, getting through the book, and meeting expectations so that faculty in other courses wouldn't muse and wonder, "Didn't you learn these concepts in this earlier course? And didn't you study the work and contributions of [fill in your favorite important person]?"

A major drawback with course designs that prioritize content is that this approach focuses attention on what the faculty member is doing, thinking, and talking about and not on the interaction and engagement of students with the core concepts and skills of a course. Trends in higher education since the late 1990s have encouraged a focus on learners as a priority, resulting in many publications such as *Launching a Learning-Centered College* (O'Banion, 1999) and Weimer's *Learner-Centered Teaching* (2002, 2013). This movement refocuses instruction on the learner and away from the content, a shift that encourages faculty to develop a habit of asking questions such as, "What is going on inside the learner's head?" "How much of the content and the tools can he or she actually use?" "What are learners thinking, and how did they arrive at their respective positions?" This focus on the learner has evolved to trends on accountability, student success, personalized learning, and analytics to capture what works (Johnson et al., 2015).

We have much more to learn about effective and joyful and meaningful teaching and learning, and more about teaching and learning in the variety of online, blended, and face-to-face environments. The good news is that we now know much more than what we did and have much more research evidence on what works.

Summary—and What's Next

This set of best practices is really just the tip of the iceberg in developing expertise in effective teaching and learning, but we hope you find it a useful set of practices as you get started in whatever new environment you will be using. Chapters Five through Nine provide tips and examples, as well as summaries and themes for what is happening in the four phases of a course.

Exercise and Reflection

If you are using this book for a course in faculty development, here are two activities to consider using to have faculty think more deeply about these best practices and to share their ideas and beliefs with their colleagues.

1. What top three best practices resonate with you? What would you add to this list as your personal best practice?
2. Spend time reflecting on these best practices. Where do your weaknesses lie? How will you strengthen those areas?

Chapter 4

Technology Tools to Support Teaching and Learning

THIS WAS AN intimidating chapter to write, as digital tools are changing faster than we can describe them. To avoid mentioning or describing specific tools that will be obsolete before the book is published, we primarily discuss tool categories. We describe the following three sets of technology tools for teaching in online, blended, or enriched classroom environments:

- The basics—the essential set of tools for teaching and learning wherever you are

- An enriched set of tools, building on the basic set

- A set of tools for practicing contextual knowledge and emerging possibilities

A high percentage of the tools mentioned and recommended in the tips are likely part of the learning management system (LMS) at your institution. These systems are so full-featured that it is possible to design almost any learning experience similar to those you may have designed for a face-to-face environment. A good strategy is to pick the three to four essential tools that are best suited for your learning goals and discipline and use those well. Then with each succeeding term you can expand your use of the tools. Remember, too, that while tools are constantly changing, they are often (though not always) getting easier to use, and many are free.

Choosing which technologies to use can be daunting. The next section of this chapter provides five guidelines to help you make initial choices for choosing and using technology tools. This is followed by descriptions of the three sets of tools.

Guidelines for Choosing and Using Technology Tools

Guideline 1: Pedagogy First, Technology Second

This guideline reminds us that learning design decisions take priority over decisions about technologies. In other words, technology should serve pedagogy. Dewey's philosophical core, that all learning is growth (1938), suggests that the most important decision of any learning experience design is the end goal, the desired outcome of the experience. This means that in designing a course, the starting point is clearly identifying and stating the desired learning outcomes. Once the learning outcomes are determined, we design the experiences for achieving the learning outcomes appropriate for our learners. At this point we make decisions about the technologies to best achieve the results.

Of course, it doesn't always work this way. Sometimes the technology decisions are mostly all in place. Institutions create the learning infrastructure and the technologies that learners are expected to have, and instructors are expected to design within this set of tools. This guideline encourages a mindset of designing your course with an eye on the available and best tools. In practice, all design is iterative, an interaction of design goals, expected students, and probable learning environments.

Guideline 2: Keep It Simple

The first time you teach in any new environment or with a new set of learners, it is wise to keep it simple and use the basic set of tools well supported by your institution.

If you focus on the essential tools and build your course around those tools, you can branch out later as you teach a course a second or third time and gain experience, confidence, and a sense of exploration.

Guideline 3: Involve Your Learners in Choices and Use of Digital Tools and Resources

We often forget about another resource for tools that is readily available: our learners. Many times our students will have experience with a tool that is an excellent fit for the learning experience. Or you might not have much experience with one of the tools, and feel a little apprehensive. Ask your learners for help and let them help you. They will feel part of the process and proud to be part of your learning too.

Your students can also be sources for rich media materials and tutorials and websites that might be effective supplements or alternatives for core concept or choice learning experiences. Students can be very resourceful in finding free materials and even developing learning materials themselves.

Guideline 4: Have Choices and Backups for When the Cloud Disappears

Always have a Plan B for when the technology you need the most fails. And yes, we're saying "when," not "if." It's inevitable that sometimes technology doesn't work as it should. Be ready to postpone or adjust a test, an assignment, or an expert event until the technology is available. For example, if a technology interruption is impacting assignment submissions, allow students to submit their work later, or in another way—by e-mail, text, or blog. Above all, assure students that their grades will not suffer because of the technology failure. Also, be open to solutions they may propose. This will help everyone relax and stay focused on the learning tasks, not the technology glitch.

Another element of providing technology choices is making certain that essential technology tools are readily available and affordable for learners. Sometimes it makes sense to let learners choose their favorite technology for producing important course products so they don't have to lose learning time using a course-mandated tool they won't be using again.

Guideline 5: Review Your Technology Tool Set Every Two to Three Terms

After you have taught a course for two or three terms, it is good to look at it with a fresh eye, using feedback from your students to see if there are resources or tools that can energize or better facilitate your desired learning goals. It is always good to also refresh your thinking about the expectations of your students and their experiences coming into your course.

As technologies appear that you think have possibilities for your course or for your students, evaluate them in light of the learning experiences framework. It is wise to introduce new technologies slowly to give you time to become comfortable with a tool. Introducing one new tool at a time is usually a good strategy.

When using a tool for the first time, it can be prudent to use it in the early middle or late middle of a course, when course processes are well established. This gives everyone a chance to try something new with minimal risk. Introducing new tools at the beginning of a course can interrupt the flow, affecting how well your course gets off the ground, and can impact the tone of the course more than at any other phase.

Basic Set of Technology Tools for Online and Blended Teaching and Learning

Teaching learners in any environment requires a core set of essential skills, tools, and habits. The primary task for any instructor is to develop and nurture a set of habits and skills to achieve the goals of guiding learners' growth within a community of learners. Digital technology tools help to achieve these goals.

When it comes to technology tools, there is good news and bad news. Tools help us accomplish teaching and learning communications much more easily and more efficiently than in the past. At the same time, tools are similar to pets, plants, and cars. They require investments of money and training, and regular updating to keep them in sync with the world around us.

In this section, we describe the basic set of technology tools and their purposes. A minimalist might say that the only tools anyone needs for teaching and learning are tools for communication and building relationships. Communications tools support presence, dialogue, and community. As we look at the basic tool set, communication and relationships are the purposes we will be focusing on. Everything else is enrichment, enhancements, icing on the cake. Fortunately, most basic communication tools for teaching and learning are now included in institution-provided learning management systems (LMS). Many communication tools are integrated as well, in less complex systems used for learning, such as blogs, and social media tools. Let's look now at the communication tools bundled into many large institutional teaching and learning systems.

Basic Set of Digital Technology Tools with Their General Teaching and Learning Purposes

1. Communication tools for supporting *instructor presence* (social, teaching, and cognitive) as described in Best Practice 1, and for building community, as described in Best Practice 2.

These communication tools include all the tools for talking to each other: e-mails, announcements, texting, tweeting, blog postings, discussion forums, and social media places, such as Facebook, and meeting places such as Blackboard Collaborate and Skype, and GoToMeeting. Also consider smartphones. How do we categorize these? Are they communication tools, creation tools, cameras, watches, flashlights, encyclopedias, or all of the above? Smartphones even

(continued)

support individual and small group meetings with e-mailing, messaging, or air-dropping photos, text, and media documents.

Communication tools also support explicit communication expectations (Best Practice 3), different size groupings (Best Practice 4), synchronous and asynchronous activities (Best Practice 5), and getting feedback early (Best Practice 6). Discussion forums support informal and formal sustained intellectual communications (Best Practice 7).

2. **Communication tools** for supporting *learner dialogue* with the instructor and with fellow learners, including all those already listed for instructor communication and presence and more. Learners may choose to create and use small groupings of two or more using tools such as Skype and Google Hangout as well as tweeting and other social media tools for just staying in touch and sharing ideas. Learners may be the ones who lead their instructors and fellow learners into use of new tools. This is a great engagement opportunity and should be welcomed as appropriate.

3. **Physical devices** of all shapes and sizes for content access, sharing, creating, and unlimited fast connections to the Internet. These physical devices include laptops, tablets, smartphones, watches, and wearables and are essentially multipurpose communication, content resource, and content-creating devices. These devices are essential for learners and instructors and to support Best Practice 8 on digital content resources.

Basic Set of Digital Technology Tools: Their Teaching and Learning Purposes

Communication Tools in the Learning Management System

The primary tool that you want to become very adept and familiar with is the learning management system (LMS) at your institution or organization. These systems are a bundled set of integrated tools that support almost any type of teaching and learning experience.

What are the key communication elements of an LMS? The sidebar "Basic Communication and Media Tools in the LMS" lists the primary teaching and learning communication features of these systems. These tools support teaching presence with ways of communicating with students and providing direction and access to content resources.

Most courses now have an online course site that is used as the primary gathering place, similar to a physical classroom. The course site is an online space for announcements, documents, peer-to-peer discussions, assignment submissions, and grading for online courses. It may also serve as the online space used to supplement the management of a course offered in a physical classroom. These systems now can do almost anything that you want to do in a traditional classroom with the advantage that the LMS is always "open" and available to students.

Basic Communication and Media Tools in the LMS

1. **Announcements:** This is perhaps the best tool for staying in touch with students on a daily or almost daily basis and helping to keep them focused and engaged. Announcement tools support basic text, audio, or video messages. They are ideal for short messages, ideas, and highlighting patterns, relationships, insights, and surprises in readings or forums. Announcements are essential for emergencies and late-breaking changes.

2. **Course Menu and Navigation:** The course menu is usually on the left side of the home page of your course. Most institutions provide a blank course template, customized to that institution. Templates help students by providing consistency across an institution's courses. Students then know where to find the syllabus and other course elements, such as unit resources, discussion forums, assignments, content resources, rubrics, gradebooks, and academic policies and procedures. When you start preparing your course, a template also guides you as to where to put all the materials you will be using to teach the course. If you need to prepare all the course materials, rather than using a course designed by someone else, the tips in Chapter Six will be very useful.

3. **Content Area:** This is usually one subsection of the menu just described, where the major course content parts are usually located. The course parts, which reflect the sequence and organization of the course and often correspond to the organization of books or other resource sets, are usually called either modules, units, topics, chapters, or weeks. Visualize eight to fourteen or more folders, each focusing on a key course content area.

4. **Discussion Forums:** This tool is for discussing and sharing ideas asynchronously so that discussions can carry on 24/7, wherever students or faculty might be. Faculty post a question, challenge, or task for students, and students post their responses. These discussions play the same role that face-to-face discussions play in classroom gatherings. The potential uses of these discussion forums are almost limitless, but a good starting practice is one discussion forum for each week of the course. More on using discussion forums can be found in Chapter Seven.

5. **Gradebook:** This tool is used to record and capture the points awarded for each of the course assignments. A good aid to using the gradebook is to develop an assessment plan with these five features of each course assignment: (1) assignment name, (2) purpose of the assignment, (3) due date, (4) number of points, and (5) location of the assignment rubric. Examples of these assessment plans are in Chapter Seven.

6. **Tests and Quizzes:** These tools administer tests and quizzes that are very useful as practice and self-review assignments. Tests and quizzes can be time-consuming to develop initially, but over time they will prove a great time-saver. Developed tests and quizzes are often part of a textbook offering. Depending on your course level and content, it can be helpful to adopt a textbook that provides these resources.

7. **E-mail Communications:** E-mail tools can be used in the traditional ways. As a basic tool, they are useful in handling private or confidential one-on-one messages between a faculty member and student. Group e-mails are no longer as useful as they once were, as faculty are tending more toward using the announcement or discussion forum for questions affecting larger groups of students. Students seldom use these tools for communicating with other students, as texting and other social media tools may be preferred.

8. **Collaboration Tools:** Small teams of students can use these tools for brainstorming and collaboration on small assignments or projects. These tools provide a way to meet in real time as on a conference call or phone call. They are scalable

(continued)

for small teams or large class meetings for Q&A, review, or project discussions or presentations. They can be used asynchronously by faculty or students to prepare mini-lectures on core concepts as well. More about these tools is in the enriched set of tools discussion later in this chapter.

9. **Audio and Video Tools:** These support recording, mixing, and editing audio and video. Some of the current tools that feature recording audio are simple audio, video, and note-taking apps for smartphones. Other, more-sophisticated tools include screen capture programs for laptops and web apps such as VoiceThread (www.voicethread.com). Some of these audio and video tools are integrated with large systems so you can use audio and video in your discussion forums and other tools. Other stand-alone apps support mixed-media storytelling and project work.

The sidebar "Basic Skills and Tools—Twelve Action Skills to Know" lists the action skills you need to learn to get started using an LMS. If you are associated with an institution, many institutions have workshops and tutorials introducing faculty to the particular LMS at their institution. Attending even one or two of these workshops is highly recommended, as they will often have additional documentation and tips and you will meet the support staff that you may need to call upon. If you are more independent, many tutorials and hints are widely available from vendor sites and also from publicly available resources at various university teaching and learning centers. A search often will reveal many useful resources on any of these topics.

Basic Skills and Tools—Twelve Action Skills to Know

When you attend a workshop or tutorial on the institution's LMS or meet with a support desk staff person, use this list to be sure you master these twelve actions.

1. Request or arrange for a course site.
2. Access the course site.
3. Know whom to contact for help for using the LMS.
4. Upload documents.
5. Create, edit, arrange, and delete folders.
6. Upload images.
7. Update and revise documents.
8. Use the announcement tool.
9. Set up and create discussion forums.
10. Set up assignments and major milestones.
11. Know how to access and manage course resources.
12. Set up teams and groups.

These "how to" basics are your survival skills for teaching with a LMS or online for the first time. Give yourself a break and don't expect perfection of yourself the first time you teach a course in this new-to-you environment. Just as your students are learning a new set of knowledge ideas, you are learning new digital tools, what they can do, and how to recover when things don't always go as expected. You are developing new habits of communicating and new strategies for teaching and developing relationship in a new environment.

Recall Guideline 2: <u>Keep it simple</u>. Use tools and teaching strategies as you are ready and as it makes sense for your course. If a tip suggests a tool or strategy that is not available to you or you are not quite ready for, simply adapt the tip as it makes sense to you if needed, and come back to it for further consideration at a later time. The set of basic tools in Table 4.1 are highly recommended for use in any teaching and learning situation.

TABLE 4.1

Basic Set of Technology Tools and Their Specific Pedagogical Uses

Pedagogical Uses and Purposes	Tip Number	Tools and Applications
1. Communicate with individual learners and groups of learners to guide learning and build a learning community.	CB1, CB10, EM1, EM13. LM13, LM14	Announcement tool, e-mail, text messaging, discussion forums, voice apps for synchronous exchange, such as Skype
2. Create a media-rich learning environment to provide variety, choices, and depth of processing opportunities.	CB1, CB2, EM16, LM9, IC1	Audio and video lectures and resources, such as TED Talks
3. Create audio or video announcements, short mini-lectures, or concept introductions.	CB1, EM12, EM16	Audio and video apps on smartphones, tablets, laptops, collaboration tools
4. Capture and record students' reflections, thinking, brainstorming, and peer-to-peer commenting.	CB1, CB8, CB10, CB14, EM 2, LM2, CW2	Blogs, online journals, discussion forums, presentations, wikis
5. Support student collaboration and teamwork on projects.	EM4, EM12, EM13, LM2, CW3	Wikis, or other collaborative project tools, and apps on smartphones and tablets
6. Introduce core concepts, demonstrating processes, showing visual examples.	CB 1, CB2, CB3, EM16	YouTube, Flickr, Tumblr, other apps for posting, sharing photos, videos
7. Provide a place where learners can ask general questions of the instructor or other students; reserve one place for general course questions and another for student social interaction—a place for learners to gather, meet, think out loud, learn, and practice.	CB 1, CB 6, CB 7, EM2, LM1, LM6, CW 1	Discussion forums, blogs, wikis, cyber cafés within LMSs, such as Blackboard, Desire2Learn, Canvas

(continued)

TABLE 4.1

(Continued)

Pedagogical Uses and Purposes	Tip Number	Tools and Applications
8. Remind students about assignments, emergencies, changes; give quick responses to critical questions or simple inquiries, or arrange meetings.	CB2, CB6, EM1, EM8	Announcement tool, text messages, Twitter, Facebook
9. Describe expectations for a forum posting, learning assignment, project, or team collaboration so that students understand the characteristics and features of the expected learning product.	CB1, CB16, EM2, EM4, LM3, LM8, LM11	Rubrics—scoring tools that lay out the grading criteria explicitly, often in a matrix using three or four criteria on a scale of 1 to 3 or 4 points
10. Help students to develop community and support each other and build networking with other students after courses and programs.	CB5, EM13, EM14, LM14	Social networking sites: Facebook, LinkedIn, Twitter, Google Plus, Tumblr, Flickr, SlideShare
11. Meet with students synchronously in real time for Q&A sessions, project discussions, review, and presentations. Students can use these for scheduled or spontaneous meetings. Good for inviting experts in for special sessions.	CB2, EM15, CW8, CW9	Synchronous collaboration tools and online classrooms: Blackboard Collaborate, Acrobat Connect, GoToMeeting, Google Hangouts *Zoom*
12. Give students practice in learning Bloom's lower-level learning objectives such as vocabulary and basic discipline knowledge and concepts.	CB1, EM2, EM5	Quizzes: testing subsystems within an LMS

More Thoughts on the Basic Tools

No matter who your students are or what content you are teaching, it is good to have a favorite, easy tool for creating short audio and video introductions. These might be introductions at the beginning of a course, module, or chapter, or topic overviews and expectations of learning, concept overviews, project introductions, or assessment summaries. These introductions can be text, of course, and a good way to get started, but with a little experimentation, energy, and time, you can take advantage of the audio and video tools that are so readily available today. Audio can even be more efficient, as you don't have to worry about spelling or formatting.

Our favorite audio, video, and image tools are in our pockets most of the time. They are the apps on our smartphones. A favorite audio tool for simple recording is easy to remember—AudioMemos—but there are many others. For video and image recording the camera app on most smartphones works very well. The only additional tool that makes recording easier is some type of tripod or selfie stick to position your phone to get a good angle when you are talking. Most computers also have audio and video tools, making audio and video lectures easy to create as well. All you need to do is find a quiet space and prepare some notes. Do this when you are ready and feeling adventuresome and can take a little time with it. You might even encourage your students to try it first and then learn from them.

Once you have recorded audio and video files or captured a set of images, it is easy to upload or e-mail these files to your course site or to a site such as YouTube. YouTube is one of many social networking sites that make it easy to upload and share videos. If you travel to a conference during the middle of a teaching term and want to stay in touch with your students and share insights from your conference, you can capture a short three- to five-minute interview with an expert or colleague and send it back to your students.

Most LMSs have built-in voice tools that also make it easy to record audio announcements, provide audio feedback, and have asynchronous audio discussions. When you are ready, look into your LMS's voice tools.

Blogs and wikis are mentioned in a number of tips for all phases of a course. Blogs are online journals or diaries that are organized with the latest postings appearing first. They can be used as reflective or outreach documents by individuals or groups. Blogs often have many levels of access, with opportunities for commenting and review so that you can customize the blog to your teaching style. Free blogging tools are widely available, and many LMSs have built-in blogs. Microblogs, smaller versions of blogs, might be great for status reports, thoughts, and questions on assignments or projects.

Wikis are web applications that support modification, extension, or deletion of their content and structure by individuals or groups. Wikis are particularly well suited for organizing and storing information that might be helpful for managing and producing collaborative group projects. The most famous example of a wiki is the modern encyclopedia project Wikipedia. Suggestions for teaching strategies using blogs and wikis are sprinkled throughout the tips.

Instant messaging is a text-based communications method that enables real-time conversation using pop-up windows on mobile smartphones and similar devices. The language of instant messaging can sometimes appear in discussion boards, such as LOL for "laugh out loud" or ?4U for "I have a question for you." Most online courses have a policy of discouraging instant messaging vocabulary in forum postings, but it is acceptable for text messaging and Tweets.

Facebook and LinkedIn are also mentioned in a number of tips, including CB Tip 4. On these social networking sites, users find and communicate with friends using pictures, blogs, videos, profiles, and "What I am doing now" messages. Many of your learners will be very familiar with these sites and can probably suggest ways to use some of the techniques from these sites in your course.

Zoom

Synchronous online tools, such as GoToMeeting and Blackboard Collaborate, are real-time web conferencing tools useful for a wide range of teaching and learning real-time interactions. Some of the most popular uses are live discussions, presentations by faculty and students, Q&A sessions, and general collaboration. These tools make it easy to prepare asynchronous short lectures or concept demonstrations as well.

Table 4.2 provides an *enriched basic* set of tools that you can choose to add to your repertoire of skills when you are ready. In fact, you may want to scan this table for any tool that might be particularly suited to your course and level of students. However, it is important to be comfortable with determining the point at which to start using specific tools. After teaching a course only once, you may just be developing a level of comfort with the course management system; thus it may not be worth your time or energy to test out any new tools. This is a personal choice. The basic set will serve you well. However, if you are fairly confident, the second time you teach a course is a good time to explore the enriched basic tool set.

When you are ready, identify a tool from the enriched basic set that makes sense for you, your students, and your discipline strategies. Once you select a tool, you can focus your energy on reading and finding ways to use it. The tips can help you with ideas and strategies. For example, you may choose to experiment with adding audio or video or images to your teaching. Choosing a tool or teaching strategy specific to a teaching goal is good practice, as it often energizes your thinking and your passion for your discipline.

One learning strategy that many faculty enjoy is learning from other faculty or from your students. You may hear about other faculty using these tools, or your own students may ask about or use these tools for their own learning and communication purposes. You can also encourage students to use graphics and audio and video media in their work as it fits the content and their own comfort and skill level.

TABLE 4.2

Enriched Set of Technology Tools and Their Pedagogical Uses

Pedagogical Uses and Purposes	Tip Number	Tools and Applications
1. Help students develop understanding and awareness of plagiarism and how to avoid it.	CB3	Software for detecting plagiarism, such as Turnitin and SafeAssign. Many institutions have a site license linked to the LMS.
2. Learners need a suite of productivity tools for writing essays, papers, and blogs, and for creating projects and presentations. Creating and producing content stimulates learners' engagement with and understanding of content.	EM9, EM12, LM9,	Students probably already have a suite of productivity tools on their devices. Institutions often have a site license for a standard set, such as the Microsoft or Apple suite. Other docs are freely available on the Web. Students might want to expand their set of tools for writing and creating to include audio and video capture and editing.
3. Learners engage more vigorously with the content when they talk and discuss assignments and readings with others. Using collaboration tools supports feelings of relatedness and deeper processing of content ideas. Collaboration tools can be particularly helpful when working on team or group projects, as they provide tracking and revision history.	EM13, EM15, LM10, CW8, CW9	Popular options for synchronous collaboration tools include Skype, Google Hangout, and live classrooms in LMSs. These can be used synchronously for live-action brainstorming and discussion, and reviewed asynchronously if they have been recorded.
4. Podcasts are a great content resource. They can provide variety and choices for required and recommended materials to support learning anywhere, anytime, and any while. Many tools support learners' creating and sharing their own podcasts.	EM10, EM16, LM9, LM14	Podcasts are audio or video files that can be created by using apps on smartphones, tablets, or laptops or within LMSs. Free podcasts are also available using these same apps. Podcasts are available on almost any topic from many discipline sites, and general public sites such as NPR, TED Talks, NASA, Smithsonian, and the Kahn Academy.

(continued)

TABLE 4.2

(Continued)

Pedagogical Uses and Purposes	Tip Number	Tools and Applications
5. As we encourage learners to use audio, image and video tools for their projects and for collaboration, learners need places and applications for creating and storing these content assets.	CB5, EM16, LM9, LM14, CW5, CW6	Flickr is one of many photo sharing sites; YouTube is a major video-sharing site; Dropbox is a useful cloud tool, as are the social media sites of Facebook and others. Concept maps are useful for graphically organizing and representing ideas, relationships, and patterns.
6. Faculty have management and assessment tasks in addition to teaching and mentoring. Systems that support these tasks often provide at-a-glance statistics about student presence in a course, grades, and discussion board participation and status of assignments.	CB15, CB17, EM2, EM6, EM10, LM12	Performance Dashboard is an example of a subsystem within Blackboard that provides a concise, up-to-date report on student activity. Other systems have similar features that can be valuable for managing, supporting, and helping to track student engagement and progress.
7. Soliciting informal feedback is especially valuable early in a course to identify the small changes that can make a big difference in learning and satisfaction; these tools make it easy.	EM3	Polldaddy/Survey Monkey survey tools

Tools for Practicing Contextual Knowledge and Exploring Possibilities

The next set of tools focuses on two teaching and learning goals: practicing new content knowledge in a variety of contexts and staying alert to emerging possibilities with new tools. Table 4.3 describes some tools that are particularly useful for embedding practice of core concepts into more complex and sophisticated contexts. For learners to really make knowledge their own, they need to see the concepts applied in a variety of contexts, which requires problem-solving and critical thinking and anticipating and dealing with consequences, both expected and surprising. This practice is

TABLE 4.3

Tools for Contextual Practice and Emerging Possibilities

Pedagogical Uses and Purposes	Tip Number	Tools and Applications
1. Demonstrate and practice the use of core and applied knowledge using problem solving in increasingly complex authentic learning scenarios.	EM8, EM14, LM4, CW1, CW2, CW6, IC1, IC3	Gaming apps that embed the complexities of design, operation, and decision-making in various disciplines can be a rich source of complex practice scenarios. These gaming apps can have literally hundreds of levels, creating infinite possibilities for analysis and critical thinking. Other apps that support simulations are also attractive options.
2. Content resources that explain core concepts or ideas or demonstrate the thought processes that experts use in solving math, engineering, or any type of problem can be invaluable in providing contextual practice. These can be open source resources; published resources available as part of a purchased set of course resources; or part of the lecture resources.	EM8, EM14, LM4, CW1, CW2, CW6, IC1, IC3	Open educational resources (OERs) consist of any types of useful learning resource, such as short concept tutorials and videos and image libraries for just about anything, such as bugs, plants, skin rashes, weeds, hospital rooms, children with speech problems. Search yourself or have your students search for resources to expand practice experiences and contextual examples. YouTube is a good place to go to for resources, as well as a place for posting videos and demos so students can see you and see process demonstrations; students can also post videos of practice and presentation on YouTube to reach a larger audience.
3. Give students practice in solving problems and working with multiple variables using virtual three-dimensional worlds that can be used for what-if scenarios. Assumptions and variables can be changed in these virtual worlds, either intentionally or randomly.	EM8, EM14, LM4, CW1, CW2, CW6, IC1, IC3	Animations that can be manipulated can be powerful aids to developing true and useful concept knowledge because the patterns and relationships become much clearer. Data from wearable devices is sure to become a rich resource for understanding people's behaviors, feelings, and creative processes.

(continued)

TABLE 4.3

(Continued)

Pedagogical Uses and Purposes	Tip Number	Tools and Applications
4. Visual representations can capture and communicate difficult-to-observe patterns and relationships. Challenge students to prepare a graphic representation of their developing knowledge by showing integration of new with existing knowledge.	EM8, EM14, LM4, CW1, CW2, CW6, IC1, IC3	Concept maps such as CmapTools and iMindmap can be used for problem solving using focus questions and to support organization and framing of knowledge.
5. As students often work on projects throughout a course, it is good to recommend a place for students to share and keep images, photos, and videos.	EM8, EM14, LM4, CW1, CW2, CW6, IC1, IC3	YouTube is only one of many websites for posting short videos; Flickr is one site for posting photos. Many students are now using Facebook as well for all types of media sharing.
6. Learners often want to learn the basics of a topic or advance their knowledge of a topic without being part of a long or overly structured educational experience. Other learners do not have the money to attend a formal university program.	EM8, EM14, LM4, CW1, CW2, CW6, IC1, IC3	MOOCs are massive online open courses that encourage enrollment of hundreds, if not thousands, of students simultaneously. MOOC courses are free and open to anyone interested in a topic. Processes are developing so that these courses include interaction among the students. Processes are also evolving so that more formal assessment and credit can be awarded to those successfully completing a course. This is good to see, as lowering the cost of higher education is a worthy goal, and this effort may inform our other systems.
7. Engaging in problem-solving and exploring tools with hands-on environments such as workshops and campus both support deeper learning. Some of the emerging edge tools can provide stimulating, innovative learning experiences.	EM8, EM14, LM4, CW1, CW2, CW6, IC1, IC3	Some of the emerging edge tools to watch for are robotic tools and applications, 3D printing to support design and prototype experiences, augmented reality with Google Glass, and literally thousands of apps.

Note: The Centre for Learning and Performance Technologies (C4LPT) at http://c41pt.co.uk conducts and publishes yearly surveys on the Top 100 Tools for Learning.

consistent with a novice-to-expert journey in any discipline or in the acquisition of any skill.

Some of the tools in Table 4.3 are just emerging as learning tools. They are what we call "emerging edge" tools, still on the periphery of the mainstream. We list these so you're aware of their potential to help your students in your discipline. Add them to your "alert list" and watch for them to become more widely available. All disciplines are changing with the advances in technology, and it is useful to see how these advances can help us bring our students greater convenience *and* deeper learning.

Staying in Sync with Tools

Staying in sync with technology tools in the twenty-first century is now part of all that we do. And as technology is totally integrated into our daily lives, it will continue to impact, change, and energize our teaching and learning experiences. Here are a few resources for monitoring new developments and tools.

1. Your own campus faculty support organization. They will be a great resource for staying aware of what you need to know about the tools on your campus.

2. The organization of your own discipline. It is highly probable that your discipline site will be recommending apps and resources and tools for your specialty.

3. The website run by Jane Hart—the Centre for Learning and Performance Technologies (C4LPT) in the UK. Jane also publishes a blog, Learning in the Modern Workplace, that adroitly addresses generic-learning issues as well: http://www.c4lpt.co.uk/blog/.

4. The website by Kathy Schrock for apps and Bloom's taxonomy: http://www.schrockguide.net/bloomin-apps.html.

5. The yearly NMC Horizon Report, published jointly by the New Media Consortium (NMC) and the EDUCAUSE Learning Initiative (ELI). The Horizon project was begun in 2001 and continues to identify and describe "merging technologies likely to have a large impact over the coming five years in education." This is our go-to yearly report to help keep our eye on current and future challenges and projects.

6. The Pew Research Center (www.pewresearch.org), a think tank that publishes reports on a wide range of issues, attitudes, and trends shaping America and the world. Their reports on access and use of technology and the Internet are particularly helpful in gaining a good measure of students' level of access to and knowledge about technology tools

and their associated behaviors. For example, their June 26, 2015 report on technology access finds that 84 percent of adults now regularly access the Internet. One of their conclusions is that for the young, highly educated, and affluent, Internet access is all but a given. This is good to know when designing and planning programs.

7. Friends, family, especially young adults ages 18 through 27.

8. Let's not forget checking Facebook and Twitter topics regularly with colleagues and friends. Identify some leaders or innovators in your field whom you might want to follow on Twitter.

Self-Directed Exercise/Application

1. What tools are supported by your institution?

2. Choose two or three tools that will support the learning outcomes of your course.

Chapter 5

Four Phases of a Course: Themes and Happenings

AS INTRODUCED IN Chapter One, every course—or planned sequence of learning experiences—has a natural ebb and flow. This flow generally has four phases: beginnings, early middle, late middle, and wrapping up. Each phase has specific goals and tasks for the learner and for the instructor. Each phase has recommended teaching and learning behaviors that can help to achieve those goals.

This chapter describes the themes and happenings of the four phases. For each phase we first describe the guiding themes, followed by its key happenings and goals and the recommended behaviors for achieving the goals. A table summarizes the learner experiences, key goals, supporting principles, best practices, and relevant tips for that phase.

Phase 1 Course Beginnings: Starting Off on the Right Foot
Course Beginnings: Themes

The guiding themes for course beginnings are *presence, community,* and *clear expectations*. These themes capture the basics of the teaching and learning goals and relationships that are essential features of any course. Some faculty like to post these words as a mantra on their cell phone, watch, or calendar. Some faculty like to add patience and energy as important guiding themes in the first weeks as well, as it takes a good measure of both to launch a course well!

Keeping an eye on these themes during course beginnings can help you feel confident about your teaching in the first weeks of an online or blended course. In fact, these themes are of continuing importance throughout any course. See Table 5.1 for a summary of the themes and desired actions in Phase 1.

TABLE 5.1

Phase 1: Course Beginnings—Starting Off on the Right Foot

Four Elements of Learning Experiences	Key Goals, Activities, and Events	Supporting Learning Principles*	Supporting Best Practices
Learner	Posting background and pictures and getting to know fellow learners	LP1 Learner is at center.	BP1 Social presence; cognitive presence
	Familiarizing self with course goals, setting personal and customized objectives	LP2 Learner brings existing mind to learning.	BP2 Supportive community
	Understanding course framework and requirements	LP6 Learner's zone of readiness may be narrow.	BP3 Clarify expectations
Faculty-Mentor	Establishing quick trust, promoting social presence	LP3 Faculty/mentor directs and supports learning.	BP1 Social presence; cognitive presence
	Getting acquainted with learners' backgrounds, points of readiness, and personal learning goals	LP8 Instruction should match goals.	BP2 Supportive community
	Ensuring that all learners are present and engaged		BP3 Clarify expectations
	Making course expectations clear and explicit		BP6 Early informal feedback
			BP11 Assess as you go
Content knowledge	Access to supplemental content resources is in place.	LP4 Learners must learn core concepts.	BP7 Discussion forums that challenge, inspire, provide practice
	Learners have core required resources.	LP7 Concepts are organized, interconnected knowledge clusters.	BP8 Think digital for all content
	Learners have access to and are familiar with rubrics.	LP8 Instruction should match goals.	BP9 Resources for core concepts and customized work
			BP12 Connect content to concepts
			BP13 Content frame for course

TABLE 5.1

(Continued)

Four Elements of Learning Experiences	Key Goals, Activities, and Events	Supporting Learning Principles*	Supporting Best Practices
Environment	Learners have required tools and know how to use them.	LP5 Environment and context influence learning.	BP3 Clarifying expectations
	Institutional tools for the learning experiences are in place, and learners know how to use them.	LP9 More time on task generally equals more learning.	BP4 Variety of experiences
	Learners know how to use, access library resources.	LP10 Tools shape us; we shape tools.	BP5 Synchronous and asynchronous activities
	Learners know how to meet and collaborate with peers.		BP14 Experiences to support novice-to-expert journey

*This table is built around core learning principle 1: "Every structured learning experience has four elements, with the learner at the center."

Presence

Presence is the most important best practice for an online course. This is the first of the best practices described in Chapter Three. Many course beginnings (CB) tips in Chapter Six describe specific actions and behaviors for achieving social, teaching, and cognitive presence in a course What is "presence" in the context of a teaching and learning experience? The simplest description of presence is "being there." Here are descriptions of the three presences and how they interact and work within the teaching and learning experiences of a course.

Social Presence

One of the best ways to get an online course off on the right foot is to ensure the social presence of the instructor and all the learners. Social presence is "achieved in the community of inquiry (CoI) model by faculty and students projecting their personal characteristics into the discussion so they become 'real people'" (Garrison, Anderson, & Archer, 2001; Swan & Shih, 2005). It is imperative that you establish trust so that content discussions can be open and substantive. One of the first tips (CB Tip 7) focuses on strategies for getting acquainted at the social level, sharing personal favorites such as drinks, food, ideas, books, or movies in the first week. This encourages expression of feelings, perspectives, and openness.

Cognitive Presence

A good companion to social presence in the first week of the course is a forum at which the learners identify their learning goals for the course, discuss their thinking about the course content, and share their personal learning goals. Finding out about each learner's personal goals helps an instructor gain insights into learners' knowledge, confidence, and experience with the content. It is a way of gaining insight into learners' individual zones of proximal development (ZPD). This question also encourages relatedness and connections as learners discover their shared and complementary experiences and goals.

Cognitive presence is defined as the "extent to which the professor and the students are able to construct and confirm meaning through sustained discourse (discussion) in a community of inquiry" (Garrison, Anderson, & Archer, 2001, p. 89). Cognitive presence is cultivated by students' expressing a desire to understand ideas more deeply and by dialogue that discerns patterns, connects ideas, and identifies relationships. Getting a sense of what students know and how they know it lays the foundation for the learning experiences that follow.

Teaching Presence

Teaching presence in an online course consists of at least two major categories of teaching direction. The first consists of all the course materials that are prepared before the course begins: the syllabus, concept introductions, discussion forums, assessment plans, and lists of resources. The second category consists of all the monitoring, mentoring, questioning, and shaping of the growing knowledge of particular learners in a course. The first category of teaching presence is developed based on the assumptions of what students probably know and understand—the "mythical" student for design purposes. The second category, "facilitating reflection and discourse for the purpose of building understanding" (Garrison, 2011, p. 58), is customized to the particular set of students. A potential third category of teaching presence includes the work of direct instruction coaching and clarifying any intellectual issues with individual students (Garrison, Anderson, & Archer, 2010).

Community

Building a sense of shared understandings, knowledge of one another, and mutual support, even if values are not shared, are elements of community. The goal of community in an online course is twofold: building knowledge and competencies in learners and building a network of mutual respect and sharing of ideas and perspectives (Brown, R. E., 2001; Rovai, 2002).

Clarity of Expectations

Clear and unambiguous guidelines about what is expected of learners and what they can expect from an instructor make a significant contribution to ensuring understanding and satisfaction. Watch for how this theme of managing expectations surfaces in many of the tips. Teaching and learning at a distance and sometimes over time zones, plus using a set of tools and systems that might not always work quite right, carry the potential for many misunderstandings. Clarifying how all this will work and sometimes might not work can help create a smooth and trusting learning environment. In the initial week of a course, it is particularly good to have procedures in place for what to do when tools and life don't work as expected. This is also true for weeks with key milestone and grading events.

Patience

It is important to be patient with yourself and with your learners in the beginnings of any learning experience. Everyone needs to develop a mutual understanding regarding content expectations, goals, and tools. If you are new to online or blended learning, you have a number of new skills and habits to develop. Also, your students may need to adjust to unfamiliar processes and to assuming more responsibility for what they know and the skills and values they want to develop.

Energy

Energy and enthusiasm are infectious. As you share your own excitement, knowledge, curiosity, and questions within your discipline, learners will respond. As learners, we crave innovation, novelty, questions that we can test ourselves on, and cool surprises. See what you can do to design these into your courses' learning experiences.

What's Happening in Course Beginnings

Getting off to a good start in any learning experience means creating enthusiasm for the learning to come, clarifying expectations, and creating an atmosphere of trust and support. Social presence is getting to know others as people with hearts, minds, and personal interests. Getting acquainted at a social level creates a trusting and understanding environment that makes it safe to step out intellectually and risk stating beliefs and thinking in the forum discussions. Think of the social gatherings you've attended. You enter the room, introduce yourself to various people, and find connections with one another before revealing any of your personal beliefs and values.

A similar process happens in a course. If we expect learners to be open and vulnerable in expressing what they do or do not know, especially without seeing one another, encouraging social interaction first is a must. Only then can learners shift to a content and knowledge focus. The importance of social presence means the getting-acquainted postings by faculty and learners have great value and meaning. Recall the suggestion for also getting acquainted intellectually, with cognitive presence, sharing our thinking about the course content and personal learning goals.

During the course beginnings, one of the instructor's responsibilities is to ensure that all learners are engaged, present, and participating. The role of the faculty member at this time is sometimes referred to as a "social and cognitive negotiator" (Conrad & Donaldson, 2011). The faculty member focuses on providing positive, supportive, and encouraging comments about the overall course process and clarifies course expectations and the types of learning experiences in the course requirements. The instructor also introduces other members of the instructional support team.

Another major goal of the course beginnings phase is launching the course community. This means ensuring that students are engaging in the core concepts of the course and "thinking out loud" about the course concepts. One characteristic of community is identifying and sharing common values and being respectful of others' ideas, even if they are quite divergent. The instructor helps to guide this process with a combination of social, teaching, and cognitive presence activities.

In summary, during the first week or two of a course, this is happening:

- Learners are getting acquainted with each other, examining and discussing course requirements, getting acquainted with the course content and resources, and setting personal and working learning goals.

- In the week or two prior to the course launch, the instructor is finalizing the course and ensuring that all is ready for the learners. Once the course begins, the instructor focuses on creating a comfortable and trusting learning environment and begins implementing the course plan for the first weeks. The instructor models thinking behavior by making connections among the learners, the content, and the desired learning outcomes. Other important actions are making course requirements and processes for communicating explicit, leading the launch of the course learning community, and ensuring that all students are engaged.

- The content resources are in place, and students have acquired the content resources required for the course. If there are problems with access to these resources, the community comes together with ways to address the problems.

- Institutional tools for the learning environment are in place. Learners have the tools they need and know how to use the required applications and tools and whatever help they might need.

Phase 2 Early Middle: Keeping the Ball Rolling

Early Middle: Themes, Best Practices, and Principles

The themes for the early middle phase of a course intensify the themes of the course beginnings. These themes include ensuring that social presence is well established, your teaching presence is working for all your students, and you are nurturing the growth of community. On a personal development level, the early middle is also a good time to expand the set of technology tools for the online and blended environment.

In the community of inquiry (CoI) model developed by Garrison and others (Garrison, Anderson, and Archer, 2001), there are three presences—social, teaching, and cognitive—all of which have a role to play in each stage of a course. The roles that these presences play, however, ebb and flow throughout the course, as do the dependencies between them (Akyol & Garrison, 2008; Garrison, Cleveland-Innes, & Fung, 2010; Kozan & Richardson, 2014). In the first phase of a course, establishing social presence and teaching presence is a very high priority. Establishing social presence, getting to know each other, and building trust launches the community; the teaching presence provides the framework for guiding learning and setting out the goals and expectations for the course learning experience. The third presence, cognitive presence, is launched with the discussion of learning goals and is less prominent, but quickly gains importance.

In the early middle of a course, the emphasis shifts into a higher gear of teaching presence and cognitive presence as learners begin deeper engagement and learning of the course content and develop group cohesion. In the two later phases, 3 and 4, the teaching presence becomes even more specialized as learners receive direct guidance from the community, the instructor, and fellow learners on their projects. At the same time the overall cognitive presence of the community grows and deepens. This shift in emphasis parallels the development of how the faculty role shifts during the stages of a course.

Let's take a closer look at the themes for the early middle. See Table 5.2 for a summary of the Phase 2 themes.

TABLE 5.2

Phase 2: Early Middle—Keeping the Ball Rolling

Elements of Learning Experiences	Key Goals, Activities, and Events	Supporting Learning Principles*	Supporting Best Practices
Learner	Actively engages in forums and assignments with core course concepts	LP1 Learner is at center	BP1 Social presence; cognitive presence
	Settles into a weekly rhythm of readings, postings, collaborating with fellow learners	LP2 Learner brings existing mind to learning	BP2 Supportive community
	Intensifies work on personal learning goals	LP6 Learner's zone of readiness may be narrow	BP14 Novice-to-expert journey practice
Faculty-mentor	Continues strong teaching presence, guides practice of core concepts	LP3 Faculty/mentor directs and supports learning	BP1 Social, teaching, and cognitive presence
	Supports community and work in small teams	LP6 Support learners' personal zones of readiness and interest	BP2 Supportive community
			BP11 Assess as you go
			BP12 Connect content to concepts
Content knowledge	Learners are intensely exploring, engaging, and identifying more content resources and sharing with community.	LP7 Concepts are organized, interconnected knowledge clusters	BP7 Forums that challenge, inspire, practice
	Faculty-mentor increases focus on cognitive presence, supporting learners' practice, exploration, and testing of ideas.	LP8 Instruction should match goals	BP9 Resources for core concepts and customized work
	Course community collaboratively builds knowledge base of content.		BP12 Connect content to concepts
			BP13 Content frame for course

TABLE 5.2

(Continued)

Elements of Learning Experiences	Key Goals, Activities, and Events	Supporting Learning Principles*	Supporting Best Practices
Environment	Community has settled into a routine of using a set number of tools for collaboration, teaming, and learning.	LP9 More time on task generally equals more learning LP10 Tools shape us; we shape tools	BP4 Variety of experiences BP5 Synchronous and asynchronous activities BP14 Experiences supporting novice-to-expert journey

*This table is built around core learning Principle 1: "Every structured learning experience has four elements, with the learner at the center."

Social Presence

By the early middle of a course, learners should be relatively comfortable with their fellow learners. In particular, after some small group work with two or three students, learners may have identified one or two others with whom they feel some particular kinship, and they feel a general kinship with the larger group, based on their shared experiences with required readings and work. With this type of trust and community developed, it is a good time to take advantage of assigning additional peer review and peer consulting and to continue collaborative work in the discussion forums and other short assignments. By this time learners should feel that it is safe to inquire, share, and challenge comments in a positive and inquiring way.

Teaching Presence

Teaching presence in the early middle of the course is in high focus as learners navigate through readings, assignments, and interactions with peers. Recall that the first category of teaching direction is embedded in the course materials prepared before the course begins, and the second category of teaching presence includes those activities that arise spontaneously based on actual student skills, interests, and needs. The mantra that we "design for the probable learners and teach to the actual students" succinctly captures the major work of teaching presence. This category of teaching presence includes the communication and activities associated with directing, monitoring, and mentoring the particular community of students. As any veteran teacher knows, each group of students develops a unique personality as it moves through the course.

Cognitive Presence

As noted earlier, cognitive presence is launched in the first week, using an assignment to review course learning outcomes, to identify one or two key learning outcomes important to the learner, and to customize at least one of the learning outcomes so that it is a very specific, focused, and achievable goal. Work on cognitive presence, started in a general soft immersion in the course beginnings, deepens through discussion and practice of core concepts in discussion forums and short assignments.

One approach to achieving cognitive presence in your course builds on the strategies for problem formulation and resolution strategies: think of it as a process of inquiry with four phases as described in the practical inquiry model (Garrison & Vaughan, 2008), beginning with a triggering event. We like to think that setting specific goals is one example of a triggering event. Learners develop a knowledge structure of core concepts as they progress through the stages of inquiry: a triggering event, exploration, integration, and resolution.

In the early middle, if not before, is the time that students identify a major course project and begin serious exploration of the question or problem of their project.

Nurturing of the Content and Learning Community

Cultivating and nurturing the learning community is a high priority continuing during the early middle. In this phase of the course, the learners and the learning community itself might be compared to seedlings, striving to root themselves using an appropriate combination of water (teaching direction), light (reflection), and wind (dialogue). Part of the teaching presence task is to provide a sheltered and safe place for this rooting. You will have many questions about your teaching presence during this time. How little presence is too little? How much presence is stifling? Will learners feel alone, or will they feel too directed? There are no easy or "this always works" answers here. Just as in the classroom, you will develop a sense of what is right for a particular group of students. Recall the following core understandings about community and cognitive presence:

- Developing community means building a sense of shared understanding, knowledge of one another, and mutual support, even if these values are not shared (Dede, 1995; Sergiovanni, 1994).

- Cognitive presence is the process of constructing meaning through collaborative inquiry (Garrison, 2006).

- "We use the concept of cognitive presence to describe the intellectual environment that supports sustained critical discourse and higher-order knowledge acquisition and application" (Garrison, 2011, p. 42).

- Cognitive presence is sharing how our brain is adapting, integrating, thinking and sometimes struggling with concepts, ideas, and structure (Boettcher, 2007).

What's Happening in the Early Middle

After you have made a good start on launching your course and getting to know your students, both in their heads and as whole persons, the early middle is the time that the focus on content, concepts, and application of concepts begins to get intense. Your top two teaching goals during this early middle are as follows:

- Ensure that all students are engaged with, learning, and using the course content knowledge to grow their own knowledge base

- Nurture the growth of the course community so the communication and support of the community strengthens and encourages curiosity and learning

By the early middle weeks, learners have generally settled into their weekly rhythm, are feeling comfortable about the course content, and are developing relationships with some of the other learners. The learning community is evolving, with all the learners participating.

During this time, it is essential that the faculty member continues a strong teaching direction presence. The faculty role in this stage of the course is evolving to assume the role of a structural engineer, overseeing how learners are supporting and querying each other in discussion forums (Conrad & Donaldson, 2012). This is also a time for teams of two or three to work on collaborative assignments or peer review or consulting.

The course content is at center stage as learners are actively exploring and learning new concepts. This is also the time when learners are applying core concepts in various scenarios and problem settings.

One barrier to community development can be the pressure of needing to cover content. A feeling of community often arises following a "long, thoughtful, threaded discussion on a subject of importance after which participants felt both personal satisfaction and kinship" (Brown, 2001, p. 18). Pressure to keep moving into new content can short-circuit the time for exploration and for sorting through issues and ideas. Sometimes it makes sense to introduce small changes in content readings in the middle of a course to accommodate the spontaneity of learning.

In summary, this is what is happening in the early middle:

- Learners are engaging with the course concepts and applying the concepts within relatively accessible scenarios and problems. These can be ill-structured or well-structured problems. Well-structured problems are those that have right or wrong answers; ill-structured problems are more complex and mirror problems in real life, meaning that students need to formulate the question and examine the possibilities and assumptions within the problem. You may want to refresh your thinking about Learning Principle 4 (learners do not need to learn all the course content, but all learners need to learn the core concepts) and the slice of content pie.

- Learners are establishing their personae within the community and sharing what they are thinking and why. They are working on small teams on various assignments and sharing ideas and comments within the community.

- The faculty member is in high gear, focusing on the core concepts and ensuring that all students are engaged with the content problems. This means that the instructor is exerting a relatively strong teaching presence but is also encouraging the learners to be clear about what they are understanding and to take the lead on course experiences such as reporting out, sharing, and wrapping up discussions.

This early middle period is a very intense time, but less so than the first weeks. This is the time to nurture the learning community and guide and mentor learners as their personal interests and goals begin to emerge.

Phase 3 Late Middle: Letting Go of the Power

Late Middle: Themes, Best Practices, and Principles

The themes for the late middle—questioning, assessing, project coaching, and empowerment—capture the essence of the work for this phase. This is where the learners come into their own as to what they are thinking and knowing about the course content. This is also the place in the course where they use their questioning and thinking skills to integrate the course knowledge into their personal and customized knowledge base. Almost all curricula goals include critical thinking as a desired learning outcome. Critical thinking is also one of the cross-functional skills recommended by the well-known report, *Building a Nation of Learners: The Need for Changes in*

Teaching and Learning to Meet Global Challenges (Business-Higher Education Forum, 2003) and a similar report, *Framework for 21st Century Learning* (2015) from the Partnership for 21st Century Learning Planning. Doing course projects is another strategy that encourages student learners' individual content integration, resolution, and critical thinking processes.

A 2013 report, *Promoting Effective Dialogue Between Business and Education Around the Need for Deeper Learning*, also affirmed the need not only for critical thinking but also for "deeper learning." The report defined deeper learning as "mastery of core content knowledge in a given field and well-developed workplace competencies, such as the ability to think critically and solve complex problems, work collaboratively, communicate effectively, and learn how to learn (e.g., self-directed learning)" (p. 1). These are the fundamental skills that will prove valuable to students in all segments of their lives as well as being most valuable to business and our country's competitiveness. Watch for the tips that emphasize critical thinking, questioning, problem-solving, and working with ill-structured, messy real-life scenarios.

Let's take a closer look now at the late middle themes. Table 5.3 presents a summary of themes and suggested faculty actions for Phase 3.

Cognitive Presence

Cognitive presence begins to take center stage following the phases in the process of inquiry: a triggering event, followed by exploration, integration, and resolution. In the late middle, the exploration phase for one's key course project is drawing to a temporary close as the focus on integrating the knowledge into a meaningful structure begins to take shape, with the goal of reaching a resolution point by the end of the course.

As noted in the literature (Swan, Garrison, & Richardson, 2009; Rourke & Kanuka, 2009), we reach the resolution phase of the inquiry process less often than we would like. It may be our course structures, teaching strategies, lack of reflection time, or administrative constraints that limit these possibilities. Capstone courses that focus on projects and complex scenario building are the courses that probably come closest to the goal of completing a process of inquiry cycle.

Questioning

Questioning is at the core of teaching and learning. It is through questioning that we learn what students know, why they think what they do, and what they want or need to know next. Questioning is one of the tools that enables us to learn each learner's ZPD, that is, what he or she is ready to

TABLE 5.3

Phase Three: Late Middle—Letting Go of the Power

Elements of Learning Experiences	Key Goals, Activities, and Events	Supporting Learning Principles*	Supporting Best Practices
Learner	Works on applying and using core concepts in increasingly challenging problems and scenarios	LP1 Learner is at center	BP1 Social presence; cognitive presence
	Actively searches for examples of patterns and relationships	LP2 Learner brings existing mind to learning	BP2 Supportive community
	Reviews, consults, supports, challenges others' ideas and proposals	LP4 Learners focus on core concepts	BP4 Variety of experiences
	Contributes to and becomes a member of the course community	LP6 Learner's zone of readiness may be narrow	BP5 Synchronous and asynchronous activities
			BP14 Novice-to-expert journey practice
Faculty-mentor	Monitors processes, which are well-established	LP2 Supports learners' personal zones of readiness and interest	BP1 Social, teaching and cognitive presence
	Supports community interaction and dialogue that is mostly working well; monitors and challenges and clarifies as appropriate	LP3 Faculty/mentor directs and supports learning	BP2 Supportive community
	Shifts from large group teaching presence to more personalized and small group teaching presence	LP8 Instruction should match goals	BP7 Forums that challenge, inspire, practice
	Supports more learners-as-leaders experiences		BP11 Assess as you go
	Reviews, mentors learners' projects		BP12 Connect content to concepts
	Provides feedback on assignments		BP14 Experiences support novice-to-expert journey

TABLE 5.3

(Continued)

Elements of Learning Experiences	Key Goals, Activities, and Events	Supporting Learning Principles*	Supporting Best Practices
Content knowledge	Learners are creating content as they learn and sharing with others in wikis, blogs, projects.	LP4 Learners don't have to learn all content	BP7 Forums that challenge, inspire, practice
	Learners are applying knowledge in assignments and peer consulting review and forums.	LP7 Concepts are organized, interconnected knowledge clusters	BP8 Think digital for all content
	Learners are actively creating knowledge representations of the course content.	LP8 Instruction should match goals	BP9 Resources for core concepts & customized work
	Content frame for the course helps organize data, examples, experiences.		BP12 Connect content to concepts
			BP13 Content frame for course
Environment	Learners are actively using course tools and may be expanding beyond and personalizing tools and bringing examples and tools back to the community.	LP5 Environment affects learning	BP4 Variety of experiences
	Learners have identified and are using their most effective learning environments.	LP9 More time on task generally equals more learning	BP5 Synchronous and asynchronous activities
		LP10 Tools shape us; we shape tools	BP14 Experiences support novice-to-expert journey

*This table is built around core learning Principle 1: "Every structured learning experience has four elements, with the learner at the center."

learn. Effective questioning also reveals misconceptions and sources of possible confusion. By hearing students' thoughts, voices, and questions through text, audio, and video postings, we come to know their minds and their knowledge structures. Some of the tips for this phase address how questioning makes students' knowledge visible to us. The techniques include turning questioning upside down and inside out by having students pose the questions to try to stump the instructor. The tips offer references for classic resources such as Bloom's taxonomy and the updated Bloom's taxonomy by Krathwohl (2002) and examples of the categories of Socratic questioning.

Assessing

Assessing is a major management and administrative task that we sometimes avoid because of the potential conflicts and disappointments that can occur. One major difference between campus and other digital courses is that an online course design plans for continuous and multiple points of assessment (Moallem, 2005): individual, small group, and larger group team assignments; feedback cycles and self-review; and peer and expert review. Continuous feedback and assessment means that assessment grading usually brings few surprises. With continuous and ongoing feedback, students should have a fairly clear idea of how they are doing throughout the course. Assessment tasks that focus on a combination of core concept practice and customized learning goals create enthusiasm and energy that often promote very satisfactory learning.

Project Coaching

For us, projects are where the rubber meets the road. In most of the first half of a course, students are encountering and experiencing resources in a domain of knowledge that may be quite unfamiliar to them. Learners are being exposed to content at a rate that can seem as if it is coming at them through a fire hose. There is usually insufficient time for pausing, reflecting, and thinking. We hope that the course design recommendations in the first chapters encourage a more realistic and practical, while still challenging, approach to acquiring course knowledge and achieving the performance goals of a course. It is one thing to have the goal of covering a certain amount of content, but it is even more important for students to engage with and process course content.

Projects are excellent knowledge integration tools; projects are also excellent tools for supporting personalization and customization goals. Projects should be designed with multiple assessment points so learners start their projects early, staging their project work throughout the course. With multiple assessment points—such as an initial proposal and concept review, an initial draft and a final paper and presentation—you, other students, and potentially invited experts get to know the students and the problem that they may be grappling with or focusing on. With multiple assessment points, students can review, discuss, and provide feedback on other learners' ideas and projects. Projects can be individualized so that students have an opportunity to focus their learning on topics of interest to themselves while still learning the core content. An additional value is that every course expands your own expert knowledge as you coach students through the design, selection, and execution of projects that the learners really care about.

Empowerment

The subhead of this Phase 3 section on the late middle, "Letting Go of the Power," captures what should be happening as the learners progress through their growing acquaintance with core content. The ideal mentor coaches his or her apprentices so that they outgrow their master. A learner's performance goals should challenge the learner to grappling with real-life complex problems. We know that simulating real-life disaster scenarios prepares people to respond automatically when met with real disaster. For example, pilots practice in flight simulators so they are prepared for complex real-life challenges. The same is true for the learning environment. We want to simulate, as much as possible, the types of scenarios that learners will encounter in life and prepare them for those situations and problems. The theme of empowerment means encouraging students to think about, respond to, and analyze each other's work. By supporting each other with problems, learners get multiple opportunities to practice and apply the course content. One of the future learning shifts may be to include the learner within a more hands-on community context resembling past apprenticeship models (Hagel, Brown, & Kulasooriya, 2014).

What's Happening in the Late Middle

With the arrival of the late middle, you and your students are likely well acquainted with each other from both a social and cognitive perspective. Your teaching direction is actively guiding both group and individual learning goals. Use of collaborative tools, such as blogging, wiki, and meeting tools, is increasing to support desirable learning outcomes, such as critical thinking and effective problem solving.

Interaction and assignment processes are established; a certain equilibrium and rhythm is in place. The course learning community has a history of trust, and a feeling of comfortable camaraderie has been established from the work learners have been doing in supporting, challenging, and helping each other. With these processes operating smoothly, you can relax a little and continue your shift from directing the learners' activities to increased facilitating and mentoring. Rather than focusing on actively directing learning experiences, you are devoting more of your time and energy to responding to questions and supporting learners as they engage with and apply the content. Time on project work is intensifying, and this is the time to individualize the mentoring and coaching for personalizing learning. Learners need to be progressing well on their course projects and interacting with the other learners on those projects.

The growing confidence of the learners makes it easier for faculty to begin letting go of power and sharing it with learners. While an instructor continues to make key course decisions—such as the timing of certain events in a course, appropriateness and fit of projects, and major grading—learners can share other responsibilities, such as conducting peer review, expanding learning outcomes, helping others to develop knowledge, and leading in the development of activities in the course.

During the late middle, a key teaching responsibility is to encourage students' movement from exploring and researching ideas to integrating knowledge and producing knowledge products that capture some of their new knowledge. This follows the stages of the practical inquiry model referred to earlier: a triggering event, exploration, integration, and resolution. This is the time to support students as they complete the exploration stage and begin integrating that explored knowledge into a usable knowledge representation. Course activities should help students move beyond integrating core concepts to defining problems and brainstorming resolutions.

Other important cognitive teaching responsibilities during this stage are to highlight patterns and relationships in the content and cycle back as appropriate to earlier course content. New core content is often concentrated in the first three-quarters of a course, and the last part of the course focuses more on the integration and application of content in solving problems. The late middle can be the best and last time to identify and correct misconceptions.

In summary, this is what is usually happening in the late middle:

- Learners are moving from the rapid and expansive knowledge exploration stage to working with problems and scenarios that require the integration of some of the core course concepts. They are responding to others and providing comments and suggestions on other students' proposed projects. Learners are generally working in small groups during this stage.

- The instructor is focusing on providing feedback to learners on the shaping and fit of learners' projects and how the projects are progressing. The role of the faculty is shifting to being primarily a facilitator of learning experiences and supporting the learners as they lead, summarize, and integrate content experiences. Faculty are striving to encourage the building of relationships, patterns, and connections and spiraling and layering the core content concepts. The instructor continues in high gear, focusing on the core concepts, but also shifts to challenging the learners even more, sometimes with complex discipline problems for which there are no known answers.

Your task as an instructor in this late middle phase of the course is to subtly shift the responsibility for directing learning more and more to the learners, their projects, and their learning outcomes, while at the same time ensuring that the course core concepts are well integrated into their knowledge frameworks. The tasks for students in this phase of the course are to move aggressively to complete the exploration stage of their learning, refine their course project plans, and complete sections of their projects while assisting and supporting the projects of their fellow learners.

The late middle is our favorite part of the course: the learners are actively engaged, the community is functioning well, we are developing insights spontaneously with our learners, and the stress of the final weeks is still in the future.

Phase 4 Closing Weeks: Pruning, Reflecting, and Wrapping Up
Closing Weeks: Themes, Best Practices, and Principles

The principal themes for learners in the closing weeks are learner independence, learners' reflecting on course knowledge, and completing the course projects and assignments. The major themes for the instructor are mentoring the students in how they apply core concepts and relationships, and coaching the learners in their projects and assignments. By this time, work on course projects is well under way, and discussions in the project forum should reflect learners' growing sophistication and understanding of course knowledge and concepts. Course projects and related complex scenarios generally reflect learners' progress toward identifying potential strategies for addressing difficult course or discipline issues. Table 5.4 lists the themes and behaviors for the closing weeks.

TABLE 5.4

Phase Four: Closing Weeks—Pruning, Reflecting, and Wrapping Up

Elements of Learning Experiences	Key Goals, Activities, and Events	Supporting Learning Principles*	Supporting Best Practices
Learner	Digs deeply into core concepts and resources to support project work and complete assignments	LP1 Learner is at center	BP1 Social presence; cognitive presence
	Actively reviews materials for relevance to projects and assignments	LP2 Learner brings existing mind to learning	BP2 Supportive community
	Contributes to and becomes a member of the course community	LP4 Learners focus on applying core concepts	BP4 Variety of experiences
	Leads some of the learning activities	LP6 Learner's zone of readiness may be narrow	BP5 Synchronous and asynchronous activities
	Reflects, secures personal knowledge outcomes		BP14 Novice-to-expert journey practice
Faculty-mentor	Continues shift of teaching direction to role of mentor and coach	LP3 Faculty/mentor directs and supports learning	BP1 Social, teaching, and cognitive presence
	Keeps a focus on core concepts and their relationships and applications	LP6 Supports learners' personal zones of readiness and interest	BP2 Supportive community
	Supports community and work in small teams	LP8 Instruction should match goals	BP10 Plan a good closing and wrapping and pruning activities
	Continues a strong cognitive and teaching presence, supporting learners' projects and the course community		BP11 Assess as you go
	Clarifies course wrap-up activities and requirements		BP12 Connect content to concepts
	Manages wrap-up experiences		BP14 Experiences support novice-to-expert journey
	Provides feedback on assessments		

TABLE 5.4

(Continued)

Elements of Learning Experiences	Key Goals, Activities, and Events	Supporting Learning Principles*	Supporting Best Practices
Content knowledge	Learners focus on relationships, patterns, and use of core concepts.	LP6 Supports learners' personal zones of readiness and interest	BP7 Forums that challenge, inspire, practice
	Faculty/mentor increases focus on cognitive presence, supporting learners' practice, exploration, and testing of ideas.	LP7 Concepts are organized, interconnected knowledge clusters	BP8 Think digital for all content
	Course community collaboratively builds knowledge base of content.	LP8 Instruction should match goals	BP9 Resources for core concepts and customized work
	Content resources used by learners go beyond the basics to support their personalized and customized learning goals and projects.		BP12 Connect content to concepts
			BP13 Content frame for course
Environment	Community has settled into a routine of using a set number of tools for collaboration, teaming, and learning.	LP5 Environment and context influences learning	BP5 Synchronous and asynchronous activities
	Learners are using whatever tools make the most sense for the work and their projects.	LP9 More time on task generally equals more learning	BP10 Plan a good closing and wrapping and pruning activities
		LP10 Tools shape us; we shape tools	BP14 Experiences support novice-to-expert journey

*This table is built around core learning Principle 1: "Every structured learning experience has four elements, with the learner at the center."

Learner Independence

By the closing weeks of the course, we sincerely hope that learners are familiar with the core concepts of the course knowledge and are able to say how these concepts relate to one another and to core concepts outside the boundaries of the course knowledge. Ideally, they can apply these core concepts in their projects and in the ideas they are contributing to other learners' projects. They also know how to make their contributions to their peers in a constructive and helpful manner. The learning community is operating smoothly, with the goal of everyone helping others in achieving the course goals. Learners are independent in their learning tasks, but strong links within the course community encourage them to help each other as appropriate as well. While these are a lot of optimistic expectations for learner independence and success, these expectations may need to be adjusted to fit individuals' readiness and skill levels.

Reflecting and Pruning Knowledge

Memory research confirms that we retain only a small percentage of our experiences (Schacter, 2001). Rather than railing against this natural memory process, it is best to work with it, identifying the specific and explicit core concepts that we want learners to take forward into their lives and careers. In other words, what will the learner be likely to use and remember after the course is over? Recall that each learner begins the course with his or her own particular area of interest and readiness. This means that the particular integration work of core concepts and examples that the learner will grapple with most often will be unique to each learner.

The probability is high, given appropriate study and experiences, that most learners will develop mastery of the core concepts, the center of the content pie described earlier. However, there is also a high likelihood of a fair amount of divergence in the learners' knowledge, especially in the application of the concepts. This divergence is natural and rooted in the processes of encouraging learners to customize and personalize course knowledge. At the end of a course, an assignment specifically asking students what they have learned and how they plan on using the knowledge is beneficial. This strategy is similar to the technique of a one-minute summary (Angelo & Cross, 1993; Light, 2004; Barkley, Major, & Cross, 2014) recommended for use in lecture classes. A one-minute summary asks students to respond to a question, such as "What was the most important thing that you learned in this [class, paper, reading, podcast]?" or "What important question do you have that has not been answered?" This can be the focus of one of the closing forums.

Course Project Completion

Ideally, course projects and other creative assignments are the expression of the integration of the course content and the newly acquired knowledge skills of the learner. The project is where it can all come together. Course projects enable the creative expression of course knowledge. The steps in creating a course project require the full range of learning experiences: reading, writing, research, listening, and revising and restructuring ideas. Rather than just covering content, this is where students use and apply content in their projects and help other learners do so. Thus, time dedicated to projects—such as proposals, design, draft, review, revision, and presentation—is a period of active learning. Be sure to think broadly about the possibilities of project expression. The project doesn't have to be a paper (Boettcher, 2011)!

Coaching

Some instructors feel that the closing weeks of a course are easier than the early weeks. During the closing weeks students are actively engaged in projects and, ideally, supporting and helping each other. The role of the instructor during these closing weeks is most similar to the work of a coach or mentor. To coach well, instructors need to balance providing their guidance and encouragement with providing neither too much nor too little help. That means staying in close touch with what each of the learners is doing. It also means keeping the learning community moving forward with individuals or teams helping each other. This is also a good time to review the literature on cognitive apprenticeship (Collins, Brown, & Holum, 1991; Brown & Adler, 2008) and the steps in helping learners develop expertise: modeling and observation, scaffolding, and increasingly independent practice (Ericsson, 2000; Ericsson, Prietula, & Cokely, 2007). While this time may be easier for some instructors, it is probably more appropriate to say that the focus of teaching practices is different. Faculty work now is directed to coaching, to ensure learner independence, and assessing, to provide feedback and closure.

What's Happening in the Closing Weeks

The closing weeks of a course bring a mixture of feelings, often ranging from concerns and worry about getting everything done to feelings of relief, satisfaction, joy, and camaraderie. As an instructor, you want your students to be feeling confident about the new skills and knowledge they have acquired. And you want to be fair and efficient in your assessment of their learning.

Your role as a coach should be front and center as the students direct more of their own learning and contribute to the learning of others. Your goal is to help your students know how they will likely use the skills and knowledge they are acquiring in their lives and careers. In these closing weeks, support your learners as they integrate their knowledge and reach some level of resolution with what they know now and want to know in the future.

Some of the tips in these closing weeks could be put to good use much earlier in your course, but just as the content for a course needs to be sequenced in some way, so too it is not wise to try to do too many things at any one time. When we started planning this book, we decided that it would be great for new online teaching faculty to move from a novice to an expert online teacher state in a twinkling. Without that as an option, we had to make some choices as to which tips, which tools, which ideas might best be introduced or used in each phase of the course. Also, some tips may well favor certain disciplines. For example, problem-solving strategies are essential for more hands-on courses such as mathematics, statistics, and practicum types of courses. We decided to trust your judgment and your book-scanning skills.

In this phase, the course is pretty much in the hands and minds of the learners, and the key tasks of the faculty member are to direct, mentor, and support learners as they integrate and frame their new knowledge and finish projects and other course requirements. The major cognitive push is to ensure that the learners receive feedback on their knowledge work and hear, see, and benefit from the results of the creative work of the other learners. The students want to bring their learning together in a form that leaves them with a sense of satisfaction and fulfillment at what they have gained. They should be clear about what concepts, skills, perspectives, and goals they have developed. In addition to bringing the current session to an end, it is also desirable for faculty and students to reflect on the course collaboratively, determine what elements worked best in this course, and consider what changes might be good for the next set of learners.

In summary, this is what is usually happening in the closing weeks:

- Learners are finishing up the course projects and requirements. They are taking the lead in community discussions and integrating their knowledge by grappling with difficult problems and working on challenging tasks such as concept mapping, scenarios, and integrating feedback from learners and possibly experts beyond the course. They may be feeling stressed and a bit overwhelmed with what they need to do.

- The instructor is directing learning at the community level and at the individual or small team level. The instructor is also coaching and encouraging the learners through the final weeks and what needs to be done. A high priority is to provide customized and personalized feedback on projects and other assessment tasks in a timely and efficient manner to ensure that students have time to reflect and act on the feedback. The faculty member also supports the learners in establishing appropriate follow-up and future networking with learners, particularly important in online courses and programs.

- To-do lists are important for both learners and faculty to ensure that the work of teaching and learning is well coordinated.

Summary—and What's Next

As noted earlier, these four phases of a learning experience apply irrespective of the length of the learning experience. If you think about a workshop you have designed or attended, the workshop cycles through the phases of initial getting acquainted and setting the rules, and continues through setting expectations, some demonstrations, and then hands-on and closing activities. What is unique and different is what learners are able to learn and the experience they will have to help them on their learning journey.

The next chapters of the book provide tips to guide, inspire, challenge, and support you as you continue in your own particular novice-to-expert journey of becoming an expert in teaching in both online and blended environments.

Exercise and Reflection

If you are using this book for a course in faculty development, here are two activities to consider using to have faculty think more deeply about the themes of each phase.

1. What top three themes resonate with you? Why?
2. Which of the themes will be challenging for you? How will you strengthen those areas?

Part Two

Simple, Practical, and Pedagogically Based Tips

Part TWO

Chapter 6

Phase 1: Course Beginnings: Starting off on the Right Foot

GETTING OFF TO a good start has a positive impact on an entire course experience. Students are excited; all learning seems possible. Launching well can energize students through many difficult tasks. This is a good time to refer back to the summary of the themes and tasks for course beginnings as described in Chapter Five. Table 5.1 highlights the tasks essential for an effective online course launch and the beginnings of building a course community.

The first set of tips for course beginnings guides you through the steps in getting ready for teaching your online and blended course. It is important to complete these steps in advance of meeting with your students. The second set of tips describes the types of interactions, experiences, and behaviors for achieving success in the course beginnings. These tips focus on the first days of your course, getting to know students, and the three types of presence. The third set focuses on discussion forums, creating questions, managing the forums, and the faculty role.

Tips for the Course Beginnings

There is much to do before your students arrive at your course. Preparing for an online or blended course requires more preparation than a face-to-face class, because the content, directions, and plans for student interaction, assessment, and experiences ideally should all be present in the course management system a week prior to the course launch. Online students generally expect to see a holistic view of a course right at the beginning of a course so they can plan their work and personal responsibilities around the course assignments and major projects. This means you must do more planning before the students "arrive" at your course site.

Getting your course ready can seem overwhelming, but as with any new and unfamiliar task, it is manageable if you first get an overview of the work and then break it into actionable tasks. Also, if you're like most instructors you have taught in other face-to-face environments and can leverage the habits and processes you use in preparing any course.

The first set of tips in this chapter walks you through these basic tasks in preparing and launching an online or blended course. Good instructional design practices are embedded in these tasks of preparing your syllabus and your course site, but many more tips on instructional design are described in the standards for quality online learning in the special section at the end of the first tip (CB Tip 1).

For planning purposes, these preparation and design tasks require a minimum of twenty to thirty hours if you are familiar with the tools and if you have taught the course before in a face-to-face mode. If the tools are new to you, this preparation time will usually be a little longer because you will be learning new habits and processes. If you are learning and preparing simultaneously, it is not unusual for this preparation to take forty, fifty, or even sixty hours over two, three, or more weeks. And if you like to feel very ready, it can take even longer. During the first cycle of a fully online course, the time in preparation and delivery is similar to the first time teaching a new course in the face-to-face environment, plus time for learning new tools and developing new working habits and strategies. Learning the tools can involve attending classes or workshops and then getting help with the staff at technology help desks.

The first phase of any course is generally from two to four weeks, depending on the total length of your course term. If you are teaching short courses, you will want to adjust these phases to your particular course structure.

Entering into the world of online teaching and learning can create uncertainty and trepidation, and even a feeling of being overwhelmed as you encounter unfamiliar tools and getting to know students at a distance. However, if you have been an effective instructor in the face-to-face environment, you will find ways to work and teach in the online environment, given a little time and practice. Your first step is to work on the preparations and establish a goal of creating a set of learning experiences that engages and challenges your students. For a new online instructor, this can be the most work-intensive time.

Course Beginnings Tips Overview

This chapter provides 17 tips for course beginnings. The first set of five tips guide you through preparing the essential elements of your course. The second set of four tips focus on launching your course well. The most important initial goals in the first weeks are getting acquainted with the learners, establishing trust, and launching the learning community. These getting-acquainted experiences lay the trust groundwork for the teaching and learning relationship (Garrison, Anderson, & Archer, 2001).

The third set of eight tips focuses on strategies for creating and developing meaningful discussions, with tips on developing good questions. Creating engaging discussions is one of the highest priorities for any online or blended course. Engaging discussions draw students into the content, encourage deep processing of ideas, and support the building of a course community. Meaningful and sustained discussions are critical for effective online socialization and cognitive engagement. Discussion forums and other types of dialogue spaces such as blogs, wikis, and journals create the sense of inviting gathering spaces for sharing experiences that are part of a community. The difference is that these are online virtual classroom spaces rather than a face-to-face classroom. The final tip (CB Tip 17) describes how your role as an instructor changes over the four phases of the course.

Each of the tips begins with the questions commonly asked by online faculty and addressed by the tip. The tip then suggests practical steps and actions supported by theory, practice, and research. Here is a list of the course beginnings (CB) tips in this chapter.

Getting Started—Preparing Your Syllabus and Course Site

- **CB Tip 1:** Essential Elements of an Online or Blended Course Syllabus and Course Site

- **CB Tip 2:** More on the Significant Elements of an Online or Blended Syllabus

- **CB Tip 3:** Creating a Syllabus that Jump-starts Learning

- **CB Tip 4:** Using "Bookending" to Add Structure and Meaning to Your Course

- **CB Tip 5:** Generating Energy and Purpose with Specific Learning Goals

Getting Started—Launching Your Course

- **CB Tip 6:** Hitting the Ground Running: How Not to Lose the First Week
- **CB Tip 7:** Launching Your Social and Cognitive Presence
- **CB Tip 8:** Getting to Know Students' Minds Individually: The Vygotsky Zone of Proximal Development
- **CB Tip 9:** Getting into the Swing of a Course: Is There an Ideal Weekly Rhythm?

Creating and Managing Discussion Posts

- **CB Tip 10:** The Why and How of Discussion Boards: Their Role in the Online Course
- **CB Tip 11:** Characteristics of Good Discussion Questions
- **CB Tip 12:** Power Questioning for Meaningful Discussions
- **CB Tip 13:** Response Posts—A Three-Part Structure
- **CB Tip 14:** Discussion Wraps: A Useful Cognitive Pattern or a Collection of Discrete Thoughts?
- **CB Tip 15:** Managing and Evaluating Discussion Postings
- **CB Tip 16:** Feedback in Discussion Posts—How Soon, How Much, and Wrapping Up
- **CB Tip 17:** The Faculty Role in the First Weeks: Required and Recommended Actions

Getting Started—Preparing Your Syllabus and Course Site

The first set of tips in this chapter describes the tasks involved in creating a syllabus and a course site that is ready for online and blended teaching and learning experiences.

CB Tip 1: Essential Elements of an Online or Blended Course Syllabus and Course Site

This tip answers questions such as these:

- Which course elements, such as the syllabus, discussion questions, and assessment plans, are essential to have ready for students before the start of a course?
- What is the most important design element to ensure a good course design for effective learning for my students?

- Is there a checklist or set of standards to help me evaluate the design of my course site?

Chapter One defined a course as "a set of learning experiences designed to guide learners as they acquire and are assessed on a specific set of knowledge, skills, and attitudes." Thus designing a course means creating a set of learning experiences appropriate to learners and designing processes for gathering evidence for assessing learners. This leads to the question, "What course elements are essential to be designed and developed before launching a course?" This tip identifies those essential course elements and the steps in getting them ready.

Essential Course Pieces

Just as a new face-to-face course goes through a gradual process of refinement, faculty can anticipate that it generally takes about three cycles of teaching an online or blended course for it to become optimally designed. During the first three course cycles, faculty are very busy developing a new set of teaching behaviors for guiding, mentoring, and assessing students in a new environment. Faculty also need time to identify, select, and prepare effective learning resources and experiences that challenge and support learners.

But first one has to start. The course elements that are absolutely essential are the syllabus, weekly plans, discussion postings, and preparation of the course site. The syllabus, a familiar part of any course preparation, includes well-known elements such as learning goals, assignments, and institutional policies. Developing the online course components is less familiar, but almost all have an analogue in the face-to-face class. Table 6.1 lists these critical course pieces with capsule descriptions; you can use this as a checklist as you develop your course.

Syllabus

The syllabus for any digital course performs the same functions as for a face-to-face class, but even more critically. Learners appreciate a bird's-eye view of the entire course with key dates and responsibilities so they can integrate their learning, work, and personal lives. This is essential to online learners having a sense of control and optimism.

The best place to start in creating any syllabus is to use the syllabus template recommended by your institution. Most institutions or departments have a syllabus template set up within a course site. This template shows the required syllabus elements, for example, beginning with the learning goals, learning outcomes, and course requirements.

TABLE 6.1

Course Elements

Elements of an Online or Blended Course	Description
Syllabus	The overall plan for the course, with performance goals and requirements. It usually includes an overview of the course goals, a description of the core content resources (textbook, readings, other resources), the course schedule, and the assessment plan. A syllabus may also contain boilerplate information on policies and procedures, library access, technical support, and contact information for non-course-specific questions. Check and see if your institution has a syllabus template.
Content resources, often including textbook description and bibliography of resources; often a section of the syllabus	Required and recommended resources for core content and initial application of core concepts, plus starting points for resources for more complex customized and personalized learning experiences. These content resources may include a series of prepared mini-lectures or selected playlists of podcasts and videos.
Assessment plan; often a section of the syllabus	Summarizes the activities for assessing student learning and ideally maps the assessment experiences to performance goals and requirements. Online assessment plans include multiple assessment experiences, including low-stakes quizzes, peer responses and reviews, concept integration papers, and high-stake projects.
Papers, projects, and quiz assignments listed in the assessment plan	The usual components of an assessment plan. These are the products of students' learning and creative efforts. The requirements for each of these are in the assessment plan. The directions, specifications, and rubrics for projects and papers are often separate documents; the quizzes, if any, are within the quiz section of the course management system.
Schedule of class activities and events	The overall course calendar that summarizes the course activities. This course calendar usually needs fine-tuning to ensure a balanced course design: balanced dialogue, a range of individual and group activities, and synchronous and asynchronous events. Learners use this course calendar to integrate their life events over the course term.
The course website, a place where resources are provided and where interactions take place	Where learners and faculty gather for the course experiences and activities. Getting a course site ready means getting the syllabus ready and preparing the resources and activities. The resources include the teaching guides, the discussions, and all the assignment materials.
Teaching guides	A set of introductions and guides for each of the course topics and modules that describe the requirements and specifications for student action and learning. These teaching guides are part of the prepared teaching presence.

TABLE 6.1	
(Continued)	
Elements of an Online or Blended Course	**Description**
Discussions and interaction activities	The set of catalyst discussion questions for the forums, usually a plan for each week that focuses on the course core concepts and performance goals. These discussions are the means by which community grows, develops, and flourishes.
Individual work and reflection activities	The learning work that students complete mostly on their own: reading, writing, researching, or collaborating with one or two other learners. The resources, learning outcomes, and goals of these activities are designed in broad terms by the instructor, but can be personalized and customized by learners.

A syllabus for an online and blended course is generally more detailed than the syllabus for a face-to-face course. It needs to include the following: a description of the course schedule and activities for each week of a term, the assessment plan with dates and rubrics, policies and procedures, and content resources (textbook, readings, audio and video resources), requirements, and locations. A syllabus template may also contain the boilerplate information specific to an institution on library access, technical support, and contact information for non-course-specific questions.

It is useful to think of a syllabus as having two major sections: (1) the policies, procedures, and resources specific to an institution, and (2) the outline of the course itself. Because of its length and contractual features, students often ignore much of the content in the syllabus. What we want to achieve is an engaging syllabus that serves as an exciting course launch introduction and overview. More on how to jazz up syllabi is in CB Tip 3.

Weekly Teaching Guides

In planning a face-to-face course, many faculty devote significant time to creating and developing lectures. For online classes, the time spent in preparing lectures morphs into preparing short text, audio, or video introductions and mini-lectures, developing and managing threaded discussions, and monitoring student discussion and reflection spaces, such as forums on the course site. Lectures in the face-to-face class are the primary channel for faculty-to-student dialogue. This is important to the teaching presence (Garrison, Anderson, & Archer, 2000), as these lectures convey the special expertise and personality of the instructor. In the online classroom, the equivalent teaching presence is expressed in the weekly plans, teaching guides, discussions, and faculty comments and observations.

Weekly teaching guides are critical elements in the syllabus. These guides list the text, audio, or video resources that introduce and describe the goals and activities for the week. Expanded guides—which are on the course site, but not in the syllabus itself—also provide the rationale for the choice and design of the learning experiences and brief introductions to the core concepts.

Discussions and Rubrics

Preparing the discussions for each week of an online or blended course is one of the key differentiators between planning an online course and planning a campus course. The discussion forums play a major role in the organizing and experiencing of the content of a course.

The discussion forum in an online course is the equivalent of whole class or small group discussions in a campus class. The forum is the primary place where dialogue, discussion, and peer-to-peer interaction take place. The student postings in discussion forums and in blogs, wikis, and journals are where you can "see" and get to know your students. Rather than seeing their students' eyes and faces, the discussion postings are a way of seeing your students' minds. These postings are even more revealing of what the students know or think they know and may be about to think.

The time you invest in developing good questions for the discussion boards and planning out the scoring rubrics and evaluation of the discussion boards makes a difference in how quickly a learning community starts to form in a course. Experienced online faculty will plan out all of the discussions before a course begins. This is absolutely recommended for your first online course. You may find that you want to make changes as you get to know your students, but having the discussions planned raises your confidence and lowers your stress. Since you may decide to make changes in the specifics of the discussions, counsel students not to work too far ahead of the group as a whole. It is possible that you would like to know more about rubrics as you are developing your discussion questions. For more about rubrics, see EM Tip 4 and LM Tips 8 and 9.

Course Site

The campus classroom serves as a gathering place for interactions and sharing of learning experiences, and for small and large class activities. In an online course, these gatherings take place online, often in a learning management system (LMS) such as Blackboard, Canvas, or Moodle. A course site is the "physical virtual space" for the online and blended classroom. This is where the instructor and students gather, share thinking and ideas, and complete the course requirements. You, as the course director and learning mentor, serve as the hub, the host, the glue of the learning community. Putting all relevant course content up on the course site is a major task to be completed.

In getting a course site ready, your first step is to complete the administrative request with the information technology services group at your institution for a course site to be set up. At some institutions, this may be done automatically, but a good rule is to leave nothing to chance. Physical textbooks are often ordered many months before a course launches. For online programs, this might be done by a departmental administrative staff member in the middle of the previous term. If physical textbooks haven't been ordered or received and it is time for the course to begin, work with the support staff to offer alternatives such as digital textbooks and other digital online resources. In some cases, it might be wise to use open and free resources for a week or two to keep students moving forward in the course until they receive their textbooks.

This is also the time to review the work that needs to be done to prepare the course site. If you have enough time prior to the first offering of a course, you may find it helpful to have a practice site set up months in advance or to use an online course site with a campus class.

The other items that a faculty member is responsible for becoming familiar with are the institution's information on library access, technical support, and contact information for non-course-specific questions for online students. One rule of thumb that is a time saver is making certain this information is prominent, so that the students know whom they should contact for a variety of questions. This is a highly effective way of building loyalty to the institution as the students develop relationships with a broader instructional team.

Checklist for Preparing for an Online Course

You may find this summary to-do list useful as you develop your course. Note: this assumes that someone else is in charge of finding and recruiting students for your class, just as for a regular campus class:

1. Find the person who is responsible for setting up the template for the course site. If you don't know where to start, start with the person who assigned you the task of teaching the course.

2. Make a request for a course site. While that is under way, work on the syllabus. Pay special attention to ensuring that learning outcomes, learning experiences, and assessment plans are all aligned (Fink, 2004).

3. If you have taught this course before as a face-to-face campus class, start with your existing syllabus.

4. Review and select textbooks. If the option is available, choose a textbook available in *both* physical and digital formats with a set of rich expanded materials online.

5. Arrange for textbooks to be available quickly for students. Post this information at least a week or more before the course begins to give students time to acquire the books.

6. Inquire about the source of the course syllabus template for your college or institution. These templates contain the standard boilerplate information regarding library access, the standard institutional tool set, and other help desk and administrative help information.

7. Prepare the syllabus, using this tip and other syllabus tips such as the graphical and bookending ideas in CB Tips 3 and 4. Part of preparing your syllabus will be to divide the content into a set of topics, modules, or chapters. Then you will use these content divisions as a way of organizing the course content on the course site. You will also use these content modules to prepare a concept map of patterns, relationships, and core concepts.

8. Be sure you can access your course site and that the template for your institution and program is in place for your site.

9. Prepare your assessment plan, being sure to have multiple points of assessment and including points for discussion, assignments, quizzes, and projects. Examples of assessment plans are in CB Tip 2 and EM Tip 12.

10. Plan out the full course schedule, being sure to take note of universal holidays and events particular to your institution. Plan assignments so you can get feedback to your students in a reasonable time. Think in terms of a regular weekly rhythm. More on weekly rhythms is in CB Tip 9.

11. Prepare discussion postings and post them in the course site. Prepare the rubrics for posting. Tips on discussion postings and rubrics are later in this chapter.

12. Once your syllabus is complete, return to the first weeks and review the plans and expectations for the first weeks of your course, and for questions and expectations that will occur in the week before the course starts. Consider whether the student workload is too heavy or too light.

13. If you have any time during the process of syllabus development, share your syllabus draft with another instructor who has taught an online or blended course before and ask for feedback. Also, using a checklist of standards of excellence for online courses can help you review the readiness of your syllabus and course site. The Quality Matters rubric is highly recommended. More on that rubric follows later in this tip.

In the midst of getting your course content ready, it is easy to forget how important it is to prepare your own getting-acquainted posting for the introductory forum. The purpose of this posting is for your students to get to know you both as an expert but as a person. Consider including a formal and informal picture of yourself, also other trust-building information about your field of expertise and informal notes such as your favorite foods and the books that you are currently reading.

Aligning Outcomes, Experiences and Assessment

How do you know if you have developed an effective syllabus and course site? The most important criteria for a quality course is the concept of *alignment*. Alignment means that the intended learning outcomes, assessment strategies, and learning experiences to achieve the outcomes are consistent with each other. This concept of alignment, designing for significant and meaningful learning, is well described by Fink (2013). Before going further, the key questions to ask about your course syllabus is "Will the learning experiences you have planned support student achievement of the desired learning outcomes?" and "Will your assessment strategies provide evidence of that learning?" Related questions from the Quality Matters Rubric that you can use to help evaluate your alignment success are: "Are all learning objectives or competencies stated clearly and written from the learner's perspective?" and "Is the relationship between learning objectives or competencies and course activities clearly stated?" (see qualitymatters.org).

Quality Matters Standards for an Online Course

If you are under a great deal of time pressure, you may want to return to these quality standards at a later time. A very useful detailed rubric is available from the Quality Matters organization. This rubric was developed as part of the Quality Matters project, funded by the Fund for the Improvement of Postsecondary Education (FIPSE). The goal of this project is to provide tools for assessing and ensuring the quality of online courses. It is a "faculty-centered, peer review process that certifies the quality of online and blended courses." (Shattuck, Zimmerman & Adair, 2014, p. 25).

The rubric currently has eight general sections with forty-three specific review standards that evaluate the design of online and blended courses. The eight general sections address the key elements of online courses:

- Course overview and introduction
- Learning objectives and competencies
- Assessment and measurement
- Instructional materials
- Course activities and learner interaction
- Course technology
- Learner support
- Accessibility and usability

The rubric is now part of a for-profit entity that certifies online courses with the Quality Matters Rubric. Full access to the Quality Matters Rubric (https://www.qualitymatters.org/rubric, 2015) is limited to institutions with a subscription to the project.

Many other valuable lists of standards of excellence are available from higher education consortia, universities, and organizations worldwide. Let us mention just two. For standards on course design and excellence, the report *Elements of Quality Online Education: Practice and Direction*, by the Online Learning Consortium, is a classic (Bourne & Moore, 2002). This report highlights five areas for quality: learning effectiveness, cost effectiveness, access, faculty satisfaction, and student satisfaction. Also, a list of standards endorsed by the Commission on Colleges of the Southern Association of Colleges and Schools in 2000 (http://www.sacscoc.org/pdf/commadap.pdf) is still quite relevant.

Other tips address key issues in designing quality and engaging courses. If you are an experienced teacher and have the basics of your syllabus well in hand, check out these tips now: CB Tip 3 on creating a great launching syllabus and CB Tip 4 on "bookending" your course.

CB Tip 2: More on the Significant Elements of an Online or Blended Syllabus

This tip answers these questions:

- What are the most important sections of a syllabus or course site for an online or blended course?
- Should I really develop all the postings for the weekly discussion forums before the course starts, as part of my course design?

- What changes should I make in my testing and assessing procedures when proctored exams are not possible or convenient?

- Should the syllabus contain information and policies about netiquette and plagiarism tools?

If you are modifying an existing campus course for the online learning environment, most of the core components of a course syllabus are the same. Here are the items with minimal changes:

- Course description.

- Performance goals and learning outcomes. It is good to review these, however, for ways that learning goals and desired outcomes might benefit from the digital environment.

- Content resources such as textbooks and access to supplementary recommended resources. Don't overlook the abundance of audio, video, and interactive digital content now available. Instructions about cost and options for acquiring the textbooks or other required resources are essential. Online courses, particular intensive courses, move along very quickly, and students can get into trouble quickly if they don't have resources in hand.

Syllabus Sections

Now let's consider the sections of an online syllabus that are more particular to the online or blended environment:

- **Discussion postings:** As noted previously, discussion postings are the backbone of an online course. The discussion forum space is the place and space for writing, thinking, reflecting, and conversing with other students. It is a major venue for students to engage and struggle with the course content. Review your discussion postings. Do they require thought, reflection, and expression? Do they encourage substantive exchange and conversation? The set of tips on discussion posts later in this chapter is a great resource for developing good postings. For now, check that your postings support discussion of the issues, core concepts, and learning outcomes for your course.

- **Assignments:** A major difference between campus and online courses is in the area of assessment. Online assessment morphs into a continuous and broad-based set of assignments rather than mid-terms and final exams. Examples of assessment plans are in the tips focusing on assessment. Instructions on how to submit the assignment online are critical. It is a good idea for students to practice submitting a low-stakes assignment in the first week. A broad-based assessment plan includes points for discussion postings and comments and review on the postings of fellow students. Participation in discussion boards and forums is a significant source of information on what a student knows and his or her understanding of course content. In the early days of online courses, a colleague of ours conducted a small action research project in which the instructor did not say anything about the value of participation and just let the learners participate as they felt moved to do so. Only 20 percent of the class posted anything in the discussions. The next time the course was offered, the instructor wrote guidelines and based about 30 percent of the course grade on participation. Participation in the discussions shot up, with 80 percent of the class posting. So if you are thinking that "If you post it, they will participate," we suggest rethinking that strategy. A scoring system or rubric can let learners know the difference between superficial and meaningful participation.

- **Communication policies and procedures:** Learning and communicating effectively in online and blended courses can take time to master. Just as there are effective practices for faculty, there are effective practices and habits that learners may need to acquire. Here are resources to consider including in your syllabus if they are not in your template for the institution.

  - **Netiquette guidelines** cover how to communicate effectively and courteously online. Here are a couple of starting points:

    - *The Core Rules of Netiquette* by Virginia Shea (http://www.albion.com/netiquette/corerules.html)

    - *Top 26 Most Important Rules of E-mail Etiquette.* These are also applicable to discussion posts (http://email.about.com/od/emailnetiquette/tp/core_netiquette.htm)

  - **Emoticons:** Consider how you will use Emoticons. These symbols are used to indicate emotion in text. The most popular is the colon-dash-close parenthesis, which becomes a happy face. Two sites describing emoticons and their meanings are http://emojipedia.org and http://en.wikipedia.org/wiki/emoticon. Some faculty discourage the use of emoticons, but as long as they are used tastefully, they help to express what body language and facial expressions do in face-to-face settings. The dictionary of emoticons keeps growing. Here is the classic "happy face": ☺

- **Communication patterns:** Follow the principle of being very clear about course processes. Briefly describe your preferred communication patterns and times. For example, let students know your preferred weekend day for questions, when necessary, and the expected turnaround time for questions during the week. Communication patterns in all teaching environments are changing. In the very traditional face-to-face environments, the instructor is in front of the students, and most questions are directed to him or her, so communication patterns flow predominately between the one faculty and the many students. In online and blended environments, communications are primarily conducted in the discussion forums going between one student or more and the faculty member, or among the students themselves. The purpose of the online question forums is to encourage whole class or group participation in content discussions. All content comments are public to the class members and the instructor, unless exceptions seem prudent. This communication pattern of one to many and many to one, regardless of role, encourages community, course discussion, brainstorming, and mutual help. A separate space, such as an open forum area, can be established strictly for socializing. Other communication patterns can be used in wikis or blogs. Private e-mails between the instructor and one student are to avoided except for confidential communications.

- **Plagiarism:** A section on plagiarism, particularly what it is and how to avoid it, can be helpful. If your syllabus already includes an institutional academic honor policy, it may not address the ease of plagiarism today and how to avoid inadvertent plagiarism. Here are some sites to consider directing your students to on this topic:

  - Definition of plagiarism: http://en.wikipedia.org/wiki/plagiarism.

  - Self-detection and checking plagiarism services: Turnitin is one subscription service for use by instructors and students (http://turnitin.com). Another service is SafeAssign within the Blackboard LMS.

  - Other small free tools are available on the Web. Here are two starting points: http://www.paperrater.com/plagiarism_checker and http://www.plagium.com

  - **Expectations:** You may currently have a section on expectations; it's a good idea to make sure this section includes information on communication turnaround time—for example, "I'll reply to most e-mails and discussion posts within twenty-four to forty-eight hours during the workweek. I'll check for urgent messages on the weekend." In addition, participation guidelines provide specifics on how often to log in to the course, how often to post in the discussions, length of posts, and depth of posts. These can be specific to assignments and activities. One good rule of thumb to state is that students should plan to dedicate a minimum of six to ten hours a week to a course, excluding transition times.

- **Troubleshooting:** In the event something goes wrong in a course, learners need to know whom to contact. If you do not specify whom to call for what, students will contact you in a panic when any technical glitch occurs. This information can be in a separate troubleshooting section or a subset of the policies and procedures section of your syllabus. Stating ahead of time the contact information for the help desk and what to do in the event the course site is down and an assignment is due helps the students and helps you. Remind students to post in the question forum if something is going wrong.

Adding these sections will not ensure a trouble-free course, but it will prepare students to participate fully and effectively in the course and to be able to resolve problems without involving you every step of the way.

CB Tip 3: Creating a Syllabus That Jump-starts Learning

This tip answers these questions:

- What can I do to get my students to actually read my syllabus?

- Is there an activity that encourages my students to set their own personal learning goals for the course?

- What can I do to create a syllabus that jump-starts the learning of my course content?

Consider your syllabus. Do your students read it? Do they use it? Even small changes in your syllabus can jump-start their learning. This tip suggests creating a graphic overview as one way to change a traditional, possibly tired-looking Word document into a vibrant and welcoming introduction to your course.

As you are preparing the information for your syllabi, challenge yourself to make some changes to your syllabus that will have students saying, "Wow, and thanks so much!" To get you thinking, Figure 6.1 is a graphic overview of this tip.

FIGURE 6.1

Graphic Overview of CB Tip 3

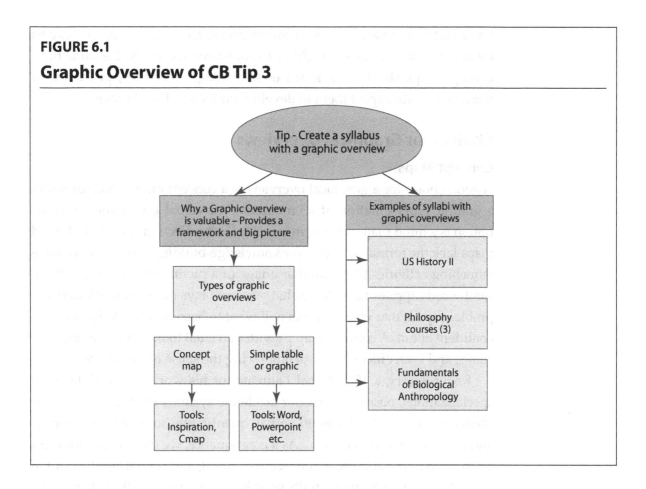

Graphic Overview: Building a Framework and Setting Boundaries

One of the most useful additions for your syllabus is a graphic overview of your course content. A graphic overview clearly lays out core concepts and relationships as well as expected boundaries for your course. It helps to communicate your expectations and can welcome your students to an intellectual adventure and community experience.

What is the value of a graphic overview? It provides a bird's-eye view of your course as a whole. This helps students build a mental framework, a mental model, a mental picture of your course. Graphic overviews can be powerful in setting course boundaries as well. Why are boundaries helpful? Boundaries serve your students by helping them to focus on the core concept essentials while also enjoying the information that is nice to know. Boundaries help your students "see" the types of content and the types of problems or scenarios they should focus on understanding and dealing with.

We live in an information knowledge world without boundaries, yet the time to learn and develop skills in our courses is definitely bounded.

So boundaries remove stress; students understand that we do not expect them to become experts in eight or ten or fifteen weeks. At the same time, concept maps show what kinds of knowledge structures, problems, or scenarios we do expect them to develop, understand, and process.

Choices for Graphical Overviews

Concept Maps

A good choice for a graphical overview is a concept map, which provides a graphic representation of a "mountain" of verbal text. (Note: Another option is a mind map, which can be useful as a reflection activity, but mind maps lack the formal structure for knowledge-building preferred in course launching activities.) The familiar adage of a picture being worth a thousand words applies here. A graphic overview lays out the knowledge and problem space that your learners will want to become knowledgeable and confident about. A concept map provides a visual look at the learning outcomes and is an efficient way of embracing the sense of the whole.

Roger Sperry, a 1981 Nobel Laureate for his work on left-right brain specializations, observed that our academic systems tend to be very left-brain oriented, with a focus on verbal, quantitative, and analytical inputs and experiences (Sperry, 1980). As a consequence, we often leave our right brain, with its dominance in the creative, visual, and spatial abilities, out in the cold. It's like learning with only half our brain. Rather than using graphics, pictures, and rich media to aid in learning, we introduce and welcome students to our courses with ten to twelve to sometimes fifteen pages of text, often wearying and overwhelming learners before they even get started. University of Illinois neuroscientist Kara D. Federmeier stated in a 2013 interview that according to more recent research, right brain/left brain characteristics are much more nuanced (Federmeier, 2013). We now understand that it takes the workings of both brain hemispheres to be logical—or to be creative. Logically speaking, it makes sense to make much greater use of visual information in all areas of our course content, starting with the syllabus.

Much more on the cognitive benefits of concept maps and graphic syllabi is detailed in the graphic syllabus and the outcomes map: communicating your course (Nilson, 2007) and other resources (Nilson & Pyser, 2012; Clark, 2015; Smith, 2014).

Using concept mapping tools requires learning another application, but that can be very useful long term for student learning. To get started with concept mapping many faculty use familiar tools such as Microsoft Word and PowerPoint, Keynote, and Prezi. More sophisticated free tools for concept mapping include the CmapTools from the Institute for Human & Machine Cognition (IHMC) and the Visual Understanding Environment (VUE) from Tufts University. Well-known commercial tools include Inspiration and Mindmap. As this field is still in flux, we highly recommend doing some research on the net and among friends when you are ready for a more sophisticated tool.

Can I Start with a Simple Picture?

Developing a graphical overview or concept map can take time, but it is time that reaps many benefits. You can start with a simple drawing, table, or course framework.

Here's how to get started. Prepare a table with three headings: (1) your core concepts—those big ideas that are captured in your learning outcomes; (2) examples of the kinds of problems and scenarios that require understanding of the core concepts; and (3) knowledge topics that support the building of understanding and skills for dealing with the problems.

Around the periphery of your table are links to the world of information beyond the course context. These links lead to additional content resources that learners may find interesting and useful individually.

This simplified course graphic can provide the big picture of a course and potentially serve as the basis from which students can develop their own more detailed concept maps. Look again at the graphic overview of this tip. Did you find it helpful in grasping a sense of the whole tip and its structure? Did your brain prepare you for what is coming next—three examples of graphic syllabi?

Examples of Creative and Graphic Syllabi

Here are some examples of creative syllabi from posts in the ProfHacker blog at the Chronicle of Higher Education.

Dr. Tona Hangen. US History II. Spring 2011 Worcester State University. Tona's syllabus is dramatic, as it launches with an iconic image by photographer Dorothea Lange of a thirty-two-year-old mother of seven from the Depression at the top of the first page. It is hard to miss the impact of this period with that image.

Another characteristic of Hangen's makeover syllabus is that she talks directly to her students as if they were right there with her. She goes over the course requirements, provides a schedule of topics and readings, and provides a grading scale in a format resembling a magazine layout. There is none of the third-person voice and dense, heavy text so characteristic of syllabi submitted to curriculum committees. By the way, research on the

FIGURE 6.2

Photo of Depression Mother by Dorothea Lange
https://www.loc.gov/rr/print/list/128_migm.htm

"personalization principle" (Clark & Mayer, 2007) has shown that learners actually feel closer to online faculty who address them in this more conversational tone. http://www.tonahangen.com/wsc/us2/wp-content/uploads/2015/07/112.Fall15.pdf. Note: Tona has shared her thought processes in making over her syllabus in her blog at http://www.tonahangen.com/blog/.

Dr. W. Mark Smillie. Three Philosophy Courses. Carroll College, Helena, MT. http://www46.homepage.villanova.edu/john.immerwahr/tp101/prep/graphic_syls.pdf. Smillie has developed graphic overviews for three courses: Philosophy of Human Being (August 2008), Perspectives in Philosophy (August 2008), and Medieval Philosophy (January 2009).

These three examples use a fairly straightforward concept mapping approach showing course topics and the relationships among topics. For example, the medieval philosophy concept map uses a three-column presentation showing the era (i.e., early Christianity); the key figure (such as St. Augustine) in the era; and the philosophical problems (such as human and divine action) that philosophers grappled with during that era. The value is that it offers a structure or a frame for holding a great deal of new and unfamiliar information. It provides a way to organize, interpret, and chunk the course content.

Dr. Susan Sheridan. Fundamentals of Biological Anthropology. University of Notre Dame. https://ltlatnd.files.wordpress.com/2015/08/bioanth-sheridan.pdf. This ten-page syllabus is enlivened by skeleton action figures sprinkled throughout and with interesting newsletter type formatting with bold headings, white space, and quotes highlighting her philosophy, such as "Remember that grades are not given by me, they are earned by you."

Two more examples of a graphic syllabi include one by Greg Haake at the University of Notre Dame on advanced French composition and another on composition by Anne-Marie Womack of Texas A&M. The syllabus by Haake on French composition (https://ltlatnd.files.wordpress.com/2015/08/advfrenchcomp.pdf) uses photographs, references to playlists of music videos and is written completely in French. The syllabus by Womack on English composition (https://dl.dropboxusercontent.com/u/610087/fall_2011_en120018.pdf) uses an attractive visual page layout featuring core questions and requirements that frame the writing projects for the course. Womack focuses the work of the course by setting out these questions front and center: (1) Why do we write? (2) For whom do we write? (3) How do we write for meaning for ourselves and our readers?

Conclusion

Your syllabus is the welcome mat for your course. It communicates many dimensions of you as an expert, a teacher, and a learning coach. Make a few changes and ask your learners what they think. Then in the next term, improve on those changes until you make great use of graphic organizers and visual treats.

CB Tip 4: Using "Bookending" to Add Structure and Meaning to Your Course

This tip answers these two questions:

- What does it mean to "bookend" my course?
- What types of activities are effective "bookends"?

Imagining Your Course

How do you imagine your course? As a series of topics or problems? As a set of concepts or ideas? As a time to reflect and think and ask fundamental life questions? This tip suggests looking at your course as a compact knowledge structure that provides confidence in an area of knowledge or skill. CB Tip 3 encourages using a concept map to show visually the structure of knowledge in a course; this tip encourages the use of a strategy called bookending.

What Is Bookending?

Briefly, bookending extends the idea of a discussion or course wrap described in other tips to the packaging and structuring of an entire course so that it feels whole, with a beginning, an ending, and a set of learning experiences in the middle that help learners develop a satisfying set of concepts and competencies.

The term *bookending* is used in many writing and speaking professions, such as screenwriting, storytelling, essay writing, and public speaking. In fact, bookending is often recommended to novice screenwriters as a strategy to "package" the film experience (Dyer, 2010). Bookending, used as a storytelling strategy, often helps viewers feel satisfied because they feel as if they experienced a whole of something, such as a meaningful and significant life experience of someone, or a whole episode, or simply a good story with a beginning, middle, and end.

How do writers achieve bookending? Writers bookend their stories by placing an interesting anecdote or scenario in their initial scene and then wrapping up the story with a resolution of that scenario or echoes of that anecdote. An example of the opening bookend from the popular 2009 film *Julie & Julia*, is the early scenes when both Julia Childs and Julie Powell are struggling with what to do with their lives. Julia's statement captures the opening problem statement for the story: "But what am I going to do?" Then the writers' closing bookend is the scene that shows Powell and her husband visiting Child's kitchen at the Smithsonian Institution and Julia Child in the same kitchen receiving a first print of her cookbook and celebrating the event with her husband. In between these two scenes is the story of how Julia Child's search for her life in the cooking profession parallels Julie Powell's challenge as she blogs about cooking her way through all the recipes in Child's first book, *Mastering the Art of French Cooking*.

The power of the opening and closing bookend provides a gentle and memorable wrap to how two women find a meaningful purpose for their creative talents. If you haven't seen it or would like a quick reminder look, there is a 2.5-minute movie trailer on YouTube (https://www.youtube.com/watch?v=ozrk7vxql-k).

Examples of Bookending Your Course

How might you use bookending in your course? First, you can build on two elements that you probably already have in place: the customized course project and your closing events. All you need is the initial problem scenario or sets of cases for launching the course that is convergent with the learning outcomes. With that simple add-on you can bookend your course.

Here's an example. In a course on managing a small company, your initial problem scenario might be a company that desperately needs to update its product line to improve its financial position. Or the company's challenge might be to diversify its sales channels.

Some of the learning outcomes from this course probably include finances, sales and marketing principles, human resources, and strategies for updating or launching new products. For an opening bookend the instructor can provide one, two, or possibly three case studies about different size and product companies and discuss possibilities and strategies for dealing with the challenges. Students might work on this in informal teams of two and record their observations and possible strategies, thereby creating a record that you and the students can refer and return to over time to see which strategies may have been a good idea. Some capstone business courses use management simulation software to see the results of some of their decision-making over the course. The closing bookend focuses on elements of those initial challenges and how they are addressed and handled in the readings and in course projects.

Let's think about an example for an undergraduate course, such as history. We know that some of the key learning outcomes of a history major are assembling evidence and then interpreting it (Glenn, 2009). A history course is particularly amenable to being designed as a sequence of topics. (I never made it past WWI in any of my courses, as the instructors wanted to start at the beginning of time.) Turning a history course into a scenario-based analysis of issues, people, and ideas requires that learners develop skills such as finding supporting or conflicting data, critical thinking, and an understanding of widely different perspectives. Other courses, such as leadership courses, can similarly use scenarios of leadership challenges and learning about oneself as a leader.

Closing course events generally include sharing, presentations, and finalizing projects. These are opportunities to look at a learner's growth over time. Phil Dyer, who writes a blog on screenwriting, notes that it's "a good idea to show how much your protagonist has grown by the end of the story by writing a bookend scene at the end of the script that demonstrates that she has overcome her internal flaw." He notes that even if the protagonist has not overcome her internal flaw, the bookend scene can capture how far she may have come. In a similar way, since all learners progress on a path of their own learning as supported by Vygotsky's zone of proximal development (ZPD), the amount of growth, change, and thinking can indicate to students how far they have come during the course.

So the course wrap itself serves as the finishing bookend to the course experience.

Conclusion

Of all the variables impacting learners' intellectual growth, course design is close to the top of the list. Try bookending and see how it can engage you and your students in creating growth experiences in your learners. More on content framing is in Chapter Ten, on intensive courses. Bookending affirms many of the core learning theory principles, including situated and authentic learning and a focus on core concepts.

CB Tip 5: Generating Energy and Purpose with Specific Learning Goals

This tip answers these questions:

- What is a good strategy to encourage students to read, process, and understand the learning outcomes?

- What learning principle supports setting very specific learning outcomes?

Do you make good use of the learning goals for your course? Or are they sitting ignored in an unused section of your syllabus? For effective learning we should be featuring, discussing, and analyzing the learning outcomes. How can we move learning outcomes into the light and put them to work in learning? An important task for students early in a course is an activity to process and discuss those goals.

Is this hard to do? Not really. In the pre-week or very early in the first week, students complete a getting-acquainted posting. This is the forum in which you and your students share who you are, where you live, and what is important to you in your work and daily life. This tip recommends a companion discussion forum that focuses on learning goals. In this forum students discuss the learning goals for the course and what these goals can and might mean for them, and they identify one or two learning goals that they customize to their own life or work purposes. The students are encouraged to restate the most important learning goals in very specific and personal terms.

This tip provides more detail on how you can accomplish this, and why setting specific learning goals is so powerful, useful, and energizing to the student learning experience.

Note: In this tip we use the terms *learning goals* and *learning outcomes* to refer to what students hope to learn and achieve during the term of a course. Other literature uses the term *learning objectives*.

Here are three examples of discussion forums focused on the learning goals for a course. This forum also begins the work of cognitive presence, described in greater detail in CB Tip 7.

Three Ways to Focus a Discussion Forum on Learning Goals

Your instructions to the student might look something like the following:

- **Example 1:** "Examine the learning outcomes for the course and rewrite in your own words the two outcomes that are most important to you and why they make sense to you. It helps if you envision yourself talking to a friend, spouse, colleague, or mentor about what you are going to be learning and doing."

  - Note 1: This activity encourages the students to translate the learning outcomes into expressions of purpose and statement that have real meaning to them. This instruction also encourages conversation about their learning goals with people who are important to them, opening up possibilities for more discussion about learning.

- **Example 2:** "Think about the time and effort you are going to be investing in the content and work of this course. How do you want your time and effort to make a difference in your life? Answer this question: How do I want to be different when this course is over?"

To help your students, you might give a couple of example statements relevant to your course content and purposes, such as:

- "I want to develop a personal code of ethics that will guide me in my life and in my work as a marketing executive."

- "I want to develop and discuss with confidence my personal philosophy about the meaning of life."

- "I want to be able to compose and write a business memo with the confidence that I am communicating effectively."

- "I want to be confident about approaching a work of art" or "I want to understand why art is important to people, and what difference it can make to me."

- "I want to develop a beginning level of expertise in a specific period of history, economics, math, music."

- "I want to be able to read a research report and be able to judge with some accuracy whether the research was well done and what the research means to the discipline."

- "I want to be somewhat knowledgeable about how to be successful in business leadership and business processes in another part of the world, such as Indonesia or China."

- "I want to be ready to lead in a particular context at a particular time.

- **Example 3:** "Select one of the learning goals and state why achieving that goal is really important to you."

One of your goals as a mentor, guide, and coach of learning is to find out where the students are coming from and where they want to go for their life and work. A discussion forum focused on learning goals helps to illuminate just what students already know and what they are ready to learn. Remember Vygotsky's statement that a learner's ZPD is what that student is really ready to learn. A forum on learning goals/cognitive presence attempts to gather these two data points: Where are the student's head and desires on this topic at this time? Where do the intended learning outcomes intersect with where the student is coming from?

The Power of Specificity: Why It Works!

Let's think about why having students write down very specific learning goals for themselves works so well. The power of writing things down is a major component of the approach used by the guru of stress-free productivity, David Allen, author of *Getting Things Done* (2015). Allen stresses that the very best question any of us can ask ourselves, when faced with a seeming mountain of complexities is "What is my next step?" In working with learning goals, the first step is to be very clear about envisioning the desired result. Then the readings, activities, and learning experiences in a course have a purpose. Each activity, each assignment is a step toward achieving that goal.

The Benefits of Specific Personal Goals

Faculty frequently ask, "But how do I get my students to read the assignments?" or "How do I get my students to engage with the content?" The answers come partly from having the students themselves choose, articulate, and discuss their own learning goals. This is not a magic bullet, but it helps students to consider and think about why they are taking a specific course, other than to meet the goal of earning another three credits toward a degree.

Over the course of our careers we have had an opportunity to see many faculty introduce learning goals and outcomes to students. Far and away the most frequently used approach goes something like this. If it is a campus-based course, the faculty member may use a "butterfly approach." They put the learning goals up on a slide, wave their hands, say, "These are the learning goals for the course, be sure to read them," and click, they are gone.

All too often in an online course, faculty may breezily say in an introduction to the first unit, "Be sure to read the learning outcomes, which are in the syllabus, a very important document as you all know." Another non-approach to learning outcomes is to never mention them, thereby missing a very valuable learning opportunity. Students remain generally clueless as to the course expectations, or purposes, other than that the course is required, it is a prerequisite, or their mother told them they had to take the course (an actual comment heard from a student).

As we start a course, we really want to invest time in discussing the questions, "What is the greater vision for the course?" and "What makes sense for our students to hope to achieve in this course?"

Conclusion

Being specific about learning goals has other benefits, such as preparing one's brain for what is to come by creating a framework, an open structure for knowledge, skills, and attitudes. Creating a structure for recall is a technique used by orators for thousands of years. St. Augustine in *Confessions* (Book X, about 399 A.D.) referred to this technique as a "memory palace." Having a mental place prepared for the issues, questions, and problems of a discipline creates hooks and nodes in one's mind. It is also helpful to revisit the course learning goals, particularly at the beginning and close of important learning activities. Journals and blogs are good places for students to track their progress on their customized goals. This recurring focus keeps goals and core concepts front and center in your course.

Getting Started—Launching Your Course

The second set of tips in this chapter describes actions that help to ensure a smooth launch for your course. Key contributors to a smooth launch are the initial gathering experiences. Many of the tips describe strategies for developing a social and cognitive presence so that students and faculty get to know one another as people and as learners.

CB Tip 6: Hitting the Ground Running: Maximizing the First Week

This tip answers these questions:

- Should I contact students prior to the course start date?

- How do I ensure that students have the right set of tools and know how to access their courses, the library, or technical help?

- How should I interact with the technical support staff and the other members of the instructional team?

Students new to a campus generally arrive a few days early to settle in and become familiar with their physical surroundings. A similar recommendation applies to digital learning; students should sign into their course site a few days before the course start date to check that they have what they need. This means that a course site needs to be ready with "getting ready for the course" information. Using the course site for this information is best, as it is available 24/7. This information should include data on the required learning resources, such as books, as well as learning tools, both hardware and software. Some institutions make information on textbooks and related required resources available as soon as students sign up for a course.

Most online programs require a laptop and/or some handheld mobile device with camera, high-bandwidth network access, and headphones. Basic software requirements generally come bundled with purchased devices, or are available through institutional licenses. Alternatively, the hardware and software requirements can be stated elsewhere on an institution's site for online courses and programs.

The learning skills and technical skills expected of students in online and blended courses are now simply assumed. But it is good not to leave these expectations to chance. Highlight technical expectations on your course site. Faculty find it useful to provide a list of contact numbers and descriptions of the people and resources prominently on the course site. This information is usually available on a general informational site, but the closer it is to the students when they need it, the more likely they are to contact the support personnel rather than you. Online learning is a 24/7 activity, but faculty need to sleep, and have a profusion of other professional and personal responsibilities.

Some institutions have instituted an official pre-week. During the pre-week students can access the course site, review the course requirements, post their getting-acquainted note, and get to know the other students by reading their postings. This can be a very useful time to post sample activities that check the following:

- Are the students able to get their passwords and access the course site? Are they able to navigate their way through the university portal to the course site?

- Do the students know how to access the library resources?

- Are the students encountering challenges with acquiring the textbook and other required resources? Do they need any help with this?

- Do the learners know how to post on the discussion board? Have they posted their getting-acquainted posting? Students are more relaxed at this time and often explore their abilities to post audio or pictures.

- Will the course schedule work for students? It is a good time to discuss preferences for any planned synchronous experiences.

Some experienced online faculty contact their students by e-mail a week prior to the course start date and invite them to the course site to check out access, complete the getting-acquainted posting, and generally ensure that they are ready for the course. If a student doesn't have a getting-acquainted post up by the end of the pre-week, contacting that student can be a good idea. Another strategy is to post an announcement reminding all students to post their getting acquainted note. A text message to any student who has not appeared at the site or communicated in some way can help to ensure that the course starts well.

If you don't have an official pre-week, take time during the first days of a course to ensure your students' familiarity with your preferred communication processes and resources. It is good practice to create an open discussion space on your course site such as a cybercafé or learner corner, similar to a physical student union, for informal interactions and support among students. Of course, the policies and procedures section of the syllabus includes your schedule indicating when you are going to be online and available for phone, e-mail, or chat. Post this information prominently in your course site, either in a general posting area or in a couple of announcements.

With all these preparations you and your students can begin to get acquainted personally and be ready to start engaging with the course content with a minimum of technical or resource problems.

CB Tip 7: Launching Your Social and Cognitive Presence

This tip answers questions such as these:

- Why is presence so important? What is social presence? What is cognitive presence?

- What can I do to establish social and cognitive presence?

- What are good examples of getting-acquainted postings for discussion forums?

Interaction and Presence as a Key Point of Satisfaction for Learners

Regular and timely interaction of faculty with students is one of the key quality indicators of online courses. A number of studies (Richardson & Swan, 2003; Burnett, Bonnici, Miksa, & Joonmin, 2007; Gould & Padavano, 2006; Young & Norgard, 2006) suggest that learner satisfaction with their online learning courses is directly related to the presence of their faculty member. Research on the community of inquiry model identified three types of presence: social, teaching, and cognitive. Just as the three most important things in real estate are location, location, location, the three most important things in online learning are presence, presence, and more presence. Here are some ways to be present for your students.

A Getting-Acquainted Social Post

A getting-acquainted posting helps to build social presence and launch the feeling of community. It also helps to establish connections and trust between faculty and students through knowing "where you are coming from" (Coppola, Hiltz, & Rotter, 2004). Not only do students want to know you, but they also want to know something about their fellow students. The getting-acquainted discussion post is an opportunity to tell a story about yourself and encourage students to share something personal about themselves. This can be done by simply asking students to complete a statement, such as, "My favorite movie, or book, or learning place is . . ." You can also ask students to share or post one or two of their favorite pictures. Students often choose pictures of themselves on vacation, with pets, with family, or even a hobby, such as refurbishing an antique car. Sharing at this level elicits a wealth of information, so that everyone connects with each other on several levels.

Many faculty forget how important it is for them to post their own rich and substantive getting-acquainted postings about themselves. You may wish to share with your learners the many places you've traveled or lived. For example, I (Judith) grew up in Minneapolis and lived in Milwaukee for six years while doing undergraduate and master's work at Marquette University. Then I had brief sojourns in Huntsville, Alabama, and Birmingham, Alabama, where my four children were born. I later lived in Orlando, Florida, and State College, Pennsylvania, and then in Tallahassee, Florida, because of my association with Florida State University. Rita grew up in Chicago and also landed in Tallahassee at Florida State University by way of Arizona and California, and as of this writing lives in California again.

What is fun about sharing this personal information is that you can almost visually see and feel the connecting threads that you and your students are weaving among the group as you discover common points of life experiences. Part of the power of social media sites such as Facebook, LinkedIn, and Twitter is derived from this feeling of closeness that comes from sharing personal, often inconsequential information that builds social links and an ongoing social ambience between people. Part of the challenge of understanding people from other cultures is that we do not share as many common data points, and thus links between minds can be more difficult. Online courses that are international in character want to be sure to recognize this and find ways of bridging those gaps and creating those connections.

Here are elements of getting-acquainted postings that you might use:

- Picture—a formal professional photo and a fun photo with family, on vacation, at a conference
- Short bio with links to published papers
- Link to your favorite professional publication
- Sharing your personal current research question that shows your curiosity about learning

Other favorite personal photos could feature family, pets, music, cars, vacation spots. The "getting acquainted" forum is also a great place to use short audio segments. We learn a lot by hearing each other's voices!

This initial posting focuses on creating social presence in your course, that is, the "ability of learners to project their personal characteristics into the community of inquiry, thereby presenting themselves as 'real people'" (https://coi.athabascau.ca/coi-model/description-social-presence/).

A Getting-Acquainted Cognitive Post

Another good practice is to have a companion posting to the getting-acquainted-socially posting: a getting-acquainted-cognitively posting. Its purpose is to get to know your students' minds. This posting focuses on what is in a learner's mind at the beginning of a term. The first week is a good time to discuss and process the course goals, objectives, and projects. We often develop ambitious syllabi, assuming that students will read and digest the information. A discussion forum that requires students to review the course learning goals and to develop some personal and customized goals helps to focus students and give them something specific and personal to grow toward. You may want to ask students to select the most important learning outcome for them in their current/future plans, or to ask them to identify the learning outcome that they believe is most fundamental/difficult/easy for them.

One of the core learning principles (Principle 6) focuses on Vygotsky's theory of the ZPD (Vygotsky, 1978). Applying this principle requires that we know what students know as individuals. How do we know what students know? How do we know the kinds of experiences they have had? We ask them to tell us in various ways.

The Announcements Tool and Just Being on the Course Site

A simple and very useful strategy for staying in touch with your students and being present is to use the announcements tool three or four times a week. These messages can be used for a quick hello inquiring how the readings are going, a reminder of a discussion posting content or challenge, a comment about the relevance of a current event, or a quick-check quiz. We often forget how intellectually stimulating a *Jeopardy*-like question can be!

Faculty often ask, "How often and for how long should I be on my course site each week?" Although there are no hard-and-fast rules, the best practice is to start being present every weekday and one of the weekend days. Most online learners do much of their learning work during the weekend, and thus your checking on how things are going can make a huge difference to them. Seeing if any critical questions have been posted can usually be done in fifteen to twenty minutes. You might also consider using text messaging for any assignment-related emergencies, particularly in the days before a major task assignment.

Being there every day is most important in the first week or two of a course. In those first days in particular, learners tend to panic if no one answers their questions in what to them is a timely manner. Be sure to let your students know when you can be reached in real time if needed. Convey the message that you are interested in how they are doing with their assignments, readings, and general progress. Your presence, as conveyed by messages and responses to postings and questions, encourages conversation among the students to think aloud, so that they can process information and link ideas and concepts. Students, like colleagues and friends, often just need to hear an occasional "uh-huh" to feel as if their efforts are being recognized and to keep going.

For faculty accustomed to teaching a face-to-face class and meeting students one, two, or three days a week for a fixed time, the demands of teaching an online course can be shocking. Students often expect faculty to be available all the time. This is why setting policies and expectations for feedback and presence is essential to student satisfaction. This is also why a question forum space is a good practice. The expectation for a question forum space is that all questions unrelated to course forums are posted there and all members of the course community can post and answer questions. The faculty mentor then answers questions and shares suggestions and comments in a public space. Use of a general public question forum increases faculty presence while minimizing, and even eliminating, all e-mail associated with content questions.

Some online faculty find it a useful practice to schedule virtual meeting times on the course site—for example, on Tuesdays, Thursdays, or Saturdays when they will be available for questions. In the first week or two it is good to schedule these times every day, if possible.

Faculty presence and involvement change over the weeks of a course. According to the phases of engagement (Conrad & Donaldson, 2012) in a course, your role in the first phase is that of a social negotiator. Later you shift to being a structural engineer, designing opportunities for students to form teams of two or three and having the students engage in critical thinking and sharing of ideas. More on how your presence changes over the course of a term is in CB Tip 17.

Presence on the Discussion Forum

The discussion forum is the online gathering place for the course, and faculty's presence is essential to the overall teaching and learning experience. Regularly posting substantive questions, challenges, and comments related to assignments or discussions is an extremely important part of the cognitive presence and creation and support of intellectual community.

Live Synchronous Collaborative Gatherings

We now have many ways of meeting with learners in real time. Designing synchronous sessions into your course contributes to community building and intellectual curiosity building. Having a live collaborative time with your students early in the term is a good practice. It can be a very informal question-and-answer session about the course and what the class as a group will be doing. If your students are located in widely varying time zones, such as military serving around the globe, this can be an optional activity that is recorded. The many synchronous meeting tools include Blackboard Collaborate, GoToMeeting, WebEx, and public tools such as Google Hangout and Skype. These tools are powerful for conveying presence and caring.

Conclusion

It is hard to overstate the importance of communication in the beginning of the course. Recall Best Practice 1: "Be present at your course." This practice means using multiple communication channels early, regularly, and consistently.

Communication and collaboration foster strong learning communities, counteracting the often isolating nature of online, digital, or blended learning (Rovai, 2002). Providing a variety of communications channels—messaging, e-mail, discussion forums, online chats—encourages student-to-teacher and student-to-student interaction and communication, essential for learning.

CB Tip 8: Getting to Know Students' Minds: The Vygotsky Zone of Proximal Development

This tip answers questions such as these:

- How do I get to know my students individually when I can't physically see them?

- What are some strategies for having students set their own learning goals?

- What is an example of a getting-acquainted-cognitively posting and sample responses?

One of the core learning principles (Principle 2) states, "Learners bring their own personalized and customized knowledge, skills, and attitudes to the experience." If that is true, getting to know our students and what they know is essential to mentoring them. In the tip on getting acquainted socially (CB Tip 7), we recommend a forum on getting acquainted cognitively.

Why do we do this in the first week? Because nurturing the growth of a learner's knowledge structures is the end-goal of all learning experiences. This means that the best way to help them grow is to find out what they know. In other words, you want to know sooner rather than later what is actually in their minds, what they think they know, and what they want to learn.

When the concept of the zone of proximal development was introduced, you may have been asking yourself, "Just how do I get to know my students' ZPDs? How do I find out what they know now?" One example of a getting-acquainted-cognitively post is to ask the students to review the course learning outcomes and have them respond, in 250 to 400 words, to how and in which contexts they hope to use the knowledge, skills, and perspectives. The discussion post may be as simple as asking the students to complete this sentence: "What I hope to be able to do as a result of taking this course is . . ." The responses to this statement might be "Be a better leader in a non-profit or tech organization" or "Read and understand a balance sheet" or "Solve differential equations and recognize when I need them." If they don't know how or when or why they will be using the information, encourage them to take a day or two to think about it and then propose some ways it could be important.

The syllabus states the expected general learning outcomes. The purpose of a goal-focused forum is to ensure that students examine those goals and personalize and internalize them. These getting-acquainted posts help us learn more about the students and make it easier and more natural to build associations and relationships, developing core concepts based on what students already know.

Keeping the Students Straight in Your Mind

The tricks of the memory trade work online as well as in the physical face-to-face settings. The best strategy is linking something personal, unique, and unusual about the learner to the learner's name, personal goals, or something else. Learners can be encouraged to post something that will help you individualize them by asking them something that will likely result in a memorable posting.

Here are a few suggestions for questions to include in the getting-acquainted postings:

- What do you think is particularly unique about how you think?

- What is your most memorable "Aha!" learning moment?

- What is your highest-priority goal for the course, and why?

- What's your best secret for being a successful online learner?
- What do you have in common with at least one other learner in the course?

And remember that learners individualize themselves to you and others through their writings.

Summary

The concept of cognitive presence, part of the community of inquiry model (Garrison, Anderson, & Archer, 2000), is often described as the extent to which the professor and the students are able to construct and confirm meaning through sustained discourse (discussion) in a community of inquiry. Reading a student's postings on how he or she thinks provides baseline information for the faculty mentor. This information helps a faculty provide teaching direction based on what students already have in their heads.

CB Tip 9: Getting into the Swing of a Course: Is There an Ideal Weekly Rhythm?

This tip answers questions such as these:

- Should I have a weekly rhythm for my course?
- What are the different types of activities that need to be scheduled and planned for?
- How much time should I estimate for monitoring and responding to discussion posts in the first weeks?
- When should learner-to-learner engagement be started?

A weekly schedule for campus classes usually revolves around scheduled face-to-face classes. These classes serve well as pacing events for students. Regular weekly assignments and activities keep students engaged with the course content. Students find that a weekly rhythm for an online course provides similar benefits. Is there an ideal weekly rhythm? Not really, but a predictable weekly rhythm helps to set clear expectations that an online course requires regular commitments and interaction.

Students have schedules for many competing responsibilities, such as working, parenting, and personal chores; thus a predictable schedule is a useful planning aid for everyone. Many faculty like to use the discussion forum as one of these pacing activities. For example, the discussion forum might open with a problem, question, or challenge on Monday, requiring an initial posting or progress response by Wednesday and comments on other students' postings by Friday or Saturday. The faculty member then commits to commenting on the posts by the following Monday. Readings, assignments, projects, and other content assignments can orbit around these class discussions.

Table 6.2 provides a sample weekly schedule for students in an online class based on a six-day schedule. This schedule anticipates that most online learners will be using one of the two weekend days for their learning. It also assumes about five to seven hours a week for one online course, or about an hour a day. Although it is not necessary for students to work on a class every day, learners should plan on logging in to their online course at least two or three times a week. This sample schedule encourages this level of participation.

This schedule may change in the second half of the course when project and team work are more intense. When group work is required, it is useful in the first phase of a team project for learners to identify a time that works for synchronous or almost synchronous collaborative activity.

Note that the schedule categorizes activities into individual and group activities and also suggests weekly collaborative times when the instructor might be available by phone, e-mail, instant messaging, or live classroom time. Of course you determine the days and times for your monitoring and scanning of students' work, responding to students' questions, and providing feedback to students. Note the insertion on the schedule of Tuesday as "Special availability hours." This might be a time for you to schedule an audio or audio and video question-and-answer time. Remember that these sessions can be recorded and archived for students who are not able to participate in a synchronous event. Faculty using synchronous online sessions often schedule these events on different days—alternating Tuesdays and Thursdays, for example, or even offering them twice a week, but always in consideration of their own schedule and perhaps special considerations of students' family and work schedules.

The tasks and activities for a course are primarily of three types, each corresponding to the three types of dialogue in a course (Moore & Kearsley, 1996; Moore, 2007). One dialogue type is the tasks and assignments that students do by themselves when engaging in a learner to resource experience. Examples of these dialogues are reading assignments, watching or listening to streaming lectures or presentations, analyzing and solving problems, reading and responding to online discussion forums, online postings in blogs or wikis, online quizzes, sending or receiving instant messages, e-mail, and general research or thinking. Although these activities can be done at any time, a time to do them needs to be scheduled.

TABLE 6.2

Sample Weekly Schedule for an Online or Blended Course

	Monday	Tuesday	Wednesday	Thursday	Friday	Saturday/Sunday
Individual activity 1 (L–R)	Assignment: Listening, reading, creating (1.0 hour)		Assignment: Listening, reading, creating (1.0 hour)		Assignment: Listening, reading, creating (1.0 hour)	
Individual activity 2 (L–L)		Discussion board reading and postings (1.5 hour)		Discussion board reading and postings (1.5 hour)		
Individual activity 3 (L–R)			Self-test quiz/review (30 minutes)		Occasional survey/feedback	
Individual activity 4 (L–L)	Discussion, informal collaboration with peers (20 minutes)	Discussion, informal collaboration with peers (20 minutes)		Discussion, informal collaboration with peers (20 minutes)		Discussion, informal collaboration with peers (20 minutes)
Group or team activity (L–L)		Possible group activity or synchronous activity		Possible group activity or synchronous activity		Possible group activity or synchronous activity
Faculty-mentor activity	Opens discussion forum for week; feedback to students on previous week discussions	Special availability hours; monitoring of student posts	Monitoring and scanning student interactions plus possible Q&A session	Special availability hours; monitoring of student posts	Monitoring and scanning student interactions plus possible Q&A session	Monitoring of student activity for critical messages

Experience suggests that if something can be done anywhere and anytime, it usually never gets done.

Other types of learning activities are learning events that students do with other students or with the instructor. The dialogue between students is expressed as learner-to-learner (L-L) or peer-to-peer dialogue; dialogue between students and faculty is expressed as faculty-to-learner (F-L) dialogue; individual learners' private resource use is expressed as learner-to-resource (L-R) dialogue. Examples of L-L activities include participation in team or group meetings and study or review sessions. Examples of F-L dialogue include participation in review or presentation sessions as well as all the asynchronous monitoring and commenting. Examples of L-R dialogue are reading of textbooks or researching online information.

Creating and Managing Discussion Posts

The third set of tips for the course beginnings focuses on the purpose and effective use of discussion boards. One of the tips describes the characteristics of questions that elicit engagement, reflection, and community, followed by a tip on strategies for managing and evaluating discussion postings as one tool in assessing student learning. The last tip in the section focuses on the faculty role in the threaded discussions and how the faculty role changes over the phases of a course.

CB Tip 10: The Why and How of Discussion Boards: Their Role in the Online Course

This tip answers questions such as these:

- What kinds and types of learning goals are discussion forums good for?

- How many discussion questions should be posted in a course each week?

- Are there guidelines or requirements for student responses to discussion questions?

- Are there any other digital tools, such as wikis and blogs, that can be used for engaging in course discussions?

The purpose of discussion forums in online and blended learning is similar to that for discussions in a face-to-face course, only much more so. We like to think of discussion forums as the "campfire" around which course community and bonding occur at the same time that learners are engaging in content processing and knowledge development. Discussion forums are threaded, meaning that learners post their comments and respond to one another in the same space, asynchronously over time. Learners can see how thoughts develop, diverge, and converge while determining what they believe or think.

This means that discussion forums are a valuable expressive space for learners. Discussion forums are a place for learners to process, analyze, and make connections among ideas. Sometimes a large percentage of course activities are receptive or passive. Learners are reading, listening, or watching. By contrast, discussion forums require learners to reflect on the ideas in the content resources or the ideas expressed by other students, and then to write about what they think, know, and reason. It is this cycle of reading, reflecting, considering, and making connections that actually changes the knowledge structure inside the learner's brain.

Often it is only when students are responding to a question or to another student's ideas that they begin to know what they think or know—or, sometimes more important, what they don't know. Discussion activities give students a way to describe how they are integrating incoming knowledge with their existing knowledge structures. The discussion boards provide time and opportunity to explore and develop ideas collaboratively and recognize and build shared values. These expressive activities help crystallize students' thoughts and increase confidence in what they think and why. Bonk and Zhang (2008) discuss a similar cycle: read, reflect, display, and do.

Best Learning Goals for Discussion Boards

One distinction between online discussion questions and class discussion questions is that the instructor plans out the discussion forums in more detail with more specific goals in mind. Why is this important? Planning questions in advance helps to ensure congruence with the desired performance goals, skills, and behaviors.

A good design strategy is to focus discussion questions on core concept topics. The purpose of forums is for learners to develop awareness and understanding of core concepts in contexts that are close and personal to learners. Rather than asking questions for which answers are readily discovered, ask questions that can direct students to the application of concepts in various contexts.

Research (Bransford, Brown, & Cocking, 2000; Haskell, 2000; Donovan, Bransford, & Pellegrino, 1999; Byrnes, 1996) suggests that learners do not easily transfer knowledge from one setting to another. In other words, they can be incredibly literal; this means problem-solving in particular contexts, particularly for novice learners, is invaluable. Research on developing expertise also requires deliberate practice applied in many contexts

(Ericsson, 2009). Discussions targeting core concepts help students build knowledge frameworks around the core concepts and link this new knowledge to existing knowledge. In the process, they can also personalize and customize their learning. Keep in mind how unique learners are and how each builds his or her own knowledge structures.

The Number of Discussion Questions Each Week

How many discussion questions should you put up each week? As with so many things in life, it depends. It depends on whether the questions are short answer essay questions that require students to apply core concepts in relatively simple problem situations, or complex questions requiring students to think deeply about what they can confirm, or problem-solving questions that require students to search out new information and develop or work with scenarios. Also, some discussions will require students to respond to and evaluate postings from the other students.

Another consideration is the number of other assignments and activities due in a particular week. For short-answer essay questions seeking responses to readings or ideas, a general rule of thumb is no more than two or three discussion questions each week if there are no other assignments due at that time. For more complex questions, one or two discussion questions per week is probably realistic. For weeks when major projects or exams are scheduled, there may be no discussion questions requiring reading or research. In those weeks, students may use the general class posting areas for giving and receiving help on their projects.

Requirements for Student Responses to Discussion Questions

Faculty also want to know when learners should post responses and how often. In general, learners should be encouraged to post early in the week to maximize the opportunity for peer and faculty response and dialogue. For example, one strategy for short-answer essay questions is for learners to post a response to the question by midweek and then respond to the posts of one or two peers in the latter part of the week.

Here are additional guidelines to share with students about their responses to discussion questions.

- Postings should continue a conversation and provide hooks for additional continuous dialogue. For more ideas on encouraging substantive postings, see the Course Beginnings (CB) Tip 13 which encourages learners to respond with answers to "What?" "Why?" and "What do I wish I knew?"

- Postings should be evenly distributed during the discussion forum time, rather than concentrated on one day or at the beginning or end of the discussion time.

- Postings should be a minimum of one short paragraph and a maximum of two to three paragraphs for short-answer essay questions.

- Postings that are limited to "I agree," or "Great idea" are not specific enough. If you agree or disagree with a posting, say *why* by supporting your statement with concepts from the readings or by bringing in a related example or experience.

- Address the question or topic as much as possible, keeping on topic and not letting the discussion stray.

- Incorporate, where possible, quotations from the articles that support your statements in the postings, and include the reference and page numbers.

- Recognize and respond to others' responses to create threads of thought in a discussion, showing how ideas are related and linked.

- Weave into your posting, where possible, related prior personal knowledge gained from experience, prior course work or work experience, discussions, and readings.

- When posting, use proper language, spelling, and grammar, similar to the tone and manner of expression that you would use in a professional environment. Refer to netiquette resources.

A Rule of Thumb for the Length of Discussions

One week is the most common length of time for discussions, although a discussion board or conference involving an external expert may be shorter. Discussion boards with complex topics might be open or run for longer, up to two weeks.

CB Tip 11: Characteristics of Good Discussion Questions

This tip answers questions such as these:

- What are some basic do's and don'ts for good questions for discussion forums?

- How do I develop good questions for discussion forums?

- Is using Bloom's taxonomy of questions as a guide a good idea?

- Is it practical to use problem-solving questions in discussion forums, or are those better used in written assignments?

- What types of questions should be avoided on discussion boards?

Getting Started on Developing Great Questions

This tip describes the characteristics of good questions for discussion forums and provides many examples as inspirations.

Developing good questions for discussion forums takes practice. Often the most important thing to do is to start and then refine questions over time. Students themselves are good sources of feedback and questions. Most importantly, good discussion forum questions are open-ended and exploratory. Open-ended questions require learners to apply and integrate information from multiple resources, including their own work or life environments. Questions to be posted early in the course might focus on how core concepts can be discerned within one's particular work or life experiences.

In a public health course, for example, questions might direct students to research water or air quality in their local area. This requires learners to develop skills in how to find the information they need and understand the measures used to evaluate the air or water quality. The results of these mini-research questions can be shared with other students and used to create a regional or national map with those specific data points. In a course on leadership, learners can be asked to state their personal leadership philosophy along with the story of how it has evolved. Or learners can work in teams to develop an ideal philosophy statement with teams commenting on one another's final statements. A course on conflict scenarios can leverage personal experiences and have the benefit of rich contextual information.

Here are some additional starting guidelines:

- Good discussion questions are open-ended and exploratory. They require learners to "inquire within" about what they currently believe and know and then to provide evidence to support their beliefs.

- Avoid objective, factual questions that have a single answer. Once one student answers a question, there is not much left for anyone else to contribute. If you do want discussion of core knowledge objective facts, have students apply them in personal and local situations.

- Good discussion questions require understanding and use of core concepts, applying the new knowledge to varied scenarios, preferably researched and customized to learners' interests.

- Factual questions can best be practiced in automated quizzes. For example, according to Peter Senge, factual knowledge in a course on organizational development might entail knowing that systems thinking is the fifth discipline that integrates the other four disciplines of any learning organization: personal mastery, mental models, building a shared vision, and team learning (Senge, 1990). Other examples might be the formulae in a math course, such as the area of a triangle, or the laws of thermodynamics in a physics course.

Developing Questions Using Bloom's Cognitive Taxonomy

The dilemmas about developing questions that faculty face often sound something like this: "I have tried to use a range of questions, from those that are very objective—such as definitions and core processes—to those more complex, following Bloom's taxonomy of the cognitive domain (1956) and the revised cognitive taxonomy of Krathwohl (2002). But I am still struggling to find the best balance for a question: one that elicits thoughtful and substantive discussion without overwhelming the students. Is there a set of guidelines somewhere?"

First of all, Bloom's and Krathwohl's revised taxonomy is an excellent starting point for developing questions, as they provide a step-by-step process by which we build our knowledge structures. It is a useful sequence as we journey from a novice state to an expert state of knowledge. Here are the five levels, from Krathwohl's revised taxonomy that focuses on cognitive processes: remember, understand, apply, analyze, evaluate, and create. The following is a description of three question categories linked to the five levels of the taxonomy:

1. Factual content questions, which often represent multiple data elements and knowledge bits required for developing core concepts. Remember that "concepts are more than words; they are organized and intricate clusters of knowledge bits" (Vygotsky, 1978). Learning concepts is a complex multistage process.

2. Questions using the Socratic method, requiring students to inquire within themselves.

3. Problem-solving questions that intersect three areas: a learner's zone of proximal development, core concept development, and complex and customized learning.

Factual Questions

Factual questions are generally those with a known answer. This includes short-answer essay questions, such as the pros and cons of different leadership types. These are often straightforward questions and facts that are part of more complex concepts. Students can sometimes apply these straightforward questions to their own experiences. These questions can include basic principles, guidelines, and accepted practices. For these types of questions, students can also be asked to identify or find ideas from relevant topic resources. A good way to ensure the learner's attention to these fundamental enablers is to use the quiz function within LMSs and provide a low point value to a completion requirement.

Socratic Questions

Questions based on the Socratic method encourage students to go within themselves and do the following: (1) clarify what is known to them, (2) provide the assumptions behind their reasoning, and (3) provide the data behind those assumptions (Paul & Elder, 2008). Here are some typical clarifying questions that can be incorporated into discussion questions and into question debriefings:

- What is your main point? And how is it related to x?

- What do you think is the main issue here?

- How does this relate to our discussion, problem, or issue?

- What do you think John meant by his remark? What did you understand John to mean? Jane, would you summarize in your own words what Roberto has said? Roberto, is that what you meant?

- Could you give me an example?

With these types of Socratic questions, learners often shift easily into the roles of questioner, summarizer, and encourager. Much more on Socratic questioning and the analysis and assessment of thinking is at the Center for Critical Thinking and Moral Critique (http://www.criticalthinking.org).

Problem-Solving Questions

Problem-solving experiences are generally good for the following situations:

- Serious thinking about complex issues

- Customizing learning and making it relevant and meaningful

- Incorporating challenges from current events using multidimensional issues

- Getting learners involved and grappling with real-world issues such as access to water and technology

- Working on learner projects, either individual or group

Problem-solving questions can range from relatively straightforward scenarios in which the recommended strategies and solutions might be known or well accepted, to very complex scenarios in which answers and solutions are not known and call for truly creative and innovative thinking.

As faculty, we also get inspired and enthusiastic when we challenge our students to work on questions for which there are no known answers or strategies. Examples of problem-solving questions for specific disciplines follow.

Discussion Questions on Core Concepts in a Course

A good design approach is to develop questions that incorporate or use one or more core concepts. These discussion questions can map directly back to the general and personal performance goals and learning outcomes of a course. These concept-focused questions can provide opportunities for students to see how the core concepts reveal themselves in very different scenarios, researching and citing examples from real life. The goal is to structure questions that lead students to think through the applications of those core concepts, resulting in more transferable knowledge.

The following are some brief examples of discussion questions focusing on core concepts.

Business case studies

- What types of marketing programs work best for small businesses? For technology innovation companies?

- What are the different ways of translating a good idea into a company?

Biology and genetics

- What if your doctor could choose medical treatments based on your genetic makeup that are guaranteed to be effective?

History/environment/anatomy

- Students assume the role of an osteologist and are tasked with identifying the bones a farmer found in a field.

Microbiology

- Students attempt to cure a sick paramecium.

- Students analyze the crud from a field, shoe, or baseball.

Tech and society topics

- Feasibility of driverless cars

- Global climate change

- Recycling

More Resources for Discussion Questions

One of the modern classics in using discussions for learning is *Discussion as a Way of Teaching* (Brookfield & Preskill, 2005). Brookfield and Preskill have found the following categorization of questions to be useful for starting and maintaining momentum in discussions:

- Questions that ask for more evidence
- Questions that ask for clarification
- Open questions
- Linking or extension questions
- Hypothetical questions
- Cause-and-effect questions
- Summary and synthesis questions

Here are more ideas on all levels of questioning selected from a much larger set developed for encouraging reasoning across the curriculum (Peirce, 2001):

- Conduct brief opinion or thought polls related to course readings to arouse interest in topics and assess and estimate students' prior knowledge.
- Create cognitive dissonance. Provoke discomfort, unsettle confirmed notions, uncover misconceptions, inspire curiosity, and pose problems.
- Present activities that require considering opposing views.
- Assign a mediatory argument promoting a resolution acceptable to both sides.
- Ask students to evaluate Internet resources.
- Ask students to reflect on their responses to the course content and on their learning processes in private journals.

One of these strategies might be particularly well suited to your content and desired skills and behaviors and knowledge of your students.

Core Assumption of Constructivism

In developing questions, keep in mind a core foundational assumption of the constructivist educational philosophy: that we know the world through our existing mental framework and bring in, transform, and interpret new information as it fits into this framework. An "Aha!" insight experience can shift and reshape areas of this knowledge base. This assumption highlights how important it is for us and for students to think deeply about what we know or believe we know, because new knowledge is built on and integrated with what is already in our heads.

CB Tip 12: Power Questioning for Meaningful Discussions

This tip answers questions such as these:

- How do I develop questions that encourage critical thinking?
- What kinds of questions stimulate learner curiosity?

This tip offers four questioning strategies with "thinking power" to encourage more interesting discussions. These questions are derived from the critical thinking work of Paul and Elder (2008) and from research on increasing the quality of discussion in discussion forums (Beuchot & Bullen, 2005; Baran & Correia, 2009; Hull & Saxon, 2009; Brookfield, 2012; James & Brookfield, 2014). The set of questioning strategies is followed by three facilitation strategies for encouraging expansive discussion forums.

The research on dialogue and discussions is suggesting that we need to pay greater attention to matching the content and learning purpose to the types of questions and activities in discussion forums. See if one of these questions or strategies might be a better fit for one of your discussion forums, given your particular students and learning goals.

Power Questioning Strategies

Here are four power-questioning strategies that you can use immediately with only slight revision. These questions can refer to assigned readings, videos, or recommended resources.

1. Ask students to provide evidence and justification of their thinking from course readings or other relevant resources. For example, one of the statements in your rubric might include some of the following requirements: "Be sure to include evidence and justification in your rationale. Evidence means quoting and citing relevant phrases or sentences. Then state how and why you agree or disagree with the author or with your peer." Providing evidence and justifications encourages accuracy in thinking.

2. Include questions on motivation and purpose. This means answering questions such as "Why did x choose to do y?" You might ask, "Why did Socrates choose to die rather than go into exile? What did he state as his reasons? What else might he have chosen to do? What would you

have chosen to do?" Questions on motivation and purpose encourage clear and logical thinking.

3. Encourage reflection on actions and consequences of actions. For example, ask students to debate the short-term and long-term consequences of a leader's decisions, or the consequences of the leader's actions. Questions on actions and consequences encourage breadth and depth of thinking.

4. Encourage comparisons and contrasts with the thinking of peers. For example, ask students to highlight how the perspectives of others differ from or overlap with the perspectives of others. These types of questions encourage fairness and breadth of thinking.

Facilitation Strategies for Expansive Discussion Forums

Depending on the characteristics of a concept or course topic, there may be times when it is beneficial to have a discussion forum span a two-week timeframe.

Each of the following three facilitation strategies (Baran & Correia, 2009) describes a multiphase design for a discussion topic. These longer discussion designs can provide more time for reflection and co-construction of meaning that invites students to integrate multiple ideas and perspectives; they go beyond simple message-posting to exploration and problem solution.

1. "Know, want, learn" structure

In the know, want, learn facilitation approach, the discussion leader, who could be a student, selects a core topic, idea, or principle. Students are then asked to reflect on this topic from three perspectives, in sequence, during the discussion forum period. This is a framework that is best used for difficult and comprehensive concepts, because it requires tapping into what is already known and then using new data and information to integrate and construct the concept.

In the first posting, which can be done at the end of a week's cycle before the formal forum begins, learners answer these kinds of questions:

- What do they or others think or *know* about a particular topic, philosophy, or person?

- How, when, or from whom did they acquire this knowledge?

- How have they used this knowledge in the past?

- What images and words come to them in their mind about this concept?

The results of this first phase reveal what students think or know about a topic before they do a lot of reading or research on the topic. This is a way of learning, of discerning what students' ZPDs are, what they are ready to learn.

In the second posting, students focus on these kinds of questions:

- What do they *want* to know about the information, encouraging them to specify the importance or rationale for wanting to know? For example, they may want to know *how* to solve a particular problem, or *what strategies* are recommended in certain areas. Getting to a specific question almost always focuses the mind toward a specific action or response.

In the third posting, learners reflect on what they have learned after completing the unit readings, or other resources. Learners post a comment or reflection that might do one of the following:

- Describe how what they know has changed from the readings and conversation.

- Share how the knowledge might impact future decisions, or actions.

- Consider what their next question might be as it relates to them personally.

At this point, you may be asking, "Where does the interaction between the students and sustained conversation happen?" In the first *know* posting, students can be encouraged to notice the sources of their knowledge information, the potential impact of such beliefs or knowledge, and how that knowledge relates to other experiences or life demands. Students can work individually or in teams to identify potential misconceptions, challenges, and knowledge sources. By the time of the third posting, on *what* they have learned, students might specify why the information is important to them, and how they expect or want to use the information.

2. Dream initiative strategy

This facilitation strategy invites students to go beyond the content and beyond traditional thinking, to propose innovative solutions, raise challenging questions, search for inner goals, develop idealistic scenarios, and discuss ways to achieve them. Here are some example dream initiative strategies. (Baran & Correia, 2009):

- A question from an instructional design course might be, "If you had the opportunity to design and teach a dream course, or classroom lesson, "How would you go about implementing it at your institution?" (Baran & Correia, 2009).

- A dream question from a course on web technologies might be, "What business app would you like to develop that would solve a pressing daily problem?"

- A dream question from a course in basic philosophical questions might be, "What philosophy would you like everyone to be guided by or base their decisions on?"

3. Practice-focused discussions

This facilitation strategy focuses discussions on examples of real-life scenarios. With this strategy, the faculty member or student presents a case and students immerse themselves in the case, analyzing it from a number of perspectives. Over the course of a discussion forum, students might be asked questions such as the following:

- What other questions or data might be relevant to this case?

- Have you heard about or experienced cases that share some of these characteristics or might have implications for this case?

- What actions are definitely not to be recommended?

- What actions might be recommended from your experiences or readings?

Discussion Forum Research and Questions for Reflection

The research on discourse has many characteristics with implications for designing conversations for discussion forums. An important design question to ask is whether we are using discussion forums for gathering evidence of learning or for stimulating thinking about issues and exploring more creative and innovative ideas (Dennen & Wieland, 2007). In the first case of gathering evidence for grading, the discussion forum is a learning product that we may want to use for individual evaluation. In the second case, the message discourse may illuminate the process of thinking and learning, revealing how students' thinking evolves as they gather and organize new information. It is the second case that is sometimes referred to as the negotiation of meaning and co-construction of knowledge.

Criteria for Rubrics

Researchers are making progress on clarifying issues that help us create more substantive dialogue and discussion exchanges. Research by Nandi, Hamilton, and Harland (2012) resulted in a framework for evaluating interaction quality between students. This framework identifies eleven posting criteria and suggests the characteristics of a poor, satisfactory, good, and excellent message or posting. You might find these criteria helpful in creating or enhancing your rubric for discussion forums.

Asking questions

Answering questions

Providing justification

Clarification posts

Critical discussion of contributions

Ideas from interactions

Posting opinions

Providing feedback

Sharing knowledge and experiences

Relevance

Using social cues to engage other participants

CB Tip 13: Response Posts—A Three-Part Structure

This tip answers these questions:

- What makes a good discussion post?
- How can post responses grow community?
- How can real conversation be sustained, avoiding routine turn-taking?

Discussion Boards Is Where Community Happens

The major question for this tip is what makes a good discussion post. As has been suggested in other tips, the discussion forum is where we express what we know and why, what we don't know, and occasionally what we wish we knew.

One of the authors of the Community of Inquiry model, D. Randy Garrison of the University of Calgary, has observed that a key advantage of online learning is that the interaction pattern of online courses tends to be "group-centered" rather than "authority-centered." This observation encourages thinking about course behaviors at the level of groups rather than individuals. In other words, we want to supplement learner-centered teaching with group-centered teaching and occasionally focus attention on how the group as a whole is moving toward key understandings.

Individual learners, of course, have important roles in community as was suggested in Brown's (2001) study. Each individual has responsibility to "make the group and the learning happen" by (1) embracing the content that is brought to the course, (2) integrating with their own knowledge, and then (3) creating and contributing ideas in a process of knowledge creation and discovery. Community depends on each of the learners' fulfilling these responsibilities.

Shift from Turn-Taking to Reflective and Developed Conversation

Garrison also observed that asynchronous online discussions allow time for reflection and can usefully shift groups away from the frantic turn-taking atmosphere that often characterizes discussions. Thoughtful posts and responses to posts can build on the thoughts and knowledge that the learners bring to the conversation. It is this type of discussion post, thoughtful and reflective and building on what others have expressed or inquired about, that makes for good discussion posts. It is these types of posts that create sustained conversation about important ideas.

Does this happen naturally? We don't think so. As with most new types of communication, effective use of tools requires practice and analysis. Also, how many of us know how to have sustained conversation, responding to and building on others' thoughts when we are face to face? How do we then encourage students to not just post what they believe, but to read and "hear" what a fellow student is saying and to integrate those thoughts with their existing thoughts and mental models?

This may mean that a faculty member needs to not only observe, monitor, and comment, but also to model and describe the process of how the content is being taken in, absorbed, and integrated. This may be an elusive goal for many of us. So what is the answer?

Here are two suggestions for encouraging discussion posts that support sustained conversation and more community thinking.

Three-Part Post—What, Why, and What I Wish I Knew

When you have posted an open-ended question that asks students for their recommendations and ideas about a particular problem, challenge, or idea, encourage them to create postings with these three parts.

- Part 1: State what your considered thought or recommendation might be. In other words, answer the question, "What do you think?"

- Part 2: State *why* you think what you think. This is a good place for learners to dig inside their heads, their experiences, their beliefs. It is a good place for learners to provide references and links to experts, events, or belief statements that share and support their thinking.

- Part 3: State what you wish you knew or what problem or challenge will follow or result from the original question.

CB Tip 14: Discussion Wraps: A Useful Cognitive Pattern or a Collection of Discrete Thoughts?

This tip answers questions such as these:

- How do you close out a weekly discussion? Do you summarize key points? Restate a core concept? Highlight an innovative relationship or pattern?

- Do you get your students involved in bringing a discussion to a close?

Closing or Wrapping Up Discussions

These most recent tips have focused on how to make discussion forums work well in engaging students, building knowledge, and nurturing community. Remember, the primary purposes of discussions are to gather evidence of learning and to stimulate thinking. This means that discussion forums play an important role in showing what students know and what they think they know. Closing out discussions well is just as important if not more so.

One question to ask yourself and your students is "What idea or thought do you take forward from a week's discussion of ideas?" Do the weekly discussions often just end in a flurry of thoughts and ideas on the last day of the week, with no clear outcomes, resolutions, or direction?

Envision having a conversation with a colleague: you are enthusiastically talking about how wonderful the last week's discussion forum has been. Can you distill into one or two sentences what you believe your students are going to remember or think about or question from that discussion?

Here are two teaching practices for making discussions more memorable and useful in building knowledge.

1. Summarize the Key Ideas from the Discussion Forum

What are our minds doing when we are learning? Our minds are growing by making new and stronger connections among the neurons in our brains. We are identifying patterns, finding hidden relationships, delighting in new insights, and pondering challenges and questions.

As students are discussing ideas in the weekly conversations, their responses, perspectives, questions, and ideas tend to be broad-ranging and dispersed. Often, just as the conversation gets to the point of identifying key challenges and interesting relationships emerging, the week ends and a new topic begins. Often the students are left with questions such as these:

- What have I learned? What do I know now that I did not know before?

- Have I changed how I think about these ideas, or about this problem?

- What is next? Are there actions that we should pursue at some point?

- Where has this conversation taken me? Taken our group?

- What are the new challenges ahead?

- What are the experts' opinions on this question?

- What does our faculty leader think? Note: it is not important for students to agree with their faculty leader, but it is important for students to know their instructor's thoughts as a representative of an expert in the field.

A summary of the week's discussion forum helps to address some of these questions and bring some closure or direction. This does not mean having answers, but rather identifying the ideas to go forward and pruning to the essential concepts. We know from memory research that we remember very little of what we experience, with good reason (Damasio, 1999). Continually searching for meaning and discarding irrelevant information helps to grow an organized and useful knowledge base. Summarizing a discussion is an opportunity to help the students focus and reflect on the essential ideas and key concepts, to help isolate out key issues and develop useful knowledge, rather than be left with vague recollections. Who should prepare the summary wrap? When? And how long should it be? Some of these questions are addressed next.

Effective Formats for Discussion Summaries

The discussion summary can take one of many formats. Here are a few popular ones.

- Create a closing discussion forum labeled "summary," "wrap-up," or "key ideas" or labeled with a core concept for the week. These forums will help students with course reviews. Faculty who teach a particular course each term can create a template for reinforcing some of the core concepts and then deftly weave in comments and observations from current students.

- Create a separate summary document that captures the key postings of the week, integrating these statements with the core concepts.

- Create a group summary by asking each student to identify the core concept from the week's discussion. The students' concepts can be an insight, challenge, relationship, pattern, or next step idea.

- Hold a live synchronous session with your students and review key ideas from a unit of two to three weeks; then create a summary from that activity.

- Have a summarizing discussion and review the concepts from the readings and comment on the discussion and conclusions that ensued.

2. Involve the Students in Wrapping Up Discussions

Keep in mind that the creative process of preparing a summary from a week's discussion requires advanced thinking skills such as analysis, synthesis, questioning, linking ideas, and identifying patterns. These are just the types of critical thinking skills that we desire for our students. So finding ways for students to do some of the summarizing is also an effective learning activity.

Summarizing as a Small Group Activity

Summarizing a week's worth of discussion ideas can be somewhat daunting the first time around. This is where models and examples can be very useful. To start this process you can model the first two or three examples of a discussion wrap. A next step can be to form teams of two students to develop future weekly wraps. This works particularly well in smaller graduate seminars.

The timing of the summary work is important, as it provides a transition and bridge to the next topic. So, if your students take on the role of summarizer, remember that your teaching or expert voice must be present in the complementary steps of providing confirmation, affirmation, or enhancement of the students' summary. Your opinion is a key element of the community summary from that week's discussion work.

Wrap Up

Summarizing work or guiding the development of discussion wraps is part of your teaching presence. It is an effective way to use insights and comments from your students and affirm your students' intellectual growth. Summarizing is also a major element of cognitive presence, as the summaries pull together many discrete pieces of information into a cohesive and useful knowledge structure that each student is constructing. As you or your students create these summaries, you are likely to create new knowledge as well. This is an engaging and exciting process.

CB Tip 15: Using Discussion Forums to Gather Evidence of Learning

This tip answers questions such as these:

- How do I manage discussion postings so that everyone responds in a timely manner with substantive comments?
- How do I support the students without squelching brainstorming ideas?
- How do I grade or evaluate discussions?
- How many points for a course should be allocated for discussion postings?

Purpose of Discussion Postings

One of the benefits of the discussion forum being asynchronous and requiring every learner to post is that it encourages more learner-to-learner dialogue and encourages the instructor to "talk and tell" less. This means that discussion boards support the creation of teaching and learning communication patterns in which the instructor's voice is more in the background, guiding, observing, challenging, and monitoring the discussions.

As has been noted earlier, reading, commenting on, and evaluating student postings all provide a window into a student's knowledge structure. A student's conceptual development becomes very clear, sometimes wonderfully so and sometimes painfully so. But it is a way of seeing "mind-to-mind" rather than simply "eyeball-to-eyeball." Thus discussions in this asynchronous and thought-captured space in text or audio can be many times more effective than a classroom discussion.

Three Basic Communication Models

Three basic communication models built on the transactional distance theory (Moore, 2007) are seen in discussion forums. The first model is basic and quite straightforward: student-to-faculty and faculty-to-student communication. In this model students respond to one or more questions or tasks in the discussion forum, while the instructor reviews and analyzes the responses and summarizes the major ideas or insights. This model can seem quite familiar to an experienced classroom instructor who is coming from the lecture model.

The second model is a communication pattern of learner-to-learner or peer-to-peer communications. In this model, students read, respond, and post responses to other students. This establishes communication strands in which the faculty member is more of a coach and observer, ensuring that students are on track and confirming what is going on, but not being in the forefront. To maintain the teaching presence, the faculty member might question, comment, suggest links in wrapping up the discussion at the end of the week, or make comments on the discussion summary if students prepared it.

The learner-to-learner model can also be used by advanced and mature online learners. In this model, students might work in teams to review, analyze, and stimulate thinking. In this model students can also act as surrogate faculty, summarizing, monitoring, and tracking responses.

The third model is a self-directed communication between a learner and resources, as learners use any type of resource or tool or combination of resources to teach themselves. The most common mode of learner to resource is that of a learner to a book, article, or video. With the abundance of YouTube videos showing how to do almost anything, learners can be very independent and then bring their new knowledge to the class discussion forums.

Monitoring Discussion Boards

The design of discussion boards makes managing multiple themes and ideas easy. The subject lines (topics or themes) of the discussions drive the postings by the students and encourage exchange, analysis, and synthesis of ideas. The design encourages a thought product, which can be text as well as audio enriched with pictures, including links to other resources. If a student wants to start a new conversation, or thread, it is a matter of making a decision and clicking a button. All comments related to that topic then flow under that topic heading. This threaded feature makes sustained conversations over time possible and makes tracking, monitoring, and engaging in multiple conversation threads quite easy. The visual layout of the discussion forum is also helpful in providing a quick visual look at how many students are participating and when. These features encourage topic-driven, multivoice discussions. Other tools such as blogs and wikis share some of the characteristics of discussion boards, but these tools may be better suited to individual or group reflection and in-depth thinking over a longer period of time. (For more about blogs and wikis, see LM Tip 14.)

How to Ensure Lively Participation

One way to ensure that students do *not* participate in discussions is to not allocate any assessment points to discussion forums. To avoid this pitfall, be sure to allocate points to discussion postings and participation. If you are reluctant to assign points to the discussions, start by providing bonus points for the discussions; however, we highly recommend that you move quickly to the required mode. The minimum number of points for discussion board participation is about 15 percent, increasing to 35 percent, depending on the complexity and requirements of the postings.

Allocating Points and Using Rubrics for Evaluating Postings

Table 6.3 presents a draft rubric for evaluating postings that you can adapt to your teaching style and your content. A rubric is a scoring system set up as a matrix with the two or three desired characteristics in the left-hand column and a three-point scale for each of those desired characteristics in the remaining three columns. In the Table 6.3 example, the rubric includes measures of time (when and how often postings are posted), quantity (a length appropriate to the discussion topic), and content (resource related,

TABLE 6.3

Draft Rubric for Discussion Forum Postings

Desirable Characteristics	Poor: 1 point	Good: 2 points	Excellent: 3 points
Timely and quantitative discussion contributions	One to two postings per discussion; somewhat distributed, with first posting later in the week.	Two to three postings per discussion; postings distributed throughout the week, with first posting occurring early in the week.	Three to four postings per discussion; well distributed throughout the week, with first posting midway through week.
Responsiveness to discussion; demonstration of knowledge; understanding gained from assigned reading	Postings had questionable relationship to reading material or topic under discussion, with little or no evidence of understanding.	Clear that readings were understood and that concepts and insights were incorporated into responses.	Very clear that readings were understood and ideas were incorporated well into responses; postings continued the comments and insights of other learners.
Followed online protocols for clear communications; correct grammar, spelling, and understandable statement flow	Two to three online protocols were not followed; organization unclear.	Most online protocols were followed; statements were mostly organized and clear.	All online protocols were followed; statements were well organized and clear.

thoughtful, and substantive) that factor into the points earned. Another measure often used in rubrics is format, which includes adherence to appropriate written English. Instructors often invite or assign students to take a supportive monitoring role for some discussions, such as the role of evaluator or summarizer with additional points.

For more ideas and hints about building rubrics, the section on discussion rubrics at the pedagogical repository at the University of Central Florida is a good starting point; you may also find the resources in the Guide to Rating Critical and Integrative Thinking at the Washington State University website useful.

Here are links to a few additional sample rubrics. Most are from a web page—https://topr.online.ucf.edu/index.php/discussion_rubrics—at the University of Central Florida; the last is in the cited article. You might find using one of these rubrics as a starting point good for your needs.

- Online Discussion Rubric—Farah Cato, instructor in UCF's Department of Writing and Rhetoric at the College of the Arts & Humanities. https://topr.online.ucf.edu/index.php/file:cato_2110_discussion_rubric.pdf

- Online Discussion Rubric—Dr. Susan Wegmann, Professor of Education and the Director of Program Development and Special Programs at the Baptist College of Florida. https://topr.online.ucf.edu/index.php/file:wegmann_online_disucssions_rubric.pdf

- Online Discussions Participation Rubric—Dr. Kelvin Thompson, Adjunct Instructor in UCF's College of Education and Human Performance. http://ofcoursesonline.com/wp-content/uploads/2011/11/weekly-online-discussions-rubric-eme5050.pdf

- Online Discussion Rubric—IDL6543, Instructional Design Team, Center for Distributed Learning, UCF. https://topr.online.ucf.edu/index.php/File:IDL6543_Discussion_Rubric.pdf

- "Designing and Orchestrating Online Discussions" (Baker, 2011). http://jolt.merlot.org/vol7no3/baker_0911.pdf

CB Tip 16: Feedback in Discussion Posts—How Soon, How Much, and Wrapping Up

This tip answers questions such as these:

- How do your students want feedback?
- When do your students want feedback?
- What are the three most important goals of feedback?

Most Pressing Questions About Feedback

The most pressing questions about feedback usually revolve around how and when to provide it for the discussion postings. Students in general seem to desire more feedback earlier and more frequently. Yet striking a balance between too much and too little feedback and presence can be difficult. Some faculty feel that jumping in too early with feedback dominates and skews the dialogue. Other faculty share that it is hard to know just what to say when.

One important teaching goal is to provide enough reflecting and thinking time early in the week so that learners can think through what they think and why. Faculty often wish they could simply nod their head or say "Keep going." Or simply "Good." And then invite another to comment. So the question arises: how do we do that with our virtual presence tools?

Here is a feedback model that corresponds to key time points in a discussion forum. This model builds in time for reflection and exploration while also acknowledging and encouraging thinking and sustained conversation.

A Feedback Model for a Discussion Forum: Early, Middle, and Late Points

In the early part of the discussion week your feedback goal might be just simple acknowledgment: letting your students know that you are listening and considering their thinking and the questions or difficulties that they may be having in completing the readings or the postings. Simple acknowledgments let the students know you are present and that you are aware of what thinking and sharing is going on. This can mean feedback such as, "Scott, thanks for getting us started this week," or "Christina, thanks for stating your position so clearly; you might also think about extending your thinking to a similar or related pattern in X's thinking," or "Andrew, keep thinking along these lines and also think about how this experience might relate to x or y or to Scott's thinking."

As the week progresses, the goal of your feedback might expand to encourage the students to be listening to each other, and to note similarities or contrasts in the thinking or experiences of others. Your feedback at this point is to gently channel or shape the learners' thinking and their expression of that thinking. Remember that it is often effective to include requirements in your rubrics for learners to provide feedback to one another on their thinking. This helps to create a participatory sustained conversation, rather than just turn-taking of isolated unrelated postings. This is a good time to question, challenge, or suggest patterns in a concept, with a link to a current happening or event.

Providing significant "expert" feedback is probably best done later in the week. At the same time, it is important not to wait so long that the expert feedback does not serve to shape and channel thinking and provide time for reflection and integration of the core concepts and significant groundings. As always, it is the learner who must be doing the work of thinking and integrating, and there must be time for this.

Feedback to Wrap Up a Discussion Forum

One of the closing postings in the discussion forum should be from the faculty member in his or her role as the course expert and facilitator. (See CB Tip 14.) This post serves two purposes: to wrap up and summarize the thinking and ideas generated by the group, and to provide a bridge and transition to the next set of learning experiences.

Value of Rubrics for Feedback

Another very important tool for feedback in discussion postings is rubrics. Rubrics are very efficient and effective. They are particularly valuable in providing models of excellent postings and thereby communicating expectations. Remember that it is almost impossible to be too clear about expectations. While rubrics can initially take a little time to develop, they can then be readily modified for other assignments.

It is hard to overstate the value of rubrics in (1) codifying the criteria and standards for an assignment, thus making grading easier; (2) communicating the academic and professional expectations of an assignment or project; and (3) providing a tool for self-review and peer-review. They can range from a simple three-point rubric for discussion postings to more complex rubrics for projects and for emphasizing specific skills such as critical or innovative thinking.

Summary: Three Purposes of Feedback

It is tempting to think of feedback primarily in the context of assessing or grading. However, the purpose of feedback is more multidimensional. In fact, the goal of feedback is to help learners grow in their knowledge and their expertise, and is thus forward-looking. Here is a three-point summary of the purposes of feedback.

- Convey the sense of caring, relationship support, and "being there"
- Guide the development of skill, knowledge
- Guide metacognitive and lifelong learning competencies

For example, providing feedback on what is standard written English shows that you care about and wish to support the student's professional competency. By encouraging self-assessment and peer review, faculty can help guide a student's development as a skilled writer. By providing resources for good writing and keeping expectations high, faculty can encourage awareness and lifelong competency in writing.

CB Tip 17: The Faculty Role in Blended and Online Courses

This tip answers questions such as these:

- What is the role of an instructor in an online or blended course? How do I convey content without lecturing? How do I cover content?
- What is my role in the first weeks of a course, and how does it evolve over the phases of a course?

A framework described by Conrad and Donaldson (2011) defines four stages of faculty and learner roles throughout a course. Table 6.4 describes

TABLE 6.4

Phases of Engagement with Activity Categories

Phase	Instructor Role	Student Role	Process	Activity Categories
1. Connect	Social negotiator	Newcomer (individual student)	Activities are interactive and allow learners to become acquainted. Instructor provides expectations for engagement and orientation to the course and keeps learners on track on a one-to-one basis.	Icebreakers, individual introductions, discussions re: community issues (such as netiquette)
2. Communicate	Structural engineer	Peer partner (two-student pairing)	Instructor forms student dyads and provides activities that require critical thinking, reflection, and sharing of ideas.	Peer reviews, activity critiques, pro-and-con discussions
3. Collaborate	Facilitator	Team member (three- to five-member groups)	Groups of three to five students form. Groups collaborate, solve problems, and reflect on experiences; also establish a group contract on group expectations, and determine final group project.	Content discussion, role playing, debates, jigsaws*
4. Co-Facilitate	Community member/subject matter expert	Initiator or partner (continued member of same group)	Activities are learner-initiated or learner-led. Learners direct discussion and facilitate interaction. Projects are developed collaboratively with instructor guidance.	Group presentations and authentic projects, learner-facilitated discussions

*In a jigsaw activity, the content is broken into parts with each team member of a group responsible for learning one of the parts and then teaching it to the rest of the team (Sellers et al., 2007).

Source: Conrad and Donaldson (2011).

the four stages. Notice that as learners become more actively engaged in working the content, the instructor moves from more direct instruction and interaction to participating and facilitating in activities as needed. As students assume more independent and collaborative roles and responsibilities, a faculty member can step back from being the leader of the learning community to being a co-community member.

Recall that one of the goals in faculty communication in any course is to balance the three dialogues of faculty-to-learner, learner-to-learner, and learner-to-resource dialogues. A campus classroom often has a high percentage of faculty-to-learner dialogue, with the faculty at the center of many classroom activities. One of the goals in increasingly learner-centered experiences is to move from a transmission-of-knowledge mode to a coaching-and-mentoring mode. Increasingly, instructors are shifting to the role of a coach, a mentor, and a director of learning. In that coaching role, instructors help learners build, reshape, and extend their knowledge structures. When instructors are talking, learners assume the role of listening, which is a less active role than talking, writing, and discussing; more learning occurs when learners are processing, writing, analyzing, and questioning.

One of our favorite stories is from an online instructor who was somewhat frustrated with what he perceived as sterile and almost pro forma postings on the discussion boards. Then he had a family emergency that required him to be away for a few days. He told the students to continue the class discussions while he assumed a less visible, but still affirming and monitoring role during the week he needed to be away. To his surprise and delight, the learning community that he had been striving to achieve started to happen. The discussion postings took on a new vibrancy of intellectual inquiry and analysis. It is this level of involvement that you want to achieve in your course. As always, the value of a faculty's presence and confirmation of content accuracy and intellectual vigor cannot be overstated, but there must always be room for learners to step forward, take a stance, and be heard.

Guidelines

Here are a few simple guidelines for refining your decisions as to when to be in the foreground and when to be in the background:

- Provide a virtual forum or space in your course site for learners to talk to and help each other that is totally faculty free. Think in terms of a social gathering place or a residence hall environment for your learners to freely comment, wonder, and ask for help. If students want or need your input, they can post it in the general course area.

- Be specific about your role for each of the discussion board activities. For example, for the getting-acquainted discussion postings during week one of a course, you might want to state that you will be reviewing these postings but not commenting on them until all have responded. You might also encourage learners who post later in the week to share or note common interests and experiences. In this way, you are building in some natural grouping or processing of these postings. Later in the course, for a more concept-oriented discussion, it might be appropriate for small groups of two or three learners to review or grade each other's postings according to the prepared rubrics. Your role would be to read the reviews and summarize and comment on the evaluations completed by the learners. This is often a good time to plan to comment on the links, relationships, and applications as noted by the learners.

- At times, your appropriate role may be the active Socratic questioner on a more complex topic requiring analysis and problem solving. In this case you would be more of a facilitator, encouraging learners to search within themselves for what they know and think. This means asking questions such as, "What do you think is the main issue here?" and "How does this relate to other core concepts?" With Socratic questioning, an instructor is present, asking questions but not proposing or suggesting the answers.

- Design some course activities where you are in the background, off stage center, and students take over the role of questioner, summarizer, and encourager.

Summary—and What's Next

The first few weeks of a course are time intensive. By the close of the first weeks, everyone should be acquainted, engaging in conversations, and interacting with the content resources and core concepts. It is time to stop and breathe deeply and feel satisfied that you have gotten off to a good start. In the next chapter we explore strategies that further community growth and move learners forward in achieving the learning outcomes.

Exercise and Reflection

If you are using this book for a course in faculty development, here are three activities to consider.

1. Identify two of the tips you are using now that have been very effective.

2. Which of the tips stimulate your excitement that you want to use in your next course?

3. Which of the cognitive presence ideas would you like to explore more deeply?

Chapter 7

Phase 2: Keeping the Ball Rolling in the Early Middle

CONGRATULATIONS! BY THE beginning of Phase 2, you have likely made a very good start on launching your course, getting to know your students, and engaging your students with the course content. Your teaching goals during this early middle are twofold: ensuring that students are engaging in activities that will help them achieve the learning outcomes, and supporting your students' project work. Another major goal during this time is to nurture the growth of the course community, expanding learners' confidence in knowing and sharing course content with their peers.

Tips for the Early Middle

The early middle tips focus on three main topics: managing your course well, ensuring the cognitive growth and presence of all learners, and strategies and tools for building community.

The first set of tips, Managing Your Course, focuses on your role as a manager, directing and supporting learners through the course experiences. This set of tips answers questions about how and when to use basic communications tools. It includes reminders of the tools that make tracking and mentoring students efficient and effective.

The second set of tips focuses on engagement with the course content. These activities have the most direct impact on students' learning outcomes and performance goals for the course. The tips in this set describe strategies for encouraging learners' growth from problems they can handle confidently at the beginning of a course and the problems they can handle competently later in the course.

The third set of tips focuses on the strategies and tools best suited for the early stages of building community. These strategies describe ways to promote peer interaction, including the use of small teaming and peer review.

Here is a list of the early middle (EM) tips in this chapter.

Managing Your Course

- **EM Tip 1:** Tools for Teaching Presence: E-mails, Announcements, and Discussion Forums

- **EM Tip 2:** Monitoring Student Progress Using Learning Management Systems

- **EM Tip 3:** Early Feedback Loop from Learners to You

- **EM Tip 4:** Early Feedback Tools: Rubrics, Quizzes, and Peer Review

- **EM Tip 5:** Steps in Memory-Making: What Teaching Behaviors Make a Difference

- **EM Tip 6:** Tips for Making Your Grading Time Efficient and Formative for Learners

- **EM Tip 7:** Dealing with Difficult Students—What Do You Do?

Building Cognitive Presence

- **EM Tip 8:** Building Cognitive Presence Using the Practical Inquiry Model

- **EM Tip 9:** Core Concepts of a Course—Do You Know Yours?

- **EM Tip 10:** Designing Assessment Plans for Online and Blended Courses

- **EM Tip 11:** Three Best Assessment Practices

- **EM Tip 12:** Assignments that Tap into the Evaluating and Creating Levels of Bloom's Taxonomy

Strategies and Tools for Building Community

- **EM Tip 13:** Collaborating with Groups of Two or Three—Casual Grouping

- **EM Tip 14:** Group Projects in Online Courses: Setting Up and Structuring Groups

- **EM Tip 15:** Using Synchronous Collaboration Tools

- **EM Tip 16:** Using Audio and Video Resources to Create More Engaging Learning Experiences

Managing Your Course

This set of tips focuses on your role as manager of the course teaching and learning experiences. Paying attention to the engagement and progress of *each* of your students and contacting and encouraging them as needed is essential. Students have higher expectations of support and attention from instructors in online and blended courses than in more traditional campus courses (Harris, Larrier, & Castano-Bishop, 2011; Bork & Rucks-Ahidiana, 2012).

EM Tip 1: Tools for Teaching Presence: E-mails, Announcements, and Discussion Forums

This tip answers questions such as these:

- Will teaching an online or blended course require seemingly endless hours of communicating by e-mail and other social media?

- How can I manage my time well when teaching online and blended courses?

- What course policies help manage learner expectations? Will I need to be accessible twenty-four hours a day?

- When and how often should I use the announcement feature?

E-mail, Announcements, and Discussion Forums

Many questions about teaching online and blended courses deal with *when* to use *which* communication tools for *what*. In this tip we consider four useful communication tools: e-mail, announcements, texting, and discussion forums. More questions will arise soon with social media tools. For example, you may have questions about using Facebook and Twitter. One way to help decide which current and future tools are good for what is to think about the characteristics of these tools, how students use the tools, and what you are hoping to achieve.

Here are a few simple rules of thumb. Keep in mind that these rules may evolve as the technologies evolve.

- *E-mail and texting:* If you absolutely must reach all students quickly and without exception, e-mail sent as text messages is a great choice. Texts are push technologies, meaning that students do not have to actively "go to" anywhere. A text message lands in the student's mailbox on whatever their favorite tool is: computer, smartphone, or tablets. If a message is particularly urgent, repeat it in an announcement on the course site. So in this case, it is not either/or, but both.

- *Announcements:* The announcement tool is good for general messages and reminders, such as the following:

  - General schedule reminders, such as holidays, assignments, and project deadlines

  - Reminders or descriptions about the week's activities

  - Announcements about special resources and events

  - Reminders about general course processes, such as the importance of making discussion postings early in the week

Be sure to keep announcements short, even Twitter-short. Many students send alerts and announcements to their smartphones and other mobile devices, and long announcements can be unwieldy. If the announcement refers to a longer message or resource, providing a link to that resource is the way to create a welcoming, useful announcement. Also, consider using the release features of announcements, which can be a time saver and reminder for yourself as well.

The best tool for private and confidential one-on-one communication is e-mail. This is the tool of choice for providing individual feedback on assignments or responding to personal questions. The telephone is also an effective and convenient tool that we often neglect, and the free phone and video applications such as Skype work very well. You may want to schedule a phone meeting with a student when personal life events are impinging on a student's course work or if you need to discuss a particularly sensitive issue, such as exceptionally poor-quality work. Whenever the message might come across as harsh or unfeeling without voice inflection, use the phone.

What about using e-mail for general course updates, answering questions, or shaping students' responses to postings? This is where experience comes into play, as these are the cases when the right answer is, "It all depends." Here are three considerations to help guide your choice of communication tool.

- One primary teaching goal in the online environment is building a learning community. This means creating an environment in which ideas are shared, knowledge is created, and dialogues of one-to-many and many-to-many are encouraged. With this goal in mind, the discussion board, the announcement tool, or a dedicated faculty discussion forum are first choices for answering questions. These postings become part of the captured course resources and are always available. An early teaching practice was to use e-mail as a way of wrapping up discussions, summarizing ideas, or touching on important current events.

However, this practice separates this content from the course site and thus is no longer recommended.

- A second goal is faculty efficiency. A good general rule is that any question worth answering for one student is probably worth answering for all of them. Much of the value of a teaching presence concerns the spiraling of content, relating ideas to previous revelations and possible future contributions. As an expert, you can enlighten students with subtleties and nuances that develop over time with many experiences. Sharing these observations in the open space of the discussion forum means the questions and responses are seen, if not read, by everyone.

- A third goal is to encourage peer-to-peer communication. Networking is one element of a course learning community. Most course templates create an open forum space for students to post questions. As appropriate, you can establish a policy that students should first respond to each other. Depending on the class and the students, this approach can work very well, as students learn and confirm what they know and think by responding to others, and it saves you time for responding to more difficult and challenging questions.

Text Messaging, Tweeting, and Whatever Short Messaging System Is Next

Text messaging has features similar to e-mail or announcements in that it is a push technology that goes out to all learners. The rapidly increasing use of text messaging for informal conversations has become part of the culture; indeed, text messaging may already be getting old. Teenagers and young adults in particular have embraced the near-synchronous capabilities of text messaging, chat tools, and Tweeting. While most knowledge exchanges of any significant nature require more time and sophistication than what is usually available with instant tools, such as the 140-character constraint (under pressure) for tweets, these tools can be useful for quick questions and for setting up times and venues for longer discussions or meetings.

The use of short messages of all kinds is emerging as a favorite tool of daily life and thus can be a useful tool to support learning communications. In a study on the use of messaging in teen life, one subject, an undergraduate teaching assistant, used text messaging to communicate the times that he would be available for discussing computer programming problems with students (Grinter & Palen, 2002). The authors of the study noted anecdotal evidence that faculty were using messaging to "field questions from students." A Pew Internet study on smartphones (Smith & Page, 2015) suggests that cell phones are now almost ubiquitous among older teenagers; they are used by 85 percent of those 18 to 29, and 79 percent of those 30 to 49. This means that students are in almost constant contact with each other—and that reaching students with important reminders is easier than ever before.

Making a Choice

The most important guideline for which tool to use for a particular purpose is that it depends on you and your students. The goal for communications in any course is to cultivate a sense of curiosity and a search for truth and wisdom and to do it regularly and meaningfully, while being as accessible as appropriate. Tools are just tools. Your student group as a whole may have preferences. So adjust as you go, and consider the benefits of the tools as they become mainstream.

EM Tip 2: Monitoring Student Progress Using Learning Management Systems

This tip answers these questions:

- What tracking and managing tools can help me monitor my students efficiently?

- What types of questions should I ask myself about how my students are doing?

Learning management systems (LMSs) provide a sophisticated set of tools for tracking student engagement in course activities. Getting a quick look at how your students are progressing gives you needed information quickly and can help you determine whether any adaptive action might be in order. This tip describes some of the features of LMSs that can be used to track and evaluate student progress.

Monitoring Student Engagement and Progress

Monitoring student engagement and activities within LMSs is easy and useful, but the systems can take time to learn. Time spent exploring and using these systems helps develop good practices in getting to know your students and in assessing their progress. These monitoring systems can provide at-a-glance statistics about student access, grades, and discussion board participation. Early warning tools allow you to set rules for expected performance and to monitor students based on those rules. You can also retrieve reports showing the number of times and the dates on which each student accessed individual course components, course content, discussion forums, and assignments. Other tools offer a student-centric view of one student's postings if you want to focus on one student in more depth. In short, the tool makes it easy to answer, quickly and with little time or mental effort, questions such as the following:

- Have all my students started accessing the course site regularly? (This is particularly useful to know in the first ten days or so of a course.)

- Are all my students actively working on their course assignments?

- Has a particular student, Mario, begun accessing the course regularly? How many days has it been since his last course access? Has he been able to address his access and work schedule issues?

- How is Sharmayne doing with the required discussion postings? Do her postings reflect increased sophistication and understanding over time? (You can determine this by looking at a collective view of her postings over time.)

- Is the class as a whole progressing on schedule for the course assignments and check tests?

- Does the overall learner engagement picture for the course suggest the need for any adjustments in the course in the next week? The next two to three weeks?

If you are a Blackboard user, you'll know the monitoring system module as the Performance Dashboard. The Performance Dashboard can show you a roster of your students showing the date of last access, the number of days since last access for each student, how many items they have marked as reviewed, and direct links to that student's postings on the discussion boards and the student's grades in your gradebook. This feature can save you time in watching your students' progress and knowing how they are doing both overall and individually. A tip sheet from *Hunter College* of the City University of New York discusses these features in more detail. (www.hunter.cuny.edu/it/blackboard/repository/files/blackboard-9.1-documents/trackingstudentperformance.pdf).

EM Tip 3: Early Feedback Loop from Learners to You

This tip describes in more detail how to practice Best Practice 6: Ask for Informal Feedback Early in the Term. It answers questions such as these:

- How early can I ask for some feedback from students?

- How formal or informal should this feedback be?

- What are some typically effective questions that seem to draw out feedback?

- What should I do with the feedback?

Ten days into a fifteen-week term, you may be wondering about your students' perceptions of how their course experience is going. A student's experience usually falls into one of three categories:

1. The content of the readings. (Are they enjoying the content? Do they find it interesting, stimulating?)

2. The overall design of the course and the course requirements. (Is the structure clear? Does it make sense to them? Are the course expectations realistic, doable, and personally enjoyable, despite the work to be done?)

3. The communications from the faculty member. (Is the instructor responsive, present, caring?)

Next, we discuss some ways to gather that information.

Using a Survey

Your institution may have survey tools at the ready for you to use; in fact, a survey tool may be part of your course template. Surveys work best if some of the questions are simple and direct. Providing for open-ended comments is also recommended and often leads to unexpected, and enlightening comments. Here are some questions that you might want to include in an early feedback survey ranked on a Likert-scale of 1 to 5:

- I understand what the course requirements and assignment due dates are.

- The instructor responds promptly to student questions and concerns.

- I have a clear idea how to make a substantive contribution to the weekly discussion through my postings.

- I understand how the rubrics work.

- The weekly discussion questions posted by the instructor are stimulating and cause me to think about the content.

- I feel free to voice an opinion that my instructor may not agree with.

If your institution provides a prepared survey, you may want to modify it and make it shorter or longer to focus on getting feedback on a new activity or process that you are using.

Many survey tools are readily available. Two of the survey tools listed in the *Top 100 Tools for 2015* by the Centre for Learning and Performance

Technologies (http://c4lpt.co.uk) can be useful for early term feedback. One is SurveyMonkey (www.surveymonkey.com), an online survey tool that allows users to design surveys, collect responses, and analyze the responses of their created surveys. Another survey tool in the 2015 list is Quizlet (www.quizlet.com). This website provides learning tools for students, including flashcards, study and game modes. One other survey tool to consider is PollDaddy (https://polldaddy.com).

Using a Discussion Forum

Another way of getting early feedback is using a feedback forum that is active for only a week. Ask students to comment on what process or activity has been working particularly well, changes they might suggest, or questions they might have. Here are some sample stimulus questions for a feedback forum. You probably want to pick the top *two or three or four* that fit you, the course, and your students:

- Do you have any "just wondering" questions?
- Are the directions and expectations for the discussion forum clear?
- Are the course expectations and assignments clear?
- How intellectually stimulating and interesting are the selected readings and resources so far?
- What communication tools do you use every day or almost every day?

Can Students' Responses Be Anonymous?

Students may or may not want to be identified with their responses. Responses to survey items are generally automatically aggregated and anonymous unless students choose to provide their names. Sometimes allowing anonymous posting is an option you can select when creating a new forum. Remind learners you are looking for constructive feedback that is actionable.

Obviously the purpose for asking for feedback either early in the course or after the course is to ensure that students are having a quality course experience. An end-of-course questionnaire looks to the future; this early feedback loop focuses on the present, making changes for the current students.

A key element of feedback is closing the loop back to the students about their comments and making any changes as a result. Sometimes students suggest a different time or a different process for an activity. Small changes in course activities that complement work and life schedules and goals can make a difference in learning and overall satisfaction. Summarizing the forum results, indicating what you will be changing or not, sends a signal that you take their feedback seriously and are listening.

EM Tip 4: Early Feedback Tools: Rubrics, Quizzes, and Peer Review

This tip answers questions such as these:

- What are some good simple rubrics for discussion posts?
- How much individual feedback do I need to provide?
- Should discussion posts be worth any points for grading?
- Should rubrics be part of the original posting or assignment?
- How should I use quizzes? Should quizzes be worth points for grading?
- How can peer review help in the early phases of a course?

All students want to know how they are doing. Yet providing feedback can be time-consuming, making time management difficult. These two competing goals can be balanced by using rubrics, quizzes, and peer review.

The basic rule of thumb regarding assigning points for discussion forums or quizzes or peer review is this: If you feel it is important for students to do, it is wise to have some points associated with the action or behavior. Remember that online learners, although they are motivated for learning, can be ruthless in doing only what is truly needed to satisfy course requirements. Assigning points to discussion forums and peer reviews is your way of telling the students that engagement and participation in these activities make a difference in learning and in building relationships.

Rubrics

As discussed in the tip on Managing and Evaluating Discussion Postings (CB Tip 15), rubrics are very valuable in communicating expectations about learning to students. We recommend using simple rubrics for discussion forums. The primary goal of discussion forums is to generate interest, critical thinking, and engagement with the content and with each other. These are the activities that support learning. Gathering evidence of learning from the forums is secondary in most cases. Table 7.1 shows a very simple zero to three (0–3) point rubric. This rubric can be part of the discussion forum's instructions, and students can even self-grade themselves. With a rubric such as this, you can focus on content references or comments in

TABLE 7.1

Three-Point Rubric for Evaluating Weekly Postings

1 point: Minimal response to the forum discussion or question	2 points: Posting responds to the discussion or question but does not stimulate further class discussion	3 points: Posting fully responds to the question or discussion and stimulates at least one substantial follow-up posting

Source: Adapted from early postings on discussion board rubrics. This table and other rubrics are available at Illinois Valley Community College website. http://www2.ivcc.edu/eng1002/rubric_online.htm.

TABLE 7.2

Rubric for Participation and Levels of Thinking

Points	Criterion	Thinking Levels
0 points	Minimum number of postings not met	Level I—Introduces problems or poses questions
7 points	Minimum postings met; discussion at Level I thinking	Level II may identify assumptions
8 points	Minimum postings met; at least one example of discussion above Level I thinking	Level III may draw conclusions "based on evidence"
9 points	Minimum postings met; at least one example of discussion above Level I and a second above Level II	Level IV may include expressing an opinion on the relevance of an argument
10 points	Minimum postings met; at least two examples of discussion above Level I with at least one above Level III	Level V may propose solutions

Source: Palloff and Pratt (2003, p. 91).

your feedback to students. Students often hold themselves to a higher standard than the faculty member does.

Another example of an approach to assessing online discussion board participation and levels of thinking is offered by Palloff and Pratt (2003) in their book *The Virtual Student*. This rubric uses the quantity of postings combined with a thinking measure (Table 7.2). Palloff and Pratt use five levels for measuring critical thinking. For example, level I introduces problems or poses questions; level II may identify assumptions; level III may draw conclusions based on evidence; level IV might include expressing an opinion on the relevance of an argument; and level V might propose solutions.

Quizzes

The quiz tools in LMSs are excellent for keeping students on track, increasing learning, and minimizing instructor time on grading. Quiz tools are really robotic assistants for you. If you have been using quizzes of any sort in your classes, it is usually a relatively straightforward task to move those quizzes online. The quiz tools in most LMSs are sophisticated, and once you have quizzes in the system, creating and setting them up is quickly done. Of course, straightforward does not mean that it doesn't take any time.

What about issues of proctoring and ensuring that the students registered in the class are the ones who are actually taking the quizzes? Let's address each of these issues. First, most quizzes should be low stakes. This means that they are worth points, but not many. Students are most likely to cheat and find ways around doing the work if the point value of an assignment is quite high, they are behind in their work, or they are finding the work too difficult. Quiz questions usually focus on facts, discipline-specific knowledge, and core concepts. When unproctored online quizzes were introduced in a very large lecture campus course, students commented that they could find ways to cheat, but they really did need to know the material, and the point value was not worth the trouble to get someone else to do it.

There are other strategies to encourage learning rather than cheating: be clear about the purpose and content of the quizzes, set strict time limits for the quizzes, and provide sufficient but low point value. Also, providing students options to retake the quizzes for a higher point value can encourage the twin goals of competency and self-competition. The goal is for all students to do well. So the bottom-line recommendations on quizzes are to use them for important core concepts, factual knowledge, and beginning concept applications; provide a low point value for completion; and let the course management system do its work after you have done your work, which is creating worthwhile and effective quizzes.

Peer Review

One of the challenges in online learning is that we really don't get a chance to be in the same physical space with our fellow learners. The synchronous tools at our disposal do reduce the distance for interacting, but it is not quite the same. Peer review and consulting both encourage online learners to work and learn with one another and have meaningful discussions with one another. Early in the course, as students are getting acquainted and establishing trust in one another, setting up learning tasks and experiences that students can do jointly has many positive dimensions. Peer review sets the tone that learning is a social and collaborative experience.

EM Tip 5: Steps in Memory-Making: What Teaching Behaviors Make a Difference

This tip answers questions such as these:

- What activities help students remember new and unfamiliar content?
- What activities encourage deep processing of content so that it becomes useful knowledge?
- What are the steps in learning new content?

Do you know what actions of your teaching or cognitive presence make a difference in what students learn? This tip suggests some behaviors that can make a difference.

If you had to estimate the percentage of the key concepts in your course that your learners integrate into useful knowledge, what would you say? Do you think it is only 10 percent, 30 percent, 50 percent, or 80 percent? How confident are you about your estimate?

Data on exactly what students master during a course is difficult to obtain, but we do have a couple of data points. One data point is the summary data from a test on core physics concepts from students in fourteen different traditional lecture-based courses. This research suggests that the mastery of core concepts from lecture-based physics courses is consistently about 30 percent or less (Hake, 1998, cited in Wieman, 2008). Are you surprised that it is that high? Or surprised it is that low?

Does this mean that students' memories aren't working very well? Would you agree with the Red Queen's observation to Alice in Lewis Carroll's *Through the Looking-Glass*, that we all have poor memories, particularly if they only work backward? Recall that the queen's memory worked both forward and backward. While that is a bit hard to get our heads around, the truth is that our memories work in very specific ways and not always best for our particular needs.

While this data is from students in lecture-based courses, do you think we would get similar results about concept mastery in online courses? As we move forward in teaching online and blended courses we do want to think about how memories work and consider how much of a course content it is important to commit to memory.

Using a Memory Process Model to Increase Learning

This tip is about the steps in creating long-term memories and a memory process model to increase the percentage of learned concepts in our students. This is the question for you: What change(s) might I make to the learning experiences in my course to increase the likelihood that students will integrate and apply core concepts?

A Look at a Memory-Making Process Model

How does memory work? Is it a one-time event or a series of events? Here are two useful definitions:

- Memory is the acquisition, storage, and retrieval of information (Gleitman, Reisberg, & Gross, 2006).

- Memory is a linear process beginning with "sensory registration and finally leading to the consolidation of some information into long-term and/or remote memories" (McLeod, 2007b). During the first stage—*acquisition*—an event is perceived and information about it is initially stored in our short-term memory. In the second stage—*storage* or *retention*—information is resident in long-term memory. In the final stage—*retrieval*—memory is searched and pertinent information is retrieved and communicated.

So what does this mean? It definitely means that memory of a particular data item is not a one-time event. It also means that reviewing, interleaving (presenting a mix of problems), and practice is key to useful acquisition of knowledge (Brown, Roediger, & McDaniel, 2014). Acquisition of knowledge—whether declarative or procedural knowledge—begins with a stimulus to our visual, auditory, or touching senses that results in sensory registration or memory. If we don't pay any attention to the sensory input, it usually goes away. Moving the sensory data into short-term memory requires attention to the sensory inputs. Once the data is in short-term memory, we need to encode and organize the data and move it into long-term memory. This step results in the knowledge being integrated and connected with other memories in long-term memory (McLeod, 2007a; 2007b; Roediger, Dudai, & Fitzpatrick, 2007). Once data is in long-term memory it may or may not be available for retrieval, depending on how much it is used. Figure 7.1 shows the steps in the making of memories.

Note the approximate time for data to reside in sensory memory, and then be encoded in short-term memory and moved into long-term memory (Atkinson & Shiffrin, 1968). Since making memories takes time, attention, and processing, it reinforces the need to build attention and processing time for encoding core facts, concepts, and applications. This research underscores the core learning principle that learning takes time.

FIGURE 7.1

Steps and Processes in Memory-Making

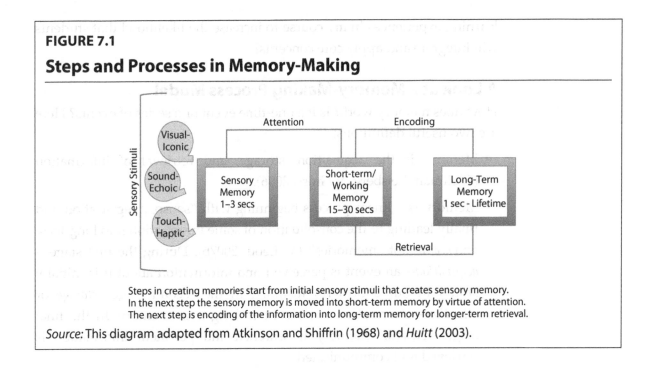

Steps in creating memories start from initial sensory stimuli that creates sensory memory. In the next step the sensory memory is moved into short-term memory by virtue of attention. The next step is encoding of the information into long-term memory for longer-term retrieval.

Source: This diagram adapted from Atkinson and Shiffrin (1968) and *Huitt* (2003).

Teaching Strategies with the Memory-Making Model

At this point, let's return to one of the main questions for this tip. What teaching strategies are important for mastery of concepts? We often design our online courses on a weekly basis, setting up a *weekly rhythm* for the course, mapping to the topics and modules within a course. Thinking about memory as a linear process with at least three to five steps suggests strategies such as the following:

- **Structure** the initial learning of core concepts into steps emphasizing the sensory aspects of the learning, creating experiences that ensure processing time for stimulus and sensory registration steps. This approach supports the acquisition step, requiring attention to the stimuli.

  - Ask questions such as, "What caught your eye? Had you heard or talked about ideas such as these before?"

  - Engage the learners with the concepts, helping them in making connections and relationships to existing or earlier concepts. These activities help to move knowledge into short-term memory and to organize and encode the information so that it moves into long-term memory, supporting the retention stage.

  - Ask questions such as these:

    - "Can you describe how these concepts might be linked or related to other memories or knowledge that you have? What do you know already that is similar or different from these ideas?"

- "Do you see a pattern emerging in this data? Can you draw a map with a fellow learner showing the relationship of these data?"

- "Is there anything that is confusing or strange about how these ideas, processes, actions relate to each other? Are there cause-effect relationships here? Or other possible associations?"

- **Consolidate** ideas with opportunities for creative use of the concepts in complex unstructured contexts

- Ask questions such as, "Can you reproduce, write, or describe what those ideas mean to you?" This is a great use of the student blogs, by the way.

- Have the students apply the ideas in a simple to more complex scenario, so they can see the application of the concept and its probable relationship to earlier, similar concepts.

As an ongoing practice throughout the course, remind students and yourself to refer to key concepts. Each time the concepts are applied or discussed as occurring in other contexts helps to build a richer concept.

Can Sleeping Help the Encoding of Memories?

Eons ago or so it seems, scientists vehemently rejected any possibility that we might be able to learn as we sleep. It now appears that while we might not learn new things while we sleep, sleeping is very important to learning and memory. Researchers are still working on determining precisely how the brain strengthens and enhances memories, but it appears certain that "Sleep does something to improve memory that being awake does not do." Research seems to suggest that "Sleep makes memories stronger, and it even appears to weed out irrelevant details and background information so that only the important pieces remain" (Stickgold & Ellenbogen, 2008, p. 24).

This finding suggests that we can increase our mastery of concepts by getting more sleep. That is a welcome finding for all of us. Imagine this instruction to our students: Read the instructions on solving quadratic equations, solve or work on two or three of these problems, and then take a 20-minute nap.

Summary

Our memories work in complex ways. We are still learning exactly how they work. But we do know that memory and learning take time with repeated exposures and practice and a mix of problems. We also know that our memories work more or less well most of the time, but that they don't always work the way we wish they might. And they definitely only work backwards, unlike Carroll's queen, who gets giddy from working with her memories that go forward!

EM Tip 6: Tips for Making Your Grading Time Efficient and Formative for Learners

This tip answers questions such as these:

- How can I make the most of my grading time?
- What are some assignments that make grading go smoothly?
- What kinds of feedback are more used, appreciated by learners?

On another planet in a galaxy far, far away, we might have lots of time in which to read and review forum postings, provide feedback on project proposals, and individually mentor and coach our students. Teachers with a passion for teaching want to provide useful feedback and mentoring to their students, but the reality is that time is scarce and limited. Here are some ideas on assessing students' work quickly and well.

First, keep in mind that there are different types of student work to assess. Student work includes items such as (1) straightforward objective tests that can be graded by LMS quiz robots, (2) slightly more complex forum postings, (3) community participation, (4) shorter concept or reflection papers, and (5) multiphased projects.

This tip focuses on strategies and suggestions for grading concept or reflection papers, blog sections, and various project segments, including the proposals and final projects. First of all, be sure to use rubrics. Rubrics generally guide students so that assignments come closer to meeting expectations and thus are a more pleasant and rewarding experience to assess.

Rubrics can help in three ways. First, rubrics set clear expectations and standards. Second, learners can peer review each other's proposals or insight papers and provide feedback to each other before you read them. Third, students can evaluate their own work with rubrics. Self-evaluation is an important skill that can become part of an assignment as well. Let's move on now to some tips that focus on the actual process of grading.

How to Make Grading Pleasant, Fast and Effective

In our efforts to put students first, we sometimes don't make enough effort to be good to ourselves. Here are a few practices to help you be good to yourself while also doing a better job on grading.

- Set yourself up in a pleasant spot, perhaps with great music and some treasured tea or coffee. Using a quiet place reduces distractions, and working with full concentration saves a lot of time. Another benefit is that you can think of grading as a pleasant experience.

- Do an attitude adjustment on yourself, if need be. Rather than thinking about how much work it is, think about how much you can learn about your students during this time. This can be very satisfying in confirming or setting plans for subsequent teaching.

- Before grading any one paper, scan a few of the papers to get a sense of how the students as a whole did. As appropriate, record a few of your thoughts about how well the students seemed to be meeting the expectations and standards of the assignment.

- Don't start editing the papers. The purpose of reviewing and grading papers is to provide feedback and help students improve their writing and to guide their learning. However, many faculty do find that it is valuable to keep a record of common writing or expression errors and suggest tools to support their improvement. This can be a list that evolves over time as well as one specific to a particular assignment.

- Once you have reviewed the papers as a whole, start reading/reviewing and grading the papers using the assignment rubric. For example, if the rubric calls for references or quotes to a reading or developing a research question, you can provide x points on that particular dimension without the need to provide much detail. The detail more often than not will be in the rubric.

- Set a time limit for each paper. Is this possible? Not always. But it helps one to focus and be realistic.

- If you find a paper with particular difficulties, set it aside for a bit. The goal is to provide students with ways to improve. Make any feedback reasonable and doable.

- Include some self-evaluation as part of each assignment. This self-evaluation can be in the form of a rubric, which might be a simple checklist. See the example below.

The final step of your grading event should be the creation of a feedback statement to the students as to how they as a group did on the assignment. The best time to do that is just as you finish the grading of the papers. This consolidates your own understanding of how and what they are learning, and possibly suggests follow-up activities or changes. This summary statement will probably include some insights and innovative or challenging ideas from the student's works. Another strategy is to prepare this summary statement and then sleep on it, and review it before posting it.

A Checklist for Students

Here is a checklist for students to complete and attach to their papers (Walvoord & Anderson, 2009). Adapting it to any particular assignment would be even more useful.

- I read the short story at least twice.
- I revised this paper at least once.
- I spent at least five hours on this paper.
- I started work on this paper at least three days ago.
- I have tried hard to do my best work on this paper.
- I proofread this paper at least twice for grammar, spelling, and punctuation. I know that I cannot trust just using a spellchecker.
- I asked at least one other person to proofread the paper.

Another section has a few questions that you might ask yourself when writing comments. Here is a sampling.

- What were the strengths in this piece of work? What were the weaknesses?
- What stands out as memorable or interesting?
- Does the author provide sufficient evidence or argumentative support?

Another resource that you may want to explore is by B. G. Davis, author of *Tools for Teaching*. An excerpt on grading practices is available at http://facstaff.necc.mass.edu/wp-content/uploads/2012/01/Grading_Practices_Barbara_Gross_Davis_article.pdf.

One of the strategies that Davis recommends is to "consider allowing students to choose among alternative assignments." This suggestion is similar to what we have encouraged as a way of customizing and personalizing learning. Davis suggests a contract approach to a course grade or section of a course. She starts by developing a list of activities, with the possible earned points based on the educational value, difficulty, and likely amount of effort required. Students are told how many points are needed for an A, a B, or a C, and they choose a combination of assignments that meet the grade they desire for that portion of the course. Here are some possible activities from that excerpt:

Writing a case study

Engaging in and reporting on a fieldwork experience

Leading a discussion panel

Serving on a discussion panel

Keeping a journal or log of course-related ideas

Writing up thoughtful evaluations of several lectures

Creating instructional materials for the course (study guides, exam questions, or audiovisual materials) on a particular concept or theme

Undertaking an original research project or research paper

Reviewing the current research literature on a course-related topic

Keeping a reading log that includes brief abstracts of the readings and comments, applications, and critiques

Conclusion

Making the best use of grading time means taking care of yourself in two ways: Don't go overboard with too much feedback, and create assignments that mean that you are learning too.

EM Tip 7: Dealing with Difficult Students—What Do You Do?

This tip answers questions such as these:

- How do you handle students who are only marginally participating?

- What do you do when a student makes inappropriate posts to forums?

- What do you do when a student posts suggest serious underlying problems?

There are several behaviors that can cause deep concern and worry for online faculty, such as:

- Postings that elicit disquieting or uncomfortable feelings

- Off-topic postings with little relevance to the learning assignment

- Chronically late postings or assignments

- Postings that are only minimally participatory

- Postings that suggest serious underlying problems of potential harm to self or others

As a director of student services (Leister, 2014) observed in a personal communication, "Difficult students can be disheartening for everyone . . . and it is very important that instructors know they have the support and backup from the entire student services team."

What actions should instructors take in the face of such events? Are there ways to discourage and prevent these behaviors? Is it possible to create an environment that encourages positive focused learning?

Types of Difficult Students

The literature (Braxton & Bayer, 2004; Bart, 2012; Sorcinelli, 2002; Sull, 2012) on challenging behaviors of students describes student behaviors in categories such as *disturbed, disrespectful,* or *difficult. Disturbed* students are the most worrisome; they could be a danger to themselves or others. *Disrespectful* students are those students who display rebellious, contrary, or openly combative behavior, distracting other learners from the learning experiences. *Difficult* students might best be described as time-consuming, annoying, or just plain worrisome. Difficult students do not fully engage in the course experience, are frequently late with their work including their postings, and do not interact or encourage support and learning with their peers. They stall, make up excuses, and can take up a great deal of time from an instructor.

A primary difference between disrespectful students and difficult students is that the conduct of disrespectful students impacts the entire learning community, whereas difficult students primarily hurt their own learning while also creating more work for the instructor. The lines blur, of course, as both disrespectful and difficult students can cause distressing ripple effects within a learning community.

Unique Challenges of Difficult Students

Much of the literature on difficult students describes troublesome behaviors of students in physical classrooms. In fact, many of the problems encountered by faculty in online situations pale in comparison to the problems faculty might face in classrooms. In online courses, faculty don't have to worry about inappropriate behaviors such as arriving late, leaving early, talking on cell phones, eating pizza, reading newspapers, or sending text messages, or even unpleasant odors or inappropriate dress. In this respect, what we can't see while in virtual online synchronous or asynchronous gatherings can be a real blessing!

In synchronous online gatherings when only the video of the person talking is visible, uncivil or inappropriate behavior is neither seen nor (ideally) heard. In fact, side conversations in the chat room are encouraged and can support engagement by more than two or three students simultaneously. On the other hand, if students are trying to multitask their presence and try to also read, write, or even parent during the online gathering, the learning community eventually notices and is impacted by that partial presence of their peers.

Prevention Is the Best and First Strategy

As with any difficult human behaviors, the best strategy is prevention. Prevention strategies generally consist of actions such as (1) clarifying expectations up front with codes of conduct and appropriate learning goals, (2) creating an environment that invites and rewards positive behaviors, and (3) modeling appropriate conduct and expectations (Tarr & Lang, 2006, 2015). This means ensuring that course materials describe expected rules of conduct for online and blended courses. And it means that students review a code of conduct that includes netiquette, course expectations, and descriptions of how to relate and interact with the instructors and peers. Depending on the context and the level of student experience, a forum where students state their expectations and recommendations can be useful.

The diversity of students, particularly at the undergraduate level, can make prevention difficult. One academic advisor (M. Barefoot, personal communication, May 7, 2014) noted that while some students are really on top of things, other students might have problems that are persistent and deeply embedded.

How Can I Recognize Disturbed Students?

The following are some of student behaviors that suggest more serious underlying problems that can benefit from professional counseling. These types of behavior merit immediate attention.

- Discriminatory, abusive, or bullying language directed toward another student, instructor, or staff member
- Obstruction or disruption of the teaching or learning experiences
- Negative or flaming postings that persist over time despite gentle or not-so-gentle intervention
- Failure to respect the rights of others to express their viewpoints
- Out-of-context unusual, strange, or bizarre remarks

In many cases, the first step to take is to contact the student's academic advisor. Most universities have offices dedicated to responding and managing these types of behaviors.

How Can I Recognize Disrespectful Students?

Disrespectful students can impair community cohesiveness and support in an online course. A weak online course community detracts from effective learning and the joy that we hope to cultivate in course experiences.

Responding to these types of behaviors often requires a multistep process. If the comments are particular inflammatory or distressing or simply merit deletion, an instructor has the right and probably *should* delete the posting immediately and follow up privately by phone or e-mail with the offending student. This action can be handled between the instructor and the student and may not need to go any further. As noted by M. Leister (personal communication, April 10, 2014), "there is a fine line between freedom of opinion and not being sensitive to the other students in the class, and this is hard for some students to understand." Most useful might be her advice, "If it raises an eyebrow in the instructor we should probably look at it. I would rather be safe than sorry."

Students who have recently experienced traumatic or very challenging life experiences may still be working through issues and processing all that they have experienced. Their postings can sometimes cause concern and/or discomfort in others. Such situations call for early and gentle intervention to differentiate what is appropriate in a learning context from what is appropriate in other types of group settings.

Recognizing Students with Difficult Behaviors

It's an unusual course that doesn't have one or two difficult students. These students provide the most angst to themselves and the instructor and by extension minimize the potential richness of the learning community.

The reasons why students might be difficult can vary considerably. Students may have signed up for too many courses. They may feel unprepared, outflanked, or overwhelmed. Family and work responsibilities may have mushroomed unexpectedly or problems with their health may have surfaced. Or the course turns out to be a poor match for what they expected.

Processes for Dealings with Difficult Students

So what is one to do? Depending on the type of situation, here is a seven-step strategy for managing difficult and disrespectful students.

- Contact the student privately by phone or e-mail or in person. It is always best to act quickly, particularly if you have had to delete a posting. Acting quickly helps to stop problems before they fester or escalate. Acting quickly is also good for the community as a whole, as you reinforce a code of conduct and expectations. It is good to err on the side of encouraging and modeling good behavior.

- Describe the student's behavior as explicitly as you can and its impact on their learning success and that of others.

- Listen to the student's perspective and response.

- Discuss appropriate behavior and suggest helpful resources as appropriate.

- Agree on next steps and consequences if the desired change is not achieved.

- Summarize the conversation.

- Document the meeting or conversation.

- Set up a follow-up conversation and checkpoint as appropriate. (Adapted from Brian von Brunt as in Bart, 2012)

Some disturbed or very difficult students need to be encouraged to meet with their advisor sooner rather than later. This is also the best route for students who have serious underlying health or emotional problems or who are displaying real problems with getting course work done.

More Preventive Strategies in Your Hands

One of the more important prevention strategies for preventing incivilities is creating a positive and supportive course community. We already mentioned one strategy, that of modeling the kinds of posting and interactions that support learning and communicate a sense of caring to all the students. Some of the other strategies suggested by Sorcinelli (2002) include the following:

- Decrease anonymity by getting to know the students as individuals with specific course goals and expectations. We do this through the use of the social introductions and specific course goal setting in the early weeks of the course.

- Engage students one-on-one so that each student feels as if they are contributing to the overall learning of the course community. One way of achieving this is for each student to be working on specific learning goals that are of personal importance, but also useful to the overall community.

- Encourage active learning. This reinforces the goal of having students be personally responsible for their learning and engages their creativity.

Building the Cognitive Presence

This set of tips describes strategies for continuing a strong focus on building cognitive presence—the process by which faculty and students work on increasing knowledge and expertise in the content. The tips provide more background on cognitive presence and discuss the need to keep a focus on the core concepts fundamental to course knowledge. Other tips focus on assessment strategies and practices, and design practices to make learning interesting and meaningful to the learner.

EM Tip 8: Building Cognitive Presence Using the Practical Inquiry Model

This tip answers questions such as these:

- What is cognitive presence?
- What are some of the behaviors that help to create the stages of cognitive presence?

Presence—social, teaching, and cognitive—is fundamental to any teaching and learning relationship. The most important presence for knowledge creation is cognitive presence. As noted earlier, cognitive presence is "the extent to which the participants in any particular configuration of a community of inquiry are able to construct meaning through sustained communication" (Garrison, Anderson, & Archer, 2000, p. 89).

As research on the community of inquiry (COI) model has progressed, the processes involved in creating cognitive presence and the stages of the process have been further defined. Garrison and Vaughan (2008) offer a definition of cognitive presence that includes four stages of a knowledge-building process: "a recursive process that encompasses states of puzzlement, information exchange, connection of ideas and creation of concepts, and the testing of the viability of solutions" (p. 22). They called this recursive process the "practical inquiry model."

Practical Inquiry Model

Applying this practical inquiry model to knowledge-building requires time. And often, depending on the state of knowledge-building on the part of learners, only a partial process may be completed during a course. If we look at knowledge-building as a recursive process, what should we be doing in the early middle phase of a course? Let's answer this question by mapping the four stages of the practical inquiry model to the four stages of a course.

Puzzlement Stage or Triggering Event

In the course beginnings, the focus may be on the initial set of questions students have about the core concepts of the course. This set of questions would include the personalized and customized questions developed by the students.

Exploration Stage

In the later weeks of course beginnings, continuing into the early middle, the focus is on gathering information and exchange of ideas. We also like to frame this stage as the initial and ongoing data-gathering stage.

Integration Stage of Connecting Ideas and Theory-Building

In the middle of a course, the work of cognitive presence might be connecting and relating the ideas within the course framework, which includes theory-building and identifying patterns and relationships.

Resolution Stage through Problem-Solving and Testing

The closing weeks are for theory-testing, problem-solving, and scenario-building. Figure 7.2 presents the practical inquiry model that graphically shows its four stages (http://cde.athabascau.ca/coi_site/documents/practicalinquiry.pdf).

Using the Practical Inquiry Model in a Unit

Another way of applying this knowledge-building process is to use the four stages in a unit or module of a course. Use the puzzlement, exploration, theory-building, and problem-testing cycle with simpler problems, and complete a cycle in one or two weeks. This can build confidence in a

---

FIGURE 7.2

Practical Inquiry Model

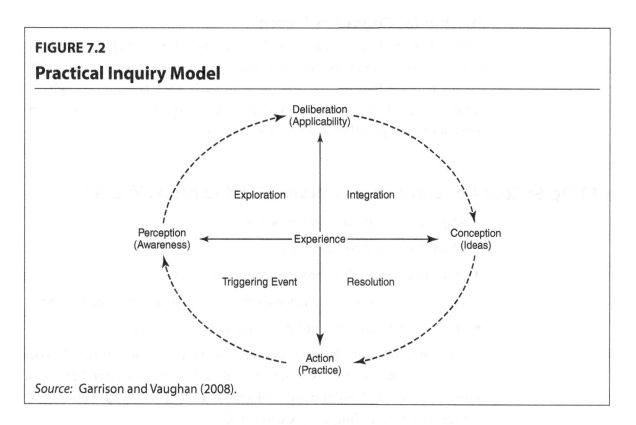

Source: Garrison and Vaughan (2008).

core concept while also teaching the process of problem-solving and knowledge-building.

Tools and Behaviors for Building Cognitive Presence

Knowledge-building requires reflection, discussion, and confirmation of meaning. This means going beyond repetition and awareness of ideas to an understanding of relationships and confidence in issues. This also means that deep processing and problem-solving is to be favored over simple conceptual awareness. Here are some behaviors that help to create and sustain cognitive presence and learning growth by the learners:

- Faculty set high expectations for student inquiry.
- The faculty member examines student responses and probes, challenges, and questions, encouraging analysis of ideas and content.
- Learners participate thoughtfully in the discussions, responding to content and thoughts and questions from other learners so that a sustained communication occurs.
- Faculty and students strive to ensure that project outcomes are long-lasting and meaningful.

Striving for Cognitive Presence

Achieving cognitive presence requires significant and ongoing emphasis on core concepts. In evaluating student responses, it is helpful to explicitly refer to the states they may be experiencing, such as Garrison and Vaughan's puzzlement, information exchange, connection of ideas, creation of concepts, and testing of the viability of solutions.

EM Tip 9: Core Concepts of a Course—Do You Know Yours?

This tip answers questions such as these:

- What exactly are core concepts?
- How do I identify the core concepts in my course?
- What is the difference between a core concept and a learning outcome?
- How do I reinforce and build core concept knowledge?

This tip returns to the topic of concepts. Have you identified the core concepts of your course? Are you confident in your selection? Do your course readings and assignments help your students develop their knowledge and understanding of core concepts?

It is generally assumed that faculty know what the core concepts of their course—or discipline—are. Unfortunately, this is seldom the case. Identifying core concepts, and then designing experiences for learners to grow in their knowledge of them, is a complex design process that requires digging deeply into the foundational thinking, beliefs, and models of our disciplines.

A common question from faculty goes something like this: "I have designed my course with the goal of helping my students achieve the learning outcomes. What is the difference between a learning outcome and a core concept?"

Let's define our terms and see if that helps. A *learning outcome* is a skill or knowledge set that enables students to use knowledge well. A *concept*, on the other hand, is a building block for learning outcomes. In most cases, developing a skill requires learning concepts and then practicing applying those concepts.

Two of the core learning principles—Principle 4: *All learners do not need to learn all course content; all learners do need to learn the core concepts* and Principle 7: *Concepts are not words but organized and interconnected knowledge clusters*—provided a definition of concepts and a stage process (initial concept awareness, concept formation, refinement, application, and revision) for teaching concepts. This tip provides examples of core concept discovery and application from two faculty.

A Concept Is . . .

Let's review the definition of a concept. Our personal favorite is Principle 7 expanded: "Concepts are more than words; they are organized and intricate clusters of knowledge bits."

It is easy to recognize when we experience "getting" a concept. It happens when we hear ourselves say, "Ah, it is all coming together" or "Now it finally all makes sense. I see how this is all connected." Cognition experts refer to this as an "Aha!" experience. Detectives in mystery novels often experience a related phenomenon, as a final piece of a puzzle falls into place, and suddenly all the disparate, seemingly unrelated elements of a case make sense. Similarly, although students entering a new discipline are often overwhelmed with terms, examples, and unfamiliar expressions and ideas, after multiple experiences with the content it all begins to come together into a meaningful and useful knowledge set.

Memory researchers Roediger, Dudai, and Fitzpatrick (2007) define concepts as "mental representations that encode sets of attributes that describe real or imaginary classes of items, processes or relationships" (p. 2).

This definition is helpful in affirming that a concept is a real object, neurologically speaking, and providing examples of concepts.

The definition from Harvard psychologist Susan Carey (2009) is similar: "Concepts are units of thoughts, the constituents (building blocks) of beliefs and theories." Carey also suggests a possible categorization of concepts as either *sensory/perceptual*, as in what things in the world look like, feel like, sound like, smell like; or *conceptual*, as in those representations that describe objects for which we have little sensory evidence, such as *electron*, *galaxy*, and *wisdom*. Many of the concepts in courses fall into this second, nonsensory category.

Process of Identifying Core Concepts

Identifying core concepts in your course requires stepping back and thinking critically about what skills the course is hoping to develop. While we often do this when submitting courses for review by curriculum committee, the focus is usually on learning outcomes, and not as often on skills. To illustrate how the process works, here are descriptions of interviews with two faculty as they work through the process of identifying the core concepts of their course.

Experience of an Information Science Faculty

The first example is a course in information literacy for adult learners, or using a library well in the twenty-first century. This course focuses on developing "information literacy skills for academic success and lifelong learning." As we talked about identifying the concepts in her course, the faculty member (we will call her Dr. Search) noted that information literacy is not a discipline but a skill. Given the absence of disciplinary content, we shifted in our interview to talking about the core ideas behind the coursework. This led Dr. Search to observe that one of the most important beliefs that she works to develop in her students is that "research is an iterative process." Any research process involves proposing a question, identifying potential big ideas, making changes based on the initial research, and refining one's focus over time. She went on to say that developing research skills requires knowing how to access, interpret, and evaluate information and information resources. One of her teaching strategies involves each student's meeting with her to discuss and brainstorm their topic, and in the process, to refine it. This discussion led to the realization that the research process requires learners to think critically about information. Yet we did not yet feel we had identified a core concept.

We continued our discussion, wending our way through skills such as problem-solving, evaluating, interpreting, and ethical use of information. These were all thinking skills. We challenged ourselves with the question, "What is the core idea, big idea of the course?" We gradually arrived at considering an important chapter in the textbook, called "Lateral Thinking," and there we paused. For under the skill of thinking laterally is a very big idea, core to everything we do in research. That big idea is that all information is linked to everything else. We felt as if we had it. The following two core concepts probably link all the other aspects of the course together:

- Research is an iterative process, requiring time, critical evaluation, and caring about the information.

- All information and bodies of information are linked to others. What may not appear to be relevant initially is often worth a second look.

Before moving on, Dr. Search wanted to share one of her assignments that focus on evaluating information. In this assignment, students select an urban legend and then search out and analyze information sources to discern the elements that may or may not be true. One of the critical questions is, "How does the knowledge contribute to your project, if at all?" Students enjoy this assignment and often suggest other urban legends or assumptions for analysis.

Experience of a Leadership Faculty

The second faculty member we interviewed taught a graduate foundation course in leadership. Her pseudonym is Dr. Vision. In contrast to Dr. Search's course on information literacy, Dr. Vision's course had the entire field of leadership to examine for core concepts.

Learning outcomes are always a good place to start, so Dr. Vision talked about what knowledge, skills, and abilities were important for her students to develop.

Dr. Vision started discussing a leadership model called the Leadership Diamond, developed by Peter Koestenbaum. This model introduces the idea of one's leadership capacity as defined by four leadership orientations: ethics, vision, courage, and reality. Roediger, Dudai, and Fitzpatrick (2007) note that concepts are "products of mental models and theories." This suggests that the idea of one's leadership capacity might be a core concept, and part of that core concept is that it depends on those four orientations.

Dr. Vision shared that she and colleagues have struggled for years with the task of identifying the core concepts of the field of leadership. In fact, she commented that it is one of the oldest arguments in the discipline. Part of the challenge, she explained, is that leadership is so ubiquitous. This led us to posit that a working core concept for her course might be as follows: "Leadership is a highly adaptive activity that manifests itself somewhat uniquely in various human contexts." This concept can serve as a linchpin for examining the broad spectrum of leadership research, theories, case studies, and models in disciplines as disparate as education, business, communication, engineering, and science, to mention a few.

This concept provides a framework for a broad, encompassing view of leadership. At the same time, going back to Koestenbaum's model, Dr. Vision noted a companion concept: Leadership, no matter how diverse, shares certain elements. The elements that she focuses on are slightly different from Koestenbaum's four—communication, vision, ethics, and followership.

Conclusion

Time invested in identifying core concepts is time well spent in becoming an expert teaching and learning professional in your discipline. As demonstrated by the search for core concepts with Dr. Search and Dr. Vision, it can serve you well in clarifying the goals and purposes of your teaching and learning. After you have identified your core concepts, the next step is to review your course design and assignments to ensure that your course activities promote the learning and integration of these core concepts.

EM Tip 10: Designing Assessment Plans for Online and Blended Courses

This tip answers questions such as these:

- What does an assessment plan look like?
- Should discussion forum postings be part of my evaluation plan?
- When should learners start on their course projects?
- What are some guidelines for designing projects and tasks that really matter to the learner?

Designing Assessment Plans

Assessing our learners is a task critical to all teaching and learning experiences, but all too often it is a task we like to avoid. We equate assessing tasks as judging and tough decision-making choices with potentially difficult consequences if students don't agree. Assessing learners' progress can often mean reading lengthy papers, ranging from dreadful to inspiring, or reading hundreds of forum postings. Is there a better way?

The focus of assessment in online learning often shifts from a set of two or three proctored tests or quizzes to multiple assessment activities. The most important of these activities are the creative projects, or what might be called learner performance tasks. Some online courses are now totally structured around the project that the students design and complete during a course. These courses demonstrate an important shift toward an apprenticeship model of learning and a focus on doing well in addition to knowing well.

The Assessment Plan

The assessment plan summarizes the points of assessment that generally include four or more types of experiences for gathering evidence of learning. For example, most assessment plans will have points assigned to these types of learning activities.

- Participation in discussion forums—the class conversation

- Automated, low-stakes quizzes

- Individual projects that include the steps in the practical inquiry model as well as communication of those ideas to others in a final product, such as a paper, interview, report, podcast, or presentation

- Short essays, papers, or tasks such as moderation of forums

- Peer review and consulting projects of various sizes and purposes

A Three-Step Process for Developing Your Assessment Plan

Your assessment plan is an essential part of your course design, and the easiest way to develop one is to go with your previous plan, simply updating the dates. But it is good to rethink your assessment plan on a regular basis. Learners change, technologies change, and learning outcomes and teaching strategies shift. Wiggins & McTighe (2005), authors of *The Understanding by Design Handbook*, suggest a three-step process for designing or rethinking an assessment plan. These three steps are as follows:

1. Return to your course goals and prioritize the results that you want for your learners. These desired results will probably include goals such as the following:

   - Developing *enduring understandings* or core concepts

   - Knowing the framework and vocabulary of a discipline domain

- Developing knowledge and use of the "exemplars of a discipline," which might include the most famous representative articles, cases or theories

- Developing competencies in applying and using the core concepts and key understandings

2. Determine the *acceptable evidence* with which the learners will demonstrate their knowledge, understanding, and integration of each of the top goals and results.

3. Design the series of course experiences, including assignments, to ensure learner accomplishment of these understandings and the activities and experiences for demonstrating their learning.

This process can help ensure that your assessment plan supports an integrated course design linking goals with experiences and with assessments.

An Assessment Plan That Is Distributed and Continuous

Learners like to see the assessment plan in a table that gives a bird's-eye view of the course experiences that require them to provide evidence of their learning. Table 7.3 is an example of an assessment plan in this format. A discussion of the various types of assessments follows.

TABLE 7.3

Assessment Plan

	Assessment Plan Elements	Percent of Grade
1	Automated quizzes and tests	10 to 20
2	Discussion forums participation and contribution	10 to 20
3	Discussion wrap/summary/other leadership work	5 to 15
4	Blog, journal, or wiki entries	5 to 15
5	Short concept papers, small team review	15 to 20
6	Project Phase 1 (plan/proposal/concept)	5 to 10
7	Project Phase 2 (resources, sections)	15 to 20
8	Project Phase 3 (paper, media, presentation for sharing)	20 to 30
9	Project Phase 4 (final submission)	20 to 30

Note: Percentages in the right-hand column total over 100%, as you will probably develop an assessment plan with only a subset of the listed elements.

The value of using a variety of experiences means that assessing is done over time and in some cases by automated robots—as in automated quizzes and tests—and in some cases, in collaboration with peers.

Take note of the assessment points dealing with a course project. A course project is best designed with a minimum of three or four milestones. The first is a proposal that can be vetted and discussed by peers as well as by the instructor. A second milestone captures some progress point in the project, and a third milestone is a presentation, sharing or session with other learners. In the example above, a fourth milestone is the submission of the final evidence.

EM Tip 11: Three Best Assessment Practices

This tip answers questions such as these:

- How can my assessment plan capture the competencies in the six levels of Bloom's taxonomy?

- How do I assess the core concepts of my course?

- How can I design an assessment plan that helps my students succeed?

This tip reviews three of many possible best practices in assessing student learning. The last section of the tip suggests other resources to explore.

These three best practices range from simple recall assessment strategies to complex and sophisticated knowledge creation. If you are creating your first assessment plan, keep your assessment straightforward while focusing on core concept development. Experienced online faculty might be particularly interested in the ideas on expanding student choices for course projects. These choices can include creating podcasts, webinars, talk show interviews, wikis, and blogs.

Best Practice in Assessment 1: Assess Across the Six Levels of Cognitive Skills of Bloom's Taxonomy

This best practice suggests framing your assessment plan with activities at three levels: (1) facts and concepts, (2) simple "doing" applications, and (3) more complex "creation" projects. These three levels are readily discernible in a course in math or biology. The first level of facts and concepts requires learning core vocabulary, concepts, and discovery stories; the second level generally includes hands-on exercises with relatively simple problems; and the third level is grappling with more complex problems, even including those problems with no known answers.

Bloom's 1956 cognitive taxonomy and the updated version by Anderson, Krathwohl, et al., in 2001 have six levels of cognitive processing. One important difference between the two taxonomies is that the revised taxonomy uses verbs rather than nouns to describe the cognitive processing. A second important difference is that the top level in the revised taxonomy is creating, rather than evaluating. As we all enjoy the creative process and usually the results of that creative process, this is a fitting top-level experience.

The updated taxonomy is illustrated in Figure 7.3. Reading from the bottom up, the two foundation processes, remembering and understanding, might be compared to the assessing of facts and concepts. The middle process, applying might be compared to the simple "doing" applications, which includes manipulating and working with content. The top processes, analyzing, evaluating and creating, are involved when learners are planning and creating complex objects or course projects. These processes are also in play when learners review the work of peers and respond with critiques or commentary.

The pyramid depiction of the six core cognitive processes also serves as a good reminder that acquiring new skills requires a series of steps, and each step involves developing links or making changes to our existing knowledge base. Recall the discussions about concepts and that core concepts are clusters of elements that require time and experiences to get firmly in our neuronal structures.

How can you effectively assess the range of Bloom's taxonomy? Here are a few strategies.

FIGURE 7.3

Bloom's Cognitive Taxonomy Updated by Krathwohl, 2002

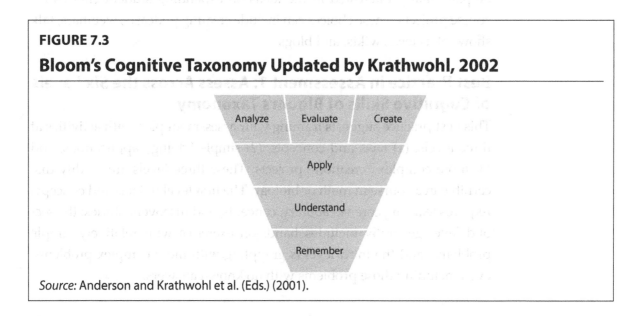

Source: Anderson and Krathwohl et al. (Eds.) (2001).

Assess Facts and Concepts:

- Use the quiz function for basic vocabulary, discipline-specific seminal facts, concepts, ideas, quotes, story lore, or biographies. Story lore can be part of learning when, where, how, and why a story became part of a discipline's history.

- Consider soliciting questions from each group of students or having a *Jeopardy*-like game contest.

- Develop a discussion forum assignment that encourages integration of basic content knowledge with existing knowledge. You can encourage this type of thinking by asking students why and how they know content or concepts and how they have used or will use the information in the future.

Assess with Simple "Doing" Tasks:

- Students enjoy "doing" rather than just listening, reading, or watching content resources. So short assignments can be very effective and can be assessed with simple rubrics and guidelines. Examples of short assignments include evaluating web resources; doing research to find similar, alternative, or comparative content ideas; and preparing short reports/news reports, podcasts, or short blogs. These short assignments can include elements such as sharing the tracking of how ideas evolve and identifying links with others' ideas. These types of assignments require students to analyze, categorize ideas, and detect relationships and patterns. These are all examples of good middle layer assessment activities.

- Individuals or small teams can also create graphical representations or mind maps of important processes and then explain the processes with current examples or objects.

Assess with Complex "Creating" Projects:

- This level of assessment continues the theme that students enjoy "hands-on" activities that often include interaction with others. A major part of online or blended assessment is often a course project. Projects can be designed as individual, team, or group projects with appropriate modifications. Course projects are examples of the higher level of analyzing, evaluating and creating activities.

- Most course projects follow a traditional pattern of either a paper or a report of some type. Today's students enjoy alternative projects such as creating radio, television or YouTube videos, interviews, webinars, or contributions to Wikipedia or course resource databases. For additional ideas, explore the kinds of film projects that students create in the Campus MovieFest (CMF), the world's largest student film festival. This project started in 2001 at Emory University with camcorders and laptops in the hands of students. Their assignment: make a movie in one week. Since that beginning more than 1 million students at colleges and universities worldwide have "told their stories" via the big screen, learning movie-making skills such as writing, editing, and filming with current software and technology tools.

- Higher-level assessment projects generally require more sophisticated assessment rubrics. Providing the rubrics in advance enables learners to self-assess and peer-review along the creative path. The rubrics also serve to remove some of the subjectivity out of the final grading. This is particularly useful as projects become more personalized and customized.

Best Practice in Assessment 2: Assess the Core Concepts in Your Course

This best practice requires thoughtful analysis of the course content. It is essential to design recognizing that learners will learn and take away only a limited amount of knowledge and skill from your course. Determining your core concepts and then relentlessly focusing on them from multiple perspectives is what drives student's acquisition of those core concepts. Reviewing just what those core concepts are and how the course experiences and requirements assist the learners in achieving them is part of the assessment design process. See if you can answer these three questions:

1. What are the four, five, or at the most (probably) ten core concepts to which you can link everything else in your course? Can you build a concept map linking these core concepts and differentiate concepts from methods, procedures, and categories? These concepts should serve as a frame for the knowledge domain of your course and, possibly, your discipline.

2. How do the course experiences assist the learners in making those core concepts their own and integrating them into their knowledge base?

3. What assessment tools will you use to gather evidence of your students' grasp and understanding of those concepts?

Best Practice in Assessment 3: Help Students Succeed on Assessment Tasks

This best practice is #8 in the set of ten recommendations in *Best Practices in Assessment* from the American Psychological Association (APA) (Pusateri, Halonen, Hill, & McCarthy, 2009). It is worth quoting in full.

> *Students will fare best in assessment activities when faculty make expectations explicit, provide detailed instructions, and offer samples or models of successful performance. They will benefit most with opportunities to practice prior to assessment and when given detailed feedback about the quality of their performance.*

This best practice reminds us of the value of (1) explicit expectations, (2) detailed instructions, and (3) samples and models of successful performance for the assessment activities. This best practice also encourages providing opportunities for practice and detailed feedback. In other words, the best assessment is ongoing, and embedded into the learning experiences with no surprises. This means rubrics and feedback with multiple reviews (self, peer, and expert). We want our learners to succeed.

Classic Resources on Assessment

Googling the term "assessment" is a sure fire way to be overwhelmed. Here is a short set of annotated resources on assessing student learning as starting points:

- This website *Internet Resources for Higher Education Outcomes Assessment* is probably best described as the granddaddy of all assessment resources on the net. It is hosted at www.assessmentcommons.org and currently contains about 1,600 links, including over 500 college and university assessment sites.

- The most cited list of assessment principles is *9 Principles of Good Practice for Assessing Student Learning*. These principles were originally developed in 1992 under the auspices of the AAHE Assessment Forum, with support from the Fund for the Improvement of Postsecondary Education. Authors of the principles include Alexander W. Astin, Trudy W. Banta, K. Patricia Cross, Elaine El-Khawas, Peter T. Ewell, Pat Hutchings, Theodore J. Marchese, Kay M. McClenney, Marcia Mentkowski, Margaret A. Miller, E. Thomas Moran, and Barbara D. Wright. (Note: These assessment principles often combine principles assessing *individual student learning within a course* with principles assessing *the learning of student cohorts*. The set of best practices listed next is a good complement to this set.)

- *The Assessment CyberGuide for Learning Goals and Outcomes* (Pusateri, Halonen, Hill, & McCarthy, 2009) is available at the APA website. A brief listing of Best Practices in Assessment: Top 10 Task Force Recommendations is on p. 4 of this guide.

EM Tip 12: Assignments for the Evaluating and Creating Levels of Bloom's Taxonomy

This tip answers questions such as these:

- Why do students like assignments at the evaluating and creating levels of the cognitive taxonomy?

- How can I design learning experiences that encourage the *use* of knowledge as well as the acquisition of knowledge?

Designing learning experiences for learners to use knowledge as well as acquire knowledge is somewhat of a challenge because such use-of-knowledge tasks tend to be "messier." Yet these are the levels of work that most directly engage and absorb learners. Demanding cognitive levels require learners to integrate knowledge from readings and discussions with their existing knowledge and use this combined knowledge in checking, judging, generating, planning, and creating, all higher level cross-functional skills.

A faculty member who favors the use of case studies in introductory leadership courses shared his observation that learners get most engaged when they make connections between the content knowledge and some of their own life experiences. Students get excited and feel they are "making new meaning" by making these connections. So how do we design these more engaging learning experiences?

Evaluating and Creating—Cognitive Processes

As you are designing your course, a good question to ask is, "How do I envision my students using the knowledge they are hopefully acquiring from the combination of resources and my expertise? Assignments that embody the evaluating and creating processes are good steps toward effective knowledge use.

First, let's take a closer look at differentiating evaluating and creating experiences. The focus of *evaluating* experiences is on a process, product, or design *developed by someone else*, including other learners; the focus of *creating* experiences is on a process, product, or design *developed or being lived by the learner or learner group*.

What Does Evaluating Demand of Learners?

Evaluating is "making judgments based on criteria and standards." For evaluating experiences, the criteria can be identified or selected by the student; in other cases, the criteria, such as professional standards of research or practice, might be provided to students.

For historians there might be standards or criteria for assembling and interpreting information; for scientists, learners might use the accepted standards or criteria for experiments; and in business courses, learners might be expected to apply standards and practices for pricing or marketing strategies.

Two cognitive processes frequently used in evaluating are checking and judging. Examples might include experiences where learners are expected to detect inconsistencies or fallacies or determine if a process has internal consistency or is effective. Examples of judging or critiquing experiences might be having learners judge the merits of a product or operation based on specified criteria or judge the appropriateness of a procedure or solution to a problem (Meyer, 2002). The essential element of evaluating experiences is the use of standards or criteria. Fortunately, these standards or criteria often map to the core concepts or essential learner outcomes.

More examples of checking experience might include these types of activities:

- Check consistency of a leader's behavior with stated beliefs

- Identify logical flaws; affirm logical consistencies of a scientist's conclusion following from data and research

- Check internal consistencies of reports, project plans, marketing plans, mathematical solutions, plot lines, or crisis responses

  Examples of critiquing experiences include these activities:

- Critique websites based on criteria, such as design, communication, inclusivity

- Critique a CEO's responsiveness and handling of crises

- Critique plans, solutions, or approaches to challenges such as change, global business, local community development

- Critique podcasts or blogs on effectiveness of communications and suitability for various audiences

Example of Evaluating Assignment in a Leadership Course

Another leadership faculty member whom we will call Dr. Holly shared her evaluating assignment. This assignment asked learners to evaluate, in a three-page essay, one of their recent managers on qualities such as effectiveness of leadership style, communication skills, managing relationships, teaming, implementing strategic actions, political behaviors, modeling organizational behaviors, articulating organizational mission and vision, and lastly, valuing workers.

The instructions directed learners to provide examples of the manager's behaviors when assessing his/her effectiveness in those functions. Dr. Holly emphasized that her learners often need to find common ground before attempting this evaluating assignment and that she establishes that common ground by means of shared experiences from the readings and discussions in the first three to four weeks of the course. In particular, Dr. Holly noted, learners need to learn how to suspend judgment and become objective in applying standards of effectiveness.

What Does Creating Demand of Learners?

Creating experiences includes three distinct cognitive processes: generating, planning, and producing. The *generating* phase is a divergent phase in which the learners are hypothesizing and considering alternative solutions and strategies. This is the phase in which learners attempt to understand the task and generate possibilities. In social science experiences, learners might generate possible useful solutions for social problems.

The second phase, *planning*, is a convergent phase in which learners devise or select a solution method and prepare a plan of action. In mathematics, for example, learners might list the steps in solving known problems, or the steps in approaching unknown problems. The third phase of creating is the actual *producing* or constructing phase. In this phase learners implement or execute their plan. For example, in a leadership course, learners might complete their personal philosophy for leadership.

Examples of Creating Projects

Radio: Theater of the Mind, a course on old radio dramas led by Duke University faculty member Daniel Foster, was very popular when ipods were first available. Students listened to old radio dramas and then produced their own shows using existing scripts. This meant that students experienced all the writing, editing, organizing, and audio production processes of producing a radio drama show. The first cycles of the course then created a website called Theatre of the Mind to share their creative work (Varkey, 2006).

Other evaluating and creating assignments often include students serving as IT consultants, business consultants, or instructional designers, or creating their own web businesses.

Creating Projects for Wikipedia. Other creating projects have focused on discipline-specific contributions to Wikipedia. Wikipedia welcomes school and university projects as a way of adding new entries and enhancing existing ones. A website (https://en.wikipedia.org/wiki/Wikipedia:School_and_university_projects) describes current and past Wikipedia projects. Some of the ongoing projects focus on some of the more than 1,000 related psychology stubs. In a cognitive psychophysiology course at the University of Illinois, students have been creating or editing pages covering major event-related brain potential (ERP) components used to study neural and cognitive functioning since spring of 2010. Students at St. Charles Community College, Cottleville, Missouri have been contributing to this work since the summer of 2011. Another ongoing project started in spring of 2012 focuses on entries related to attitudes and social cognition (University of Kent, UK).

Rubrics

Just as planning and designing these higher-level experiences can be a challenge, assessing these experiences can require more sophisticated assessment rubrics. Here are three rubrics that you may find useful

- Student podcasting project: https://edorigami.wikispaces.com/file/view/Publishing+-podcasting+rubric.pdf

- Validating information: http://edorigami.wikispaces.com/file/view/validating+rubric.pdf

- Digital publishing, including blog entries, Wikipedia, and so on: http://edorigami.wikispaces.com/file/view/digital+publishing+rubric.pdf

Strategies and Tools for Building Community

This set of tips focuses on strategies and tools for building community. Building community is launched in the course beginnings, with a heavy emphasis on social presence. During the early middle phase of a course the focus shifts to building community while engaging in exploration and research activities with the course content. The last tip in this set discusses ways of easily adding rich audio and video resources and interaction to your course.

EM Tip 13: Collaborating with Groups of Two or Three—Casual Grouping

This tip answers questions such as these:

- When is a good time to start teaming and collaboration activities?
- What learning purposes and activities are good for small groups?
- What is the value of small teams of two or three in different types of casual grouping strategies?

Get Started on Teaming with Dyads and Triads

One challenge faced by online learners is the lack of connections with other learners. The getting-acquainted forums in the first few days of a term are good first steps in establishing trust and community. But then individual readings and discussion postings soon lure learners back into their own mobile caves. Given that learning is basically social, arising from our interaction with people and resources, how can we build more interaction into our online courses?

Research on community-building affirms that sharing goals and experiences builds familiarity, closeness, and overall feelings of caring. Yet how do we shift from the focus on the individual learner to support of groups, teams, and the larger course community? In one of our webinars, participants almost universally agreed that both learners and faculty dislike and avoid group work. So, what to do? Is there a way to take a step toward capturing the documented learning power of social interaction?

Here are a few ideas on incorporating very small group work into your courses. These ideas are low-risk steps toward social learning experiences. Try one or two and see how it goes.

Start Casually!

One step toward grouping has a simple name: *casual use* (Fink, 2013). Casual grouping is, by definition, unstructured and informal. It is a good way to explore group learning, as it can be used almost spontaneously—with little or no advance planning. This means that you can insert a casual grouping experience into a course without having designed it into the course from the beginning.

Using casual grouping early in the term can build on the first week's introductions. This keeps the momentum for building community going. In the getting-acquainted postings, learners speak to everyone in the class; in casual grouping, learners have a chance to dig a little deeper into getting acquainted with one or two other learners. And these interactions can be accomplished through e-mails, texting, or meeting by phone or other social media tools over coffee or tea. (See also Michaelsen, Sweet, & Parmelee, 2008.)

Three Casual Grouping Opportunities

Courses often begin with seminal readings introducing core concepts, big ideas, and new perspectives. Casual grouping can be used to get the students more involved with each other and with the core ideas in those readings.

- **Buzz Groups.** Buzz groups form for a specific purpose and then quickly dissolve. Buzz groups in the first two or three weeks of a course might meet to exchange ideas, opinions, or recommendations about a problem, position, or principle. After a brief conversation by phone, Skype, or e-mail in which learners discuss their reaction to, understanding of, or puzzlement with a reading and how it might apply or be used by them, they individually post their response to the discussion forum. Their posting would include describing how their "buzz" dialogue impacted their understanding or added perspective. Feedback from faculty and their fellow learners can then help to confirm, affirm, or question. Buzz groups can also be used for spontaneous problem-solving, collaborative analysis, or review of reading assignments, or for presentation practice. In intensive short courses, buzz groups can be a particularly valuable avenue for learners to talk and share difficult or complex ideas such as those posed in early philosophy texts.

- **Peer Consulting Groups.** Peer consulting groups are groups of two or three learners who gather for brainstorming and discussion of an assignment that involves evaluation, analysis, or creation of a work. Courses designed around a project generally require a project proposal in the first third of the course. Learners need to identify and then describe their thinking about their course project in a brief 150- to 400-word proposal. Peer consulting groups share their proposal ideas and thoughts at an early stage of conception and then again when the proposal is almost ready for submission to the faculty member. The faculty member then provides input and suggestions on this learner's project, which has already benefited from the thinking of two or three learners. Peer consulting groups thus support individuals in the early design and conceiving stages. Peer consulting can also be used for reviews of projects at different project points. This strategy helps learners to think more deeply about projects other than just their own and gain additional perspective on their own project. This happens naturally as learners consider a wider audience. Faculty can share ideas and feedback on all the projects with the larger group.

- **Structured Controversy.** In this strategy, pairs or triads of students assume a position on a controversial issue and then must argue for that position using data and evidence from core readings or other research (Pimple, 2002). Many variants of this strategy are possible. Some of the key benefits support critical thinking, as it requires identifying concrete evidence and considering perspectives that might be antithetical to one's own.

Ways of Pairing or Grouping Learners

The process for setting up casual groups is best kept simple and transparent. For example, you can simply start with the first two or three learners in alphabetical order and go from there. Or you can take the class list and pair the first and third learner, the second and fourth, and so on. Another approach is to use learners' birthday months in sequence and pair learners or group them in triads using that data. Another strategy is to use a formula based on geography or first names. In the case of peer consulting groups, some approach to grouping based on experiences and interest might be appropriate and valuable. More on these approaches is addressed in the next tip.

Learning Power of Groups

Small groups provide space and opportunity for learners to "talk" through their thinking with someone else. Author Joan Didion has said, "I don't know what I think until I write it down" in her 1976 essay, *Why I Write*. Something similar holds true for many learners: they don't know what they really think until they are asked to explain, with their own voice, what they know and think—and why. Casual groups provide a safe environment to "talk" through what they might be thinking and test ideas.

EM Tip 14: Group Projects in Online Courses: Setting Up and Structuring Groups

This tip answers questions such as these:

- What processes work best for setting up groups?
- Should learners form groups on their own, or should groups be formed around particular criteria matching the purpose of the learning experience?

This tip focuses on guidelines and suggestions for setting up groups, suggested optimal group sizes, and recommendations for collaboration tools during different stages of the projects. These suggestions can be adapted to fit the smaller teams that are often used early in a course.

Setting Up Group Projects

Setting up group projects in the online or blended environment is similar to setting up groups in campus courses. The primary difference is that online group projects depend more heavily on the maturity and self-direction of group members. Online groups can require more initial direction and less ongoing monitoring, but it is best to leave nothing to chance. Here are a few suggestions on setting up projects.

Group Project Directions and Rubrics

The best projects begin with clear, explicit directions about the purpose of the project and its relationship to core concepts and learning outcomes. The detail for group projects can be quite lengthy, and a rubric is an essential element of the assignment. If the group project is less complex, such as a short discussion summary, the directions can be simpler, but a rubric is still recommended.

Presenting directions for group projects in different formats can also be helpful for students. For example, the group project directions in a syllabus may be text based. For some projects, especially significant course projects, a synchronous Q&A discussion can help students process and understand the purpose of the project more fully.

Students find it helpful if information about project processes, resources, and tools is included in the project directions. For example, students may find process suggestions useful for different stages of project communications and presentations. For example, when starting a project, students often find synchronous tools such as phone conferences and chats work well, providing spontaneous brainstorming and problem solving; later stages of a project, which can involve drafts and thoughtful analyses, can often be best accomplished through discussion forums or shared online collaboration spaces or online breakout rooms.

Criteria and Processes for Setting Up Groups

The criteria and processes for setting up groups can be highly dependent on your course content or program. Some cohort programs set up groups at the beginning of a course and keep those groups intact for the full course; other faculty prefer to vary the groups for different types of projects and learning experiences. If you have no experience or requirements to dictate otherwise, we suggest the following:

- Don't let students set up their groups themselves; they often do not consider all the factors that make a good team.

- Let the course goals and purposes guide the formation of groups. Ask yourself, "With what learning or skills do I want the students to emerge from the group experience?" For example, learners might be grouped according to their interest in developing skills for working with for-profit or nonprofit organizations or for working with retail or technical organizations.

Other Factors for Setting Up Groups

Here are other potential factors to consider in setting up groups:

- Amount of content familiarity or expertise of students
- Types of professional contexts in which the students are working
- Types and number of roles the group needs
- Learner goals for the course experience
- Culture, gender, and age (it is often beneficial to mix these)
- Students' online work habits
- Time zones where students are located

It is easy to forget about the impact of time zones and online work habits on team projects. As it turns out, there is nothing more destructive to online teamwork than having a team composed of both members who like to work early in the week and members who prefer to work late in the week. As part of the group setup process, you might ask each learner to submit information similar to that in Exhibit 7.1 before you structure the project teams.

Additional Considerations for Setting Up Groups

Depending on the purpose and context of the groups, you may want to form groups of learners with mixed backgrounds and experiences. In other situations it may be useful to form groups on the basis of similar backgrounds.

Smaller groups of three or four learners generally seem to work better than larger ones. The reasons are many, including working out the roles and responsibilities for the project and arranging times and places to meet to work on the project. A team of two can also be a good choice depending

EXHIBIT 7.1

Group Availability and Contact Info

Enter your available hours for group work or study.

Example:

Sunday

	Sunday	Monday	Tuesday	Wednesday	Thursday	Friday	Saturday
John Doe	Generally not available for meetings	After 6 pm. EST	Before 3 p.m. EST	After 6 pm. EST	5:30-7:30 pm EST	5:30-7:30 pm EST	After 10:00 a.m EST

Study Habits: I log on Wed-Fri and generally make my group contributions on Friday.

Contact Info: 555-123-4567 (H) 555-123-4568 (w)

Preferences: I prefer text messages for initial contact; and then to work by phone, e-mail, and Google hangout or Skype

on the project or the assignment. Some of the roles and responsibilities of team members are organizational, such as project manager, note taker, and meeting manager. Other roles and responsibilities are those focused on content, such as researcher, writer, thinker, or reflector. Obviously, in smaller groups learners need to assume more than one role or task.

The purpose of groups is to increase the time and space available for each learner to express his or her ideas and for you and other students to hear the learner's voice. Groups also, by their very nature, can produce more content for review and feedback. It is extremely important for the faculty member to stay involved with each of the groups and monitor and mentor their activities and learning outcomes and products. Without the instructor's active involvement and feedback, learners can discuss topics and possibly reach conclusions without adequate expert overview and guidance. In a classroom, faculty float and walk around, checking on how discussions are proceeding. This same type of overview and guidance is essential to the online group experiences.

A Note about Post-Millennial Students

We know that the Millennials—those born between roughly 1981 and 2000—enjoy doing, creating, and talking more than listening or reading. They prefer rolling up their sleeves and immersing themselves in projects; they like to find ways to complete learning requirements as quickly as possible without too much of what they refer to as hassle. We also know that members of this same generation are more likely to chat, use Twitter, instant message, play games, and create their own profiles, blogs, and wikis (Lenhart, Madden, Macgill, & Smith, 2007). The post-Millennial students— those born from around 2000 onward—have grown up with Google, Wikipedia, and Wi-Fi as an assumed part of their environment. With these tools, they collaborate and share freely. This generation and future generations of online learners are comfortable with online spaces (they have always been there) and social networking tools, but not necessarily with using these tools and spaces for learning. A very useful resource for staying current with the mindset of your students is the Mindset resource updated each year (Nief, McBride, & Westerberg, 2015).

EM Tip 15: Using Synchronous Collaboration Tools

This tip answers questions such as these:

- Why should I design synchronous gatherings into my courses?
- Why do learners and faculty find these types of gatherings desirable?
- What tools should I use for synchronous meetings? Aren't they expensive and difficult to use?
- Do online learners avoid synchronous time commitments?

"Where are you now? And what are you doing and thinking?" "What is happening where you are now?" This is often the opening line of our social exchanges. We enjoy relationships that are synchronous, social, and interactive. Online and blended learning is no exception. We want tools that are flexible, engaging, affordable, and instantly available. Synchronous collaboration environments support open dialogue, Q&A reviews, presentations, and project work. Spontaneous collaboration also supports learning activities such as brainstorming, producing, and revising.

Synchronous gatherings support constructivist and social learning strategies; they support as well the social, teaching, and cognitive presences that combine to make learning effective and satisfying. And they support students' desires to be socially active and related while learning. These are all good reasons to design synchronous gatherings into your course.

Web Conferencing Tools

Web conferencing tools for synchronous collaborative gatherings are still in rapid change mode. Some of the tools frequently mentioned in higher education circles include Blackboard Collaborate, WebEx, Adobe Connect, and GoToMeeting. Some of these tools overlap with business applications as well. For small team or group meetings, Skype and Google+ Hangout are good options as they are free and widely available. However, when considering a purchase of a web conferencing tool, it is always wise to check web conferencing software websites for the latest and greatest features and options. The web conferencing solutions that work best have most of these very important features:

- Audio and video capabilities
- Document sharing capability
- Ability to archive and play back
- Mobile compatibility
- Real-time polling capability
- Breakout rooms

Full-function synchronous collaboration tools are invaluable for teacher-led gatherings and smaller group project gatherings, making possible the types of synchronous interchanges between teacher and learners that we value so highly in face-to-face classrooms. Once again, teachers and learners can discuss in real time, bringing real-time spontaneity back into teacher-learner interactions.

Sara Cordell, a writing professor at the University of Illinois-Springfield who also teaches British Victorian literature, commented that she values her online classroom for the real-time give-and-take with her students (J. Boettcher, personal communication, January 3, 2008). She added that the synchronous environment provides a way of "pulling things together for her students." She noted that the synchronous online classroom saves her time because she can talk through an essay; for example, discussing how the argument and flow of a student's essay works or not, and weighing the thoughts of other students in real time. She commented that her students have shared with her that they feel as if there is more of a "real person teaching the class." (More about how Cordell uses synchronous tools for teaching is in an NPR interview in Abramson, 2007.)

Faculty often ask how students respond to the expectation of participating in synchronous events, particularly because one reason they are taking an online course is for the flexibility. Anecdotal data gives us some insight. Sara Cordell, for example, requires her literature and writing students to participate in ten of thirteen live classes and to watch the archives of the classes they miss, setting up a separate forum discussion for those students. These classes also extend her day: she meets with her students for between two and three hours, starting at 6:00 p.m. After using the live classroom for five terms, Cordell has concluded that although students find it difficult to participate in the synchronous events, they enjoy the real-time spontaneity. Other faculty provide flexibility by offering a choice of synchronous sessions or by making the synchronous sessions optional.

Mixing and Matching for Spontaneous and Customizable Instant Collaboration

Learners can mix and match the tools to create whatever type of collaboration environment is needed at the time. In other words, they can create their own customized synchronous environment—in a sense, their own mobile ecosystem that fits their particular needs at the time. Learners can set up collaborative environments in these ways:

- Using their cell phone text messaging and calendaring for setting up meetings

- Using their phones and websites for initial brainstorming of projects, determining roles and responsibilities, and setting up time lines with calendaring applications

- Using group text chat and documents combined with phones for creating, planning, editing, and revising reports and other learning content

The only major constraint in setting up these mix-and-match environments is the need for relatively good and predictable network access and relative quiet in physical spaces. Quiet is often hard to come by in popular "offices" such as noisy bookstores, cafés, and other public meeting places. Particularly as a 2014 report suggests that 30 percent of web conferencing participants are using a mobile device and may well be multitasking including driving, walking, or doing chores to participate in the conversation (Blue Jeans Network).

What is also promising about these tools is that they are currently either free or free for education and are readily available on the Internet, resulting in fewer demands on IT infrastructures. Learners can be more in control and can reach out and be productive with other learners without much preplanning, as schedules are often so unpredictable.

EM Tip 16: Using Audio and Video Resources to Create a More Engaging Course

This tip answers questions such as these:

- Why should I use audio and video resources and tools?

- How can I prepare audio and video segments for my online course? (I find it difficult to create quality audio and video segments in a reasonable time.)

- How do I find quality audio and video resources if I don't have much time?

- How long should podcasts or other media resources be?

You probably know that your students would enjoy using audio and video resources in your course, but wonder just how to do it within your time and energy limits. The good news is that it is easier than ever before—filmmakers are making headlines by making movies with iPhones.

More specifically, consider the following:

- Audio adds personality, feeling, and tone to discussions and comments.

- Using audio can save time. It takes less time to provide feedback with your voice than to write the same feedback. This reason alone makes it worthwhile to do it occasionally.

- Audio makes doing learner presentations and project reports much more realistic. This means that students can practice the skills of real-time discussions, reporting, and presenting.

Keep in mind that audio, as any resource, can be overdone or used inappropriately. In other words, using audio is not an opportunity for you to think, "At last I can lecture online." For great teaching and learning, long, rambling lectures are definitely out; quality mini-lectures, concept introductions, dialogue, and interaction are in. Podcasts and audio introductions are best if they are brief. Most teaching and learning podcasts range from three or four minutes to twenty minutes. There are exceptions, of course. Professionally produced webcasts are often in the range of forty-five to fifty minutes. YouTube videos and the TED Talk webcasts are both great resources. These sites also provide many good and bad examples for students. When you are ready to make your own podcasts, you may want to make a podcast that is three to five minutes long by using your smartphone. Think of it as a video selfie.

Strategies for Getting Started

There are two choices for getting started with media resources. The first and easiest way is to use what someone else has created. The second way is to create your own. Here are some virtually painless ways to get started.

Using Published Audio or Video Resources

The easiest way to get started using audio and video in your course is to find and use published audio and video resources. If you don't have time to search out quality resources, you can enlist students to do this. Here's how: Begin with a text reading. As part of the assignment, require that students do some research to find an audio or video podcast or interview on that topic. Your instructions to the student might go as follows:

> *"One of the topics that we will be studying over the next week is X. This might mean a topic such as consumer markets in China, the characteristics of leaders, the ethics of open software, or the pros and cons of intellectual property. To support the ideas in your posting, find an audio or video resource from a reputable reference discussing these issues. Include the URL and a short description of the resource in your posting. Then other students can review these resources as part of their response to the postings."*

This is a good initial audio experience, as it means that you and your students need to ensure that your personal learning devices work well with audio and video.

Add Audio to Your Biography and Introductory Posting

Our voices are another dimension of our personality and part of getting to know someone. Think about how CNN uses audio. When correspondents are in far-flung and sometimes dangerous places such as war zones they use the correspondent's picture in an inset with the audio, frequently accompanied by a Google Earth shot of the terrain where the correspondent is. So we hear the voice, and our mind almost fills in the missing video.

You can make a voice audio file with an app on your smartphone, usually with a format such as WAV or MP3, and e-mail it to other devices. The same processes work for creating your own podcasts and course announcements.

As with learning any other new tool or application, use audio in noncritical course elements as you develop confidence and introduce your students to this way of bringing voice energy into your course.

Use Audio in Course Announcements or for Discussion Feedback

Two other easy starting places for using audio are course announcements and discussion board postings. Think of announcements as ways of talking naturally with your students and giving them reminders of what's next, what might be happening in the world that is particularly relevant to their course content, and schedule changes.

Summary—and What's Next

We hope these tips for the early middle will prove useful and helpful. By now, your learning community is growing and projects are planned, if not already well under way. Your teaching presence has likely already started a subtle further shift into more coaching, mentoring, and deeper questioning which is the focus of the next phase and chapter.

Self-Directed Exercise/Application

If you are using this book for a course in faculty development, here are some questions and activities to consider. What are the priorities for the early middle of your course? Is it content engagement, developing questions, firming up course projects? Is your community developing? Which of the tips address the most important areas of growth for yourself?

Develop a particular exercise for sharing in a blog or journal entry or that you might share with your students as part of your teaching presence.

Chapter 8

Phase 3: Letting Go of Power in the Late Middle

YOU ARE NOW at the halfway point of your course. By this time, you and your students are likely well acquainted with each other from a social and cognitive perspective. Your teaching presence is actively guiding individual and group learning goals.

In this chapter we expand on tips and strategies for deep learning with questioning techniques, assessing growth, project coaching, and empowering learners. These tips and strategies all support critical thinking and effective problem-solving within a given field, accompanied by "well-developed workplace competencies" (Business-Higher Education Forum [BHEF], 2013). Obviously all of these outcomes are achieved through an entire program, rather than one course, but each course plays a role in the larger mastery of knowledge and use.

Take time to enjoy the late middle of a course—this is the time for deep thought, exploration, sorting out confusions, and grappling with the core concepts and deep unanswered questions of your discipline. Students are coming into their own in terms of developing content knowledge and pursuing creative projects. Students bring a host of new perspectives, relationships, and patterns from other disciplines. This can be a stimulating time for discipline insights and for novel approaches to traditional perspectives.

Overview of Late Middle Tips

There are four sets of tips for this "letting go of the power" time. The first set, Going Deeper: Leveraging the Power of Questions, explores how questions and students' responses provide insights into what learners know and what they think they know. These tips provide examples of probing questions for querying learners as to what they think and why they think what they do. These techniques encourage peer-to-peer dialogue that supports creating community. Of all the skills developed for online teaching and learning, effective questioning skill is one of the most important.

The second set of tips, Feedback for Cognitive Growth, offers suggestions on providing feedback to learners. These tips provide guidelines and hints on strategies for ensuring timely, efficient ongoing feedback to learners. Ongoing assessment ensures that you get to know your students as individuals and thus minimizes the potential for cheating or other types of fraud. As you become familiar with the manner of a student's expression and perspectives, you can detect any abnormalities in his or her work.

The third set of tips, Assessing Learning as You Go, describes ways of enhancing assessment so that the evaluation of student work emphasizes learning growth rather than judgment. The first tip in this set describes strategies for personalizing and customizing learning and the power that these strategies bring to learning. Other tips focus on the tasks of managing and assessing an individual learner's projects as well as group projects. These tips complement the earlier ones on projects and include a rubric for analyzing critical thinking and a set of best practices during project time.

The last set of tips, Community Empowerment and Social Networking, brings together hints on using social networking tools such as blogs and wikis for putting conversations into high gear.

Going Deeper: Leveraging the Power of Questions

- **LM Tip 1:** Questions and Answers: Upside Down and Inside Out

- **LM Tip 2:** Three Techniques for Making Your Students' Knowledge Visible

- **LM Tip 3:** Developing Rigor in Our Questioning: Eight Intellectual Standards

- **LM Tip 4:** Moving Beyond Knowledge Integration to Defining Problems and Finding Solutions

Feedback for Cognitive Growth

- **LM Tip 5:** "Are You Reading My Postings? Do You Know Who I Am?" Simple Rules for Feedback in Online Learning

- **LM Tip 6:** Feedback on Assignments: Being Timely and Efficient

- **LM TIP 7:** Substantive Feedback: Doing It Wisely and Well

- **LM Tip 8:** A Rubric for Analyzing Critical Thinking

Assessing Learning as You Go

- **LM Tip 9:** Customizing and Personalizing Learning Projects
- **LM Tip 10:** Managing and Facilitating Group Projects
- **LM Tip 11:** Assessing Group Projects
- **LM Tip 12:** Four Effective Practices During Project Time

Community Empowerment and Social Networking

- **LM Tip 13:** Course Middles and Muddles: Souped-Up Conversations That Help Build Community
- **LM TIP 14:** Using Social Networking Techniques to Build a Learning Community
- **LM Tip 15:** Experts: A Touch of Spice

Going Deeper: Leveraging the Power of Questions

These four tips expand on techniques and strategies for Socratic questioning and for involving students in creating questions.

LM Tip 1: Questions and Answers: Upside Down and Inside Out

This tip answers questions such as these:

- What are alternatives to the questioning model in which instructors pose questions that students answer?
- Why are students hesitant about asking questions?
- How can we make questioning more natural and more open?

Faculty ask questions and students answer questions. Then we know what students know. Right? Well, maybe not. We may want to turn this questioning model upside down and inside out. In the late middle of a course, students have been working with the course content for some time. You want to know the state of their concept development. Remember the principle that concept development is not a one-time event. Research into concepts confirms that students build knowledge over time as a result of a *series* of experiences. The likelihood that students will be familiar with and conversant with key concepts from the first part of a course is generally low (Hake, 1998, cited in Wieman, 2008). We know it is important to revisit, discuss, review, and reference core concepts continually throughout a course.

One technique to determine how students' concept development is progressing is to probe each learner's knowledge and skills by designing activities that require students to ask questions. Questions reveal the structure of how and what they know. The downside is that they may ask questions that show they have acquired very little. They may also ask difficult or complex questions that may lead the course conversation in unplanned but needed directions. If that happens, it may mean shifting gears and revising the course to meet students where they are.

Student Questioning: Inquiry as a Reflection of Knowledge

We often can't move forward on a problem or learn something new until we can specify what we *don't* know. By stating what we don't know, we are creating a holding space within the structure of our knowledge base for that new knowledge.

Consider the thinking processes for asking good questions. Learners need to think, review what they know or what has just been discussed, and identify what they don't know or wonder about. Learners are often afraid of asking questions, with good reason. A question reveals the structure—or lack of structure—of existing knowledge, links, and relationships. Answering factual questions, for example, is often a simple stimulus-response action, requiring little deep thought or analysis. More complex questions, such as clarifying questions, require tapping into a learner's state of conceptual development and examining the links and relationships that are either formed or beginning to form.

Discussion Forums for Student Questioning

The discussion forum is often used for questions to the students—for example, "What do you know? What do you think you know? How do you know what you know?" and "What is the basis for your knowledge, and what are the relationships and data required for that knowledge?" We ask students to analyze articles, news reports, websites, or podcasts. We ask them to respond to statements and support what they know with references and research. We ask them to research topics specific to their own interest area or region. The students' task is to answer, analyze, and suggest possibilities and strategies for addressing the problem or scenario.

These types of discussion requirements are excellent and can stimulate desirable sustained conversation and inquiry. But teachers and students like a variety of experiences, so asking students to do the questioning is a way to provide variety.

Here are a few specific ideas for challenging students to come up with tough questions. These activities can also be used as team activities. The simpler activities could be dyad activities; the more complex activities involving scenarios might be done with teams of three students:

- Play a variation of "Stump the Faculty Member" in which the learners generate scenarios or questions for the faculty member, hoping to "stump" the faculty member in their area of expertise. Another strategy is to have an external expert participate in a discussion and be available for answering questions over a few days. This variation could culminate with a "Stump the Expert" in an interview. Either of these experiences could be a wrap-up activity in a synchronous event using an online classroom.

- Post a statement, article, scenario, or video news clip on the discussion forum, and ask students to generate a set of data-gathering questions to help address that situation, problem, or question.

- Create a discussion forum for capturing content problems or questions that students have or are wondering about. Students can do research for examples of such problems.

- Establish an open forum for a week. Have the students generate questions and problems related to the readings and challenge others to find the answers.

- Encourage students to question the information they gain from their research. Questions that should be encouraged include: "Who asserted this? What are this person's credentials? Who had the opportunity to critique this idea? Who supports and who disagrees with it?" (Bruckman, 2005, p. 36).

Using these strategies means you turn the tables on the questioning model and encourage deeper thinking by the students. Questioning by students can become a form of testing and evaluation; it can also build useful critical thinking skills, inquiry skills, and cognitive inquisitiveness about what it is we really do know and even how we came to know something.

LM Tip 2: Three Techniques for Making Your Students' Knowledge Visible

This tip answers questions such as these:

- What are examples of questions that reveal a student's state of knowledge?

- What types of questions show how students are linking new information and core concepts to what they already know?

- How can I develop a questioning mindset in my students?

- What is concept mapping, and how might this technique make students' knowledge visible?

Getting to know your students' state of knowledge and zones of proximal development is an essential part of the teaching process. Knowing what your students know helps you to match their learning experiences to appropriate growth experiences.

Here are three techniques that help stimulate learners to balance the input experiences of reading, listening, and watching with output experiences such as reflecting, questioning, exploring, and producing learning products for you to observe and evaluate.

Technique 1: Interviewer-Expert Modeling

As part of a reading research or listening assignment, ask your students to develop two or three questions to ask, as if they were preparing to interview an expert, leader, fellow learners, or you. For example, what in your career prepared you for your current role?

Developing questions requires the student to pause, reflect, and assimilate knowledge or content. An interview questioning activity can assign the role of interviewer to some of your students and the role of expert to others. The interviewers' task is to develop the questions and post them to the discussion board, and the "expert" students then have the task of responding to the questions as best they can. If it makes sense, students can switch roles for a follow-up activity.

The questions that students ask and the student responses to questions help you to observe how students are putting things together in their heads and whether they are creating a useful and accessible body of knowledge. These questions can also stimulate thinking about questions for which additional research and study is needed.

Technique 2: Identifying Patterns, Relationships, and Linkages

Making new knowledge one's own requires linking ideas and new incoming knowledge to existing neurons in our physical brain and knowledge structures. These knowledge-integration processes include identification of patterns and relationships, and differentiating the characteristics of one item from another. Here are some questions that might elicit this type of knowledge work in your students:

- What do the ideas in [a chapter, reading, discussion, podcast, or news article] remind you of?

- What relationships are fundamental or inherent in these ideas?

- What patterns, if any, are you observing?
- Are these patterns or relationships present in recent or significant past events or experiences?

Technique 3: Identifying Insights

Part of being a lifelong learner is an awareness of how our minds work; that is, an awareness of when insights happen and when we are aware of discrete data elements and information pieces coming together. Here are a couple of questions that can lead students to think about their own minds and how learning happens.

- What insights or "Aha!" experiences have you had in the past week or so?
- What do you know or understand now that you did not have at your intellectual readiness a few days ago?

Students' responses to these questions and your affirmation of what they observe can help students develop their metacognitive skills—one of the goals recommended by the How People Learn research analysis (Bransford, Brown, & Cocking, 2000).

LM Tip 3: Developing Rigor in Our Questioning: Eight Intellectual Standards

This tip answers these questions:

- What are some intellectual standards that can guide the creating of questions and the responses to those questions?
- Can I suggest that question responses focus on just one or two intellectual standards?
- What are some learning activities that can make use of these intellectual standards?

Are you stumped for ways to ensure that you are asking stimulating and relevant questions? Would you like to have more confidence that your questions help your students internalize the core concepts of your course? Here is a way to tap into the power of Socratic questioning. This tip describes a set of eight intellectual standards. Using these standards can help raise the level of intellectual thought, clarity, and purpose in your communications.

As you know from previous tips, concept formation is not a one-time event; it takes time, thought, and a series of exposures and uses. Systematic questioning can serve as a framework for revealing the accuracy, breadth, and depth of how learners are doing in their process of acquiring concepts. If a concept is really core to a discipline, learners must approach that concept from a number of directions. They must experience that concept in virtual, simulated, or even hands-on contexts if possible.

Concepts as Knowledge Clusters

Recall that concepts are more than words; they are "organized and intricate clusters of knowledge bits." This means that while we must often teach in a linear fashion, building up concept information step by step, learners need to experience concepts in the contexts of complex problems and case studies. Effectively learning concepts—as we know from novice and expert studies—requires a focus on patterns and relationships, not merely learning discrete facts or vocabulary.

What are some examples of core concepts? The next part of this tip provides three core concept examples and then lists eight characteristics of intellectual rigor with sample questions.

Core Concept Examples

Here are examples of three core concepts:

  In the discipline of learning: Learning is growth that occurs with the acquisition of new knowledge and experiences associated with that knowledge. Growth can be observed by new behaviors.

  In leadership studies: Leadership is rooted in a shared, well-articulated, and worthy vision.

  In biology: Deoxyribonucleic acid (DNA) is a nucleic acid that contains the genetic instructions for the development and functioning of living organisms.

Now let's move on to the eight intellectual standards that you might use to help learners to acquire these concepts.

Rigor in Questioning: Eight Intellectual Standards

Developing concepts requires thought and reasoning work by the learner, similar to the processes used in solving problems, puzzles and in detective work. These eight intellectual standards help ensure your learners are developing the core concepts of your course. Each standard is followed by a generic sample question and then an example of a question applied to a core concept.

These standards provide an explicit system to help achieve the power of Socratic questioning.

1. Clarity

   - A sample generic question for clarity might be: Can you give an example or illustration of your idea?

   - A sample of the **clarity** standard for the core concept of **leadership** might be: Can you give an example of a leader who articulated a vision well?

2. Precision

   - A sample generic question for precision might be: Can you be more specific about your concerns?

   - A sample of the **precision** standard for the core concept of **learning** might be: How can we best see evidence of growth in learning? What are the some of the possible ways to evaluate learning that has resulted in a change in behavior?

3. Accuracy

   - A sample generic question for accuracy might be: What evidence do you have that supports your statements? Is this evidence verifiable and from a reliable source?

   - A sample of the **accuracy** standard for the core concept of **leadership** might be: Can you verify the sources and the time, place, and occurrence of the clearly stated vision?

4. Relevance

   - A sample generic question for relevance might be: Can you explain how your example, statement or story is connected to the current issue? How is it relevant? What is its relationship to the issue at hand?

   - A sample of the **relevance** standard for the core concept of **biology** might be: How is the genetic information that resides in our DNA of particular relevance today? What are the possible future impacts of DNA processes shared by living organisms? How has our understanding of DNA as the genetic material enabled us to prevent certain birth defects and cancers? What are some possible future impacts of genetic engineering of humans and other living organisms?

5. Depth

   - A sample generic question for depth might be: What makes this concept so complex? What are the components of the concept that must come together?

- A sample of the **depth** standard for the core concept of **learning** might be: Why is learning so complex? What does learning interact with that is internal to each individual? What is shared? What is unique?

6. Breadth

    - A sample generic question for breadth might be: What other points of view should we consider?

    - A sample of the **breadth** standard for the core concept of **leadership** might be: What are other perspectives or consideration for the vision of this leader? Are there ethical, economic, justice issues?

7. Logic

    - A sample generic question for logic might be: Does the solution make sense? What is the line of reasoning that brought you to this point?

    - A sample of the **logic** standard for the core concept of **biology** might be: What line of research substantiates the workings of the genetic material and how it manifests itself in different living organisms? Why were early researchers able to exclude proteins as the carrier of genetic information? Why does a skin cell produce different proteins than a heart cell, even though they both contain the same DNA?

8. Fairness

    - A sample generic question for fairness might be: Who has vested interest in these issues? What assumptions is an author making?

    - A sample of the **fairness** standard for the core concept of **learning** might be: Is merit pay based on test scores an appropriate measure for K–12 teachers? Why or why not? What does this approach assume?

Background of the Set of Eight Intellectual Standards

The set of eight intellectual standards described in this tip is just one of many resources available at the website for the Foundation for Critical Thinking (http://www.criticalthinking.org/). This site is sponsored by a cross-disciplinary group promoting excellence in thinking. The many small guides available from this group are rich resources for ideas on developing critical thinking. These same resources can be useful in developing rubrics for discussions, assignments, and general course dialogue.

The two primary authors of these materials are Richard Paul and Linda Elder. Richard Paul was an internationally recognized authority on critical thinking and founder of the Center for Critical Thinking at Sonoma State

University. Linda Elder is president of the Foundation for Critical Thinking and executive director of the Center for Critical Thinking. Other resources include guides on *Asking Essential Questions* and a *Guide to Scientific Thinking*. One resource—*Thinking with Concepts*—loops us back directly to the question of how concepts are related to critical thinking. In the words of Paul and Elder (2002):

> *"To become a proficient critical thinker, they (students) must become the master of their own conceptualizations. They must develop the ability to mentally 'remove' this or that concept from the things named by the concept and try out alternative ideas, and alternative names."*
> *(paragraph 4)*

This quote is a bit complex to process, as it is a cluster of concepts itself. It reminds us that concepts are the building blocks of our thinking, and that people who are successful at thinking critically need to be able to reshape their concepts as new information becomes available. This can mean "removing" and recalibrating our thoughts. For example, we do depend on language and memory as tools for building concepts; but in addition, culture is a significant influence on our concepts. Our concepts are steeped in our culture and the society of our life experiences. Critical thinkers learn to examine their concepts and identify the experiences that resulted in those concepts and adjust accordingly.

Using Intellectual Standards in Learning Activities

Individual assignments might focus on one or two of the intellectual standards. For example, the assignment instructions might coach students in analyzing one of their course readings and ferreting out the underlying implicit concepts and assumptions. Here are some other examples of learning activities making use of these intellectual standards.

- Use a breadth (perspective) question in one or more initial discussion postings to help ensure a broad look at the issues.

- Use precision or clarity questions when probing with follow-up questions on discussion conversations and reading or writing assignments.

- Design a learning activity that requires students to use two or three of these eight standards in an analysis of an assumption.

The practice of explicitly designing excellence in thinking into our courses supports learners in developing explicit and implicit knowledge of the standards and means for critical thinking. These eight standards—clarity, precision, accuracy, relevance, depth, breadth, logic, and fairness—are tools for faculty and learner inquiry. Using these standards is a means to higher-level thinking and effective critical analysis.

LM Tip 4: Moving Beyond Knowledge Integration to Defining Problems and Finding Solutions

This tip answers questions such as these:

- Getting students to formulate the problem space can be difficult. Are there any models that help in defining problems?

- What are examples of good problem definitions?

- What are examples of effective problem resolution?

- Can learners arrive at a problem resolution during a course?

The early stages of the practical inquiry model by Garrison and Vaughan (2008) focus on clarifying the issues and challenges of a domain, and researching and exploring ideas. By the late middle of a course, it is time to encourage more complex use of knowledge, including active and creative use of the content to propose solutions and strategies.

A learner's awareness of and exposure to the content knowledge has expanded by the late middle, but the ability to use the knowledge in any meaningful way may not be developing. New knowledge will be lasting only if it is used. Defining problems—getting to one or more questions—and then deciding on a way to approach them are steps three and four in the practical inquiry model. As a reminder, the four steps in the model are (1) the triggering event where the issue or problem is identified; (2) exploring the problem and gathering relevant information; (3) making sense of the data and defining some possible solutions; and (4) testing the possible solutions. These steps help develop students' critical thinking and problem-solving skills and provide rich opportunities for mentoring by the faculty member.

Defining Problems and Deciding on Resolution Strategies

It is helpful to recall that the underlying process of all learning is growth (Dewey, 1916). Part of the learning process requires identifying areas of dissonance and inconsistency in content resources. As noted in the tip on intellectual standards (LM Tip 3), it is essential to identify dissonance and inconsistency in learners' own beliefs as well.

The process of identifying areas of dissonance can be difficult. A study that defined cognitive actions and behaviors in problem formulation and resolution is helpful. Murphy and Manzanares (2006) identified a set of nineteen behaviors that can be used in defining and formulating problems and working on finding a resolution. Eleven of the behaviors focused on formulating problem statements, and eight of the behaviors were those often used in resolving or testing solutions to problems. See which of these you have been using and which you may want to adopt.

Eleven Problem Formulation Behaviors

In their analysis of the transcripts of online discussions, Murphy and Manzanares identified behaviors helpful in formulating or defining a problem. These behaviors can be helpful in providing suggestions and guidance for students as they proceed in their own problem formulation. These behaviors are also useful for developing rubrics for assessment or simply as guidelines:

- Agreeing with the problem as presented
- Specifying ways in which the problem may manifest itself
- Redefining a problem within a modified problem space
- Minimizing or denying the problem
- Identifying the extent of the problem
- Identifying the causes of the problem
- Articulating the problem outside the problem space
- Identifying unknowns in knowledge
- Accessing and reporting on sources of information
- Identifying the value of information

Eight Behaviors Supporting Problem Resolution

Murphy and Manzanares associate three types of high-level cognitive behaviors with problem resolution: identifying solutions, evaluating solutions, and acting on solutions. Here is the list of behaviors they identified as used in problem resolution:

- Proposing solutions
- Hypothesizing solutions
- Agreeing with solutions that others propose
- Weighing and comparing alternative solutions
- Critiquing solutions
- Rejecting or eliminating solutions judged unworkable
- Planning to act
- Reaching conclusions or arriving at an understanding of the problem

Developing Problem Solvers and Critical Thinkers

Many reports and books on the state of higher education stress the need for graduates who are good problem solvers and effective team players (Bransford et al., 2000; Business-Higher Education Forum, 2003; Bok, 2007).

Becoming familiar with and using these behaviors helps students develop an understanding of the processes and the knowledge needed for problem formulation and problem solving. In many cases, the work done in formulating and clarifying a problem often takes us halfway to a solution, and this is a valuable lesson as well. Working with others on sustained and thoughtful interaction to clarify and solve problems results in the shared knowledge discovery and co-creation that are also characteristics of a successful learning community.

Feedback for Cognitive Growth

The importance of timely substantive feedback to learners has always been recognized, but it is now being acknowledged as a key factor in deep learning. In a *Chronicle of Higher Education* article (2012) describing the strategy of flipped classrooms, reporter Dan Berrett compares the professor's role to that of a cognitive coach. In his words, "A good coach figures out what makes a great athlete and what practice helps you achieve that. They motivate the learner to put out intense effort, and they provide expert feedback that's very timely."

In this section, LM Tips 5 and 6 offer guidelines and suggestions on providing timely feedback to learners and suggestions on efficient habits of staying in touch with learners on their discussion posts, assignments, and general participation. LM Tips 7 and 8 focus on rubrics as a way of providing direction and feedback. In particular, LM Tip 7 provides a rubric for analyzing critical thinking and LM Tip 8 describes three scenarios for actively involving learners with rubrics, so that feedback becomes more of a community experience.

LM Tip 5: "Are You Reading My Postings? Do You Know Who I Am?" Simple Rules for Feedback in Online Learning

This tip answers questions such as these:

- How important is feedback?
- How many types of feedback are there?
- When is feedback important?
- Does feedback always have to address an individual's work, or can it address and summarize the work of groups?

Research is showing that mastering the art of giving students feedback in an online course makes a substantive difference in student satisfaction and retention (Kim & Moore, 2005). This study affirms that "students' interaction with classmates and their instructor have an impact on their satisfaction with web-based courses." In other words, getting feedback right often results in good feelings about a course and, by extension, about an institution. Here are quick answers to the questions for this tip:

- How important is feedback? (Vital!)
- How many types of feedback are there? (Lots!)
- When is feedback important? (Almost always!)
- Does feedback always have to address individual's work, or can feedback address the work of groups? (Both types can be very useful!)

This tip focuses primarily on traditional feedback from instructor to learner. Other types of feedback are peer feedback, feedback from students to faculty, automated feedback, and media-rich feedback, including the use of audio.

What is feedback? Feedback is a key element of any communication or dialogue. In fact, there is no real communication or dialogue without feedback. Feedback continues, enhances, or closes a train of thought. The image of a train of thought is very useful, because you don't want to interrupt a train that is moving along. The image of a train of thought is also useful in thinking about how individual learners' thoughts might diverge from each other and follow a train of thought or inquiry important to their own knowledge construction and integration.

In online learning, the type of feedback that first comes to mind is that from faculty to student. This is the most important feedback from a student's point of view. Learners want to know what an instructor thinks about the work they are doing. Next we will discuss the most important rules about feedback from faculty to student, which are straightforward:

Provide feedback early and often.

Provide feedback on assignments when expected.

Provide feedback that is personal and formative for learning.

Provide Feedback Early and Often

Providing feedback early in a course can mean giving feedback as soon as students begin introducing themselves. Personal data about your students can be used to help students connect their goals and purposes to the content and goals of the course. The simple act of taking a personal data element and incorporating it into feedback to the student sends the message that postings are not going into a black hole. Other connections that you might comment on can include shared working environments and similar life experiences, such as a love of baking or biking or having roots somewhere in the Midwest. These observations create connections that build a foundation of community.

Here is an example of how you can make connections between course content and goals and a student's background experiences and goals. You might observe, "Your background in the XYZ industry may be especially relevant to the rest of the class when we discuss ABC topic in weeks five and six." This observation signals to the student that you have connected with him or her in a unique way. Making these kinds of observations requires first noting the connections between what learners reveal about themselves and what we know of the content and also students' work context. This personalizing and recognition of individuality helps keep students engaged and motivated. Fortunately, everything that a student posts online, such as the getting-acquainted posts, is captured and can be returned to at any time.

One technique that works for some faculty is to take the time to mine the information about learners' expected learning goals and purposes for the course and create a reminder that profiles key information about each student, such as the name of the company that he or she is working for and his or her particular area of interest.

Feedback Early in the Course—How To and When

- As in any relationship, the first interactions in a course lay the groundwork for what follows. Students want to know about you and your expertise; your students want you to know them.

- In the pre-week and week one, read the students' introductions carefully and respond to one or more of each student's statements by acknowledging where they are coming from and also to highlight important connections between the students. Remember, too, that you have (probably) asked them to customize at least one learning outcome to be very specific to their interests. With that information, you can acknowledge their goals, and sometimes their worries and anxieties, and encourage them to find common ground with other students, while reinforcing shared content goals. While doing this, be sure to share connections between your own expertise and, as appropriate, your life experiences, just as you would do in a face-to-face encounter.

- In the first two weeks of any course, making frequent postings is an extremely high priority. How frequent? The standards suggest postings on four or more days of each week. Graduate students need a little less handholding, but a focus on developing expertise is highly desirable, and the first week is a great time to focus on core concepts to come.

- Remember that the first two weeks are special in establishing connections and relationships. As the course progresses, students will be able to take on more responsibility for self-assessment, peer-assessment, and community roles. Substantive comments in the first two weeks means careful reading and analysis of students' first postings. Use multiple types of feedback, such as group feedback via announcements and forum postings as well as individualized feedback via posting conversations and first assignments. It is important, time-wise, to make good use of group feedback that integrates a focus on course content while recognizing individual work.

- One strategy for saving time is to have the students use their own self-assessment skills by having them specify the thoughts, ideas, or observations on which they most want your feedback. For example, you might direct them as follows: "After you complete your initial posting on the first assigned reading, add a postscript that identifies the idea, comment, or observation on the reading that you most want me to respond to."

Provide Feedback on Assignments When Expected

If you do not tell students when to expect feedback on their assignments, they will expect it within minutes of hitting the send or upload button. So state your general rules for feedback turnaround times clearly and provide regular reminders.

Since the feedback turnaround on assignments can differ, the assignment information should be part of any assignment information. This does mean planning assignment deadlines around your own teaching and life patterns and special events. For example, if a week's postings close on Saturday, you will likely need to schedule time on Monday for review and feedback on the week's postings and summaries.

For large projects, the turnaround time may be longer; other times you may want to adjust deadlines, given your own schedule. Also, if you know your final course grades are due three days after the end of the final week, you may want to move the submission deadline for a final assignment up a few days or a week to give you adequate time to provide feedback to students. The average turnaround time for larger projects is around seven days, depending on variables such as the length of a course.

Online learners are particularly concerned about the first cycle of assignments and feedback because it is a benchmark for what will likely follow. They will use the feedback from the first assignment as a marker for what you think about their ideas and how they express themselves. It often determines how much time and effort they put into subsequent assignments. Some of the questions learners often have include: "How closely do you follow the assignment rubrics?" "Do you count timeliness?" "How much do you recognize or expect analysis, innovation, or creativity?" "How much research do you expect?" and "Do you notice grammar and spelling?" Rubrics included with assignments generally help answer these basic questions.

Provide Rapid Response to Questions

For general discussion questions, it is important to answer questions promptly or have a system for ensuring that questions are answered in a timely manner. For example, you might state that your general rule of thumb for answering any and all questions is twenty-four hours during the usual workweek, but that you do try to respond sooner when you can.

A good rule of thumb is that if a student asks a question, three to five others are probably also wondering about the same issue but didn't have the courage or take the trouble to ask. Thanking students for their questions is feedback that says, "I value your questions. There's no such thing as a dumb question, so keep the questions coming."

Provide Feedback That Is Personal and Formative for Learning

Providing feedback to learners can be very time-consuming. To aid you in your effort to save time, systems with automated or embedded feedback are available, and some of these are proving to be excellent and effective, as in the example of using rich feedback in quizzes in large introductory biology classes (Cooper, Tyser, & Sandheinrich, 2007). Nevertheless, these systems do not provide personal feedback or a relationship with a live faculty member.

The best feedback is personal and formative for learning. Effective feedback assumes that the faculty is reading or listening to a learner and then analyzing and reflecting on his or her work and ideas. Personal feedback means that you are getting to know the student as a person and as a mind, and that you are helping to shape and challenge the learning of the student. This type of feedback creates long-lasting and satisfying links and connections. No wonder that feedback is an element of student satisfaction and loyalty! Many of us have stories where feedback to a student has made all the difference in someone's life or learning. Quality feedback means that you have taken time to know an individual and to care about him or her as a person and a learner.

LM Tip 6: Feedback on Assignments: Being Timely and Efficient

This tip answers these questions:

- Does feedback to students always have to be private? Can I use the open community forum or a faculty blog for summarizing feedback?

- What are more examples of rubrics to guide learners' self-feedback and peer feedback?

- How do I provide feedback that recognizes a student's individual content and concept mastery?

The ideas in this tip are a good fit for the late middle phase of your course when you are handling individual feedback on assignments. We discussed feedback on weekly discussion postings that are public, open, and part of the course community dialogue in EM Tip 4. Feedback on assignments is more private. It is typically part of the faculty-to-learner dialogue and ideally is personalized and customized to shape an individual's growth. This is the feedback that often contributes to the grading requirements.

It is worth noting, however, that as we design more collaborative work into courses, more feedback is shifting to the open community, where it contributes to the intellectual growth of the entire community and advances sustained conversation and inquiry. Blog and wiki assignments are examples of this more open work and feedback.

Timely Feedback

Always let students know *when* they can expect feedback on their assignments; include this information in the assignment. The announcement tool is often a great reminder tool to use as well. The standard time for providing feedback for larger or major assignments is one week. If assignments are stacked, one building on a prior one, as happens in course project assignments, you may be able to provide feedback more quickly. Posting a note about the expected feedback schedule is also an opportunity to change this time frame if your schedule requires such an adjustment.

Also tell students the process by which you will provide feedback. Will you be making embedded comments in a Word document, with detailed observations based on a rubric? Or will you be providing more of a holistic grade and comments? For example, the "how" will likely change with the phases of a project. Feedback on early phases of a project may be more open, even soliciting input from others to contribute brainstorming ideas in a synchronous session.

In the early parts of a project you may choose to provide two levels of feedback: first a summary feedback for the entire group, later supplemented by more private feedback to individual students.

Feedback Using a Rubric

Using a grading rubric for assignments guides student projects and saves you time. A rubric lays out the criteria for grading and becomes useful as a checklist. You can counsel students to work on the assignment with one eye on the rubric as a way of self-assessment. (Examples of rubrics are provided later in this tip.) A grading and assessment rubric also helps to avoid unwelcome surprises because students generally can predict their own grade from the rubrics.

Part of the assignment direction might include a discussion of the rubric. If the highest points are reserved for papers or presentations that show evidence of research or deep thinking about the issues evidenced by noting patterns, relationships, and insights, are there any examples or models from earlier courses that students might examine? Will the grade include assessment of communication elements, such as writing, grammar, clarity, and citation accuracy? LM Tips 7 and 8 provide more background and help on using rubrics.

Conceptual Feedback Reminders

Here are other reminders for feedback to individual students that particularly address content issues:

- Keep an awareness of a student's particular zone of proximal development front and center. Recall that learners cannot learn everything in a flash until the "Aha!" moment. Our brains process information chunk by chunk and piece by piece, depending on the knowledge structures already in our heads, and create structures over time. As you review the student's assignment and prepare your feedback, structure your comments so that you tap into where the student's ideas are coming from based on what they likely know, and then mold or shape their thinking by reinforcing the strengths of their ideas and guiding them to the next steps of integrating those ideas. Viewing an archive of the student's postings, including a personal archive, so that you refresh your view of the student's state of thought can help in providing effective feedback.

- If you prefer a more holistic approach that combines simple criteria with personal comments, create a template for feedback; for example, to use for a brief thought paper. This template can consist of two sections: the first section lists the criteria you are using for the assessment, the second sets out examples of how you might encourage, challenge, and reinforce the core concepts. Providing thoughtful conceptual feedback can take time. Building a template that includes reinforcing concepts and principles can make this process more efficient.

- This technique can be used with assignments or a long and rich discussion forum. Review the assignment, and respond with one summative cohesive discussion and analysis, weaving in and making reference to contributions by students by name. This feedback technique has the advantage of taking less time than individual responses to students while creating a useful summary.

- Audio feedback tools offer new strategies for providing substantive feedback to individuals or to the class as a whole. For summary feedback to the class, you can comment back to the public forum or discussion board and highlight the strengths of the work of the learning community. This is an opportunity to reinforce, praise, coach, and direct.

Examples of Rubrics

Here are two examples of rubrics that you can use for written assignments. The first is a rubric for a significant written assignment; the second is a simple checklist for a shorter assignment. In each case the assignment instructions direct students to use these rubrics to check their papers before submitting them.

A Rubric for a Written Assignment

In this example, the final paper or project is an individual project and is worth 20 percent of the final grade:

- The paper/media project is well organized, easy to understand, and well written or produced. The project is presented well, with no major grammatical or spelling errors, and citations are styled in accordance with APA guidelines, as appropriate. The project is the right length for the assignment. It includes a descriptive title, an introduction, a conclusion, and appropriate section headings. 5 points.

- The paper/media project is responsive to the content of the assignment. It includes a summary statement of your thoughts, the research, and the rationale supporting your recommendations. 12 points.

- All tables and figures presented are thoroughly discussed in the paper / media project. Additional resources are included as appropriate. 3 points.

A Checklist for a Short Written Assignment

This example of a checklist guides students through an evaluation of their own writing. This can be very useful, as it increases the student's own judgment of his or her own work for the long term, while reducing the amount of time for faculty in review and evaluation of the student's work.

Directions to the student: Before submitting your assignment, use this checklist to ensure that your assignment is complete. If you find problem areas, revise. This checklist is used in grading your assignment, so you can even self-grade your work.

1. Do you have a clear introduction? Does it identify the thematic and organizational structure of the essay? Does it indicate the point of view you will argue?

2. Have you organized the material effectively? That is, is the sequence of presentation appropriate for the content?

3. Is the content presentation user-friendly? Do you "talk to the reader" and clearly indicate the transitions from one section/argument/theme to the next? Do you use headings and subheadings appropriately?

4. Do you make a persuasive argument to support your point of view? Have you considered other points of view?

5. Have you used relevant source material? Have you referenced all your sources, including those you have quoted directly and those that you have paraphrased?

6. Do you provide a conclusion and summary?

7. Have you included a bibliography?

8. Have you spell-checked your work and reviewed it for word choice, punctuation, and grammar errors?

9. Is your assignment the required length?

Some faculty also direct their students to attach this checklist to their assignment and ask students to respond or answer the questions even to the point of self-grading. This checklist can be adapted for use with peer review as well, with pairs of students reading each other's papers and giving them feedback, and then allowing time for student revision before the formal submission to the faculty member.

Here are two additional rubrics for your consideration among the many that are available online. You can use these as is or adapt to your needs.

A rubric for a short paper assignment (Parsell, 2015):

http://staff.mq.edu.au/teaching/curriculum_assessment/ curriculum_design/engagement/podcasts/engagement_rubrics/

A rubric for participation in discussion postings (Frey, 2006): http://www.udel.edu/janet/MARC2006/rubric.html

LM TIP 7: Substantive Feedback: Doing It Wisely and Well

This tip answers these questions:

- What is the definition of substantive feedback?

- How can I use self-assessment and peer feedback to improve feedback and save time?

- What are more examples of rubrics to guide learners' self-feedback and peer feedback?

Feedback makes a difference in students' learning and their engagement in course content. And research suggests that feedback is one of the key factors in student satisfaction (Yang & Durrington, 2010).

In keeping with the goal of increasing the quality of teaching and learning, standards for excellence in online teaching have begun defining what excellence in feedback means in practice. For example, excellence might mean "to review and respond to student posts with substantive comments throughout the week."

This tip suggests ways of providing substantive feedback by integrating personalized coaching. This tip also discusses ways of using personal and peer feedback to increase total feedback to keep students' growth on track, while saving faculty time.

You may want to start this tip with by scanning Table 8.1, which shows four different types of feedbacks, two purposes of feedback, and suggested tools for each type of feedback.

What Is Substantive Feedback?

First of all, what kind of feedback can be recognized as "substantive feedback"? Palloff and Pratt (2003) suggest that a substantive post by a student does one of the following: supports a position with evidence, begins a new topic while building on the previous post, critically reflects on the post, or moves the discussion in a new direction.

In contrast, an instructor's substantive feedback, we believe, is *individualized and actionable*. Substantive feedback clearly responds to the individual's work, while providing suggestions for taking action for increasing knowledge, skills, or attitudes. If substantive feedback is personal and actionable, it is natural that we combine substantive feedback with personalized coaching. The best coaching guides, advises, and models the specifics of a student's direction for growth. This type of feedback takes time and is most appreciated by students, as it is the most valuable to an individual. You may wonder how an online instructor can do this within reasonable time limits. This is where student responsibility plays a role. Effective formative assessment requires the student to share what is going on in his or her head, while sharing the results of a created work/assignment. This means that students might submit a statement assessing how they used and interpreted the assignment rubric, which can help an instructor interpret the student's level of engagement and understanding. Obviously, this type of interaction requires an environment of trust that the information primarily supports a student's growth.

Use of Self-Assessment and Peer Feedback Strategies and Tools

Two feedback types that are generally underutilized are self-assessment and peer feedback. Yet each of these can improve learning and reduce instructor workload. Both, however, require a level of maturity and metacognition on the part of learners. One definition of self-assessment is "the ability to be a realistic judge of one's own performance" (Cornell Center for Teaching Excellence, 2012). The benefit of self-assessment for learners is that they develop a greater awareness and appreciation of the created work or production. Self-assessment requires a rubric that clearly communicates expectations and a student who reads and understands the rubric, who can then judge or evaluate the work based on that rubric. This can set a relatively high bar and one that students might need help in developing skills to meet. The benefit to the instructor, once students know how to do this, is that a higher level of conversation about skill and content can be reached.

Peer feedback also requires that students understand both how to use rubrics and the content and goals of a course. When a course uses a project with multiple milestones—such as a proposal phase, a partial development phase, and a final published and presentation phase—peer feedback can be used to great advantage. For example, at the proposal phase, students can discuss and evaluate early ideas and offer and hear suggestions and the thinking behind project proposals. This builds understanding and an appreciation of the cognitive processes and work required for the

TABLE 8.1

Types and Purposes of Feedback Using Five Types of Tools

Type of Feedback	Purposes of Feedback		Tools for Five Types of Feedback				
	Focus on understanding and engagement with course concepts.	Focus on learner's growth areas.	Automated, canned feedback; e.g. testing	Asynchronous communication using announcements, forums	Combination of automated, personalized feedback using a database of comments and rubrics	Asynchronous feedback using e-mail and individualized comments on assignments based on rubrics.	Synchronous meetings using Skype, Google Hangout, Collaborate
Group feedback by instructor	Useful throughout course. Use announcements, forums and large synchronous gatherings.	Highlights of students' achieved and practice growth areas.	NA	Announcements and forum postings can provide quick alerts, feedback to course group or subgroups	NA	Instructor summarizes student's work, highlighting what is working or not, what is fantastic, insightful, etc.	Students share their created works to larger group(s) and instructor. Instructor provides feedback.
Personalized feedback by instructor or expert	Useful on created works and discussion postings.	Highlight individualized ways of growing, next steps.	NA	One-on-one communication by e-mail, phone, Skype, or social media tools	Takes time to develop, but more efficient, over time, for reinforcing core concepts, skills	Instructor "meets" with student via e-mail or other asynchronous tools.	Student and instructor meet one-on-one using phone or other synchronous meeting tools.

TABLE 8.1
(Continued)

	Purposes of Feedback*		Tools for Five Types of Feedback		
Peer feedback	With peer feedback, students can develop expertise and build networks.	Small 2- to 3-student teams do peer consulting on created works and postings.	NA	Small teams collaborate and consult and discuss on forums, blogs, journals, wikis	NA	Students consult, discuss, collaborate with each other.	Students consult, discuss, collaborate with each other and report, present back to others.
Self-review or assessment	Students can review, reflect, and create.	Students review, revise, edit, and share created products.	NA	Students practice, develop confidence and speed on basic content data	NA	Students use rubrics to self-evaluate, then share results with peers and instructor.	NA

* Purposes of feedback might include a third category, that of building community.

Source: Boettcher, J. V. (2015).

expressive output of each phase of a project. This means that students and instructors all become quite familiar with projects and students' skills, so that feedback and assessment take much less time, while providing much deeper understanding and joy in the development of expertise.

Purposes and Types of Feedback and the Tools

A critical element of any course is the assessment plan. Providing feedback for course assignments is a major time commitment for instructors. Using Table 8.1 can help you design an assessment plan with maximum substantive feedback and reasonable time expectations.

Deciding What to Do Next in Feedback Practices

Developing expertise in feedback is challenging, as the demands of students and time are so great and the literature and research can be overwhelming. Using a mix of feedback, as suggested earlier, is the best starting point. Here are two starting points to explore when making more decisions about your feedback practices.

1. Cornell University Center for Teaching Excellence. Assessing Student Learning (http://cte.cornell.edu/teaching-ideas/assessing-student-learning/index.html). This site features short descriptions of seven assessment topics, such as Using Rubrics, Self-Assessment, Peer Assessment, and What Do Students Already Know.

2. Center for the Study of Higher Education at the University of Melbourne, Australia. Good Feedback Practices: Prompts and guidelines for reviewing and enhancing feedback for students (http://www.cshe.unimelb.edu.au/resources_teach/assessment/docs/Good_Feedback_Practices_2014.pdf).

LM Tip 8: Rubrics for Analyzing Critical Thinking

This tip answers these questions:

- What are the four levels of proficiency for critical thinking skills?

- How can I create instructions for assignments that encourage critical thinking skills?

Earlier tips in the course beginnings chapter suggested that the best discussion questions invite reflection and responses from students. Every success is often followed by another challenge. If you have developed a very effective post question and the students start responding thoughtfully and expansively, your existing rubric for analyzing the discussions might not be as robust as you would like it to be.

Three important rubrics for analyzing critical thinking follow in this tip. Choosing which to include was difficult, but these are good starting points. These can be used as a basis for developing or adapting your new or existing rubrics.

The VALUE Critical Thinking Rubric

The first rubric is one of the VALUE rubrics developed by teams of faculty experts organized by the Association of American Colleges and Universities (https://www.aacu.org/value-rubrics). The VALUE rubric for Critical Thinking offers this definition:

Critical thinking is a habit of mind characterized by the comprehensive exploration of issues, ideas, artifacts, and events before accepting or formulating an opinion or conclusion.

The definition is useful in clarifying that critical thinking is a series of steps and not just a single event. It includes exploring issues and then making decisions. The VALUE rubric has five criteria: (1) explanation of issues; (2) evidence—selecting and using information to investigate a point of view or conclusion; (3) influence of context and assumptions; (4) student's position—perspective, thesis/hypothesis; (5) conclusions and related outcomes—implications and consequences. This rubric is available at the organization's website at https://www.aacu.org/value/rubrics/critical-thinking. Additional rubrics addressing problem-solving, teamwork, inquiry and analysis, and quantitative and information literacy are also at this site. While the site states that the rubrics are "intended for institutional-level use in evaluating and discussing student learning, not for grading," they can be very useful data points for developing rubrics.

The Guide to Rating Critical and Integrative Thinking

The second critical thinking rubric, A Guide to Rating Critical and Integrative Thinking (http://www.cpcc.edu/learningcollege/learning-outcomes/rubrics/WST_Rubric.pdf) was the result of a multiyear research project at Washington State University. It uses a four-point scale with this range: no/limited proficiency, some proficiency, proficiency, and high proficiency on criteria relevant to critical thinking. Here are the seven criteria for evaluating a learner's progress in developing critical thinking skills:

1. Identifies, summarizes and appropriately reformulates the problem, question, or issue

2. Identifies and considers the influence of context and assumptions

3. Develops, presents, and communicates his or her own perspective, hypothesis, or position

4. Presents, assesses, and analyzes appropriate supporting data/evidence

5. Integrates issue using other (disciplinary) perspectives and positions

6. Identifies and assesses conclusions, implications, and consequences

7. Communicates effectively

These are the desired critical thinking skills for learners; they are independent of any particular discipline or course of study. Here is a link to a rubric that expands and builds on this basic set of seven criteria: General Education Critical Thinking Rubric (short version), Northeastern Illinois University (https://www.etsu.edu/cbat/economics/documents/ NIU_Critical_Thinking-short.pdf).

Example Statements of Three Levels of Thinking on Issues

This guide to rating critical thinking goes beyond listing criteria: it expands each criterion and lists examples of the types of evidence pointing to stages of critical thinking skills: emerging, developing, and mastering. These example statements can be used to measure the maturity of a student's critical thinking skills. Table 8.2 shows examples of these three stages for critical thinking criterion 5.

TABLE 8.2

Examples of Critical Thinking Criterion 5: Integrates Issues Using Other Perspectives and Positions

Stage 1: Emerging critical thinking

- Deals with a single perspective and fails to discuss others' perspectives.
- Adopts a single idea or limited ideas with little question. If more than one idea is presented, alternatives are not integrated.

Stage 2: Developing critical thinking

- Begins to relate alternative views to qualify analysis.

Stage 3: Mastering critical thinking

- Addresses others' perspectives and additional diverse perspectives drawn from outside information to qualify analysis.
- Integrates own and others' ideas in a complex process of judgment and justification. Clearly justifies own view while respecting views of others.

Source: Washington State University (2006).

The Socratic Questioning Rubric

The characteristics of Socratic questioning described in other tips are useful for input into the design of critical thinking rubrics. The website of the Center for Critical Thinking and Moral Critique (www.criticalthinking. org) is an excellent resource. With minimal work, you can use some or all of the items in these critical thinking rubrics to develop your own rubrics and instructions for assignments. You can include examples from the rubric in your teaching instructions and grading rubrics to make your expectations of the students clear and explicit.

A web search on critical thinking rubrics quickly reveals many additional resources. Here is a good starting point: http://www.etsu.edu/cbat/economics/RubricExCriticalThinking.aspx.

Why Rubrics Are Catching On: Nine Advantages

The advantages of rubrics are many. Here is a list of nine advantages identified by higher education assessment expert Linda Suskie in her 2009 book, *Assessing Student Learning*, (2nd ed.) These advantages share a common theme of clear expectations, a focus on student growth, and efficiency for both faculty and students.

1. Rubrics help clarify vague, fuzzy goals.

2. Rubrics help students understand your expectations.

3. Rubrics can help students improve themselves.

4. Rubrics can inspire better student performance.

5. Rubrics make scoring easier and faster.

6. Rubrics make scoring more accurate, unbiased, and consistent.

7. Rubrics improve feedback to students.

8. Rubrics reduce arguments with students.

9. Rubrics improve feedback to faculty and staff.

Assessing Learning as You Go with Projects

Projects are excellent learning activities. Projects stimulate learners' thinking so they integrate and consolidate content knowledge into their own knowledge structures. Projects are by their very nature somewhat messy, involving false starts and often requiring iterations and revisions. Acknowledging the messiness of projects from the start helps everyone be realistic while learning.

LM Tip 9: Customizing and Personalizing Learning Projects

This tip answers these questions:

- How much flexibility for student choice should be designed into project assignments?
- What are some guidelines for project teams?
- What are the three components of a task model for a course project?

During a faculty workshop celebrating ten years of a faculty support center, a faculty member in charge of an online master's degree program in nursing administration had a question regarding teams. His program had been online for almost five years and was doing very well, but he was looking for ideas on the design of team projects. One of the courses had a significant team project, with the students working in groups of five. The feedback from the students was that the team project didn't work well. Some of the problems centered on communication challenges and how difficult it was to coordinate the team across distance, work, and family responsibilities; other problems centered on appropriate sharing of roles and responsibilities; still others focused on the choice of topics that didn't quite fit. And then of course there is the ever-present challenge of team evaluations.

Have you faced similar quandaries? How might you change project requirements to accommodate learners' interests and learning conditions while still respecting the performance goals of a course? Here are some guidelines and hints for developing project requirements with built-in flexibility.

Guidelines for Developing Project Requirements

Reduce the Number of Team Members or Vary the Size of the Teams

Striving for consistency and fairness is important, but there is no reason that all groups need to be the same size. Projects can usually be adapted quite easily to varying sizes, and the learners can be responsible for proposing how they will do that. So the default project team size might be three or four learners, but those who want to do projects in groups of two or five, or even alone, can propose a revised project for approval.

One good place to communicate flexibility regarding teams is in the project description. The project description provides an overview of the course project, including the learning goals for the project, dates, and reporting processes. As part of this overview, you can indicate flexibility in the team size, giving students the responsibility of preparing a revised project team plan for approval by a specified date—probably a week earlier than the initial proposal date, to leave time for a conference or negotiation with the instructor. Recall that your directions to the students are a key component of your teaching presence, and that it is hard to be overly explicit about processes and requirements.

We like to recommend team assignments of just two or three members, as this reduces the challenges of communications, meetings, and roles, and also increases the input from each of the members.

Broaden the List of Possible Topics for the Project

Many online and blended learners are working adults and have preferences and interests that influence their choice of project and commitment to course requirements. Just as providing flexibility in team size is important, so is flexibility in the choice of a topic. Early in the course, even in the first two weeks, focus the students on choosing a topic and developing a proposal for their course project. One strategy that increases dialogue is to have the students post their project proposals in a forum, blog, or wiki. This makes it easy to invite comments and recommendations from the other students.

For faculty, the most important reason for having a course project is that a project is a focused and complex type of learning experience that engages students in the course content, helping them to consolidate concepts and make meaningful connections, and aiding in their achieving the course performance goals. A course project is also a primary tool for assessing online learning because high-stakes proctored tests are not generally part of an assessment plan for online courses.

For students, the most important part of a project (other than meeting course requirements) is doing something that will be meaningful to them in their current or future lives. A student working on a meaningful, relevant project usually willingly and enthusiastically expands the time and energy invested in it. For employers who are providing tuition aid, project choices that have positive and visible ripple effects in the workplace are also a win-win scenario, creating a closer relationship with a program or institution.

Describing the Course Project: The Task Model

Task model is a term that captures the three variables of any assessment task: (1) the key features of the task, such as the content area and the level of difficulty or complexity; (2) the directions provided to the learner; and (3) the expected work product that "allows one to observe the students' performance" (Gibson & Swan, 2006). Effective task models describe the expected work product in general terms, leaving room for learners to customize and personalize learning by selecting how and by what means they will complete the work product. The task model requires that directions be clear and explicit about the need for a professional end product while still providing flexibility and choice for learners.

Complement the Task Model Guidelines with Process Guidelines

Course projects have many purposes relating to content acquisition and integration, but another important goal is developing the cross-functional skills of project planning, teamwork, and project management. Thus, providing guidelines and coaching for the process of completing projects is as important as the directions and explicit guidance on the task model for the project. The skills developed from a process model are often among the most useful learning outcomes.

Encourage Course Projects That Combine Challenge, Confidence, and Interest

Vygotsky's zone of proximal development (ZPD) is a good principle to guide us in how flexible we might want to be in the design of course projects. Recall that the ZPD defines the space that the learner is ready to develop into useful and independent knowledge and skill. Ideally, if the project task model is sufficiently flexible, learners can define and select a project that fits their personal zone of proximal development. Because this zone of learning readiness combines a confidence level with a challenge level, learners naturally gravitate to a project that more or less fits their learning needs. A key role of the faculty mentor is to ensure a good choice and guide learners to a project fit that combines challenge and know-how. The time it takes to ensure this fit will be well spent.

To determine whether a project is a good fit, ask if the learners are doing it mostly for the teacher or for themselves and whether the student cares enough about the work to make a significant investment in it. These questions help to balance the trade-off between gathering evidence of learning and a product that will be of lasting value to learners (Gibson & Swan, 2006).

The process of fitting the project to the learners and to the course goals and content simultaneously takes time and energy, but the result is committed, enthusiastic, and customized learning that can also be shared with the other students.

LM Tip 10: Managing and Facilitating Group Projects

This tip answers questions such as these:

- What are some simple guidelines for facilitating group projects to ensure that all students contribute to the project?

- How many project checkpoints are recommended?

- What communication and presentation tools work well for students when working on projects?

- What should I do if teams aren't working well together?

This tip provides suggestions for matching the appropriate tools for different stages of group projects and techniques for helping to ensure that students stay on schedule.

Monitoring and Guiding Group Projects

With project work, it is important to check regularly with each project team to ensure that everyone is participating and that the project is moving along. Here are a few suggestions for doing this monitoring and guiding. The suggestions also work well for individual projects.

- If students are working in groups on a project, set up a group space online as a place for students to share ideas, resources, and drafts of their projects. This group space might be a blog, a wiki, or a group discussion forum. If you have offered the flexibility of learners to do a project on their own, it is still recommended that the learner have a personal space such as a blog or discussion space for capturing and tracking project progress. Learners can then invite classmates to this project space for comments, suggestions, and brainstorming.

- Establish a minimum of three checkpoints. The first checkpoint is a project proposal that describes a project's goals and purposes; the second is a project design or definition that serves as a blueprint for the project, plus a set of initial or probable resources for the project; and the final checkpoint is the project paper or presentation. Other useful checkpoint products might be a team task schedule, an ongoing summary of discussions and decisions, and an outline of final project components.

- Monitor the team project space, and make comments or suggestions as appropriate. If the group seems to be proceeding appropriately, you can offer affirmation or challenges. If little progress is evident, you can ask what questions they might have or suggest a conference call or live classroom meeting. Also, there are useful team tools in most LMS that enable you to monitor and track team participation and activity, such as those that track discussion participation in group areas.

- Provide reminders of the schedule using a milestones approach—for example: "We are now halfway through the time allotted for the project, so you should have completed the following . . ." or "The project proposal or design is due by Friday of next week, so you should have met with your team and have a draft of your sections under way" or "If you would like feedback at this time, let's meet in the open forum space."

One principle for facilitating online projects is to provide enough instructor presence to remind team members that their activities and progress are not invisible to you and yet not provide so much presence that the project shifts from being team led to instructor led.

It is easy for students to get lost in the process of group work, especially in larger groups. One team member could be the project or group manager; this person directs the project and monitors to ensure that each student is working on his or her particular role or responsibility and doesn't get lost. This is a good leadership role.

Communication and Presentation Tools

Synchronous tools are particularly useful in the early stages of a project when groups need to reach consensus as quickly as possible about project content and tasks. Simple low-tech conference calls sometimes can be the best tool for group formation and task negotiations. Synchronous communication tools such as the telephone and online conferencing tools such as Skype (www.skype.com) are free, easy to use, and familiar to almost everyone.

Once the team has organized itself, asynchronous tools such as the discussion forums, wikis, and blogs are useful for sharing progress and resources, collaborative writing, and critical reviews by team members and other teams. Students can also use Google Docs as preliminary work sharing spaces for Word documents, spreadsheets, and presentations (https://www.google.com/docs/about/).

Many of these tools are free and readily accessible. Students may have their favorite tools to use as well: they may want to chat, Tweet, or instant message. So we recommend focusing on the task—the project—and letting the students decide which communication tools work best for them. Provide help and suggestions as needed or requested.

When learners are ready for reviews of their proposals before presenting projects to the larger group, asynchronous tools work well so that everyone in the course has an opportunity to review the projects. Group project presentations can be made synchronous with the use of live classrooms or a combination of audio and video conferencing tools.

Managing Groups: Additional Thoughts

When problems arise with one of the project groups—and the law of averages pretty much ensures this will happen at some point—a set of guidelines for students as to how to proceed will be useful. The usual rule of thumb is that the problems are best resolved within the group itself. Resolution by the faculty member should be reserved for the most difficult problems—those the group cannot come to terms with by itself. Faculty, of course, can be asked general questions to help guide the students as they work through difficulties, but the best outcome is for the group to resolve its problems. A good resource for both faculty and students working in teams is *Building Blocks for Teams* (http://archive.tlt.psu.edu/suggestions/teams/student/) from the Teaching and Learning with Technology Group at Penn State (2001–2012). You can post this resource in the same folder or space as the group project directions and rubrics. The resources for remotely collaborating continue to improve in both functionality and ease of use. The best advice for selecting technology tools today is to pick a tool that is available and works, and simply go with it. This can avoid you or your students wasting time making decisions concerning virtually identical tools.

LM Tip 11: Assessing Group Projects

This tip answers these questions:

- How do I assess group projects?
- Is there a way to have students participate in the review and grading of projects?

This tip focuses on strategies for assessing group projects. A common thread among all projects, whether individual or group, is that they are powerful and satisfying teaching and learning experiences. Projects provide an opportunity for students to customize course performance goals to their particular life and work goals, making the learning experience meaningful and satisfying. Papers, presentations, interviews, podcasts, talk shows, and other projects also make students' thinking and learning visible. They require students to link the new content to their existing knowledge, creating a larger networked knowledge base and structure.

Techniques for Assessing Group Projects

Online and blended course group projects can be assessed in much the same way that they are assessed in classroom environments. However, our recommendation is to assess both the process and the final product. The process includes the interim milestones such as a project proposal and the project design. Assessment of these interim stages mirrors professional processes more closely and provides an opportunity for peer review (Moallem, 2005). Interim reviews thus become part of the dialogue of the learning community, and comments can tap into the collective thinking and expertise of the group. The processes in the planning and the execution of the project then become part of the course content and goals.

The most useful tool in assessing group projects is the project grading rubric that you develop at the same time that you create and design the task model for the project. By referring to the rubric in your reviews and comments to the students, you help to ensure students' awareness and understanding and minimize unpleasant surprises. Here are some of the criteria areas that you may want to consider; they include metrics for the processes of teamwork and the project, as well as the completed product:

- The process of how the team worked. For example, how effective were the team members in participating in group formation, task definition and progress, and finished product?

- The end product. How well did the team execute the design for the project, and how well did the project achieve the intended goals and objectives? Criteria such as innovativeness, thoroughness, readiness for action, and professionalism might be considered.

- The presentation of the product to the larger group. Encourage the students to branch into a varied set of presentation techniques that might feature interviews and multimedia news releases as well as websites.

- Participation in the peer reviews and evaluations of the product and responsiveness to comments.

More About Peer Reviews by Students

An effective tool for encouraging effective and appropriate participation in teams is the peer review. Ideally, this is designed as an integral step in the project. It can be most useful while the project is still in the proposal or design phase. Peer review of the final project also helps with the final assessment and grading of the students addressing both process and product perspectives. Involving students in the process of review increases networking and collaboration among them and deepens the peer-to-peer dialogue that contributes to a vibrant learning community. Students often need coaching in the process of doing peer reviews, and the skills of evaluation and honest and fair review of work are valuable cross-functional skills. Exhibit 8.1 provides a sample peer assessment form that you may wish to adapt to the nature of the particular project in your course.

EXHIBIT 8.1

Team Member Evaluation Form

Team member name:

Directions: Using your best objective, fair professional analysis, complete the following evaluation form concerning your team member's performance on your team project.

1. The LEVEL of effort this team member gave toward the project was . . .

Below Expectation   Met Expectation   Above Expectation

2. The QUALITY of that effort was . . .

Below Expectation   Met Expectation   Above Expectation

3. The INPUT this team member contributed to the team discussions was . . .

Below Expectation   Met Expectation   Above Expectation

4. How would you rate this team member's level of participation?

Below Expectation   Met Expectation   Above Expectation

5. How would you rate this team member's level of time on the project?

Below Expectation   Met Expectation   Above Expectation

6. This team member participated in team meetings and work:

Below Expectations   As Expected

7. This team member met team deadlines:

Below Expectations   As Expected

8. This team member's OVERALL work and contribution to this project was . . .

Below Group Grade   Same as Group Grade   Above Group Grade

9. Additional comments regarding this team member's work on this presentation:

Each member should submit a form for every team member as well as themselves. Question 8 is really the crucial question. Sometimes a team member may be disgruntled about a particular behavior of a teammate but overall still rates the team member as having done a good job. Only in those cases that the team feels that the grade should be lowered is it good to consider doing so.

A useful resource for more detail about assessing group projects is *Assessing Group Work* (O'Neill, 2013) from the University College, Dublin, Ireland. Here is a sampling of strategies:

- All students get the same mark for the product of the group; then peers assess contributions to the process with a maximum of ten; for example, a = 23 + 9, b = 23 + 4, c = 23 + 7.

- All students get the same mark for original task and then get different marks for an additional or separate task or responsibility, or for their individual contribution to a presentation event.

Another good starting point for assessing group work is *Assessing Group Tasks* (Isaacs, 2002) at the University of Queensland. This document addresses topics such as the following:

- When should group tasks be assessed?
- Best practices in the assessment of group tasks
- Examples and theory
- Assigning marks to individuals versus the group as a whole
- Self- and peer assessment
- Freeloading and plagiarism
- The logistics of forming groups

The University of Melbourne also hosts the Graduate Centre for the Study of Higher Education (GCSHE) (http://melbourne-cshe.unimelb.edu.au/__data/assets/pdf_file/0011/1489169/Good_Feedback_Practices_2014.pdf), another good starting point. The most comprehensive of all sites on assessment is the Assessment Commons site (www.assessmentcommons.org). It currently contains about 1,000 links, including about 375 college and university assessment sites.

LM Tip 12: Four Effective Practices During Project Time

This tip answers these questions:

- What types of support do students most value during project time?
- How flexible should the projects be in customizing and personalizing them to learners' interests?
- How closely should an instructor monitor project progress?

As a course reaches the halfway point and beyond, work on projects, papers, and presentations picks up steam. Project time for students can be stressful, as the balance of course work shifts from receptive or exploring activities to creative, productive work. And of course learners are always balancing work, life, and learning responsibilities. This is a time to be sure to stay in close touch with your students. A few learners always need additional guidance, support, and encouragement at this time.

This is a good time to stop and check yourself on four best practices to guide you and your students through these creative project and teamwork experiences.

1. Be Proactive and Help Learners Get Unstuck on Projects

The most difficult part of many learning tasks is getting started. Large projects require skill at planning, segmenting, and organizing. Finding planning and collaborative time with other busy people can also present barriers. For working adults and professionals, who often turn to their course work in 15- to 30-minute segments (listening to podcasts while jogging, reading while waiting for children or between appointments), finding time to do project work that requires a dedicated effort can be a challenge. One of us used to enjoy flying because it offered the best uninterrupted thinking time.

One best practice during project time focuses on techniques for supporting and encouraging students during this time. A technique recently popularized in the business arena (Allen, 2015) is being explicit about answering the question: "What is your next step? And then what is the next step after that?" Often students find that their next step is something they can do while doing other things, and that one of their next steps is planning for learning time, getting access to a resource, or arranging a meeting.

Another technique for getting unstuck on getting started is described in the title of a book by Brian Tracy (2007): *Eat That Frog! 21 Great Ways to Stop Procrastinating and Get More Done in Less Time!* The message behind this book is, "If you eat a live frog first thing each morning you'll have the satisfaction of knowing it's probably the worst thing you'll do all day." We're not certain we agree with that, but certainly finding a way to get started on a complex task is good to do first thing in the morning if you can. A good alternative is putting it at the top of your "learning time" list. In fact, Tracy recommends that, when starting a project, the instructor build a plan of all the steps in the projects and then organize them by priority and sequence. Sometimes doing this plan is the worst "frog" of all, but it can make the difference in getting started well.

Here are a few more ideas to help students get started on projects or get unstuck if they have made a good start but then hit a wall:

- Ask students to share their questions, difficulties, and successes with their ongoing papers and projects. Sometimes they answer their own questions once they formulate them.

- Ask your students what their next one, two, or three steps on their project are.

- Ask how their teams are working, what they are working on now, and what they plan on doing next. This is a good time to reinforce the feeling of a learning community. Encourage the teams to share templates, process tools, and good ideas. The goal is for everyone in the learning community to succeed.

- Remind students about the resources, tools, processes, and rubrics that you developed to guide them through the tasks. As they share what helps them, you can expand that set of resources for future students.

- Encourage learners to customize and personalize their projects.

Consider the three types of content in a course: (1) prepackaged authoritative content (books, resources, tools), (2) director-mentor faculty teaching presence content that guides and supports learners through the course, and (3) performance content that is generated by the learners in the process of learning.

An ideal time to personalize and customize the performance content so that it is maximally useful and of most interest to learners is when they are working on projects. Encouraging them to select and perform learning tasks that are of most interest and use to them is also healthy, because it reduces their level of anxiety about how much time they are spending on their course work.

2. Coach Learners on Personalizing Their Projects

If you have used a three- or four-milestone approach of proposal and design steps in the project, you have a built-in opportunity to coach students to be wise about their selection of their project.

Defining projects and papers so they can be most useful to an individual and to a larger, potentially external group can be an excellent community brainstorming activity. Peer review of proposals also means open and public discussion about how best to personalize and customize a project. Once students have identified a project that meets these characteristics, they may find it useful to post or otherwise share in a discussion forum why they have made the selection and how they feel it will be useful to them. This can have the ripple effect of reminding the other learners in the community about potential applications that they may not have considered.

3. Ask Learners to Post Progress Reports or Updates

The best practice of posting progress reports complements the practice of learners' identifying their next step. As students are planning out a project, creating a task list, finding a needed or seminal resource, or completing one of the steps in an assignment, openly sharing that success is a way to build community. As they share their completed steps and identify their next steps, other students often praise, encourage, and suggest, building a stronger network of learners. One habit that I (Judith) have developed over the years is to always pause before putting a project away, whether it is an article, chapter, or teaching or quilting project, and make some notes about my next steps. When I return to the project, sometimes after a significant delay, my next step is right there for me. This is not foolproof, but it works more often than not and always saves time. In fact, sometimes my subconscious has been working on the next step during the project pause.

4. Communicate Your Availability and Schedule

Be sure to continue your use of the announcement tool and other communication channels to let students know your schedule. Another good strategy is to schedule open question-and-answer times by phone, e-mail, chat, or live classroom. Students then can feel comfortable about contacting you during those times, knowing that they are not intruding on your personal time.

Students may be so overwhelmed that they may not even be able to frame questions with ease, but setting a time and a place to talk some ideas through might work for them. Setting times and places when you will be more or less available is comforting even if learners do not make use of them. Also, be sure to be present on the discussion board. Students do want to hear your expert perspective while exploring the perspectives of the other students.

Community Empowerment and Social Networking

These next tips on community empowerment and social networking highlight some of the networking and social learning power possible with discussion forums, blogs, and wikis.

LM Tip 13: Course Middles and Muddles: Souped-Up Conversations That Help Build Community

This tip answers these questions:

- How can you energize your learners in the late middle when enthusiasm and energies often begin to lag?

- What are some strategies for encouraging challenging questions and substantive knowledge building?

It is easy to get bogged down in course middles. Lots of learning activities are in progress, but you may not feel the students are doing any lasting learning. Or you may be feeling that the amount of interaction and discussion is rote and uninspiring and that everyone is just going through the motions. How can you energize your learners at this time? Here are three ideas for stirring up your course middles.

Team Up for Course Discussions for a Week

Group your students into teams of two for one discussion week. Working in a pair means that the students will collaborate and discuss a topic in more depth. To do this, create a set of three or four open-ended questions for the week, and have each team select a topic to explore. Then have the students post the results of their collaboration by Friday of that week. This activity generally results in a set of more elaborate postings than usual. For the following week, select one or more of those threads for the entire class to respond to and extend.

Why do this? One of the more difficult behaviors to cultivate in students is effectively responding to their peers' comments. From a student's perspective, it is more efficient and takes less time to just prepare his or her own post and then exit the online classroom. This pairing exercise structures a learning task that requires students to respond to, comment on, and analyze the comments and responses of their peers.

In the three-stage model of building community (Brown, 2001), stage 2 requires a feeling of "sharedness." Brown found that that feeling of having shared an experience in online classes often follows a "long, thoughtful, threaded discussion on a subject of importance after which participants felt both personal satisfaction and kinship." It is this type of discussion that we want to be working toward for students. And this often does take time. Sometimes you need to be patient and provide time for exploration and even for clearing up confusion.

Plan for Time for Learners to Develop the Tough Questions

Sometimes the most difficult cognitive work is figuring out what the question is, and this frequently happens as we approach the middle and muddled part of a course. By this point, students' heads are "getting filled up to overflowing," but they don't know what they know or don't know. There's a lot of stuff in their minds, but no framework or set of relationships that helps it all come together to make sense. Students may know that they have covered a lot of material and the multiple-choice questions weren't too hard. But they probably wonder how they will be able to use this knowledge.

This is a good time to challenge the students to propose and deal with difficult questions. Here are some ideas:

- Post a statement, article, scenario, or video news clip on the discussion forum and ask students to generate a set of data-gathering questions that might help address that problem.

- Set up a discussion forum for students to describe problems that now seem easy and problems that still stump them.

- Establish an open forum, blog, or wiki for a week, and have the students generate questions and problems related to the readings. Or set up a space in Facebook, Flickr, or the latest, best video service for students to submit photos that might help in solving a problem or answering a question.

- Encourage students to question the information from their latest internet search. They might ask, "Who asserted this?" "What are this person's credentials?" "Who had the opportunity to critique this idea?" "Who supports and who disagrees with it?" (Bruckman, 2005, p. 36).

LM Tip 14: Using Social Networking Techniques to Build a Learning Community

This tip answers questions such as these:

- What are social networking tools?

- How can social networking tools help build community?

- What performance goals can blogs, wikis, and other social networking tools help learners to achieve?

Social networking tools are digital applications that make it easy to share and interact with others online. Some of the most popular sites are

Facebook and LinkedIn, Twitter, and photo and video sites such as Flickr and YouTube.

These sites use applications that go beyond the first wave of internet applications, which mostly just displayed and organized data. These tools are creating a new communications milieu created and extended by users.

This means that almost all learners, regardless of age or circumstance, are familiar with how these applications make it easy to create, share, and stay in touch with users globally. The online learning environment will seem foreign and strange if we do not integrate some of these same social networking techniques into our courses.

Social Networking Strategy for Projects

This learning strategy incorporates a social networking component and works well with course projects, personal or course blogs, or other more complex assignments. This strategy can use a discussion forum, a blog tool, Facebook, or other tool of their choice.

1. Create a personal project blog or discussion forum for each student.

2. Each student posts a project topic or abstract as the first proposed phase of a course project.

3. Students, from a designated small group or the class as a whole, review the project abstract and add comments, ideas, and suggestions and offer additional resources, adaptations, or cautions. This is similar to the comment and tagging features of the photo-sharing sites such as Flickr or blogs of all types. All comments become part of an individual project as it evolves.

4. Each student responds and makes changes and tweaks to the project as appropriate.

5. The faculty member blogs and comments on the project progress and the learners' input. This can be private or public or a combination of both.

6. Each student integrates the ideas and suggestions as appropriate into his or her project. Students also post regular notes that update the project status similar to the "What's on your mind?" Update Status feature on Facebook. This update can be something as simple as, "I am researching some of the suggestions this week" or "I am not making much progress right now."

7. Each student posts the completed project as required by the course assignment.

8. Each student's group or class members then review or see the final product and again make comments or evaluations.

This strategy can work for individuals or small groups. The cycle of posting and commenting is repeated, depending on the number of project phases or the complexity of the project. Cycles of posting and commenting shift the project from being the sole production by one student to a collaborative group project.

Characteristics of the Social Networking Tools

Here are a few observations about using blogs, wikis, journals, and discussion boards for building community:

- Using a blog for project planning and progress is almost like a student's private journal in that it is individually "owned" and created by one student. It is the student's own place, similar to one's own space in Facebook. But it is social because it can be open for review, comment, and adaptation. The student can invite and respond to comments and suggestions. With this type of blog project, there is an end product—a project report, paper, or presentation of some ilk—just as with a wiki.

- These tools share characteristics of a journal in that they are authored over time and track and record activities and progress.

- Tools such as blogs or discussion forums are organized chronologically from first posting to most recent or from most recent to earlier postings.

- Tools such as blogs, wikis, and discussion boards have the ability to include media of all types, such as pictures, video, text, and links.

Using social networking apps and practices in your course encourages peer interaction and community-building. It is likely that learners are comfortable with these apps and pleased that they are part of their learning environment. Social networking apps encourage regular, daily, and even hourly checking in and commenting and seeing where everyone is and what they are doing and thinking. This can be very useful and supportive of project work. Sharing where they are in a project and what they are thinking of doing next encourages awareness of their own thinking and working strategies (Bonk & Khoo, 2014; Rinderle & Hampson, 2014; Johnson, Adams Becker, Estrada, & Freeman, 2015).

The cycles of comments and responses also promote community because students no longer focus solely on their own projects. Through their review and support of their fellow learners, they develop ownership and critical thinking about many of the other projects. The best part of this approach is the social aspect of learning and creativity that it promotes. It also provides an inside view of an individual's knowledge and skill development for formative and growth purposes.

Essential Features of Social Networking Tools: Interconnectivity and Interactivity

One of the most fundamental truths about learning is that it is active, specific, and internal to the learner. Social networking tools empower learners to comment on and develop their own work and build on the work of peers and experts. These tools enable real-time and asynchronous collaboration and encourage, stimulate, and motivate learners to create new content and support and challenge each other in the process.

Most learning systems now have blog, wiki, and voice tools as part of their systems. Be sure to select and try one tool to see how it can support your course performance goals. The basic principle of these tools is that learners add value to the community learning experience. This means that you learn more too.

The next wave of applications, now on the horizon, is part of what is being called the "semantic web," or Web 3.0. The critical feature of this next wave of apps is that applications will not only have the power to display information and help to create information. Web 3.0 tools will also be able to extract embedded meaning and actively select pages that are likely of greater interest and use. This means we will be able to search and find faster, better, and more relevant and coherent information. The apps in the Web 2.0 wave helped build community; the apps in Web 3.0 wave will help build knowledge (Ohler, 2008).

LM Tip 15: Experts: A Touch of Spice

This tip answers questions such as these:

- What are some good times for inviting experts to a course?
- Where can I find experts?
- What types of expert learning events engage learners?

Invited experts can add a bit of spice to your course for you and your students. Most courses by necessity are planned well in advance and often use a textbook or a set of published readings and content in a field or discipline. These resources, together with the learning goals, provide the framework for the set of course experiences. Yet many of our most exciting experiences occur when we see how course content is impacting current events. This is what guest experts can bring to a course: customized and authentic application of course content as embodied in a real personality within an authentic career experience.

Expert guests also provide a change of pace for a large group community experience. Most faculty bring expertise from a particular field of knowledge; other authoritative voices come from the textbook and other resources, such as readings and podcasts. Inviting an expert provides another perspective for core concept knowledge, particularly as used within a specific context.

Bringing an expert into your course community also creates learning opportunities prior to, during, and after the experts' participation. Prior to the expert's visit, learners can research the person, organization, and subject of that person's expertise. During the event, students have a chance to inquire and dialogue. After the expert interaction, learners can be challenged to integrate the expert's perspective with the other course content. Experts often have wisdom that clarifies why and how the content matters.

Expert events help in the community-building process of a course as well. We enjoy the feelings of anticipation prior to a novel event. It is stimulating getting ready to be good hosts, preparing challenging intellectual inquiries, sharing the event experience, and then following up with the specific application of that intellectual inquiry.

By now you may be saying, "Yes, sounds like a good idea! Just how do I go about incorporating experts into my course?" Here are a few questions that you might have about how to incorporate experts into your course and some starting points for answers.

Is There a Preferred Time in the Course to Have an Expert Event?

Sometime in the second half of a course is usually a good time. By this time students have developed sufficient understanding and curiosity about a topic to prepare good interview questions. However, there are few hard-and-fast rules about inviting experts. Sometimes inviting an expert to pose significant challenges at the first part of a course can work well for advanced learners.

How Do I Go About Finding an Expert?

Experts are plentiful and often willing to participate as long as it doesn't take too much time. Serving as an invited expert is usually a pleasant and rewarding experience.

Colleagues who are part of your network are always good candidates for experts. As you become more experienced with using experts, search out national and even international experts. With online classroom technology, plain- old telephone conferences, and asynchronous discussion tools, experts can come from anywhere. Program graduates are an excellent source of experts. Alumni often have warm feelings for their institution and a natural affiliation with future graduates. Such invitations build ties back to the institution that are beneficial to all.

What Type of Content Is Good for an Expert?

You can set your own criteria, of course, but a good place to start is by focusing on one of the following areas:

- A core concept application. If you are working on scenarios with difficult leadership challenges, you may want to invite an expert who has personally experienced a difficult leadership challenge and can share some lessons learned and reinforce the need for flexibility and confidence.

- A current trend or development in a particular discipline. If a significant development in your field has occurred in the past six to twelve months—possibly in the area of impending legislation, managing response to economic conditions, significant natural events such as Hurricane Katrina and the subsequent support leadership, or new technology developments—invite an expert to share his or her perspective or analysis of that trend, event, or development.

- An area in which you have a particular strength or weakness. If you have a colleague you have worked with over time and with whom you share expertise, hold an event where you and your students can probe areas in greater depth with dialogue and debate. And if you have an area of relative weakness, try to identify an expert in that area to provide greater depth.

- You might also invite an expert in to listen to, judge, or evaluate one or two key team projects.

How Do I Set Up the Expert Event?

The best type of event is one that both feels comfortable to and challenges both experts and learners. Some of the possible structures are a mix of one or more of the following:

- A simple question-and answer-format. If the expert is sufficiently well known, the preparation can consist of a set of questions prepared by students and sent to the expert in advance. Years ago, Steve Jobs of Apple accepted a keynote invitation from a higher education technology group on the condition that he didn't have to prepare a talk. The format was a simple question-and-answer session. Of course this did mean that organizers had to prepare an appropriate and interesting set of questions.

- A magazine, journal, or other content or media resource that has been authored by the expert or features the expert, combined with the question-and-answer format.

- A short PowerPoint presentation (about ten minutes) that forms the basis for the conversation and dialogue.

- A podcast by an expert used as a base resource and then a conversation and discussion with the expert after all the students have listened to it and prepared questions.

- Experts can also be invited to be discussion forum leaders for a week. In this scenario the instructor serves as host or moderator and supports the dialogue of the expert with the students.

Generally it is important to prepare for the unexpected that can occur for an expert event. Something can always go wrong, so having a backup plan is highly recommended. This plan might be as simple as moving to a later day or time or week or substituting an article authored by the invited expert or a related resource, such as an equally relevant article, podcast, or archived presentation.

Are There Other Resources on Using Experts in Online Courses?

Here are the links to a two-part resource, "Guest Lecturers in the Online Environment," by Virgil Varvel of the Illinois Online Network.

- July/August 2001: Guest Lecturers in the Online Environment. Part 1 of 2. Learn the benefits of bringing in the outside lecture into your online courses (http://www.ion.uillinois.edu/resources/pointersclickers/2001_07/index.asp).

- September/October 2001: Guest Lecturers in the Online Environment. Part 2 of 2. Where can you find a good guest lecturer? What do students think about guest lecturers? (http://www.ion.uillinois.edu/resources/pointersclickers/2001_09/index.asp).

A professor in a graduate medical education program shared that he liked to use guest experts because "our learners are usually ready for variety in the latter part of a course, and because they can add expertise that we do not have ourselves" (Miller, 2014).

Summary—and What's Next

With the late middle of the course behind you, you probably have a set of mixed feelings. You may be feeling elated that some of your students obviously are doing very well and progressing on meaningful learning projects. At the same time you may be feeling a little disappointed that some students are still on the edge and that their projects may be only minimally successful. If this is your first online course, you are also probably feeling pleased at how the course has progressed but also anxious about the final weeks. This is all normal. Enjoy the range of experiences. In the next chapter the focus shifts to resolving the challenges of the final weeks.

Self-Directed Exercise /Application

Here are some suggestions for a faculty development activity:

- Design a collaborative activity that focuses on formulating problems for your course content.
- Write out the instructions for preparing to interview a guest expert.

- Develop your policies for feedback on the brief concept papers for your course and for the course projects.
- Develop a rubric for one or more of your assignments.

Chapter 9

Phase 4: Pruning, Reflecting, and Wrapping Up

THE CLOSING WEEKS of a course bring a mixture of feelings, ranging from concerns about getting everything done to feelings of relief, satisfaction, joy, and camaraderie. As an instructor, you want your students to be feeling confident about the new skills and knowledge they have acquired. You also want to be fair and efficient in your assessment of their learning.

In this phase of the course, your role as a coach should be front and center. This is the time that students are more in charge of their own learning and are contributing to the learning of others. Your teaching goal now is to help your students organize the course concepts and determine how they will likely use the skills and knowledge they are acquiring in their lives. In these closing weeks, you want to support your learners as they integrate their knowledge and reach some level of resolution with what they know now and want to know in the future.

Tips for the Closing Weeks

The tips in this chapter focus on complex cognitive growth, managing a vibrant and dynamic community, and wrapping up assessment and course projects.

There are two sets of tips for the closing weeks: Meaningful Projects and Presentations, and Preparing for the Course Wrap.

The first set focuses on strategies for managing, directing, and supporting meaningful projects and presentations. The strategies include learners' assuming leadership roles in the course community and determining how to tailor their learning to be most useful to themselves. The tips also address authentic problem solving, working with what-if scenarios, and strategies for achieving a stimulating and comfortable camaraderie within the course community. One of the tips describes concept mapping, also known as mind mapping, which asks learners to create a graphical representation or map of what they know, identifying the nodes, relationships, and dimensions of the course content.

The set of tips on course wraps addresses ways of planning and celebrating the closing experiences. Just as it is helpful to wrap up discussions and other assignments during the course, it is helpful to explicitly design closing wrap-up experiences for the course. One tip focuses on the pruning and reflecting processes of learning. These processes are natural to integrating knowledge and contributing to the cognitive growth of the course learning community. This tip on pruning provides a number of strategies for identifying core useful concepts that students can take away from a course. We know that no one can possibly remember everything from a course, so being explicit about what is known and not known helps learners organize and put their knowledge into perspective. Two tips in this set discuss celebrating the closing of a particular community and making plans for future gatherings and networking. The closing tip in this set focuses on the learner experience, encouraging learners to think critically about their course experience and in doing so, providing useful feedback for enhancing the course.

Here are the sets of closing weeks (CW) tips:

Meaningful Projects and Presentations

- **CW Tip 1:** Using What-If Scenarios: Flexing Our Minds with Possibilities
- **CW Tip 2:** Stage Three of a Learning Community: Stimulating and Comfortable Camaraderie
- **CW Tip 3:** Learners as Leaders
- **CW Tip 4:** Course Wrapping with Concept Mapping: Capturing Course Content Meaningfully
- **CW Tip 5:** Using Case Studies in Online Courses: Making Content Real

Preparing for the Course Wrap

- **CW Tip 6:** Pausing, Reflecting, and Pruning Strategies
- **CW Tip 7:** Closing Experiences: Wrapping Up a Course with Style

- **CW Tip 8:** Real-Time Closing Gatherings: Stories and Suggestions
- **CW Tip 9:** Debriefing Techniques: What One Change Would Students Recommend?

Meaningful Projects and Presentations

This set of tips suggests teaching strategies for managing, directing, and supporting meaningful projects and presentations. As learning is a constructive process, requiring time and energy and creativity from learners, projects are the learning activities in which students often find that it all comes together.

CW Tip 1: Using What-If Scenarios: Flexing Our Minds with Possibilities

This tip answers questions such as these:

- What are what-if scenarios?
- What are some examples of what-if scenarios?
- How do I design for these types of intense, collaborative activities?

Picture this. You are the manager of a large grocery store, but the number of new food products and variants—such as yogurt Cheerios, apple cinnamon Cheerios, milk, soymilks, almond milk, and varieties of organic products—seems endless. If only you had infinite shelf space. How would you manage it, and how would your customers navigate the space? Or picture a variant of our current political and philosophical worlds. In alternate history studies, historians ponder and explore scenarios that might have been if our familiar history was not so familiar. Some alternate history scenarios explore questions such as: "What if Socrates had died before his philosophy was written down by Plato?" (Hanson, 2002) or "What if FDR's life or circumstances had been different in the 20th century?" with seven different possible scenarios (Ward, 2002). Our students might suggest these what-ifs: "What would have happened if Martin Luther King Jr. had not been assassinated and become president?" "What if JFK had not been assassinated?" "What if we had never landed on the moon?" "What if Steve Jobs had never returned to Apple?"

In the case of the store manager wistfully desiring a world with infinite shelf space, this wish has virtually been granted, and a new world of niche culture is one of the ripple effects. This new world is persuasively described by Chris Anderson, an editor at *Wired* magazine, in *The Long Tail: Why the*

Future of Business Is Selling Less of More (2006). Anderson states that examples of infinite shelf space abound today. We have infinite shelf space for books, music, and other media, enabling businesses to profit from low-volume items desired by the specialized interests of consumers. One ripple effect of this phenomenon, Anderson argues, is that common culture will reshape itself into an array of infinite overlapping niche cultures. How the effects of this reshaping of mass culture will play out is unknown, but even a partial reshaping of mass culture will have significant effects as people become less and less familiar with the thinking of others.

Do you think that a scenario of infinite shelf space might have been the focus of a business course fifteen or twenty years ago? What types of scenarios might you want to use in your course today, looking out fifteen years or so to encourage thinking in new ways and of new possibilities?

This tip examines some possible uses of what-if scenarios in your course and when you might want to use them.

What Are What-If Scenarios?

What-if scenarios generally pose a question inquiring about a possible ripple effects if a significant event had either not happened or happened differently, as in the alternate history example presented earlier, or what might happen in the future, such as varying scenarios of the future of health care in the United States. What-if scenarios are a specific type of problem-solving experience that includes role-playing activities, simulations, and case studies. These types of activities engage students on both an intellectual and emotional level. These activities require higher cognitive workload as they research, evaluate and analyze, make decisions, observe results, and then make decisions dealing with the consequences of earlier decisions (Carnes, 2014).

Why Use What-If Scenarios?

Here are four reasons for using what-if scenarios in your course:

- Using what-if scenarios encourages spontaneity and flexibility in thinking. When a group explores these scenarios, they are basically dealing with fictionalized events. One requirement for this fiction, however, is that once a context has been established for a scenario, the happenings within the event must have internal consistency.

- What-if scenarios typically have possibilities rather than right or wrong answers. Devising scenarios is relatively straightforward because all scenarios, real or imagined, depend on a set of assumptions. Change the assumptions, and you have a new scenario. Have

Socrates die earlier, and his philosophy is not written down. Assume that you have fixed shelf space, or assume that you have infinite shelf space. Assume that gas will cost six dollars a gallon or, alternatively, two dollars a gallon. Change the assumptions, and then examine the possible consequences.

- Using what-if scenarios in your course often helps students develop confidence in what they know or don't know or might need to know of the course content and related areas. Exploring the assumptions behind the scenarios requires that students examine their own assumptions and knowledge structures, and clearly communicate what they think and why.

- Using what-if scenarios is often an excellent device for keeping the course content fresh for both faculty and students. It also offers ways of personalizing and customizing content.

Getting Started with What-If Scenarios

Here is an easy way to get started: Search out case studies in your field with ongoing challenges. Then change some of the variables and some of the assumptions. This initial step can be designed as a student activity. A team of two or three students can select a case study from a list you have created, identify the core assumptions, and suggest a different set of assumptions. If you want to control the design of a scenario, build your question for a group activity around a change in an influential figure in your discipline. In a leadership course, explore a scenario in which Al Gore was elected president in 2004 or John McCain was elected president in 2008. In biology, examine a scenario in which significant plant life is found on Mars.

CW Tip 2: Stage 3 of a Learning Community: Stimulating and Comfortable Camaraderie

This tip answers questions such as these:

- How do I know if the learning community has reached stage 2 or stage 3 in Brown's (2001) three-stage model of building community?

- Is it possible to reach the stage of stimulating and comfortable camaraderie in a single course term?

When a course is in its closing phase, it is wise to return to fundamental themes: community and collaboration. This tip revisits the development stages of a community and focuses on the characteristics of stage 3: reaching a state of stimulating and comfortable camaraderie.

Three Stages of Building Community

One of the earlier tips (LM Tip 13) referred to stage 2 of Brown's three-stage model. Here the stages are again, in summary.

Stage 1

Making friends online with students with whom we feel comfortable communicating.

Stage 2

Community conferment (acceptance and effective communication).

Stage 3

This is characterized by camaraderie. Student engagement is even more intense, as students are focusing, sharing, and working on projects, presentations, and course capstone experiences. Peer reviews and consulting on projects earlier in the course often drive a high level of commitment and mutual support.

Faculty Behaviors That Support Stage 3 Community-Building

Faculty behaviors that help a class move beyond the mutual acceptance and effective communication of stage 2 to the commitment and support of stage 3 include variations of the following behaviors. These actions also support the learner's work in integrating knowledge in each learner's knowledge base. It is a good strategy to select one of these behaviors to focus on one of the closing discussion forums for your course:

- Grappling with issues and problems together, including problems for which the answers are unknown

- Encouraging learners to brainstorm and challenge each other about innovative strategies and solutions

- Communicating with learners on the intersection of interests and core concepts in the course content

- Sharing relevant experiences that support future networking and professional collaboration

At this stage, your students' postings will likely show evidence of developing personal and professional relationships. One of the desired outcomes of learning and sharing discoveries together is the development of these lasting relationships. When we ask our students what they take with them from a course, professional and personal friendships for the future are usually mentioned.

Conditions That Can Hinder Community Development

In striving to achieve a successful stage 3 of community of stimulating and comfortable camaraderie, are we aiming so high that we set ourselves up for disappointment? Here is a reality check. In her study on building community, Brown (2001) identified fifteen lifestyle conditions that might hinder a group of learners from developing into a vibrant learning community. She called these "intervening conditions," and they include many of the familiar lifestyle and commitment issues, such as health, work, family, logistics, and technology. Other conditions that she included might not come as readily to mind:

- Personalities and how they manifest themselves online.

- Possible mismatch of learner and faculty teaching and learning styles.

- Varying expectations and needs from a course. Some students really just want the credit and the grade and have no interest in networking. For working professionals, this needs to be an acceptable option.

What does this reality check suggest? Be patient and understanding with yourself and your students. Review the list of faculty actions for building community. If you are doing many of them, the community that is evolving in your course may be what makes sense for a particular group of students. Be sure that you are enjoying the discussions and learning that are happening, and then relax.

CW Tip 3: Learners as Leaders

This tip answers questions such as these:

- Why design experiences that empower learners as leaders of course experiences?

- How can I require learners to lead forums and other activities without appearing as if I am not doing "my" job of teaching?

Part of our challenge as instructors is managing the delicate balance between directed and self-directed learning. One instructional strategy that encourages this balance is learner-as-leader experiences.

Providing opportunities for learners to take the lead in learning experiences for a group or the larger course group can give learners a sense of empowerment that is both a critical element and a desired outcome of participation in an online learning community (Palloff & Pratt, 2007).

Learners-as-leaders experiences shift the learner's mindset away from the instructor as the primary content authority. It encourages a learner to see himself or herself as a valuable resource and contributor to the learning experience of others. Learners can see themselves as knowledge generators and connectors. Having learners lead activities also supports Vygotsky's theory of the zone of proximal development (ZPD). As learners develop expertise, their ZPDs shift and expand. Ideally, course experiences are designed with flexibility to be reshaped by and for learners to adapt to these shifting ZPDs.

As shifts occur in the learner's mindsets and ZPDs, the role of the instructor also shifts, from directing and telling to supporting, clarifying, critiquing, coaching, and shaping. Simultaneously with this shift, the instructor also learns more from the students. This tip provides a few hints on designing and implementing learner-as-leader activities.

Learners-as-Leaders Experiences: Orientation and Planning Time

Learner-led activities generally succeed when learners are prepared, expectations are clear and purposeful, processes and procedures are explicit, and the activities fit learners' state of readiness and personal goals. Here are some steps to include in your planning:

- Many learners may need to be oriented to the idea of leading a group or class activity, such as a forum, discussion, role-play, debate, or project. Start talking about the concept of learner-led activities from the beginning of the course.

- Provide learners with a detailed description of the activity and the expected outcomes and responsibilities. An overview of the activity with a link to the detailed directions often works well.

- Encourage learners to begin making choices about their planned learner-led activity after the first phase of the course has been completed.

- Provide time in the course calendar for learners to begin planning the activities around the middle of the term.

- Schedule instructor-team discussion time for the activities before the team is scheduled to lead an activity. Depending on the scope and complexity of the activity, this discussion could be one week or many weeks before the activity. The instructor serves as guide, director, and consultant, keeping the focus on the outcomes and clear expectations.

Individual versus Team-Led Activities

The adage "There's safety in numbers" is often true for learner-led activities. Learner-as-leader activities can often be very effective as team-based activities. The teams should be small, to minimize the likelihood of learners' opting out of an activity. Groups of three to five students can work well for more complex projects, but experience suggests that teams of two or three work better and encourage more activity on the part of each learner. Each member's voice is heard more often with smaller teams.

Making Outcomes Explicit

In addition to knowing the purpose and outcomes of the activity, it is helpful if students know how the outcomes fit into the larger context of the course plan. If the outcomes from the instructor are clear and learners embrace them, they can also develop additional goals or outcomes for the activity.

Choosing the Type of Activity

Gagné, Briggs, and Wager (1992) describe five kinds of learning outcomes: intellectual skills, verbal information, cognitive strategy, attitude, and motor skills. Of these five, the first four lend themselves best to learner-led activities because the activities to achieve those outcomes can be accomplished almost anywhere. (Admittedly, tools and strategies for achieving the outcomes of motor skill proficiency in an online course are still early in their development.)

Some of the most common learner-led activities are leading a group in a discussion, forum, or research topic. Other good learner-led activities are working on complex problems or projects, preparing and conducting debates, and role-playing key concepts or games. Again, the keys to success are preparation, consultation, and clear expectations.

It should always be assumed that learners are novice activity leaders and therefore should be encouraged to keep their activity simple from both a pedagogical and a technological perspective.

Table 9.1 provides a list of elements to consider when including a learner-led activity.

CW Tip 4: Course Wrapping with Concept Mapping: Capturing Course Content Meaningfully

This tip answers questions such as these:

- What is concept mapping?
- What are the benefits of concept mapping? How can it support the processes of capturing and representing course content?
- Are there any software tools for concept mapping or its close relation, mind mapping?

TABLE 9.1

Checklist for an Effective Learner-Led Activity

	Yes/No	Comments
1. Are the objectives for the activity clearly stated in the syllabus?		
2. Is there a rubric for the grading of the activity?		
3. Is the concept of a learner-led activity introduced at least two weeks before learners begin planning it?		
4. Are learners provided several weeks to plan the activity?		
5. Does the topic allow a person or team to be creative in their choice and implementation of the activity?		
6. Does the participation grade include participation in the learner-led activities?		

Source: Conrad and Donaldson (2011, p. 116).

With so many priorities competing for attention in the closing weeks of a course, great learning opportunities can get lost in the shuffle. When the frantic feelings are over, our learners may be tempted to wonder, *What was that all about, and how am I and my brain different?*

Concept mapping is useful because it requires thinking structurally about concepts. When we consider what we want our learners to take with them from a course, it is usually a rich set of concepts integrated into their knowledge base that we want most to encourage. Learners also value a set of concepts that they can talk about, because it can be helpful in sharing with family and friends what their course work means to them.

This tip provides a definition of concept mapping and a description of concept mapping software. Concept mapping is a good choice for course wrapping, as it can assist learners in framing their course knowledge for future use and in pruning and focusing on core concepts. This strategy can be a powerful tool for knowledge creation and consolidation.

Concept Mapping

What is a concept map? Here are two definitions. First, the simplest: "Concept maps are graphical tools for organizing and representing knowledge." (Novak & Cañas, 2006, p. 1). A complementary definition from Wikipedia that reinforces the use of concept maps for instructional use is "A concept map is a way of representing relationships between ideas, images, or words." This is important as course outcomes rely on students constructing knowledge representations.

The development of concept mapping is generally attributed to the work of Joseph Novak at Cornell University as part of a 1972 research program seeking to understand changes in children's knowledge of science (Novak & Cañas, 2008). Concept mapping is rooted in the theories of cognitive restructuring, going back even further to the work of Ausubel in the 1960s; he stressed the importance of prior knowledge in learning. Meaningful learning, according to Ausubel, occurs with only three conditions: conceptually clear resources, a learner's prior knowledge, and the learner's active choice to learn (Novak & Cañas, 2008.)

Concept mapping is generally considered to be a tool for these types of cognitive processes:

- Integrating old and new knowledge

- Assessing understanding or diagnosing misunderstanding

- Brainstorming

- Problem-solving

In other words, it is a useful tool for meaningful learning. And it can also be useful for seeing how knowledge changes and evolves over time.

Core Concepts About Concept Mapping

As defined above, concept maps are graphical tools for organizing and representing knowledge. Figure 9.1 shows a concept map that answers the question, "What is a concept map?" Note that concept maps are generally read from top to bottom.

This concept map includes a definition of concepts, which can be seen on the low middle left. Novak and Cañas define a concept as a "perceived regularity in events or objects, or records of events or objects" (p. 10). The concept map informs the reader about the characteristics of concepts as well. Concepts are hierarchically structured; they are labeled with symbols or words; and they can be combined to form propositions.

We can talk about concepts with words alone, but as the concept map illustrates, concepts are much more than just words. Concepts are a cluster of related ideas. Single words are often used as labels for complex ideas, and we can readily think that students own a concept when in reality they own only the word. For example, leadership is a concept and works relatively well as a simple label, but like many concepts it is clearer when stated as a proposition containing multiple concepts, such as vision, influence, motivating others, ethics, and influence. Think about the number of concepts in your course and how you might represent them graphically.

FIGURE 9.1

A Concept Map Showing the Key Features of Concept Maps

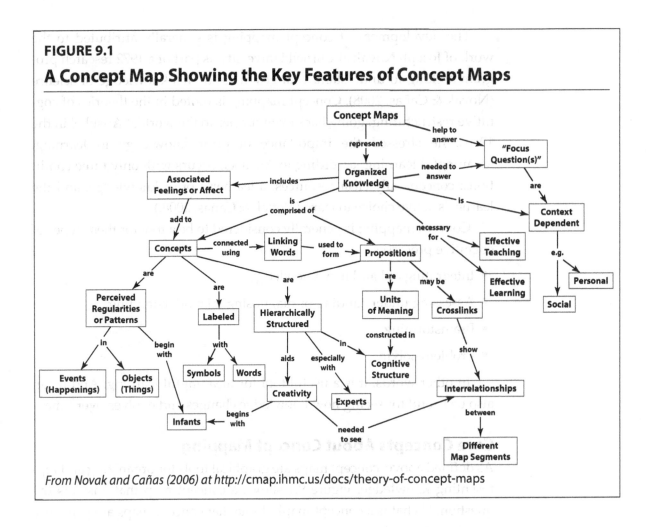

From Novak and Cañas (2006) at http://cmap.ihmc.us/docs/theory-of-concept-maps

Concept maps are organized hierarchically; however, the hierarchy of complex concepts is not always clear. The structuring of concept maps requires identifying the components of concepts, relationships, and dependencies. When we identify connections, new patterns and relationships among the knowledge concepts often reveal themselves. Nursing students using mind mapping in a clinical practicum made comments such as, "I'm finally able to make sense of all the pieces of the puzzle, and to form relationships among the pieces of data" (Cahill & Fonteyn, 2000, p. 220).

Integrating Concept Mapping into a Course

To start using concept mapping in a course, Novak and Cañas (2008) recommend starting with a focus question—one that clearly specifies the problem or issue the concept map should help to resolve. This question helps to frame the particular domain of knowledge for a learner to map. Creating concept maps requires learners to use their generalized available body of knowledge and the course content knowledge. In other words, concept mapping requires relating new knowledge to existing knowledge, highlighting the fact that the course knowledge is not independent or wholly separate from what students already know.

Developing a good focus question for a concept map is itself a useful collaborative instructional experience. As a course is coming to a close, you want the learners to think about what they knew initially about the course knowledge, what they think they know now, and what they wish they knew more about something—or how to do something. What students wish they knew can be a rich source of focus questions. Another good end-of-course activity is to modify the concept map they may have initiated at the beginning of the course.

Is There a Good Tool for Concept Mapping?

The list of tools for concept mapping and mind mapping is now extensive. Novak and others offer a tool for concept mapping that is free for higher education: CmapTools (v. 6.01.01); it is available from the Institute of Human and Machine Cognition (http://cmap.ihmc.us). There is even a Cmap app available. A listing of concept map and mind mapping software is available at Visual Thinking Center (http://www.mind-mapping.org/Visual-Thinking-Center.html). Another good source is Kathy Schrock's Guide to Everything (http://www.schrockguide.net/concept-mapping.html).

Using concept mapping as an instructional tool does require some rethinking about course design. Concept mapping encourages a shift from a topical linear approach of building knowledge to a more connectionist view of knowledge representation. Concept mapping requires propositional knowledge and knowledge of patterns and relationships rooted in deep knowledge and expertise. It requires thinking, analysis, weighing of ideas, and identifying relationships and patterns. This means it can be used at a number of different points in a course.

Concept mapping can be an effective way of wrapping up a course. For example, it can be an individual assignment with students focusing on one or more focus questions, or a small team assignment of creating a concept map focusing on a core concept and its connections to the other core concepts. Karen R. Stout, an associate professor at Western Washington University, likes to use concept mapping to generate class discussions, and for capturing what students know about particular concepts. A YouTube video (www.youtube.com/watch?v=Gm1owf0uGFM)—and script is at http://pandora.cii.wwu.edu/cii/resources/modules/concept/#intro.

CW Tip 5: Using Case Studies in Online Courses: Making Content Real

This tip answers questions such as these:

- How can we use problems and case studies in our courses and still cover all the core ideas of a discipline?

- Why is using case studies so fundamental to deep processing of content?

Do you shy away from using situations, problems, or case studies in your course? Do you do this because you worry that you have so much to tell, to cover, to share? This is a very natural response, because we, as experts, have brains chock full of a lifetime of knowledge. We worry, we wonder: *How can our students learn what they need to learn about this topic in a mere 8 weeks or even 15 weeks?*

Yet we know the following: for students to construct their own knowledge structures, we must immerse them in examples, scenarios, problems, stories, and case studies situated in real contexts (Dewey, 1938; Bruner, 1963; Brown, 1989; Ericsson, 2007). So when planning our teaching, we have a dilemma: How to we balance "telling" with "student thinking and discussing"? How can we get students to deeply process course content while ensuring that we at least acquaint them with all the core ideas of a discipline?

Start with Stories

The short answer is this: start with stories. If you are teaching biology, start with the story of solving the problem of cholera in London in 1832, or the countries where cholera is still a problem today, or the current challenge of how flu vaccine–making scientists can keep up with mutating strains of flu viruses. If you are teaching business leadership, consider starting with a company facing a corporate challenge, such as how to come up with a whole new category of product every three or four years. Or how to handle company succession when a founding father dies suddenly, or the question of why oil prices are dropping so rapidly and the effects and consequences, including employment, types of cars being purchased, and future oil exploration.

John Seely Brown, noted scientist, thinker, and former director of the Palo Alto Research Center (PARC), affirmed the role of stories when he described his theory of situated cognition in 1989 (Brown, Collins, & Duguid). What is situated cognition? It is the belief that "knowledge is 'situated,' being in part a product of the activity, context, and culture in which it is developed and used" (p.32). Thus studying knowledge in context is essential to learning well.

What This Tip Does

This tip suggests ways of integrating stories, problems, and case studies into digital learning experiences. Situating content within a particular context helps students see why, where, when, and how content is important. Stories illustrating the usefulness of course knowledge draw students in to how the content is relevant to their lives, now and in the future. Exposure and discussion of a broad set of stories and cases develops confidence and expertise in a discipline or skill.

Situating content in real-life contexts can be done with the use of stories, examples, and cases such as those populating the headlines on a daily basis. Another source are the examples and scenarios in discipline resources. Integrating case studies into your courses does not mean that you abandon your textbook. Rather, it means taking advantage of our current media environment, where students can research the stories behind the headlines and bring those questions, problems, etc. to the class for discussion and then apply the content to these real life events, with the guidance and interpretation of you, the discipline expert.

So, how do you start?

Definitions of Content Resources Containing Stories

When talking about case studies, we often think about the long, complex case studies that require many hours of work, discussion, and reflection developed by a team of scholars. However, there are many other options. Lengthy case studies are only one type of resource for bringing complexity and context into a course. Here is a list of other story type resources to consider. They are all similar to case studies in that they are rich, contextual, and multidimensional. They are listed in a rough approximation of increasing complexity.

Example

An illustration of a principle, or model, or a specimen or instance typical of the set of which it forms a part (dictionary.com). Illustrations, instances, samples, and specimens are all examples. Sprinkle liberally throughout the course.

Situation

Describes a series of events leading to an event that needs to be resolved.

Story

"An account or recital of an event or a series of events, either true or fictitious" (thefreedictionary.com).

Case study

For instructional purposes, "student-centred activities based on topics that demonstrate theoretical concepts in an applied setting" (Davis & Wilcock, 2003, pp. 3–4).

Game

"A system in which players engage in an artificial conflict, defined by rules, that results in a quantifiable outcome" (Salen & Zimmerman, 2004).

Problem

"Something that is difficult to deal with: something that is a source of trouble, worry" (Merriam-Webster). Problem-based learning (PBL) is a student-centered pedagogy that strives to "teach content by presenting the students with a real-world challenge similar to one they might encounter were they a practitioner of the discipline" (Gallow, 2001).

Simulations

A learning environment in which the student can practice difficult, exacting, life-threatening, or mission-critical skills (Epper, Derryberry, & Jackson, 2012). "Online simulations engage students with real-life management situations that require them to make critical decisions" (Harvard Business Publishing, 2011)

Scenarios

"Consistent and coherent descriptions of alternative hypothetical futures that reflect different perspectives on past, present, and future developments, which can serve as a basis for action" (Van Notten, 2006).

As can be seen, the ways in which "deliberate practice," as recommended by Ericsson (2009), can be integrated into courses range from a very short, simple story or example to more complex, demanding, and lengthy cases. It is well worth searching out stories and cases or having your students identify relevant examples and stories.

Mix Up Stories and Cases

What are some ways you can use stories and cases in your courses? Here are a few ideas. But first, an important note: Be sure to select stories, problems, and cases that reinforce your course's core concepts, skills, and learning outcomes. You want to be prepared to guide the students' analysis and understanding of the cases. Students will likely make unusual connections and suggest surprising insights, but the case must be a good exemplar of the core concepts.

Launching a Course or Topic

1. Start with a simple, but dramatic story in which someone uses course content with great results, or ignores course content with disastrous consequences. Have students respond with thoughts, insights, and suggestions.

2. Start with a problem or case study representative of the types of problems experts in the field face or grapple with. Gather ideas, strategies, thoughts, and recommendations from the students.

3. Stories or case studies can be discussed in a forum or a simple written team assignment. Ideally, this discussion can be revisited later in the course. The goal is that students will intuitively establish more purpose for learning course content, answering the question of what knowledge or skills they might need to deal with complex issues presented by such cases and stories.

4. Note: Sometimes it is effective to couch a simple story or case with the classic beginning of, "One day in the life of a leader, manager, scientist, professor, marketer, CIO."

Reading Assignments

1. When assigning a reading, assign a companion story, problem, or case for evaluation, analysis, question, reflection, or action.

2. Provide a choice of two or three stories, problems, or cases and have students research, respond to one of them. This is a great two-person team assignment, as students can assume different perspectives or roles.

3. The next step in this assignment, can be discussing the assignment in a forum for whole class sharing. This is an efficient way of exposing students to more cases and problems based on course content.

Creating or Writing Assignments

1. Create a writing, audio or media production assignment that requires evaluation or analysis of a case or problem.

2. Create an assignment for students to find stories that exemplify the problem, or maybe even search out Tweets that exemplify the concept going right or wrong.

3. Evaluate a crisis, how it evolved, and possible strategies for dealing with them.

4. Analyze or debate issues raised in a story, relying on course content for rationales and principles.

Earlier, we posed the following question: How can we get students to deeply process course content while ensuring that we at least acquaint them with all the core ideas of a discipline? The way to bridge the gap between the theory presented by course readings and the practice provided by cases, stories, and problems is to guide and support students in identifying and using the core concepts. It is a discovery, rather than a telling.

Conclusion

The power of stories, problems, and cases is that they reside in a complex context. The power of linear chapter-by-chapter content lies in its abstract simplicity. Constructing meaningful knowledge requires joining of the abstract concepts with the complexity of life. Stories, problems, and cases are one way of helping students deal meaningfully with course content.

For more about the case method of teaching, Harvard Review Publishing has many resources available to faculty. They sponsor a blog on case method teaching (http://teachingpost.hbsp.harvard.edu/questions/368/criteria-for-evaluating-class-participation.html).

Preparing for the Course Wrap

This set of tips has suggestions for preparing you and your students for the closing weeks of the course and focusing on meaningful experiences to wrap up the overall course experience.

CW Tip 6: Pausing, Reflecting, and Pruning Strategies

This tip answers questions such as these:

- Why is pausing and reflecting so important?
- How can we integrate these processes into course designs?
- What do researchers say about how memory works?

Pausing, reflecting, and pruning are elements of the learning process that are often neglected. Yet our brains and memories are not designed for remembering everything. Daniel Schacter (2001), a professor and chair of Harvard University's Department of Psychology, has identified seven "sins" of memory. One of these "sins" is well known to all of us: the "sin" of transience, or the tendency to forget things over time. While this memory trait might be considered a negative, Schacter suggests that transience and other memory traits of omission, such as blocking and absent-mindedness, are not flaws in the architecture of memory but costs we pay for benefits in memory that make it work as well as it does most of the time.

Many of the new technologies—smartphones, cameras, GPS trackers, and social media apps—are going beyond the traditional capturing of key life moments to *life-logging*, a term used to describe systems that document every conversation and movement. Twitter services, for example, enable us to share what we are doing each moment in messages to all our followers. Just as we may cringe at the thought of every moment of our lives being captured and recorded, we may well cringe at every moment of our teaching and learning processes being recorded. Learning, like life, can be messy. And a large percentage of the activities of learning are best left behind.

The big challenge for students is discerning which concepts, ideas, and examples are keepers. How do students identify the real takeaways of a course? Pause-and-reflect learning strategies help students identify and encode the core concepts and skills that are the foundation for subsequent learning. Pause-and-reflect strategies encourage elaborate encoding processes for the key important content and help to move content elements from short-term memory into long-term memory and to find a place for the knowledge in the knowledge structure we call mind. Here are a few pause-and-reflect strategies.

- Plan pausing, reflecting, and summarizing times into your course on an ongoing basis. One technique useful for this reflection strategy is the discussion-wrapping tip. You will recall that discussion wrapping is used to summarize the key points of a discussion topic and to transition to the next. When directing students to prepare summaries of the discussion, one technique is to use terms such as the *bottom line*, *core concepts*, and *implications for next steps*.

- Hold synchronous online question-and-answer sessions as concept summary sessions. With synchronicity, you can hear in real time what students are thinking and understanding. Faculty who use synchronous sessions in online and blended courses report that it is their—and their students'—favorite way of gathering and thinking out loud together.

- Ask your students to generate questions. Ask them to record, talk about, or think out loud about what is potentially confusing to them. The practical inquiry model (Garrison, Anderson, & Archer, 2000) affirms that two processes in developing useful knowledge are *integration* and *resolution*. Integration refers to reaching some group or team convergences by connecting ideas, identifying relationships and patterns, and proposing solutions. With resolution, the group or larger community applies and tests solutions in the real-world scenarios.

- Plan other activities that challenge students to describe, define, and use the core concepts in various contexts. These can be compare-and-contrast activities and scavenger hunts for how the core concepts are expressed in classic and current scenarios.

- Plan a lessons-learned paper or discussion by asking learners to discuss what they learned and why it was important to them. This technique is sometimes termed a *reverse exam*.

Pause-and-reflect activities are so important because they encourage the elaborate encoding of knowledge by identifying and seeing relationships, categories, and unique application examples.

Here are the seven sins of memory identified by Schacter (www.apa.org/monitor/oct03/sins.aspx):

1. Transience—forgetting that occurs with the passage of time

2. Absent-mindedness—forgetting probably caused by lack of attention or divided attention and preoccupation

3. Blocking—inability to recall a bit of information that we know we know

4. Misattribution—errors in recall; we remember events that never happened, attribute features of an event to a different time or place, and remember events, but find they happened to someone else

5. Suggestibility—a tendency to incorporate misleading information from external sources into personal recollections

6. Bias—the tendency to be influenced by factors, such as consistency, change, the present, role of the self, generic stereotype

7. Persistence—tendency to remember those things you would rather forget

CW Tip 7: Closing Experiences: Wrapping Up a Course with Style

This tip answers questions such as these:

- What strategies help students manage the stress and panic often induced by end-of-course projects and requirements?

- How do I design a closing experience?

The closing weeks of a course can often be quite stressful. Planning, list making, and deep-breathing exercises can be helpful in reducing stress and calming us. A favorite image of one of us is from the productivity consultant David Allen (2015). According to Allen, making a list is a powerful strategy, as it helps us to clear the "psychic RAM" of our brain, and we feel more relaxed and in control. With a list in hand, we don't have to continually remind ourselves of what needs to be done and when.

Here are a few hints for closing out a course experience with style, panache, and pleasure.

Prepare a List of What's Next and When Assignments and Readings Are Due

This tip places the burden of creating a master "Things to Do to Complete a Course" list for students on the instructor. Some faculty may think this falls into the category of helping students too much. We like to think that making such a master list benefits the instructor as much as the student. A master list is a chance to ensure that the deadlines and assessment tasks that an instructor must do is in sync with learner deadlines. Such a master list helps students stay focused on learning the course knowledge and completing their projects.

A master list is a form of teaching direction and can be posted in a prominent place on the course site. Then your voice or text announcements in the final days and weeks can refer to it. Another strategy is to use a community forum and have a community to-do list, with room for hints, suggestions, and reminders. This can be a way of developing students' responsibility for list-making.

Plan a Celebration Session to End the Course

Remember that a course is a series of structured learning experiences. A well-designed course ending provides opportunities for reflection and integration of useful knowledge. It is also a time to wrap up positive social and cognitive experiences.

When we get together for family and holiday time, we often do a lot of hugging as we disperse and return to our usual daily responsibilities. The end of a course can be closed with cognitive hugging and concept pruning, reflecting explicitly on the knowledge and skills students look forward to using in the future.

End-of-course experiences can focus on one or all of these three areas: (1) content, (2) interaction and community, and (3) the full course experience.

End-of-Course Content Experiences

Both faculty and learners benefit from end-of-course content experiences. For faculty it is an opportunity to affirm the core concepts of a course, saying, "If you remember nothing else, remember '_____' or '_____.'" (Fill in your favorite terms for what you consider the most foundational core concepts.) Many faculty like to use a course summary that includes discipline trends and encourages the development of lifelong career habits. For example, an obvious goal for many graduate students is to develop the habit of reading a specific journal, following a discipline organization, or tracking a particular expert as a way of integrating the course content over time.

For learners, the end of the course is a time to tie up loose ends and put the finishing touches on new perspectives and new knowledge. Recall that as we develop concepts, it is often necessary to identify and build relationships among ideas and concepts within our existing body of knowledge. This also requires pruning what we have learned so that we can readily access and use essential and useful concepts.

One strategy that promotes end-of-course reflection is to ask the learners to share one of their most meaningful insights. The end of the course is also a time for discussing what learners will be doing next. What courses are next on their schedule, or what learning tasks are they going to turn to next?

End-of-Course Interaction Experiences

Learners often create a helpful, supportive, and dynamic learning community over eight to fourteen weeks. Closing out such an experience can sometimes be wrenching; other times it is much easier. Providing a time and place for saying good-bye, just as we provide a time and place for learners for introductions, is a good thing to do. A simple way to do this is with a closing forum where students share a closing comment, such as the end-of-course content insight they gleaned from a collaborative experience, that they will take with them.

One of the most valuable parts of a successful learning is expanding our network of colleagues, so providing a way for students to stay in touch is also helpful. This can happen naturally in a cohort-based program. Another technique might be to encourage them to share where and when they might meet again, such as which other courses they might be in again. Other times, "until we meet again" works just fine. One faculty shared that one of the most heartwarming comments that he remembers is a student saying that he disliked "seeing the class come to an end!"

A wrap-up forum can be a good activity for the end of the last week. It might be combined with a debriefing on the projects.

End-of-Course Full Course Experience

The end of a course brings course evaluations. Although this is an important feedback mechanism for the institution, it is often less useful for faculty. To gain more value, ask the learners for feedback about particular elements of the course experience while it is fresh in their minds:

- What was the most useful resource or assignment for the course, and why?

- What problems, if any, did they have with the use of the learning tools—either "operator error" or "designer error"?

- What did they notice about the course that you think might be changed in some way? You can add your own comment here to get them started: "Here is one thing *I* noticed . . ."

- Were they ready for the course content? What might have helped if they were not?

- Include an open question for other suggestions or recommendations.

This informal feedback can be in a separate place on the course site, and it can be unstructured and anonymous. The goal is to gather data for ongoing updating and quality enhancement of the course experiences for faculty and learners. Of course, you can remind the students that you would like ideas that will improve the course for others, keeping the focus on constructive feedback.

Closing Thought

Reviewing your end-of-course experiences can reveal, sometimes with surprise, all the tasks that learners must complete during the final weeks of a course. Be realistic and, if advisable, modify the requirements. The last few weeks of a course can be some of the most stimulating and creative learning time, as learners are putting it all together. So prepare a special coffee or other favorite beverage or music and enjoy your students and their dialogue at this time.

CW Tip 8: Real-Time Closing Gatherings: Stories and Suggestions

This tip answers questions such as these:

- What are the key features of synchronous meeting rooms and what are they good for?

- I am clueless and intimidated and too busy to use the online synchronous classrooms. How can I possibly get started?
- What about the students? Are they ready to use these tools?
- Do real-time gatherings help build community?

Synchronous meeting rooms are finally easy enough to use that they are becoming an expected teaching and learning tool for online and blended courses. As discussed in EM Tip 15, synchronous sessions are particularly valuable for demonstrations, problem-solving activities, and Q&A review sessions. Synchronous sessions have great potential during the closing weeks. These rooms provide a place where participants can talk and chat interactively in real time, making them a fitting venue for presentations, project summaries and demonstrations. Holding review activities in the online classroom also makes the evaluation of student learning more transparent and collaborative.

Using Synchronous Meeting Rooms

Synchronous meeting rooms make it possible to interact in real time from wherever you might be as long as you have a good network connection. However, synchronous meeting room applications are a bundle of sophisticated technologies, so things can easily go wrong. Moreover, they require learners to be familiar with the use of headphones and the microphone settings on their devices. Learners may also require some time in developing new habits of communicating and sharing. Remembering to press a button to talk can feel strange at first. Experiences suggest that once an instructor and students use a synchronous meeting room, they rarely want to teach and learn without it. So how might you use this online classroom? Is it worth the challenges?

Faculty Stories with Synchronous Meeting Rooms

Once faculty start using synchronous tools, they often become passionate about them. One of the most enthusiastic faculty that we talked to about the online classroom taught business writing. She held twice-weekly sessions in which she and her learners collaboratively analyzed business writing samples and student work pieces for effectiveness and construction. Together they developed a comfort level with the technology that really worked for them.

Another faculty member, Debra Dinnocenzo at Duquesne University, used the online classroom when teaching a graduate course on leadership in the virtual workplace. She used it for gathering her students together in real time, both as a full class and as smaller teams for content and project discussions. The sixteen students often used the environment by themselves for team meetings and for project work, bypassing the challenges of setting up conference calls, and using the archiving feature to capture their work. Debra also highly recommends using the live real-time environment to invite experts to her class.

Using Live Classroom for a Course Closing Experience

If we think about multiple online meeting rooms as a conference center for the course, many possible uses for closing experiences become apparent. Debra used the general course room for having a course celebration closing party, complete with course trinkets, beverages, and special closing discussions. This may be more than what you want to do, but it tickles the imagination. Students sent company-logoed cups or hats to Debra, who then mailed a "party package" to all her students. Alternatives to this approach might be to simply determine the "party menu" and everyone bring their own beverage or treat to the event at their computer.

Likely Questions

One question you may have is whether synchronous activity reduces the number of postings on discussion boards. As in the case of Debra's class, with an average of over 200 messages a week, the community that develops with the real-time gatherings may be prompting even greater asynchronous interaction. This is a question deserving of more data.

Another question you may have is about how students respond to online courses using synchronous meetings when online courses are designed primarily as asynchronous and independent of time and place requirements. Informal feedback from faculty and students suggests that these gatherings work if they are optional rather than required and if the gatherings are captured and archived so that students who are unable to participate in real time can still access the experience asynchronously.

Depending on the infrastructure for your online course, creating online meeting rooms can be very easy or a little more difficult. Some questions that you will want to ask of your contact at your institution include the following:

How do I create and set up online meeting rooms for my course?

Setting up rooms in LMSs often appears as a simple option, just as you might create a forum or discussion board. The best thing to do is to ask this question of your technical support team or a colleague.

How do I record and archive the online classroom sessions?

Press the archive button at the beginning of the session and again at the close of it. You can post the link to the archived session anywhere it is convenient in your course.

How do I prepare technically for an online session?

Most online classroom systems have prerecorded or live tutorials available on their sites. Or you can prepare by attending sessions offered by your institution.

How do I prepare the content for an online session?

Preparing well for the content of online sessions is extremely important. The goals for everyone need to be clear, and everyone who is a leader for the session needs to be prepared—with either questions, demonstrations, or polls to make it useful and engaging.

CW Tip 9: Debriefing Techniques: What One Change Would Students Recommend?

This tip answers questions such as these:

- How can I know which course experiences really make a difference in learning and which ones are duds?

- What are some strategies for encouraging students to help improve future courses?

Wouldn't you like to know specifically which of the course activities and experiences really worked for your students' learning? Which activities had an impact on their knowledge, skills, and ways of thinking? The best way to do this is to ask.

Create a special "place" for the course debriefing—as simple as a new discussion forum, as quick as a survey, or as complex as a wiki that you have developed with all the course readings and resources. Once you have selected the particular place or tool, after your students' final projects are completed, ask them one or more of these questions:

- What was the best, or a very good, course experience—reading, activity, project, and discussion—for you personally? And why?

- What would you have liked to study in more detail or explore more widely?

- What course activity do you strongly recommend to keep for the next offering of this course? Why?

- What one change would you recommend?

You might focus questions on a new activity that you introduced this term, or imagine that a new learner about to enroll in the course wanted advice about how to succeed in the course. Students do have a soft place in their hearts generally for students who might be taking the course after them. For example, you might ask one of these questions:

- What did you enjoy or not enjoy about [a new resource, the use of new audio or video resources, or a new two-person team assignment, for example]?

- If you had one piece of advice for a student about to start this course, what would it be?

A simple debriefing of this sort is valuable for students, as they focus on what specific assignments, readings, and experiences worked for them. This debriefing gives immediate and specific feedback that can quickly be applied to the new course offering. Students then also feel as if they are contributing to the program quality and that their comments make a difference. Students are often asked or required to complete other questionnaires regarding their learning experiences, but these tools are most helpful to administrators. The feedback is often too delayed or too generic to be of much use to faculty in helping with course design.

When faculty use this debriefing activity, they are often pleasantly surprised. Students often respond that the best parts of the course are those that are the least work for the faculty, and that activities on which you might spend a great deal of time are not that important after all.

Conclusion—and What's Next

If you have been using this book as a guide to teaching your first online and blended course, you are likely ready to take a deep breath, celebrate, and give yourself a few pats on the back. Completing a new task as complex and challenging as teaching and coaching students in a new environment is very satisfying. By now you probably have developed a feeling of competence in at least a few areas. Be sure to take time to acknowledge your success at whatever level you have reached. Stop and write a note to yourself or a short note to a colleague, and share what you feel very good about and what your top priorities are for when you teach a course for the second time.

In the final chapter of this book, we'll look at some issues you might have faced and how to improve your next offering of this course or your next course. The following chapter is devoted to the special demands and constraints of teaching accelerated intensive courses.

Self-Directed Exercise /Application

Activity 1:

Check this list of faculty behaviors for building community, and put a check next to or circle behaviors that you use consistently. Then select one of the behaviors that you would like to use more frequently in these closing weeks:

- Supporting and encouraging peer-to-peer discussion and collaborations
- Posing open-ended questions about what students think, and what they think they know or would like to know
- Making positive observations about students' participation in the learning experiences
- Encouraging connection making and linking of ideas among the learners

- Encouraging the linking of course content to current events and problems, with links to learners' personal work and career environments as appropriate
- Challenging students to share questions, strategies, and insights about the course content

Activity 2:

Design one or two closing activities. If you are designing two activities, change their characteristics. For example, design one activity that is synchronous and one is asynchronous; design one with a focus on content learning individually and one with a small group. Perhaps one of the activities could be learner-led or learner-designed.

Chapter 10

Teaching Accelerated Intensive Courses

ACCELERATED INTENSIVE COURSES are a special type of learning experience. Faculty often feel stressed—understandably so—about how to cover all the content in a course that has been compressed from fifteen weeks into eight weeks or less. The feeling that there is simply not enough time for learning the content is well-founded. As Core Learning Principle 9 states, "Everything else being equal, more time on task equals more learning." This principle affirms that, learning takes time because it is a growing process. The neurons and synapses in our brains take time to grow. (Kandel, 2006; Brain and Research Foundation, 2013) Assimilating information does not often happen in a flash, and then not until after a great deal of data has been gathered and processed.

How do we address this challenge? The tips in this chapter provide ideas for tackling the design and teaching of intensive courses.

Tips for Intensive Courses (IC)

The first tip, IC Tip 1, provides suggestions for designing accelerated short courses by focusing on content framing and case studies. These designs shift from the traditional topic-by-topic approach to an immersive approach, focusing on problem-solving scenarios that cover the content by using core concepts to solve problems. IC Tip 2 describes some high-impact teaching strategies using patterns and relationships. With a compressed learning time, big-picture patterns and relationships are significant learning opportunities. IC Tip 3 examines how to build expertise through practice despite the challenge of time.

Here is the list of Intensive Course (IC) tips:

- IC Tip 1: Designing for Intensive Courses Using Content Framing and Case Studies

- IC Tip 2: High-Impact Practices for Short Courses: Reflections, Patterns, and Relationships

- IC Tip 3: Developing Expertise in Short Courses: Can It Be Done?

IC Tip 1: Designing for Intensive Courses Using Content Framing and Case Studies

This tip answers these questions:

- What can I do to quickly convey a useful sense of the content picture of a course?

- How do I design a course with case studies at the center, avoiding the topic-by-topic design?

- What resources do I need for implementing problem-focused courses?

While shorter courses provide less time for learning, there is no reduction in expected content "coverage" or learning. This can mean making tough decisions about content selections and learning experiences. Here are two design strategies that can help make accelerated courses lively and dynamic while not dramatically shortchanging the content exposure and awareness.

Design Strategy 1: Create a Visual Frame of the Core Concepts

This design strategy focuses on creating a visual frame or map of the core concepts of the course. We are accustomed to creating a set of learning outcomes for a course. This usually means that we give students a list of abstract, often verbose, formal learning outcomes for them to achieve. In accelerated courses, the preferred strategy is to provide an organizing visual such as a map or graphic that learners can use as a frame to attach, process, and manage the expectations of content knowledge.

Remember the four-element learning experiences framework (Figure 2.1; Boettcher, 2003–2016) for designing online teaching experiences? While designing for learning is a complex process, it can be simplified by using the frame of the learning experience created by the four elements of the *learner*, the *faculty mentor*, the *content* and the *environment*. All the elements involved in making design and teaching decisions fall into one of these four categories.

That is the type of visual frame that can provide a knowledge structure into which all the content of a course can flow. How do you build a graphic frame for your course? The most important question guiding a course frame is "What are the core concepts of your course?" Once you have determined these, you can create a visual or graphic that can hold those concepts, linking the content and relationships of your course. Don't worry about your course frame being perfect; it can be a work in progress, refined Weover time collaboratively with your students.

Design Strategy 2: Place Case Studies with Consequences at Course Center

We like to subtitle this design strategy as the "sink or swim" strategy. This makes it particularly fitting for intensive courses. How does this strategy work? Find or create a set of problems, scenarios, or case studies dependent on the core concepts of your course. Use your discipline knowledge to guide the sequencing of simple to complex problems. Then, basically toss your learners into deep enough water that they need to apply and use the course content almost immediately in a problem-solving mode. I also like to call this the "jellyfish" design, with the problem on the surface and all the core concepts dangling below, essential to solving problems and making good decisions.

Your teaching direction responsibility is to guide your learners through tackling of these problems or scenarios. This approach means that your learners are simultaneously solving the problems, making decisions for various scenarios, and discussing which of the core concepts enlighten them or lead the way for dealing with any particular case or problem.

The timeframe in longer courses encourages what some might call a leisurely linear approach, starting out slowly and then building to a crescendo project. The sink-or-swim strategy is more akin to an apprenticeship or situated learning, wherein the learners need to apply the concepts in an integrated way and learn by doing. This is an example of "situated cognition" (Brown, Collins, & Duguid, 1989; Lave, 1993; and Kirsh, 2009).

To implement this teaching strategy, you will want to have at least two of the following course resources at the ready.

1. Visual graphic or organizer for the course that shows the relationships of the core concepts

2. A list and description of the core concepts

3. A set of cases and problems that require use of the core concepts for successfully addressing or solving the cases, problems, and scenarios

If you don't have some of these items developed for your course yet, you might want to set a goal of creating these, with the help of your learners, in a blog, wiki, or straightforward discussion forum during this course and then building on it for your next iteration of the course. The first two items help to serve as a learning tool for solving problems, and learners can take them forward to their next courses or to use in their life or career. These items help to guide problem-solving and support the reasoning and thinking behind problem-solving.

The third item—a set of cases and problems—is a resource that you probably have somewhere but haven't quite decided how to use. Likely resources include current events that highlight business or leadership challenges and cases from textbooks or discipline sites.

In summary, for intensive courses, a good teaching strategy is to pose the challenges, problems, and cases at the beginning of a course and then work toward finding and using the core concepts needed to solve problems or analyze scenarios.

Collaborative Projects in Short Courses: A Hint

While teaming and collaborative projects are excellent community and learning strategies, the additional overhead of working with teams during a short course can be overwhelming. So you may want to assign group-supported independent projects (Chen, 2007), which each student can complete at his or her own pace while still collaborating with other group members for input on improving the project.

IC Tip 2: High-Impact Practices for Short Courses: Reflections, Patterns, and Relationships

This tip answers questions such as these:

- What is Kolb's four-stage learning cycle, and how does reflection play a role in that learning cycle?
- What are some examples of question clusters for stimulating reflection activities?
- What are some examples of pattern assignments and activities?

With intensive courses, it is critical to provide practice in using core concepts. This tip focuses on two effective practices for making the most of the condensed time frames of intensive courses: reflections and patterns. Try them and see what you think.

Reflection Practices

Reflection is an integral part of the four-stage learning cycle in experiential education and learning styles developed by David Kolb (1984). Where does reflection fit in the learning cycle? It is step 2, as shown in the graphic of the learning cycle (Figure 10.1) Reflection means processing the data or content after a learning experience, deciding what meaning we need to take forward.

In Kolb's learning cycle, learning begins with a concrete experience in the here and now, in some immediate and personal learning experience. The experience can be sourced in readings, cases, or simulations, even though these experiences are one step removed from direct hands-on experience. That initial experience is followed by the stage of collecting or recording data and making observations about the experience. The third stage is conceptualizing—forming conclusions based on the meanings derived from the observations—followed by the fourth stage, active experimenting using those beliefs.

Intensive courses are by their very nature condensed and seldom provide room for all of the phases of this full learning cycle for deep experiential learning, but there are a few ways we can deepen the reflection part of the cycle. We do know that if we just keep pushing content at students without designing in opportunities for reflection, learning doesn't occur. It flows through and around the brain without stopping.

Phil Race (2006) of the University of Leeds has developed a set of questions that you can use in developing activities and guiding the reflective processes that are an essential part of deep learning. These clusters of

---

FIGURE 10.1

Kolb's Four-Stage Learning Cycle

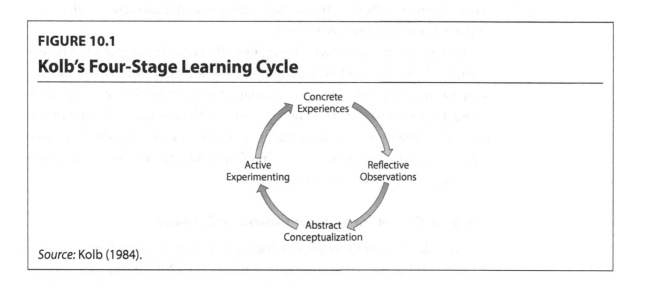

Source: Kolb (1984).

questions can be catalysts for discussion forums. Keep in mind that the overall goal of reflection is for your students to make sense of what they are learning. These types of questions can be easily integrated into many of your existing assignments, so you can try some of these questions almost immediately.

Here are two clusters of questions, adapted from Race's suggestions. One of these clusters has been adapted for traditional reading assignments. The second cluster can be used to guide a learner's reflection on a brief case study analysis.

Question Cluster for a Reading Assignment

How did this reading assignment move my thinking forward, or expand my understanding? How did one of the ideas connect with, deepen, or change the thinking that I had prior to the reading? What question do I have that I would like to answer going forward?

Here is an example of how this might work in practice from my personal growth. I (Judith) have been pushing myself to stay current with evolving learning theory developments by exploring a book by Lawrence Shapiro called *Embodied Cognition.* This is not an easy read. Making sense of what I am reading takes some work, similar to that which a student might have on a difficult reading assignment. I am fortunate that I have the luxury of reading portions of it, skipping around a bit, stopping and then going back to it a few days later. Our students don't have the luxury of time; thus, for the meanings to take root, it is essential that they stop, think, record, write, discuss, and share their thoughts with others. Questions such as these can help them to frame their thinking and make sense of the ideas and experiences in the assignment.

By the way, if you are wondering just what *embodied cognition* is, here is a starter definition. Embodied cognition—as a theory of how we know—suggests that our ability to know is shaped by how our bodies and senses interact with the world. This theory reaffirms the essential role that physical environments—such as authentic contexts, cases, and simulations—play in learning. Following this train of thought, the next question cluster focuses on cases, problems and scenarios.

Question Cluster for a Case, Problem, or Scenario

What did I find to be the greatest challenge in analyzing or judging the merits of this case? Why was this a challenge to me? What do I need to do, learn, and practice so that I will be more ready to meet a similar challenge in the future?

One or two of these questions can also be used as follow-up questions in discussion forums.

What Places Are Good for Reflection?

You may be wondering just where in the LMS reflection practices can be used. Here are three places that often work well. It is likely that many more will be emerging with social media characteristics.

Discussion Forums

First of all, reflection questions fit well in the discussion forums. Because discussion forums always need to link core learning back to individual experiences and what students already know, these questions will draw out fairly unique responses as learners make sense of the readings based on who they are and their prior experiences. Since we want the discussion forums to also build community and dialogue, we can also add a guiding suggestion for some of the forums, such as, "How are your ideas similar to the thinking of some of your colleagues?"

Blogs or Journals

The second great place to use these types of reflection questions is as catalysts for students' blogging or journaling assignments.

Written Assignments

The third place to use these question clusters is in a short written assignment. Or similarly, these questions can be part of the debriefing after a larger project assignment.

Now, let's look at two additional high-impact, high-engagement practices using pattern practices.

Pattern Practices

One of the earlier tips (CB Tip 14 on discussion wraps) focused on identifying and affirming patterns in your course content. This is a particularly powerful teaching approach in intensive courses because it helps to chunk an overwhelming amount of information into more usable and memorable chunks.

A helpful quote regarding the need for patterns is this quote of Marshall McLuhan: "Faced with information overload, we have no alternative but pattern recognition" (McLuhan, 1969).

Patterns can make your teaching easier, because learners will more quickly develop a feeling of confidence and be less stressed. How do you get started with pattern making? The first step is for you to identify what you see as the fundamental patterns and cycles in your course content. If you have not yet done this, not to worry: ask the students to share what patterns they see and what connections with other knowledge. It may well be that your learners will identify patterns that you have not seen or noticed before.

When and how might be a good time to do this? About two to three weeks into the course, include a question on patterns in your discussion forums or in your short paper assignments.

What patterns might get them started thinking? You can encourage thinking in terms of visual patterns as well as connections and relationships. Here are a couple of examples.

- A newsletter article at the University of Northern Iowa College of Education provides this example of the use of patterns in a literature class. This class studied the connections between Hamlet's "To be or not to be" soliloquy and the topic of the teen suicide rate. As stated, "This activity requires students to see patterns and make connections between the past and present, finding similarities between conditions then and now. The insights they gain will help them better understand the present through the past" (University of Northern Iowa, 2001).

- In the study of leadership, many patterns come to mind, such as the transactional (exchange something of value) and transformational (shifting of beliefs, values) leadership style concepts identified by James MacGregor Burns in 1978 and reexamined in 2004. Examining the patterns of behavior and outcomes that result from different styles is one type of pattern making. Applying these leadership concepts to other arenas such as social and personal relationships is another example.

- Consider also the power of visual patterns, parallels, and echoes. In mathematics, for example, fractals are patterns that contain self-similar patterns of complexity increasing with magnification. In other words, when a fractal pattern is divided into parts you get a nearly identical reduced-size copy of the whole. See examples of fractals in cauliflowers, snowflakes, and waterfalls at Wired Science (http://www.wired.com/2010/09/fractal-patterns-in-nature/?pid=162).

How Technology Tools Can Support Active Learning

As the capabilities of technology tools keep expanding, it is helpful to regularly ask ourselves, "What teaching strategies are improved with the new tools?" Ryan Cordell, who teaches English at St. Norbert College and is a regular contributor to the *Chronicle of Higher Education* Prof. Hacker blog, offers these suggestions. In his May 13, 2011 posting on New Technologies to Get Your Students Engaged, Ryan lists four pedagogical goals that he thinks technologies now can make a difference in learning well and with purpose. These goals fit well with our focus on reflection and pattern making:

- Conduct research using primary sources.
- Organize their work—Cordell suggests free tools such as Zotero (www.zotero.org) and Mendeley (www.mendeley.org).
- Practice real scholarship.
- Work collaboratively.

Even in accelerated courses, active learning can be supported.

IC Tip 3: Developing Expertise in Short Courses: Can It Be Done?

This tip answers questions such as these:

- What are two core requirements for developing expertise?
- How can I help my learners practice widely and deeply in short courses?

Remember that two of the core requirements for developing expertise are time and deliberate practice. This is particularly challenging in intensive courses. Providing the special kind of deliberate practice needed for developing expertise always requires explicit design, but even more so in online environments. One familiar teaching strategy is using cases and scenarios. Another great strategy that is not so familiar is using expert resources.

This tip suggests ways to use expert resources as one strategy for designing deliberate practice into your courses. While it is not truly possible to provide deliberate practice—as ideally it is customized to the learner—there are ways to approach it. An added benefit is that many expert resources feature current experts describing their experiences in video, adding media diversity to learning resources and experiences.

Included in this tip that describes two expert resources is an outline of a learning strategy for using these resources. Be sure to explore at least one of these resources.

How Expert Resources Can Provide Deliberate Practice

Experts' stories and narratives give us insight into the complex representations of knowledge that experts use when solving problems. These complex mental representations go far beyond the bare bones of abstract knowledge often presented in textbooks.

These knowledge representations include the historical, social, and practical context in which knowledge is applied. Thus access to experts' narratives and stories provide access to complex real-world contexts that engage, enthuse, and challenge learners.

Access to these complex narratives also makes it possible for students to further individualize their own learning as well (Brown & Duguid, 1995). So using expert resources can help us approach the customizing challenge of "deliberate practice" experiences.

What Does This Mean for My Course Assignments?

You, as the designer of learning, the designer of *practice* experiences, can guide learners to the types of experts and deliberate practice in which your learners can best delight and grow.

TED talks are one great expert resource for you to consider. They are freely available, feature experts on a range of discipline issues, and are growing by leaps and bounds (www.ted.com). Websites of professional organizations are also great sources for expert resources, such as webinars and expert stories.

TED Conferences and Discussions: Ideas Worth Spreading

The TED (Technology Entertainment and Design) Talks—online forums—are an expert resource not to be missed. They are called "riveting talks by remarkable people, free to the world," and this is quite accurate. TED Talks—limited to a maximum of twenty minutes—address an impressive array of topics within the research and practice of science and culture.

If you haven't experienced these TED Talks as yet, do take nineteen minutes and listen to the talk by author/educator Sir Ken Robinson on *Do schools kill creativity?* from January 7, 2007. With over 36 million views, it is one of the most-watched TED talks. In this talk, Sir Robinson "challenges the way we're educating our children" and "champions a radical rethink of our school systems, to cultivate creativity and acknowledge multiple types of intelligence." This is the lead talk in a ten-talk playlist on reimagining school. This playlist also includes a talk by Salman Khan of the Khan academy, *Let's use video to reinvent education*, influential in the concept of the flipped classroom. (Khan, 2011)

A section of the TED website called TED Studies uses TED Talks as jumping-off points for a structured educational experience. Playlists have been developed from the database of over 2,000 and growing TED Talks, and are designed to help students, professors, and self-guided learners explore important topics in higher education. Here are possible expert starting points:

- Biologist E. O. Wilson on saving life on earth
- Simon Sinek: How great leaders inspire action
- David Logan on tribal leadership
- Ed Boyden: A light switch for neurons

TED conversations provide a way for wider audiences to participate and interact with others. Transcripts accompany each talk as well.

How can you use these expert talks to support learning? These talks provide insight into the thinking of these experts and provide significant, meaningful, and current topics to evaluate and assess from the vantage point of the course knowledge.

Background and Theory on Deliberate Practice

Before closing, here is a bit of background on the concept of deliberate practice and how it is different from simple practice.

K. A. Ericsson, one of the leading researchers in this field, and his colleagues define deliberate practice as "those activities that have been found to be most effective in improving performance" (Ericsson, Krampe, & Tesch-Romer, 1993). Deliberate practice has also been defined as "intense, prolonged, and highly focused efforts to improve current performance" (Colvin, 2008). Note the emphasis on performance in both these definitions. So in using expert resources, it will enhance learning if we assign students to tasks that require doing and performing. This can mean analyzing, speaking, writing, and creating as suggested by the higher levels of Bloom's taxonomy.

Conclusion—and What's Next

We have reached the end of the chapters with tips. It has been a journey for us, and a journey we hope you have enjoyed as well. We also hope that you will continue to return to the various tip categories and charts for subsequent iterations of your course designs and offerings. Also we always enjoy hearing from readers about their suggestions and comments.

In the next and final chapter of this book, we'll look at some issues you might have faced and how to improve your next offering of this course or your next online course.

Self-Directed Exercise/Application

Intensive courses benefit from fresh approaches to design, given the challenges of time, stress, and feelings of being firehosed with content. Reflect now on one section or chapter of a course that you might redesign, given the ideas in this set of tips. In this reflection, set these three goals: First, identify a course core concept that challenges your learners, but that is one of the concepts you feel is core to the course knowledge; search out three or four possible cases or scenarios that require use of this core concept, and then create a draft assignment for your learners for that content. Keep in mind that it is good that the assignment relies on other concepts as well, so that solutions are not obvious. Also, assignments that include collaboration with a least one or two other students in a review stage can be quite effective. Good luck!

Part Three

Continuing Your Journey to Expertise

Chapter 11

What's Next: Reflecting and Looking Forward

THIS CHAPTER IS similar to a course wrap for your students. By now you've completed your review and grading of all the students' work, turned in the grades, and are probably ready for a day or two off. Do take the time to reward yourself for taking on a new challenge and making it work.

After completing an online course and relaxing and rejoicing in your new skill set, it is wise to reflect and debrief yourself. The best time to do this is while the experience is still fresh.

You want to review what worked well, what may not have worked so well, and any possible surprises that you encountered. If you will be teaching this course again, now is also the time to plan revisions, possibly using the feedback from your students as to what worked well for them. If you will be teaching a different online course, write a note to yourself about the particular strategies you want to use again.

Reflecting and Looking Forward Using the Four Course Phases

Reflecting on a course and planning for the next offering of a course can be a joy and a struggle. Very probably, there were successful moments as well as tough ones. Preparing a summary of lessons learned and revising the course to be more effective takes time and a bit of practice.

Here are some questions for review and descriptions of common problems for the four phases of a course. You can use these to guide the reflection of the course you have just completed and to guide the planning and revisions for your next course.

Design and Preparation Phase

Start your reflection by reviewing the course from the beginning: the design and preparation phase. Check yourself with these questions:

- What did you not have prepared as well as you thought you had? One area that usually takes more practice is creating the discussion forum postings and the directions for those postings. Remember that you can never be too clear and explicit.

- Was your syllabus clear enough on the policies and procedures for involving the whole instructional team, including technical and media support?

- Did your syllabus clearly map out the week-by-week view of readings, assignments, and expectations, and do a good job of launching a course with excitement and enthusiasm?

- In the assignments, did you talk to the students as if you were talking to them face-to-face in a classroom? Many syllabi state, "the students will do this" or "the students will do that." That format is appropriate for curriculum review but not for instructions to the students. In your syllabus you want to talk to the students, addressing them as "you."

- What about your assessment plan and the rubrics for each of the components of the plan? Did you and your students use the rubrics well? Or would you like to refine and adapt them more to the particular content?

Common Problem Area: Learners Were Confused About Activities

Learners are often confused despite herculean efforts to be clear. So it is always good to review your instructions on readings, assignments, and postings. Another reason for learners being confused is that they may not be reading your instructions. If that is the case, you might want to encourage more student-to-student conversation in a student course forum. Of course, you can also use this place to respond and clarify as well.

Common Problem Area: Some Students Can Be Bullies or Simply Have Bad Manners

Online courses are not exempt from the challenge of difficult students. Students can be difficult by acting or speaking inappropriately in the discussion forum, creating new topic threads when only a reply is appropriate or inserting frivolous comments within existing discussion threads.

Students who behave this way sometimes are just looking for more personal attention, and a personal e-mail can sometimes help this. A good general rule is to handle difficult students online in the same way that you would handle them in a face-to-face class: take them to one side and in a personal and confidential way provide some counsel. EM Tip 9 offers more strategies for understanding and dealing with difficult students.

Reflecting on Phase One, Course Beginnings

The themes for the course beginnings focused on social presence, getting acquainted, launching the community, and ensuring that all the content and tools for teaching and learning were in place. These questions will get you started on your review:

- How did the initial getting-acquainted experiences work? Did all your students respond in a timely and appropriate manner? Did you share enough of yourself and help to make social connections as the base for the cognitive connections?

- Did you follow up with all students to ensure that everyone was engaged in the course in the first few days of the course? If you lost any of your students, this can often be the place to focus on to ensure that students feel welcome and are in the right course at the right time.

- Launching of the learning community is often linked to course goals and objectives. Did you have a forum that focused on the learners' setting personalized and customized goals? How did it work? Did you feel that the students made a connection between themselves and the goals of the course?

- Did the students acquire the core required content resources in a timely manner? Did getting the materials pose any difficulties for your students? Do you want to make changes in the sets of content resources for the next course?

- Did the students—or you—have any unresolved technical issues regarding the tools used in the course? Was the needed technical support in place and responsive?

- Were there other administrative issues that created difficulties that need to be reported to administrators?

Common Problem Area: Discussions Were Flat or Never Got Going

If you felt as if your discussions did not take off or were generally flat without passion or energy, review the discussion questions. Did you tend to use one-answer questions or those that called for a yes or no and nothing more? If so, be sure to develop open-ended questions by using such phrases as, "In what way . . .," or "Based on your own experiences . . .," or "Using data from your particular region or discipline perspective . . ." Another question to ask yourself is whether you were too involved too early in the discussions. Did learners wait to read what you wrote or ask you what you thought before posting their own response? If so, make it clearer in the instructions that you will guide discussion and will comment primarily to encourage and facilitate and to help craft a discussion summary. Review the many tips on creating substantive discussion postings.

Common Problem Area: You Are Not Feeling Comfortable with the Course Management System

If there were activities that you wanted to design for students using the course management system but didn't quite know how to, plan to get those questions answered before teaching another online course. For example, you may have questions about setting up groups, using some audio tools, or using the synchronous online classroom. The best way to ensure that you will be ready and able to use these features in your next course is to create a "Top Three Things That I Want to Know How to Do" list and then write out the steps to make that happen. You may want to take a refresher course with your institution to expand your knowledge about the system. The second time around it will all make more sense, and you will get even more ideas about how to make better use of the tools.

Reflecting on Phase Two, Early Middle

One of the most important tasks for keeping the ball rolling in the early middle is the nurturing of a learning community for your students. This is accomplished with a strong teaching and cognitive presence. Here are some of the questions to reflect on:

- How did you feel about the process of building the learning community?

- Did you see the learners getting engaged with the content?

- Did you keep cycling back to the core concepts and linking those concepts to the learning outcomes? Or did you not review, summarize, or link back well enough?

- Did you focus time on getting to know the individual learners? Did you know where they were coming from and what they hoped to learn so that you could help them discern patterns and relationships?

Common Problem Area: A Learning Community Never Formed

If a learning community never really came together, this might be a response to your teaching presence. In some cases, you may need to revise your rubrics to place more emphasis on students' continuing the flow of a discussion and responding to other students' comments and responding to the ideas and assertions in the readings. Community forms only when learners do more than simply taking turns in response to a question. Recall that community depends on "long, thoughtful, threaded discussion on a subject of importance after which participants felt both personal satisfaction and kinship" (Brown, 2001, p. 18). A greater focus on core required readings and case studies can provide the basis of shared experiences and a deeper connection to the content and to the other learners.

Another aspect of community is equality. This means that your role as an expert can overpower the learners, so you may need to be more in the background in the discussions and reserve your more expansive expertise for the summaries, mini-introductions, and concept demonstrations and for facilitating and drawing out from the learners what they know. Another design strategy to build into your course is to assign one or two learners as a team to lead a forum discussion for a week. Review the many tips on community building as well.

Reflecting on Phase Three, Late Middle

The late middle is a time of increased exploration and engagement with the content while also shifting into a content resolution and focus stage. Here are some questions to reflect on:

- How were the students doing midway through the course? Were they engaged and working well?

- Had the students identified their course projects? Did you help to ensure that the projects were a good match for the students and the course goals?

- Were the students actively supporting and helping each other?

- How were you feeling about the course at this point? Did you feel as if you wanted to adapt some of the course readings or requirements?

Common Problem Area: Assignments Were Consistently Late

If learners were consistently turning in assignments a day or more late, you may wish to deduct points or use a clever ticket system devised by one of our colleagues. He gave each student a "one late assignment free" ticket that the learner could use when an emergency arose and he or she needed to turn in an assignment late. In other cases, you may decide on a policy of subtracting points for each day that an assignment is late. You may also want to review your assessment plan and see if you have too many assignments, making it difficult for learners to complete them all. When you review your assessment plan, consider how directly the assessment plan supports the learning of the course objectives. Some faculty also use the announcement feature and remind students two or three days before an assignment is due.

Reflecting on Phase Four, Closing Weeks

In the closing weeks of a course, you are guiding and mentoring the students in their projects. You are also finding ways to affirm and confirm the learners' understanding of the core concepts in the course and mentor the learners in achieving the learning outcomes. Here are a few questions to check how the teaching and learning in this part of the course worked:

- Were students involved in peer review of project work?

- Were the students collaborating with and challenging their colleagues?

- Were the teams working well? Or were any adjustments you had to make working?

- Did you help the learners organize themselves for the last part of the course, making sure that the goals, outcomes, and expectations all were still making sense?

Common Problem Area: The Course Could Use More "Pizzazz"

If you are feeling comfortable in your course system and would like to add more media or more variety to your course, you may want to consider using one or two of the technology tools described in earlier chapters. A good place to start is adding audio or video to your welcome message. Our smartphones now can capture short videos quickly and easily. This can be a way of touching base with your students with short reminders, or intros to challenging readings or assignments. You might also want to prepare short audio or video podcasts, with short concept introductions as mini-lectures. As always, keep it simple, and encourage students to let you know how they are working.

Common Problem Area: Final Course Evaluation Responses Unpleasantly Surprised You

If learners are feeling unhappy or experiencing dissatisfaction with your course, it's a good idea to know this before the end-of-course evaluations. As recommended in one of the tips on feedback, ask for feedback early in the course and, depending on circumstances, at other points as well, such as feedback on a project assignment or unusual resources. If you did not ask for feedback early in your first course, be sure to design in a couple of feedback points for your next course.

Common Problem Area: Something Is Not Quite Right, But You're Not Sure What

If you're feeling uncomfortable about how the course went, this is a good time to evaluate the alignment of your learning outcomes, assessments, and activities. Do they all relate to one another, or is there an objective that didn't make sense for these students? Or is there a learning outcome that should be added? If the course elements are not aligned, the course can easily go off-track without anyone noticing until a major assessment occurs. One of the tips suggested asking your students for specific feedback on a new assignment, reading, or activity. If you did that, then be sure to use that feedback as you revise your course.

Reflecting and Looking Forward with the Learning Experiences Framework

Another way of reviewing your course is to use the learning experiences framework described in Chapter Two. You'll recall that this framework has four elements: the learner, the faculty mentor, the content, and the context or environment. Here are a few questions for each of the four elements.

Learner

- What did you learn about the learners in your course?
- Did anything about the learners in your course surprise you? The amount of time they spent on the course? How they wanted to interact?
- Were the learners who you thought they would be? Were they interested in achieving the designated learning outcomes that you had planned or were they interested in refreshing or developing a different area of expertise?
- Did they have the appropriate prerequisite skills?
- Did they interact and collaborate as expected?
- Did they successfully complete the course?
- If a learner was unsuccessful, why did that happen?

If your learners did not have the prerequisite skills that you thought they would have, the course description in the course catalog or program sequence may need to be reviewed. This is a topic to be discussed with your colleagues and department chair. If there are just a couple of core concepts that students were grappling with, you may want to develop a precourse unit with resources that review those concepts. If a high percentage of learners were unsuccessful, reexamine the alignment of objectives, activities, and assessment. The assessment may have been a mismatch or too ambitious.

If interaction and collaboration did not take off and blossom, review the expectations stated about collaboration. Make sure that at least 20 to 30 percent of the course points were allocated to participation so as to send the message that interaction is important.

Faculty Mentor

- Were you adequately present in the course?
- Did you guide, but not dominate the discussions?
- In what ways could you have helped learners be more successful?
- How do you think your instruction could be improved? Think about all the areas you are responsible for: instruction, design, implementation, teaching presence, and learner response. How would you improve each of these?

If you did not develop a satisfactory relationship with the students individually or as a group, review your social, teaching, and cognitive presence in the course. Maybe you remained aloof from the students and didn't give them a chance to get to know you. Maybe your teaching direction at the general course level was effective, but you did not shift and provide any personal or customized mentoring or guidance. And review your cognitive presence. Did you help the students become knowledgeable and comfortable with the core concepts and regularly review, facilitate, and challenge the students? Review the evaluations from the early points of your course as well as the end of course evaluations. And check with your colleagues as to what strategies they find most successful in developing positive relationships you're your students. The most basic need students have is to feel that instructors care about them. Finding ways to be sure that message comes across is helpful.

Content and Knowledge Resources and Goals

- Did your choice of required, recommended resources work for the students? Were the resources at the right level of difficulty?

- Did the resources provide enough variety in terms of media? Did you have a set of text, audio, video, and current resources?

- Were the materials in a mobile and digital format that made it easy for the students to access and use?

- Were the content resources effective at helping the students achieve the course learning outcomes?

- Did you build in opportunities for learners to add to the content you had planned?

In the first cycle of a course, the resources may or may not be effective at engaging the students in the way you would like. The resources might not be a good fit, or there may not be a rich enough set to challenge, assist, or engage the students. Be sure to review the resources and add or delete, and perhaps annotate, recommended sources.

Copyright issues might also need to be addressed. Most institutions have policies and staff people to help if you need to address issues of fair use and appropriate use.

Environment and Context

- Where did the students do their best work at learning: individually, in small teams, or in larger groups?

- Which tools and resources were the best fit for the content and your students?

- Did technical issues detract from the course?

- Did the students use appropriate applications to do their teamwork and their collaborative or synchronous work? Which of these tools might you want to build into your next course?

- What information might learners need for resolving problems more effectively in future offerings of the course?

These questions are a combination of pedagogical strategy, student preferences, and the particular demands of the content and the performance goals of the course, so answering the questions might be difficult after your first course. But you may want to be alert in future course cycles to some of these questions. As for yourself, review where you do your best teaching in an online course and record the habits, strategies, and tools that work best for you.

Advice from Fellow Online Instructors

You are not alone in the triumphs and challenges you have faced in designing and implementing your online or blended course. Developing expertise in teaching online is a process of continuing dedication over time. Here are a few words that may resonate with you from those who have made similar journeys.

Advice 1: Just Do Your Best

Almost every objection raised by faculty who imagine what online teaching "must" be like has been answered by the actual experience of doing it and searching for ways to make an online course the best it can be. I still tell my students, "This is a class with no back seats," and do everything I can, whether high tech or low tech, to make it so. Nobody has it all figured out, but just do your best to be better at it tomorrow than you were yesterday, and you'll make it fine!—David W. Forman, Ed.D., Graduate Education, Georgetown College, Georgetown, Kentucky

Advice 2: It's Kind of Fun to Do the Impossible!

The reason I love teaching online is the challenges of working with incredibly unique individuals with highly diverse backgrounds. When computers began to be used in teaching, I heard a lot of negative predictions about them: "They will take away the human touch." "They will be cold and impersonal." "They just won't work." I'm the type of individual who says, "Show me!" Instead of accepting such negative predictions at face value, I look for the silver lining. What someone else sees as impossible, I learn to welcome as a challenge! This is what drew me to exploring the positive possibilities of teaching (online) when a senior faculty member said, "Why not try this? And I think you should be the one to do it!!"

I was delighted by the students' positive response to the two online courses I developed and taught that summer. They were far from cold and impersonal, and the students sang the praises of its flexibility and the individual attention that they got from me. I'll never forget how one of them, a student who had been somewhat fearful of statistics, excitedly printed out all of her study notes and went to show our department chair what she was learning. You'd think she was showing him a stash of gifts from the genuine joy and excitement in her voice.

These successes fueled my passion to keep it going. Keep peeking outside the box. Keep pushing the boundaries of what can be done in online teaching and learning. So from that humble beginning, I developed more courses . . . that led to more student demand for them . . . that in turn led to other faculty members wanting to get in on a very good thing! As Walt Disney once said: "It's kind of fun to do the impossible!"—Mary I. Dereshiwsky, Ph.D, Professor, College of Education, Northern Arizona University, Flagstaff, Arizona.

Advice 3: Begin with the End in Mind

In my first semester as an assistant professor, I was given an online course, developed by another instructor to teach. The course was Instructional Systems Design, a project-based course for graduate students. As a new professor with three new preps, I tried to make minor changes to the course rather than starting with the learning objectives I had developed. First lesson learned: modifying someone else's course to your objectives is almost harder than starting from scratch.

Because I thought the course would be "reusable" as it was, I did not plan enough time for review and revision and consequently made adjustments on the fly. The lack of congruence between my learning objectives and the existing instructional materials caused difficulty for the students' ability to readily grasp and apply the concepts. I learned that designing quality online courses must begin with the end in mind: what your learners will be able to do! Determine the learning objectives for your course first, and then choose the content, assessments, and technologies! Backward planning will also help provide an overall temporal time line for your course.

Adequate time to align the instructional materials with the learning objectives is interrelated with what I believe is the second best practice: an online course must be fully designed and developed before the first learner accesses the course. I have worked with many instructors who did not fully grasp the concept of what a complete online course entails until after they had invested an exorbitant amount of time teaching and developing concurrently!

The dual role of developer and instructor left little time for comprehensive feedback on the discussion boards or assignments, much less for teachable moments! The experience was painful for both the instructor and the students. So be sure to give yourself enough time to completely design and develop an online course. Depending on the content, support, and technology, the time required could range from six months for a new course to six weeks to revise a course. When is your course complete? When another instructor is able to teach your online course with little or no prep! — Kathy

Ingram, Ph.D., Assistant Dean of Curriculum, Kaplan University, Jacksonville, Florida.

Advice 4: New to Online Teaching? Get to Know Your Students

If you are new to online education, don't expect to produce the perfect course; don't expect to anticipate the needs of each class of students no matter how much instructional design and media production support you have access to. Prepare as much as you can for what you can anticipate, be clear on what learning needs to happen and get to know your students.

I highly recommend surveying your students sometime in weeks 3 or 4 after they have had a chance to become familiar with the rhythm and workings of the course. Ask them about the pace of the class and distribution of work, about the weekly rhythm and your choice of due dates. Ask them about what is going well and what less so. Ask them about things that you can change and be prepared to respond where it makes sense.

My start in online education (or distance education as we called it), back in the mid 2000s at the University of Alaska, was part of the larger effort of the University to provide access to the geographically isolated students in the state. Over the years, I have learned a lot about the lives of my students who live in a wide range of cities, towns, and villages. The first time I taught a summer course, I learned that subsistence and commercial salmon fishing are open each week of the season from Sunday to Wednesday, making midweek due dates out of rhythm and hard to meet. I learned that course materials that students could use offline were much more useful on a fishing boat or while at a fish camp and put a lot more energy and creativity into their design. Every improvement in my teaching has student insight to thank.

While many aspects of Alaskan life may be unique, online students respond well when you make an effort to get to know them and their life demands, which readily offers amazing insights into their learning needs.
— Deborah Barnett, Ph.D. Adjunct Professor of Biology, University of Alaska Southeast and Director of Online Pedagogy, School of Public Health, University of California, Berkeley.

Conclusion: Innovation as a Three-Phase Process

A business innovation professor at Harvard describes the cycle of innovation as a three-phase process: imitation, incremental improvements, followed by transformational processes (Rosenbloom, 1999). These phases can guide our innovation journey in online and blended teaching and learning as well. The first time you design and teach a course, you tend to do things in much the same way you've always done them but using the new technology, the new online space, the new course management system. In your next two or three cycles of teaching, you become comfortable with the base set of tools, add new tools, refine your use of the base set of tools, and refine your teaching strategies and content resources. By the third and later cycles, you venture forth and create a new course maximizing the new environment and testing innovative new strategies.

Of course, with the ever-increasing rate of change, we don't see an end to innovation. We just start the three cycles again. What doesn't change is the fundamental relationship of a teacher to student or mentor to learner. That is our treasure and one we always will have.

Appendix

Resources for Learning More about the Research and Theory of Teaching Online

BECOMING A MASTER in the art and skill of teaching and learning online is a journey. Here are some resources to help you along the way. Becoming an expert is a matter of years of dedication, not just months. Be patient with yourself, enjoy the process, and invite your colleagues and students to share and enjoy the journey with you.

As you are learning how to teach online, watch for excellent resources on topics such as research on learning, memory, and brain development. These are all areas that are changing how we think about teaching and learning. It is also useful to be alert to how your learners, and people in general, are using new technologies. This will have an impact on our teaching and learning environments, and probably sooner rather than later.

The resources listed here are just some of our favorites. In these days of the Internet, it is not possible to be comprehensive. Thus, these are just starting points.

Books

Teaching and Learning Online

Anderson, T. (Ed.) (2008). *The theory and practice of online learning* (2nd ed.). Athabasca, AB, Canada: Athabasca University.

Bates, A. W. (2015). Teaching in a digital age. Creative Commons licensed version available from https://opentextbc.ca/teachinginadigitalage/

Beetham, H. & Sharpe, R. (2013). *Rethinking pedagogy for a digital age: designing for 21st century learning* (2nd ed.). New York, NY: Routledge.

Bender, T. (2012). *Discussion-based online teaching to enhance student learning: Theory, practice and assessment* (2nd ed.). Sterling, VA: Stylus.

Bowen, J. A. (2012). *Teaching naked: How moving technology out of your college classroom will improve student learning.* San Francisco, CA: Jossey-Bass.

Brookfield, S. D. (2012). *Teaching for Critical Thinking: Tools and techniques to help students question their assumptions.* San Francisco, CA: Jossey-Bass.

Brookfield, S. D., & Preskill, S. N. (2016). *The discussion book: 50 great ways to get people talking.* San Francisco, CA: Jossey-Bass.

Conrad, R. M., & Donaldson, J. A. (2011). *Engaging the online learner: Activities and resources for creative instruction.* San Francisco: Jossey-Bass.

Conrad, R. M., & Donaldson, J. A. (2012). *Continuing to engage the online learner: More activities and resources for creative instruction.* San Francisco, CA: Jossey-Bass.

Garrison, D. R., & Vaughan, N. D. (2008). *Blended learning in higher education: Framework, principles, and guidelines.* San Francisco, CA: Jossey-Bass.

Gurung, R. A. R., Chick, N. L., & Haynie, A. (Eds.). (2009). *Exploring signature pedagogies.* Sterling, VA: Stylus.

Horn, M. B. & Staker, H. (2015). *Blended: Using disruptive innovation to improve schools.* San Francisco, CA: Jossey-Bass.

Joosten, T. (2012). *Social media for educators: Strategies and best practices.* San Francisco, CA: Jossey-Bass.

Knowles, M. (1980). *The modern practice of adult education: From pedagogy to andragogy* (2nd ed.). New York, NY: Association Press.

Laurillard, D. (2012). *Teaching as a design science: Building pedagogical patterns for learning and technology.* New York, NY: Routledge.

Means, B., Bakia, M., & Murphy, R. (2014). *Learning online: What research tells us about whether, when and how.* New York, NY: Routledge.

Miller, M. D. (2014). *Minds online: Teaching effectively with technology.* Cambridge, MA: Harvard University Press.

Palloff, R., & Pratt, K. (2013). *Lessons from the virtual classroom.* San Francisco, CA: Jossey-Bass.

Smith, R. M. (2014). *Conquering the content: A blueprint for online course design and development* (2nd ed.). San Francisco, CA: Jossey-Bass.

Stein, J. & Graham, C. R. (2014). *Essentials for blended learning: A standards-based guide.* New York, NY: Routledge.

Tobin, T. J., Mandernach, J., & Taylor, A. H. (2015). *Evaluating online teaching: Implementing best practices.* San Francisco, CA: Jossey-Bass.

Weimer, M. (2013). *Learner-centered teaching* (2nd ed.). San Francisco, CA: Jossey-Bass.

Brain, Cognition, Learning, and Memory

Bransford, J. D., Brown, A. L., & Cocking, R. R. (Eds.). (2000). *How people learn: Brain, mind, experience, and school* (Exp. ed.). Washington, DC: National Academies Press.

Brown, P. C., Roediger, H. I., & McDaniel, M. A. (2014). *Make it stick: The science of successful learning*, Cambridge, MA: Harvard University Press.

Daniels, H., Cole, M., & Wertsch, J. V. (2007). *The Cambridge companion to Vygotsky*. Cambridge: Cambridge University Press.

Johnson, S. (2004). *Mind wide open*. New York, NY: Scribner.

Kandel, E. (2006). *In search of memory: The emergence of a new science of mind*. New York, NY: Norton.

Moll, L.C. (Ed.). (1990/2004). *Vygotsky and education: Instructional implications and applications of sociohistorical psychology*. Cambridge: Cambridge University Press.

Ramachandran, V. S. (2011). *The tell-tale brain: A neuroscientist's quest for what makes us human*. New York, NY: Norton.

Roediger, H. L., Dudai, Y., & Fitzpatrick, S. M. (Eds.). (2007). *Science of memory: Concepts*. New York, NY: Oxford University Press.

Schacter, D. L. (2001). *The seven sins of memory: How the mind forgets and remembers*. Boston: Houghton Mifflin.

Shapiro, L. (2011). *Embodied cognition*. New York, NY: Routledge.

Journals

Hybrid Pedagogy: A Journal of Learning, Teaching and Technology, http://www.digitalpedagogylab.com/hybridped/

International Review of Research in Open and Distance Learning, http://www.irrodl.org/index.php/irrodl

New Directions in Teaching and Learning, http://onlinelibrary.wiley.com/journal

Journal of Educators Online, http://thejeo.com/

Journal of Interactive Online Learning, http://www.ncolr.org/

Journal of Online Learning and Teaching, http://jolt.merlot.org

National Teaching and Learning Forum, http://www.ntlf.com/

Tomorrow's Professor Postings, Stanford University, https://tomprof.stanford.edu

Organizations, Conferences, and Certifications

Center for the Integration of Research, Teaching, and Learning, CIRTL Network, http: www.cirtl.net

EDUCAUSE *Learning Initiative*, http://www.educause.edu/eli

Certified Online Instructor program sponsored by the Learning Resources Network, http://www.lern.org/events-and-education/online-courses-for-continuing-education-professionals/certified-online-instructor-coi/

International Council on Open and Distance Education, http://www.icde.org/

Online Learning Consortium, http://onlinelearningconsortium.org/

University of Wisconsin's Annual Conference on Distance Teaching and Learning Conference, http://www.uwex.edu/disted/conference/

Communities and Listservs

OL Daily and OL Weekly by Stephen Downes, Stephen's Web, http://www.downes.ca/about.htm

Online Learning Update, Ray Schroeder (Ed.), OTEL, Online@Illinois Springfield http://people.uis.edu/rschr1/onlinelearning/blogger.html

Professional and Organization Development Network in Higher Education POD, https://listserv.nd.edu/

Other Teaching and Learning Resources

BlendKit Learning Toolkit, https://blended.online.ucf.edu/blendkit-course/

Boettcher, J. V. Designing for Learning- Tips for Teaching and Learning Online, www.designingforlearning.info.

Canadian Institute of Distance Education Research at Athabasca University, http://cider.athabascau.ca

Illinois Online Network Online Education Resources, http://www.ion.uillinois.edu/resources/tutorials/

Instructional Design, http://www.instructionaldesign.org

Library of E-coaching Tips for Teaching Online by Designing for Learning, http://www.designingforlearning.info/services/writing/ecoach/index.htm

MIT OpenCourseWare, http://ocw.mit.edu/index.htm

Multimedia Educational Resource for Learning and Online Teaching (MERLOT), https://www.merlot.org/merlot/index.htm

The Open Syllabus project, http://opensyllabusproject.org

Open University at iTunes University, http://www.open.edu/itunes/
Top 100 Tools for Learning, http://www.c4lpt.co.uk

Other Articles of Particular Interest

Hayles, K. N. (2007). Hyper and deep attention: The generational divide in cognitive modes. *Profession, 13,* 187–199.

Muirhead, B. (2006). Creating concept maps: Integrating constructivism principles into online classes. *International Journal of Instructional Technology and Distance Learning, 3*(1). Retrieved from http://www.itdl.org/Journal/jan_06/article02.htm

Vesely, P., Bloom, L., & Sherlock, J. (2007). Key elements of building online community: Comparing faculty and student perceptions. *Journal of Online Teaching and Learning, 3*(3). Retrieved from http://jolt.merlot.org/vol3no3/vesely.htm

References

Abrami, P. C., Bernard, R. M., Bures, E. M., Borokhovski, E., & Tamim, R. M. (2011). Interaction in distance education and online learning: Using evidence and theory to improve practice. *Journal of Computing in Higher Education* (23). Retrieved from doi: 10.1007/s12528-011-9043-x

Abramson, L. (2007, November 28). Online courses catch on in U.S. colleges. *National Public Radio.* Retrieved from http://www.npr.org

Akyol, Z., & Garrison, D. R. (2008). The development of a community of inquiry over time in an online course: Understanding the progression and integration of social, cognitive and teaching presence *Journal of Asynchronous Learning Networks,* 12(3), 3–22. Available at http://www.aln.org/node/1397;olc.onlinelearningconsortium.org

Allen, D. (2002, 2015). *Getting things done: The art of stress-free productivity* (2nd ed.). New York, NY: Penguin Books.

Allen, I. E., & Seaman, J. (2008). *Staying the course: Online education in the United States.* Retrieved from http://www.onlinelearningsurvey.com/reports/staying-the-course.pdf

Anderson, C. (2006). *The long tail: Why the future of business is selling less of more.* New York, NY: Hachette.

Anderson, T. (2008). Teaching in an online learning context. In T. Anderson (Ed.), *Theory and practice of online learning.* Athabasca, AB, Canada: Athabasca University.

Angelo, T. A., & Cross, K. P. (1993). *Classroom assessment techniques: A handbook for college teachers* (2nd ed.). San Francisco, CA: Jossey-Bass.

Association of Colleges and Universities. (2009). *VALUE (Valid Assessment of Learning in Undergraduate Education).* Washington, DC: www.aacu.org

Astin, A. W., Banta, T. W., Cross, K. P., El-Khawas, E., Ewell, P. T., Hutchings, P., . . . Wright, B. D. (2012). *9 principles of good practice for assessing student learning.* Retrieved from http://www.learningoutcomeassessment.org/Principles of Assessment.html

Atkinson, R. C., & Shiffrin, R. M. (1968). Human memory: A proposed system and its control processes. In K. W. Spence & J. T. Spence (Eds.), *The psychology of learning and motivation: Advances in research and theory* (Vol. 2, pp. 89–195). New York, NY: Academic Press.

Bain, K. (2012). *What the best college students do*. Cambridge, MA: The Belknap Press of Harvard University Press.

Baker, D. L. (2011). Designing and orchestrating online discussions. *Merlot Journal of Online Learning and Teaching*, 7(3). Retrieved from http://jolt.merlot.org/vol7no3/baker_0911.pdf

Banta, T. W., & Blaich, C. (2011). Closing the assessment loop. *Change: The Magazine of Higher Learning*, 43(1), 22–27. Retrieved from http://college.wfu.edu/assessment/wp-content/uploads/Closing_The_Assessment_Loop-Banta_Blaich-2011.pdf

Baran, E., & Correia, A.-P. (2009). Student-led facilitation strategies in online discussions. *Distance Education*, 30(3), 339–361. Retrieved from http://www.public.iastate.edu/~acorreia/Student-led%20facilitation%20strategies.pdf

Barkley, E. F., Major, C. H., & Cross, K. P. (2014). *Collaborative learning techniques: A handbook for college faculty* (2nd ed.). San Francisco, CA: Jossey-Bass.

Bart, M. (2012, June 4). Dealing with difficult students and other classroom disruptions. Faculty Focus. Retrieved from: http://www.facultyfocus.com/articles/effective-classroom-management/dealing-with-difficult-students-and-other-classroom-disruptions/

Bennett, D. (2009). Trends in the Higher Education Labor Force: Identifying Changes in Worker Composition and Productivity. Center for College Affordability and Productivity. April 2009. Retrieved from http://www.centerforcollegeaffordability.org/uploads/Labor_Force.pdf

Bernard, R. M., Abrami, P. C., Borokhovski, E., Wade, A., Tamim, R., Surkes, M., & Bethel, E. C. (2009). A meta-analysis of three interaction treatments in distance education. *Review of Educational Research*, 79(3), 1243–1289. Retrieved from http://www.jstor.org/stable/40469094

Berrett, D. (2012, February 28). How "flipping" the classroom can improve the traditional lecture. *Chronicle of Higher Education*. Retrieved from http://chronicle.com/article/How-Flipping-the-Classroom/130857/

Beuchot, A., & Bullen, M. (2005). Interaction and interpersonality in online discussion forums. *Distance Education*, 26(1), 67–87. Retrieved from http://www.tandfonline.com/

Bloom, B. S. (Ed.). (1956). *Taxonomy of educational objectives, handbook 1: Cognitive domain*. Boston, MA: Addison-Wesley.

Bloom, B. S. (1964). *Stability and change in human characteristics*. New York, NY: Wiley.

Bloom, B. S. (1976). *Human characteristics and school learning*. New York, NY: McGraw-Hill.

Bloom, P. (2002). *How children learn the meanings of words.* Cambridge, MA: MIT.

Blue Jeans Network. (2014). *The state of the modern meeting.* Retrieved from http://pages.bluejeans.com/infographic-modern-meeting-nt

Boettcher, J. V. (1998, June). Let's boldly go . . . to the education holodeck. *Syllabus, Vol. 11,* 18–22.

Boettcher, J. V. (2000). How much does it cost to put a course online? It all depends. In M. J. Finkelstein, C. Frances, F. I. Jewett, , and B. W. Scholz (Eds.), *Dollars, distance, and online education: The new economics of college teaching and learning* (pp. 172–197). Phoenix, AZ: American Council on Education/Oryx Press.

Boettcher, J. V. (2005). *Ten core principles for designing learning—The jungle brain meets the tundra brain!* Retrieved from https://www.academia.edu/6075767/Ten_Core_Principles_for_Designing_Learning_The_Jungle_Brain_Meets_the_Tundra_Brain_

Boettcher, J. V. (2007). Ten core principles for designing effective learning environments: Insights from brain research and pedagogical theory. *Innovate: Journal of Online Education,* 3(3). Retrieved from http://nsuworks.nova.edu/cgi/viewcontent.cgi?article=1099&context=innovate

Boettcher, J. V. (2011). Evidence of learning online: Assessment beyond the paper. *Campus Technology.* Retrieved from: http://campustechnology.com/Articles/2011/02/23/Assessment-Beyond-The-Paper.aspx?p=1

Boettcher, J. V. (2007, 2012). *E-coaching tip 36: Cognitive presence in online courses — Are you doing it?* Retrieved from http://www.designingforlearning.info/services/writing/ecoach/tips/tip36.html

Boettcher, J. V., & Conrad, R. M. (1999). *Faculty guide for moving teaching and learning to the web.* Laguna Hills, CA: League for Innovation.

Boettcher, J. V., & Conrad, R. M. (2004). *Faculty guide for moving teaching and learning to the web* (2nd ed.). Phoenix, AZ: League for Innovation.

Bok, D. (2005, December 18). Are colleges failing? Higher ed needs new lesson plans. Boston Globe. Retrieved from http://archive.boston.com/news/education/higher/articles/2005/12/18/are_colleges_failing/

Bok, D. (2007). Our underachieving colleges: A candid look at how much students learn and why they should be learning more. Princeton, NJ: Princeton University Press.

Bonk, C. J., & Khoo, E. (2014). Adding some TEC-VARIETY: 100+ activities for motivating and retaining learners online. Retrieved from http://tec-variety.com

Bonk, C. J., & Zhang, K. (2008). Empowering online learning: 100+ activities for reading, reflecting, displaying, and doing. San Francisco, CA: Jossey-Bass.

Bork, R. H., & Rucks-Ahidiana, Z. (2012, April 13–17). *Virtual courses and tangible expectations: An analysis of student and instructor opinions of online courses.* Paper presented at the American Educational Research Association, Vancouver, BC, Canada. Retrieved from http://67.205.94.182/media/k2/attachments/online-outcomes-virtual-courses-expectations.pdf

Bourne, J., & Moore, J. C. (Eds.). (2002). *Elements of quality online education: Practice and direction*. Needham, MA: Olin College-Sloan-C, 2003. Retrieved from http://olc.onlinelearningconsortium.org/node/1090

Brain and Behavior Research Foundation. (2013, Fall). Frequently asked questions on brain plasticity. *The Quarterly*, 28–29. Retrieved from https://bbrfoundation .org/sites/bbrf.civicactions.net/files/file-downloads/THE%20 QUARTERLY%20FALL%202013.pdf

Bransford, J. D., Brown, A. L., & Cocking, R. (Eds.). (2000). *How people learn: Brain, mind, experience, and school* (expanded edition). Washington, DC: National Academy Press.

Braxton, J. M., & Bayer, A. E. (Eds.). (2004). Addressing faculty and student classroom improprieties (*Vol. 99*). *New Directions for Teaching and Learning*. San Francisco, CA: Jossey-Bass.

Brookfield, S. D. (2012). *Teaching for critical thinking: Tools and techniques to help students question their assumptions*. San Francisco, CA: Jossey-Bass.

Brookfield, S. D., & Preskill, S. N. (2005). *Discussion as a way of teaching: Tools and techniques for democratic classrooms* (2nd ed.). San Francisco, CA: Jossey-Bass.

Brown, J. S. (1997). Research that reinvents the corporation. In J. S. Brown (Ed.), *Seeing differently: Insights on innovation* (pp. 203–219). Boston, MA: Harvard Business School.

Brown, J. S. (2006). New learning environments for the 21st Century: Exploring the edge. *Change: The Magazine of Higher Learning*, 38(5), 18–24. Retrieved from http://www.johnseelybrown.com/Change%20article.pdf

Brown, J. S., & Adler, R. P. (2008). Minds on fire. *EDUCAUSE Review*, 43(1), 17–32. Retrieved from http://net.educause.edu/ir/library/pdf/ERM0811.pdf

Brown, J. S., Collins, A., & Duguid, P. (1989). Situated cognition and the culture of learning. *Educational Researcher*, 18(1), 32–42. Retrieved from http://edr .sagepub.com/cgi/content/abstract/18/1/32

Brown, J. S., & Duguid, P. (1995). *Universities in the digital age*. Xerox Corporation. Retrieved from http://www.johnseelybrown.com/The%20University%20in% 20the%20Digital%20Age.pdf

Brown, J. S., & Duguid, P. A. (2000). *The social life of information*. Cambridge, MA: Harvard Business Press.

Brown, P. C., Roediger, H. I., & McDaniel, M. A. (2014). *Make it stick: The science of successful learning*. Cambridge, MA: Harvard University Press.

Brown, R. E. (2001). The process of community-building in distance learning classes. *Journal of Asynchronous Learning Networks*, 5(2), 18–35. Retrieved from http:// onlinelearningconsortium.org/jaln_full_issue/volume-5-issue-2- september-2001/

Bruckman, A. S. (2005, December). Student research and the internet. *Communications of the ACM, 48*, 35–37.

Bruner, J. S. (1963). *The process of education*. New York, NY: Vintage Books.

Burnett, K., Bonnici, L. J., Miksa, S. D., & Joonmin, K. (2007, Winter). Frequency, intensity and topicality in online learning: An exploration of the interaction dimensions that contribute to student satisfaction in online learning. *Journal of Education for Library & Information Science, 48*(1), 21–35.

Burns, J. M. (1978). *Leadership*. New York, NY: Harper & Row.

Burns, J. M. (2004, 2015). *Transforming leadership*. New York, NY: Grove Press.

Business-Higher Education Forum. (2003, June). *Building a nation of learners: The need for changes in teaching and learning to meet global challenges*. Business-Higher Education Forum. Retrieved from http://www.bhef.com/publications/building-nation-learners-need-changes-teaching-and-learning-meet-global-challenges

Business-Higher Education Forum (BHEF). (2013). *Promoting effective dialogue between business and education around the need for deeper learning*. Retrieved from http://www.bhef.com/sites/g/files/g829556/f/201303/report_2013_promoting_effective_dialogue.pdf

Cahill, M., & Fonteyn, M. (2000). Using mind mapping to improve students' metacognition. In J. Higgs & M. Jones (Eds.), *Clinical reasoning in the health professions* (2nd ed., pp. 214–220). New York, NY: Butterworth-Heinemann.

Carey, S. (2009). *The origin of concepts*. New York, NY: Oxford University Press.

Carnes, M. C. (2014). *Minds on fire: How role-immersion games transform college*. Cambridge, MA: Harvard University Press.

Carroll, J. B. (1963, May). A model of school learning. *Teachers College Record, 64*(8), 723–733.

Carroll, J. B. (1989). The Carroll model: A 25-year retrospective and prospective view. *Educational Researcher, 18*(1), 26–31. Retrieved from http://www.psycholosphere.com/The%20Carroll%20Model%20by%20John%20Carroll.pdf

Chen, S.-J. (2007). Instructional design strategies for intensive online courses: An objectivist-constructivist blended approach. *Journal of Interactive Online Learning, 6*(1). Retrieved from http://www.ncolr.org/jiol/issues/pdf/6.1.6.pdf

Chi, M.T.H. (2006). Two approaches to the study of experts' characteristics. In K. A. Ericsson, N. Charness, P. J. Feltovich, & R. R. Hoffman (Eds.), *The Cambridge handbook of expertise and expert performance* (pp. 21–30). New York, NY: Cambridge University Press.

Chickering, A. W., & Ehrmann, S. C. (1996, October 1996). Implementing the seven principles: Technology as lever. *AAHE Bulletin*. Retrieved from http://www.tltgroup.org/programs/seven

Clabaugh, G. K. (2009). *Jerome Bruner's educational theory.* Retrieved from http://www.newfoundations.com/GALLERY/Bruner.html

Clark, C. (2015). *Building a visual syllabus.* Retrieved from https://ltlatnd.wordpress.com/2015/08/19/building-a-visual-syllabus/

Clark, R. C., & Mayer, R. E. (2007). *e-Learning and the science of instruction: Proven guidelines for consumers and designers of multimedia learning.* San Francisco, CA: Jossey-Bass.

Clark, R. C., & Mayer, R. E. (2011). *e-Learning and the science of instruction: Proven guidelines for consumers and designers of multimedia learning* (3rd ed.). San Francisco, CA: Wiley.

Collins, A., Brown, J. S., & Holum, A. (1991). Cognitive apprenticeship: Making thinking visible. *American Educator.* Retrieved from http://www.21learn.org/archive/cognitive-apprenticeship-making-thinking-visible/

Colvin, G. (2008). *Talent is overrated: What really separates world-class performers from everybody else.* New York, NY: Portfolio.

Commission on Colleges Southern Association of Colleges and Schools. (2000). *Best practices for electronically offered degree and certificate programs.* Retrieved from http://www.sacscoc.org/pdf/commadap.pdf

Conceição, C.S.O., & Lehman, R. M. (2010). *Creating a sense of presence in online teaching: How to "be there" for distance learners.* San Francisco, CA: Jossey-Bass.

Conrad, R. M., & Donaldson, J. A. (2004). *Engaging the online learner: Activities and resources for creative instruction.* San Francisco, CA: Jossey-Bass

Conrad, R. M., & Donaldson, J. A. (2011). *Engaging the online learner: Activities and resources for creative instruction* (updated edition). San Francisco, CA: Jossey-Bass.

Conrad, R. M., and Donaldson, J. A. (2012). *Continuing to engage the online learner: More activities and resources for creative instruction.* San Francisco, CA: Jossey-Bass.

Cooper, S. T., Tyser, R. W., & Sandheinrich, M. B. (2007). The benefits of linking assignments to online quizzes in introductory biology courses. *MERLOT Journal of Online Learning and Teaching,* 3(3). Retrieved from http://jolt.merlot.org/vol3no3/cooper.pdf

Coppola, N. W., Hiltz, S. R., & Rotter, N. G. (2004). Building trust in virtual teams. *IEEE Transactions on Professional Communications,* 47(2), 95–104.

Cordell, R. (2011, May 08). New technologies to get your students engaged. Chronicle of Higher Education. Retrieved from http://chronicle.com/article/New-Technologies-to-Get-Your/127394/

Cornell University Center for Teaching Excellence. (2012). *Assessing student learning.* Retrieved from http://cte.cornell.edu/teaching-ideas/assessing-student-learning/index.html

Culkin, J. M. (1967) A schoolman's guide to Marshall McLuhan. *Saturday Review*, pp. 51–53.

Curtis, J. W., & Thorton, S. (2013). Here's the News The annual report on the Economic Status of the Profession 2012–2013. *Academe*. Retrieved from http://www.aaup.org/file/2012-13Economic-Status-Report.pdf.

Damasio, A. (1999). *The feeling of what happens: Body and emotion in the making of consciousness*. New York, NY: Harcourt.

Daniels, H. (2007). Pedagogy. In H. Daniels, M. Cole, & J. V. Wertsch (Eds.), *The Cambridge companion to Vygotsky* (pp. 307–331). Cambridge: Cambridge University Press.

Davis, B. G. (1999). *Grading practices*. Retrieved from http://facstaff.necc.mass.edu/wp-content/uploads/2012/01/Grading_Practices_Barbara_Gross_Davis_article.pdf

Davis, C., & Wilcock, E. (2003). Teaching materials using case studies. UK Centre for Materials Education. Retrieved from http://www.materials.ac.uk/guides/casestudies.asp

Dede, C. (1995). *The transformation of distance education to distributed learning*. Retrieved from http://www2.gsu.edu/~wwwitr/docs/distlearn/

Dennen, V. P., & Wieland, K. (2007). From interaction to intersubjectivity: Facilitating online group discourse processes. *Distance Education*, 28(3), 281–297.

Dewey, J. (1916). *Democracy and education*. New York, NY: Macmillan.

Dewey, J. (1933). *How we think* (1998 ed.). Boston: Houghton-Mifflin.

Dewey, J. (1938). *Experience and education*. New York, NY: Macmillan.

Diaz, V., Garrett, P. B., Kinley, E. R., Moore, J. F., Schwartz, C. M., & Kohrman, P. (2009, May/June). Faculty development for the 21st century. *EDUCAUSE Review*, 44, 46–55.

Donovan, M. S., Bransford, J. D., & Pellegrino, J. W. (Eds.). (1999). *How people learn: Bridging research and practice*. Washington, DC: National Academy Press.

Dyer, P. (2010). *Screenwriting mistake #29: No bookend scenes*. Retrieved from http://www.doctormyscript.com/2010/11/screenwriting-mistake-29-no-bookend.html

Epper, R. M., Derryberry, A., & Jackson, S. (2012). *Game-based learning*. Research Bulletin. EDUCAUSE Center for Applied Research. Retrieved from https://net.educause.edu/ir/library/pdf/ERB1208.pdf

Ericsson, K. A. (2000). *Expert performance and deliberate practice: An updated excerpt from Ericsson*. Retrieved from http://www.psy.fsu.edu/faculty/ericsson/ericsson.exp.perf.html.

Ericsson, K. A. (2009). Enhancing the development of professional performance: Implications from the study of deliberate practice. In K. A. Ericsson (Ed.),

Development of professional expertise: Toward measurement of expert performance and design of optimal learning environments (pp. 405–431). New York, NY: Cambridge University Press.

Ericsson, K. A., Charness, N., Feltovich, P. J., & Hoffman, R. R. (2006). *The Cambridge handbook of expertise and expert performance.* New York, NY: Cambridge University Press.

Ericsson, K. A., Krampe, R. T., & Tesch-Romer, C. (1993). The role of deliberate practice in the acquisition of expert performance. *Psychological Review,* 100(3), 363–406. Retrieved from http://projects.ict.usc.edu/itw/gel/Ericsson DeliberatePracticePR93.pdf

Ericsson, K. A., Prietula, M. J., & Cokely, E. T. (2007). The making of an expert. *Harvard Business Review,* 114–121. Retrieved from https://hbr.org/2007/07/the-making-of-an-expert.

Federmeier, K. D. (2013, December 2) *The truth about the left brain /right brain relationship.* Interviewer: T. Lombrozo. 13.7 Cosmos & Culture: Commentary on Science and Society. National Public Radio. Retrieved from http://www.npr.org/sections/13.7/2013/12/02/248089436/the-truth-about-the-left-brain-right-brain-relationship

Fink, L. D. (2004). *A self-directed guide to designing courses for significant learning.* Retrieved from http://www.deefinkandassociates.com/Guideto Course DesignAug05.pdf

Fink, L. D. (2013). *Creating significant learning experiences: An integrated approach to designing college courses* (2nd ed.). San Francisco, CA: Jossey-Bass.

Freeman, W. J. (2000). *How brains make up their mind.* New York, NY: Columbia University Press.

Frey, B. (n.d.) *Rubric for asynchronous discussion participation.* Retrieved from http://www.udel.edu/janet/MARC2006/rubric.html

Gagné, R. M. (1965). *The conditions of learning.* New York, NY: Holt, Rinehart & Winston.

Gagné, R. M., Briggs, L. J., & Wager, W. W. (1992). *Principles of instructional design* (4th ed.). Fort Worth, TX: Harcourt Brace.

Gallow, D. (2001). *What is problem-based learning?* Retrieved from https://www.scu.edu/provost/teaching-and-learning/digital-resources-for-teaching-drt/teaching/problem-based-learning/

Garrison, D. R. (2006). Online collaboration principles. *Journal of Asynchronous Learning Networks,* 10(1). Retrieved from http://onlinelearningconsortium.org/sites/default/files/v10n1_3garrison_0.pdf

Garrison, D. R. (2011). *E-learning in the 21st century: A framework for research and practice* (2nd ed.). London: Routledge/Taylor and Francis.

Garrison, D. R., Anderson, T., & & Archer, W. (2000). Critical inquiry in a text-based environment: Computer conferencing in higher education. *The Internet and Higher Education*, 2(2-3), 1–19. Retrieved from http://auspace.athabascau.ca:8080/dspace/bitstream/2149/739/1/critical_inquiry_in_a_text.pdf

Garrison, D. R., Anderson, T., & Archer, W. (2001). Critical thinking, cognitive presence, and computer conferencing in distance education. *The American Journal of Distance Education*, 15(1), 7–23.

Garrison, D. R., Anderson, T., & Archer, W. (2004). *Critical thinking, cognitive presence, and computer conferencing in distance education.* Retrieved from http://communitiesofinquiry.com/documents/CogPres_Final.pdf.

Garrison, D. R., Anderson, T., & Archer, W. (2010). The first decade of the community of inquiry framework: A retrospective. *The Internet and Higher Education*, 13(1-2), 5–9.

Garrison, D. R., & Cleveland-Innes, M. (2005). Facilitating cognitive presence in online learning: Interaction is not enough. *American Journal of Distance Education*, 19(3), 133–148.

Garrison, D. R., Cleveland-Innes, M., & Fung, T. S. (2010). Exploring causal relationships among teaching, cognitive and social presence: Student perceptions of the community of inquiry framework. *Internet and Higher Education*, 13(1-2), 31–36.

Garrison, D. R., & Vaughan, N. D. (2008). *Blended learning in higher education: Framework, principles, and guidelines.* San Francisco, CA: Jossey-Bass.

Gazzerly, A. (2014, October 29). *Take a virtual tour of a WSJ columnist's brain.* WSJD Live. Retrieved from http://www.wsj.com/video/take-a-virtual-tour-of-a-wsj-columnist-brain/CB75AA89-4E10-4F83-970C-7BB142F9DE2B.html

Gibson, D., & Swan, K. (2006). *How to know what your students know!* Workshop at the 12th Annual ALN International Conference on Online Learning, Orlando, FL.

Glance, D. G., Forsey, M., & Riley, M. (2013). *The pedagogical foundations of massive open online courses.* Retrieved from http://firstmonday.org/ojs/index.php/fm/article/view/4350/3673.

Gleitman, H., Reisberg, D., & Gross, J. (2006). *Psychology.* New York, NY: Norton.

Glenn, D. (2009, November 15). A teaching experiment shows students how to grasp big concepts. *Chronicle of Higher Education.* Retrieved from http://chronicle.com/article/Teaching-Experiment-Decodes-a/49140/

Goleman, D. (1995). *Emotional intelligence—Why it can matter more than IQ.* New York, NY: Bantam.

Goleman, D. (2006). *Social intelligence: The new science of human relationships.* New York, NY: Bantam Dell.

Goodyear, P., Jones, C., Asensio, M., Hodgson, V., & Steeples, C. (2003). *Constructing the "good" e-learner*. Proceedings of the 10th Biennial European Association for Research on Learning and Instruction (EARLI) Conference, Padova, Italy.

Gould, M,, & Padavano, D. (2006, May). 7 ways to improve student satisfaction in online courses. *Online Classroom*, 1–2. Madison, WI: Magna.

Grinter, R. E., & Palen, L. (2002). *Instant messaging in teen life*. Paper presented at the Computer-Supported Cooperative Work and Social Computing02, New Orleans, LA. Retrieved from http://www.cc.gatech.edu/~beki/c21.pdf

Grogan, G. (2005). *The design of online discussions to achieve good learning results*. Retrieved from http://www.openeducationeuropa.eu/en/article/The-Design-of-Online-Discussions-to-achieve-good-learning-results

Hagel, J., Brown, J. S., & Kulasooriya, D. (2014). *A movement in the making* (pp. 24). Retrieved from http://d2mtr37y39tpbu.cloudfront.net/wp-content/uploads/2014/01/DUP_689_movement_in_the_making_FINAL2.pdf

Hake, R. R. (1998). Interactive-engagement vs traditional methods: A six-thousand-student survey of mechanics test data for introductory physics courses. *American Journal of Physics*, 66, 64–74. Retrieved from http://www.physics.indiana.edu/~sdi/ajpv3i.pdf

Hangen, T. (2011). *Extreme makeover, syllabus edition*. Retrieved from http://www.tonahangen.com/2011/01/syllabus-makeover/

Hanson, V. D. (2002). Socrates dies at Delium, 424 B.C. In R. Cowley (Ed.), *What If? 2: Eminent historians imagine what might have been* (reprint edition). New York, NY: Berkley Trade.

Harris, S. M., Larrier, Y. I., & Castano-Bishop, M. (2011). Development of the student expectations of online learning survey (SEOLS): A pilot study. *Online Journal of Distance Learning Administration University of West Georgia, XIV(V)*. Retrieved from http://www.westga.edu/~distance/ojdla/winter144/harris_larrier_bishop144.html.

Harvard Business Publishing. (2011). *Undergraduate course materials*, 16. Retrieved from: https://cb.hbsp.harvard.edu/cbmp/resources/marketing/docs/16863_HE_Undergrad%20Broch_FNL.pdf

Haskell, R. E. (2000). *Transfer of learning: Cognition, instruction, and reasoning*. Cambridge, MA: Academic Press.

Huitt, W. (2003). The information processing approach to cognition. *Educational Psychology Interactive*. Retrieved from http://www.edpsycinteractive.org/topics/cognition/infoproc.html.

Hull, D. M., & Saxon, T. F. (2009). Negotiation of meaning and co-construction of knowledge: An experimental analysis of asynchronous online instruction. *Computers & Education*, 52(3), 624–639. Retrieved from http://www.sciencedirect.com/science/article/pii/S0360131508001681.

Hutchings, P., Ewell, P., & Banta, T. (2012). *AAHE Principles of good practice: Aging nicely.* Retrieved from http://www.learningoutcomesassessment.org/Principles ofAssessment.html

Illinois Valley Community College. (n.d.). *WebCT discussion board rubrics.* Retrieved from http://www2.ivcc.edu/eng1002/rubric_online.htm

Institute of Human and Machine Cognition. (n.d.). CmapTools (v. 5.03). Retrieved from http://cmap.ihmc.us/conceptmap.html

Isaacs, G. (2002). *Assessing group tasks.* Teaching and Educational Development Institute. University of Queensland, Queensland, AU. Retrieved from https:// www.itl.usyd.edu.au/assessmentresources/pdf/Link11.pdf

James, A., & Brookfield, S. D. (2014). *Engaging imagination: Helping students become creative and reflective thinkers.* San Francisco, CA: Jossey-Bass.

Johnson, L., Adams Becker, S., Estrada, V., & Freeman, A. (2015). *NMC horizon report 2015* Higher Education Edition. Austin, TX: New Media Consortium. Retrieved from http://www.nmc.org/publication/nmc-horizon-report-2015-higher-education-edition/

Kandel, E. (2006). *In search of memory: The emergence of a new science of mind* (paperback ed.). New York, NY: Norton.

Khan, S. (2011). *Let's use video to reinvent education.* Retrieved from https://www .ted.com/talks/salman_khan_let_s_use_video_to_reinvent_education? language=en

Kim, K. S., & Moore, J. L. (2005, November). Web-based learning: Factors affecting students' satisfaction and learning experience. *First Monday, 10*(11). Retrieved from: http://www.firstmonday.org/htbin/cgiwrap/bin/ojs/index.php/fm/article/view/1294/1214

Kirsh, D. (2009). Problem solving and situated cognition. In P. Robbins & M. Aydede (Eds.), *The handbook of situated cognition* (pp. 264–321). Cambridge, MA: Cambridge University Press.

Koestenbaum , P. (2002). *Leadership, new and revised: The inner side of greatness, a philosophy for leaders* (2nd ed.). San Francisco, CA: Jossey-Bass.

Kolb, D. A. (1984). *Experiential learning: Experience as the source of learning and development.* Englewood Cliffs, NJ: Prentice Hall.

Kozan, K., & Richardson, J. (2014). Interrelationships between and among social, teaching and cognitive presence. *Internet and Higher Education, 21,* 68–73.

Krathwohl, D. R. (2002). A revision of Bloom's taxonomy: An overview. *Theory into Practice, 41*(4), 212–218. Retrieved from http://www.unco.edu/cetl/sir/stating_outcome/documents/Krathwohl.pdf

Krathwohl, D. R., Bloom, B. S., & Masia, B. B. (1973). *Taxonomy of educational objectives, the classification of educational goals. Handbook II: Affective domain.* New York, NY: David McKay.

Krauth, B. (1996). Principles of good practice for distance learning programs. *Cause/Effect*. Retrieved from https://net.educause.edu/ir/library/pdf/CEM9613.pdf

Langer, E. J. (1997). *The power of mindful learning*. Reading, MA: Addison-Wesley.

Langer, E. J. (2014). Mindfulness in the age of complexity. *Harvard Business Review*. Retrieved from https://hbr.org/2014/03/mindfulness-in-the-age-of-complexity

Lave, J. (1993). Situated learning in communities of practice. In L. B. Resnick, J. M. Levine, & S. D. Teasley (Eds.), *Perspectives on socially shared cognition* (pp. 63–82). Washington, DC: American Psychological Association.

Lave, J. (2009). The practice of learning. In K. Illeris (Ed.), *Contemporary theories of learning*. (pp. 200–208). New York, NY: Routledge.

Lave, J., & Wenger, E. (1991) *Situated learning: Legitimate peripheral participation*. Cambridge: Cambridge University Press.

Lehman, R. M., & Conceição, S.C.O. (2014). *Managing and retaining online students: Research-based strategies that work*. San Francisco, CA: Jossey-Bass.

Lenhart, A., Madden, M., Macgill, A. R., & Smith, A. (2007). *Teens and social media*. Washington, DC. Pew Internet & American Life Project. Retrieved from http://www.pewinternet.org/~/media//Files/Reports/2007/

Light, R. J. (2004). *Making the most of college: Students speak their minds*. Cambridge, MA: Harvard University Press.

Lombrozo, T. (2013, December 2). *The truth about the left brain / right brain relationship. Interview with Kara Federmeier*. Retrieved from http://www.npr.org/sections/13.7/2013/12/02/248089436/the-truth-about-the-left-brain-right-brain-relationship

McKeachie, W. J., Pintrich, P. R., Lin, Y., & Smith, D. (1986). *Teaching and learning in the college classroom: A review of the research literature*. Ann Arbor, MI: National Center for Research to Improve Postsecondary Teaching and Learning, University of Michigan.

McLeod, S. A. (2007). *Multi store model of memory—Atkinson and Shiffrin, 1968*. Retrieved from www.simplypsychology.org/multi-store.html

McLeod, S. A. (2007). *Stages of memory—Encoding storage and retrieval*. Retrieved from www.simplypsychology.org/memory.html

McLuhan, M. (1969). *CounterBlast*. New York, NY: Harcourt, Brace and World.

Means, B., Toyama, Y., Murphy, R., Bakia, M., & Jones, K. (2010). *Evaluation of evidence-based practices in online learning: A meta-analysis and review of online learning studies*. Washington, DC: Center for Technology in Learning, Department of Education. Retrieved from http://www2.ed.gov/rschstat/eval/tech/evidence-based-practices/finalreport.pdf

Meyer, R. E. (2002). Rote versus meaningful learning. *Theory into Practice*, 41(4), 226–232. Retrieved from http://www.unco.edu/CETL/sir/stating_outcome/documents/Krathwohl.pdf

Michaelsen, L. K., Sweet, M., & Parmelee, D. X. (Eds.). (2008). *Team-based learning: Small-group learning's next big step* (Vol. 116). San Francisco: Wiley Periodicals.

Miller, G. (1956). The magical number seven, plus or minus two: *Some limits on our capacity for processing information Psychological Review*, 101(2), 343–352. Retrieved from http://www.psych.utoronto.ca/users/peterson/psy430s2001/Miller%20GA%20Magical%20Seven%20Psych%20Review%201955.pdf

Miller, G., Benke, M., Chaloux, B., Ragan, L. C., Schroeder, R., Smutz, W., & Swan, K. (2013). *Leading the e-learning transformation of higher education: Meeting the challenges of technology and distance education.* Sterling, VA: Stylus.

Miller, K. H. (2014). The blessings and benefits of using guest lecturers. *Faculty Focus.* Retrieved from http://www.facultyfocus.com/articles/teaching-and-learning/blessings-benefits-using-guest-lecturers/

Moallem, M. (2005). Designing and managing student assessment in an online learning environment. In P. Comeaux (Ed.), *Assessing online learning* (pp. 18–33). Bolton, MA: Anker.

Moore, J. C. (2011). A synthesis of Sloan-C effective practices. *Journal of Asynchronous Learning Networks*, 16(1), 92–115. Retrieved from http://onlinelearningconsortium.org/synthesis-sloan-c-effective-practices-december-2011/.

Moore, J. L., Dickson-Deane, C., & Galyen, K. (2011). E-learning, online learning, and distance learning environments: Are they the same? *Internet and Higher Education*, 14, 129–135.

Moore, M. G. (2007). The theory of transactional distance. In M. G. Moore (Ed.), *The handbook of distance education* (2nd ed., pp. 89–108). Mahwah, NJ: Lawrence Erlbaum.

Moore, M. G., & Kearsley, G. (1996). *Distance education: A systems view.* Belmont, CA: Wadsworth.

Murphy, E., & Manzanares, M.A.R. (2006). Profiling individual discussants' behaviours in online asynchronous discussions. *Canadian Journal of Learning and Technology*, 32 (2). Retrieved from http://www.cjlt.ca/index.php/cjlt/article/view/55/52

Nandi, D., Hamilton, M., & Harland, J. (2012). Evaluating the quality of interaction in asynchronous discussion forums in fully online courses. *Distance Education*, 33(1), 5–30.

Newman, J. H. (1853). *The idea of a university.* Retrieved from http://www.newmanreader.org/

Nief, R., McBride, T., & Westerberg, C. (2015) *The mindset list for the class of 2019.* Retrieved from http://www.beloit.edu/mindset/2019/

Nilson, L. B. (2007). *The graphic syllabus and the outcomes map: Communicating your course.* San Francisco, CA: Jossey-Bass.

Nilson, L. B., & Pyser, S. N. (2012). *The graphic syllabus: Communicating your course creatively.* Retrieved from www.fox.temple.edu

Novak, J. D., & Cañas, A. J. (2006). *The theory underlying concept maps and how to construct and use them.* Pensacola, FL: Institute for Human and Machine Cognition. Retrieved from http://cmap.ihmc.us/docs/theory-of-concept-maps

O'Banion, T. (1999). *Launching a learning-centered college.* Mission Viejo, CA: League for Innovation in the Community College and PeopleSoft.

Ohler, J. (2008). The semantic web in education. *EDUCAUSE Quarterly*, 31(4). Retrieved from http://er.educause.edu/articles/2008/11/the-semantic-web-in-education

Oldenburg, R. (1999). *The great good place: Cafes, coffee shops, bookstores, bars, hair salons, and other hangouts at the heart of a community* (3rd ed.). New York, NY: Marlowe.

O'Neill, G. (2013). *Assessment: Assessing group work.* Dublin: UCD Teaching and Learning University College. Retrieved from http://www.ucd.ie/t4cms/UCDTLE0065.pdf

Oregon Health and Science University. (2010). *Examples of rubrics for assessing online forum posts.* Retrieved from http://www.ohsu.edu/xd/education/teaching-and-learning-center/academic-technology/upload/Assessing-Forums-with-Rubrics-Handout.pdf

Owens, M. (2014). Using social media in the classroom: Why there's a lot to like. *Faculty Focus.* Retrieved from http://www.facultyfocus.com/articles/teaching-with-technology-articles/using-social-media-classroom/

Painter, C., Coffin, C., & Hewings, A. (2003). Impacts of directed tutorial activities in computer conferencing: A case study. *Distance Education*, 24(2), 159–174.

Palloff, R. M., & Pratt, K. (2003). *The virtual student: A profile and guide to working with online learners.* San Francisco, CA: Jossey-Bass.

Palloff, R. M., & Pratt, K. (2007). *Building online learning communities: Effective strategies for the virtual classroom.* San Francisco, CA: Jossey-Bass.

Palloff, R. M., & Pratt, K. (2011). *The excellent online instructor: Strategies for professional development.* San Francisco, CA: Jossey-Bass.

Parsell, M. (2015, June 11). *Instructional rubrics (podcast, rubric and transcript).* Retrieved from http://staff.mq.edu.au/teaching/curriculum_assessment/curriculum_design/engagement/podcasts/engagement_rubrics/

Partnership for 21st Century Learning (P21). (2015). *Framework for 21st century learning*. Washington, DC. Retrieved from http://www.p21.org/our-work/p21-framework

Paul, R., & Elder, L. (2002). *Thinking with concepts*. Foundation for Critical Thinking. Retrieved from http://www.criticalthinking.org

Paul, R., & Elder, L. (2008). *The analysis and assessment of thinking. Foundation for Critical Thinking*. Retrieved from http://www.criticalthinking.org/

Peirce, B. (2001). Strategies for teaching thinking and promoting intellectual development in online classes. *The Instructional Area Newsletter*, 19(3). Retrieved from http://academic.pgcc.edu/~wpeirce/MCCCTR/ttol.html

Pelikan, J. (1992). *The idea of the university: A reexamination*. New Haven, CT: Yale University.

Pimple, K. D. (2002). *Using small group assignments in teaching research ethics*. Retrieved from http://poynter.indiana.edu/teaching-research-ethics/tre-resources/

Pinker, S. (1997). *How the mind works*. New York, NY: Norton.

Pusateri, T., Halonen, J., Hill, B., & McCarthy, M. (2009). *The assessment cyberguide for learning goals and outcomes*. Washington, DC: American Psychological Association. Retrieved from http://www.apa.org/ed/governance/bea/assessment-cyberguide-v2.pdf

Quality Matters. (2015). *The Quality Matters higher education rubric* (5th ed.), 2014. Annapolis, MD: Quality Matters Org. Retrieved from https://www.qualitymatters.org/rubric

Race, P. (2006). *Evidencing reflection: Putting the "w" into reflection*. Retrieved from http://escalate.ac.uk/resources/reflection/09.html

Ramachandran, V. S. (2011). *The tell-tale brain: A neuroscientist's quest for what makes us human*. New York, NY: Norton.

Richardson, J. C., & Swan, K. (2003). Examining social presence in online courses in relation to students' perceived learning and satisfaction. *Journal of Asynchronous Learning Networks*, 7(1), 68–88.

Rinderle, J., & Hampson, K. (2014, April 24). *Analytics in online higher education: Three categories*. Pittsburgh, PA: Acrobatiq – Carnegie Mellon University. Retrieved from http://acrobatiq.com/analytics-in-online-higher-education-three-categories/

Ritchhart, R., Church, M., & Morrison, K. (2011). *Making thinking visible: How to promote engagement, understanding, and independence for all learners*. San Francisco, CA: Jossey-Bass.

Robinson, K. S. (2006). *Do schools kill creativity?* Retrieved from https://www.ted.com/talks/ken_robinson_says_schools_kill_creativity?language=en

Roediger, H. L., Dudai, Y., & Fitzpatrick, S. M. (Eds.). (2007). *Science of memory: Concepts*. New York, NY: Oxford University Press.

Rosenbloom, R. S. (1999). *Sustaining American innovation: Where will technology come from?* Paper presented at the Forum on Harnessing Science and Technology for American's Economic Future, National Academy of Sciences, Washington, DC.

Rourke, L., & Kanuka, H. (2009). Learning in communities of inquiry: A review of the literature. *Journal of Distance Education*, 23(1), 19–48. Retrieved from http://files.eric.ed.gov/fulltext/EJ836030.pdf

Rovai, A. (2002). Building sense of community at a distance. *International Review of Research in Open and Distance Learning*, 3(1), 1–16. Retrieved from http://www.irrodl.org/index.php/irrodl/article/view/79/153

Salen, K., & Zimmerman, E. (2004). *Rules of play: Game design fundamentals.* Cambridge, MA: The MIT Press.

Schacter, D. L. (2001). *The seven sins of memory: How the mind forgets and remembers.* New York, NY: Houghton-Mifflin.

Schank, R. C., & Abelson, R. P. (1977). *Scripts, plans, goals and understanding: An inquiry into human knowledge structures* (1st ed.). Mahwah, NJ: Lawrence Erlbaum.

Schank, R. C., & Abelson, R. P. (1995). Knowledge and memory: The real story. In J. Robert S. Wyer (Ed.), *Knowledge and memory: The real story* (pp. 1–85). Mahwah, NJ: Lawrence Erlbaum.

Schechter, E., & Pacheco, R. (2015). *Internet resources for higher education outcomes assessment.* Retrieved June 4 2016, from http://www.assessmentcommons.org

Schwartz, H. L. (2009). Facebook: The new classroom commons? *Chronicle of Higher Education*, 56(6), B12–B13. Retrieved from http://chronicle.com/article/Facebook-The-New-Classroom/48575/

Senge, P. (1990). *The fifth discipline: The art and practice of the learning organization.* New York, NY: Doubleday.

Sellers, S. L., Roberts, J., Giovanetto, L., Friedrich, K., & Hammargren, C. (2007). Reaching All Students: A Resource for Teaching in Science, Technology, Engineering & Mathematics. Madison, Wisconsin. Center for the Integration of Research, Teaching, and Learning. Retrieved from http://www.cirtl.net/ReachingAllStudents

Sergiovanni, T. J. (1994). *Building community in schools.* San Francisco, CA: Jossey-Bass.

Shank, P. (Ed.). (2011). *The online learning idea book, Volume two: Proven ways to enhance technology-based and blended learning.* New York, NY: Pfeiffer.

Shapiro, L. (2011). *Embodied cognition.* New York, NY: Routledge.

Shattuck, K. (2014). *Assuring quality in online education.* Sterling, VA: Stylus.

Shattuck, K., Zimmerman, W. A., & Adair, D. (2014). Continuous improvement of the QM rubric and review processes: Scholarship of integration and application. *Internet Learning*, 3(1), 25–34. Retrieved from http://digitalcommons. apus.edu/internetlearning/vol3/iss1/5

Shea, P. (2006). A study of students' sense of learning community in online environments. *Journal of Asynchronous Learning Networks*, 10(1), 35–44. Retrieved from www.onlinelearningconsortium.org/sites/default/files/v10n1_4shea .pdf

Shea, P., Hayes, S., Smith, S. U., Vickers, J., Bidjerano, T., Pickett, A., . . . Jian, S. (2012). Learning presence: Additional research on a new conceptual element within the Community of Inquiry (CoI) framework. *The Internet and Higher Education*, 15(2), 89–95. Retrieved from http://www.sciencedirect.com/ science/article/pii/S1096751611000522

Shea, P., Hayes, S., Vickers, J., Gozza-Cohen, M., Uzuner, S., Mehta, R., . . . Rangan, P. (2010). A re-examination of the community of inquiry framework: Social network and content analysis. *The Internet and Higher Education*, 13(1-2), 10–21. Retrieved from http://www.sciencedirect.com/science/article/pii/ S1096751609000682.

Shea, V. (1990–2011). *The core rules of netiquette*. Retrieved from http://www.albion .com/netiquette/corerules.html

Sherron, G. T., & Boettcher, J. V. (1997). Distance learning: The shift to interactivity. CAUSE Professional Paper Series, 17, 40. Retrieved from: https://net.educause .edu/ir/library/pdf/PUB3017.pdf

Smillie, M. (2009). *Three examples of a graphic syllabus*. Retrieved from http:// www46.homepage.villanova.edu/john.immerwahr/TP101/Prep/Graphic_ syls.pdf

Smith, A. (2015). *US smartphone use in 2015*. Washington, DC. Pew Research Center April, 2015. Retrieved from http://www.pewinternet.org/2015/04/01/us-smartphone-use-in-2015/

Smith, R. (2014). *Conquering the content: A blueprint for online course design and development*. San Francisco, CA: Jossey-Bass.

Sorcinelli, M. D. (2002). Promoting civility in large classes. In C. Stanley & E. Porter (Eds.), *Engaging large classes: Strategies and techniques for college faculty* (pp. 44–57). Bolton, MA: Anker.

Sorcinelli, M. D., Austin, A. E., Eddy, P. L., & Beach, A. L. (2006). *Creating the future of faculty development—Learning from the past, understanding the present*. San Francisco: Jossey-Bass/Anker.

Sperry, R. W. (1980). Mind-brain interaction: Mentalism, yes; dualism, no. *Neuroscience*, 5(2), 195–206. Retrieved from http://people.uncw.edu/puente/ sperry/sperrypapers/80s-90s/215-1980.pdf

Stavredes, T. (2011). *Effective online teaching: Foundations and strategies for student success*. San Francisco, CA: Jossey-Bass.

Stickgold, R., & Ellenbogen, J. M. (2008, August/September 2008). Quiet! Sleeping brain at work. *Scientific American Mind*, 19, 22–29.

Sull, E. C. (2012, September 6). Tips for overcoming online discussion board challenges. *Faculty Focus*. Madison, WI: Magna Publications. Retrieved from http://www.facultyfocus.com/articles/online-education/tips-for-overcoming-online-discussion-board-challenges/

Suskie, L. (2009). *Assessing student learning: A common sense guide* (2nd ed.). San Francisco, CA: Jossey-Bass.

Svinicki, M., & McKeachie, W. J. (2011). *McKeachie's teaching tips: Strategies, research, and theory for college and university teachers* (13th ed.). Belmont, CA: Wadsworth.

Swan, K. (2004). *Relationships between interactions and learning in online environments*. Retrieved from: https://www.researchgate.net/profile/Karen_Swan3/publication/250700769_Relationships_Between_Interactions_and_Learning_In_Online_Environments/links/02e7e53360e0c284e6000000.pdf/download?version=vs

Swan, K., Garrison, D. R., & Richardson, J. C. (2009). A constructivist approach to online learning: the Community of Inquiry framework. In Payne, C. R. (Ed.) *Information technology and constructivism in higher education: Progressive learning frameworks* (pp. 43–57). Hershey, PA: IGI Global.

Swan, K., & Ice, P. (2010). The community of inquiry framework ten years later: Introduction to the special issue. *The Internet and Higher Education*, 13(1-2), 1–4. Retrieved from http://www.sciencedirect.com/science/article/pii/S1096751609000694

Swan, K., & Shih, L. (2005). On the nature and development of social presence in online course discussions. *Online Learning Journal*, 9(3), 115–136. Retrieved from: http://onlinelearningconsortium.org/jaln_full_issue/volume-9-issue-3-october-2005/

Tarr, T., & Lang, S. (2006, 2015). *Tips for handling disruptive student behavior*. Retrieved from http://ctl.iupui.edu/Resources/Teaching-Strategies/Tips-for-Handling-Disruptive-Student-Behavior

Teaching and Learning with Technology Group. (2001–2012). *Building blocks for teams*. Retrieved from http://archive.tlt.psu.edu/suggestions/teams/student/

Thomas, D., & Brown, J. S. (2009). Why virtual worlds can matter. *International Journal of Media and Learning*, 1(1). Retrieved from http://ssrn.com/abstract=1300470

Tracy, B. (2007). *Eat that frog! 21 great ways to stop procrastinating and get more done in less time!* San Francisco: Berrett-Koehler.

University of Northern Iowa. (2001). *Principles of learning: Patterns & connections. In Time*. Retrieved from http://www.intime.uni.edu/model/learning/patt.html.

Van Der Veer, R. (1996). Vygotsky and Piaget: A collective monologue. *Human Development* (39), 237–242. Retrieved from https://openaccess.leidenuniv.nl/bitstream/handle/1887/10346/7-703-113.pdf?sequence=1

Van Notten, P. V. (2006). Scenario development: A typology of approaches. In *Think Scenarios, Rethink Education*, 200. Organization for Economic Cooperation and Development (OECD). Retrieved from http://www.oecd.org/edu/school/thinkscenariosrethinkeducation.htm

Varkey, C. (2006). *iPods aid dramatic imagination*. Retrieved from https://cit.duke.edu/blog/2006/08/ipods-aid-dramatic-imagination/

Vaughan, N. D., Cleveland-Innes, M., & Garrison, D. R. (2013). *Teaching in blended learning environments: Creating and sustaining communities of inquiry*. Edmonton, AB, Canada: Athabasca University Press.

Veletsianos, G., Kimmons, R., & French, K. (2013). Instructor experiences with a social networking site in a higher education setting: Expectations, frustrations, appropriation, and compartmentalization. *Educational Technology Research & Development*, 61(2), 255–278.

Vygotsky, L. S. (1962). *Thought and language* (E. Hanfmann & G. Vakar, Trans.). Cambridge, MA: MIT Press.

Vygotsky, L. S. (1978). *Mind in society: The development of higher psychological processes*. Cambridge, MA: Harvard University Press.

Walvoord, B. E., & Anderson, V. J. (2009). *Effective grading: A tool for learning and assessment in college* (2nd ed.). San Francisco, CA: Jossey-Bass.

Ward, G. C. (2002). The luck of Franklin Delano Roosevelt. In R. Cowley (Ed.), *What If? 2: Eminent historians imagine what might have been*. New York, NY: Berkley Trade.

Washington State University. (2006). *Guide to rating critical & integrative thinking*. Retrieved from https://www.etsu.edu/cbat/economics/documents/NIU_Critical_Thinking-short.pdf

Weimer, M. (2002). *Learner-centered teaching: Five key changes to practice* (1st ed.). San Francisco, CA: Jossey-Bass.

Weimer, M. (2013) *Learner—centered teaching: Five key changes to practice* (2nd ed.). San Francisco, CA: Jossey-Bass.

Wieman, C. (2008). *Science education in the 21st century: Using the tools of science to teach science*. Retrieved from https://net.educause.edu/ir/library/pdf/ff0814s.pdf

Wiggins, G., & McTighe, J. (2005). *Understanding by design* (2nd ed.). New York, NY: Pearson.

Yang, Y., & Durrington, V. (2010). Investigation of students' perceptions of online course quality. *International Journal on E-Learning*, 9(3), 341–361. Retrieved from https://www.researchgate.net/publication/251881614_Investigation_of_Students_Perceptions_of_Online_Course_Quality

Young, A., & Norgard, C. (2006). Assessing the quality of online courses from the students' perspective. *The Internet and Higher Education*, 9(2), 107–115.

Index

Page references followed by *fig* indicate an illustrated figure; followed by *t* indicate a table.

Subject Index

Page references followed by *fig* indicate an illustrated figure; followed by *t* indicate a table; followed by *e* indicate an exhibit.

A

AAHE Assessment Forum, 209

Absent-mindedness, 295, 296

Accelerated intensive courses. *See* Intensive courses (IC)

Activities. *See* Communication activities; Course activities; Faculty development exercises

Adobe Connect, 220

American Psychological Association (APA) *Best Practices in Assessment,* 209

Announcements tool (LMS): description of, 67; developing presence through the, 138–139; enhancing teaching presence using, 174; use audio in course announcements, 224

Anonymous student feedback, 180–181

Apps: social networking, 271; Web 3.0 ("semantic web") vs. Web 2.0, 272

Asking Essential Questions, 236

Assessing Group Tasks (Isaacs), 264

Assessing Group Work (O'Neill), 264

Assessment: classic resources on, 209–210; comparing traditional and online course, 10; group project, 228, 261–264; Late Middle to build cognitive presence, 94; of learning during projects, 228, 255–267; prepare list of what's next and due dates of, 297; technological tools that facilitate, 74t; three best practices for, 173, 205–210; using discussion forums to gather evidence of learning, 110, 162–166; as you go by gathering evidences of learning, 45t, 58. *See also* Course evaluations; Rubrics

Assessment best practices: assess across six levels of Bloom's taxonomy, 205–208; assess core concepts in your course, 208; classic resources on, 209–210; help students succeed on assessment tasks, 209

The Assessment CyberGuide for Learning Goals and Outcomes (Pusateri, Halonen, Hill, and McCarthy), 210

Assessment plans: aligning substantive feedback tools with, 250t–251t, 252; description and functions of a, 203; designing, 173, 202–203; elements and percent of grade in the, 204t–205; three-step process for developing your, 203–204

Assignments: applying practice experiences and expert resources to designing, 314; description and course element of, 112t; evaluating and creating levels of Bloom's taxonomy, 173, 210–213; mixing up stories and case studies by creating or writing, 293–294; mixing up stories and case studies with reading, 293; plagiarism and, 121; projects, 94–95, 101, 112t; providing timely and efficient feedback on, 227, 244–248; reflection question cluster for a reading, 310; reflection questions used for written, 311; rubrics for, 245, 246–248; syllabus section on, 119–120

Asynchronous activities: best practice on using synchronous and, 45t, 51–52; comparing classroom and online, 9–10; description of, 9–10; LMS communication tools for synchronous and, 65–74t; LMS Discussion Forums, 67. *See also* Communication activities

Audio and Video Tools: AudioMemos, 71; creating a more engaging course using, 173, 222–224; creating presence with mini-lectures, 45; LMS (learning management system), 68; podcasts, 73t; published audio and video resources, 224

B

Baptist College of Florida, 166

Beginnings. *See* Course Beginnings (CB)

Best practices: assessment, 173, 205–210; Closing and Wrap Up learning experiences and supportive, 98t–99t; Course Beginnings learning experiences and supportive, 80t–81t; Early Middle learning experiences and supportive, 86t–87t; Late Middle learning experiences and supportive, 92t–93t. *See also* Teaching

Best Practices in Assessment: top 10 Task Force Recommendations (APA), 209, 210

Best practices list: 1: be present at your course, 44–47; 2: create a supportive online course community, 45t, 47–48; 3: develop set of workload and communication

Embroidery

Embroidery is the art of forming decorative designs upon a fabric background, allowing creative individual expression through the use of color, threads and yarns, fabric and stitch variations. Everyday products can be transformed into unique creations by the use of a few embroidery stitches and the motifs within this comprehensive design book.

Iron transfer onto "right side" of fabric and embroider using either wool, cotton, metallic, silk or synthetic thread or yarn. The use of stitches is limited only by the imagination and skill of the stitcher.

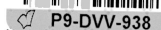
Punch Embroidery

Every single design in this huge resource book of over 1000 designs can be used for punch embroidery, a wonderfully versatile needlecraft technique. Decorate clothing, create miniature hooked rugs, produce Christmas ornaments for fund-raising bazaars—the ideas and uses are never ending. Let your creativity soar!

Since punch embroidery is worked from the backside of the fabric, iron the transfer onto the BACKSIDE. Your finished piece will 'read' the same from the front of the fabric as the transfer design appears on paper. Remember, for any design with words or numbers that read backwards on the transfer, you must adjust this for punch embroidery by redrawing the design from the backside of the transfer and then trace the words or numbers to read correctly.

Outline Embroidery

This remarkably simple and rapid embroidery style is visually striking when there is high contrast in color between stitches and fabric.

Iron the transfer designs directly onto the fabric. Then, using one of the basic embroidery stitches such as the stem stitch, embroider only the outlines of the design. Use satin stitch, straight stitch and French knots to enhance the design. For a traditional country look use blue or red floss on a white background.

KEEPSAKE TRANSFER COLLECTION

Color Key

Use this key as a guide for selecting embroidery thread, yarn or paint colors

	DMC	BATES	
A-	000	002	White
B-	001	926	Ecru
C-	739	885	Beige
D-	746	386	Palest Yellow
E-	745	300	Pale Yellow
F-	445	288	Medium Yellow
G-	307	289	Lt. Bright Yellow
H-	743	297	Pale Gold
I-	972	298	Bright Gold
J-	727	293	Light Yellow
K-	444	291	Bright Yellow
L-	783	307	Brass
M-	781	309	Dark Brass
N-	741	304	Pale Orange
O-	740	316	Light Orange
P-	608	333	Bright Orange
Q-	900	333	Dark Orange
R-	729	890	Yellow/Brown
S-	842	376	Gray/Tan
T-	840	379	Gray/Brown
U-	754	778	Flesh
V-	352	010	Dark Flesh
W-	776	024	Pale Pink
X-	894	026	Light Pink
Y-	603	076	Medium Pink
Z-	601	078	Dark Pink
a-	349	013	Light Red
b-	304	047	Dark Red
c-	891	035	Warm Red
d-	666	046	Bright Red
e-	814	044	Burgundy
f-	899	027	Rose/Pink
g-	3350	042	Rose
h-	605	050	Pale Pink

	DMC	BATES	
i-	915	089	Magenta
j-	221	897	Light Brick
k-	902	072	Dark Brick
l-	3042	869	Lt. Gray/Lavender
m-	3041	871	Dk. Gray/Lavender
n-	210	104	Lt. Cool Lavender
o-	208	110	Med. Cool Lavender
p-	554	096	Lt. Warm Lavender
q-	552	101	Warm Lavender
r-	550	102	Purple
s-	341	117	Lt. Lavender/Blue
t-	340	118	Lavender/Blue
u-	800	128	Pale Blue
v-	799	130	Light Blue
w-	996	433	Lt. Bright Blue
x-	995	410	Bright Blue
y-	926	779	Lt. Gray/Green
z-	924	851	Gray/Green
AA-	793	121	Lt. Cornflower Blue
BB-	792	940	Cornflower Blue
CC-	796	133	Dk. Cornflower Blue
DD-	823	150	Midnight Blue
EE-	798	131	Bright Blue
FF-	820	134	Dark Blue
GG-	807	168	Aqua
HH-	806	169	Dark Aqua
II-	913	209	Lt. Mint Green
JJ-	911	205	Mint Green
KK-	964	185	Pale Turquoise
LL-	958	187	Turquoise
MM-	700	229	Emerald Green
NN-	909	229	Dk. Emerald Green
OO-	500	879	Dark Green
PP-	562	210	Gray/Green

	DMC	BATES	
QQ-	561	212	Dk. Gray/Green
RR-	907	255	Lt. Yellow/Green
SS-	906	256	Yellow/Green
TT-	702	239	Light Green
UU-	904	258	Medium Green
VV-	895	346	Dark Green
WW-	890	879	Very Dk. Green
XX-	437	362	Light Tan
YY-	436	363	Tan
ZZ-	434	309	Light Brown
aa-	869	944	Cool Brown
bb-	400	351	Red/Brown
cc-	300	352	Dk. Red/Brown
dd-	801	357	Medium Brown
ee-	610	889	Dk. Gray/Brown
ff-	938	381	Dk. Warm Brown
gg-	839	380	Dark Brown
hh-	3371	382	Brown/Black
ii-	613	956	Cool Gold
jj-	611	898	Dk. Cool Gold
kk-	762	697	Pale Gray
ll-	415	398	Light Gray
mm-	318	399	Medium Gray
nn-	414	400	Gray
oo-	647	8581	Warm Gray
pp-	3024	869	Lt. Warm Gray
qq-	648	900	Silver
rr-	317	400	Light Gunmetal
ss-	413	401	Dark Gunmetal
tt-	535	401	Dark Gray
uu-	844	401	Gray/Black
vv-	310	403	Black

Using Transfers

NOTE—BLACK LINES WILL NOT TRANSFER. This key points to a Tan fill-in area.

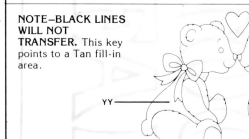

YY ——

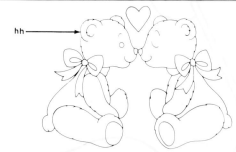

hh ——→

Color keys with arrows show the color for single lines or outlines. This key points to a Brown/Black outline.

You need—Fabric; iron-on transfer design; iron and ironing board; pins.

1. Fabric. Wash washable fabric first to remove sizing which may prevent the design from transferring. Iron fabric to remove all wrinkles. Transfers work best on fabrics that have some synthetic content and are smoothly woven. They will not transfer on 100% linen. The transfers will not show up on dark fabrics. If you wish to use dark fabrics, apply the design using white dressmaker's carbon. Simply sandwich the carbon (carbon-side down) between fabric and motif and trace with a ballpoint pen.

2. Ironing board. Pin a piece of sheeting or smooth scrap material to the ironing-board cover to prevent the transfer from going through embroidery fabric onto the cover.

Hint: to obtain darker impressions on subsequent applications of transfers, place a piece of aluminum foil on the ironing-board cover.

3. Test Transfer. It is always important to test fabric, heat of iron and optimum transfer time by applying one of the test transfers to a scrap of fabric. By using the shortest time possible, you'll get more repeats from the transfer. Preheat the iron to 400 degrees (Cotton or linen) for five minutes. If the design appears too faint, adjust heat to a higher setting. However, check to make sure iron temperature will not damage the fabric.

4. Design Transfer. Cut out motif, allowing paper margins for pinning to fabric. Place fabric on ironing board and press to warm fabric. Immediately pin design ink-side down to fabric and while fabric is still warm, use a press-lift motion to transfer the design. Do not slide iron as it may blur the design. Carefully lift one side of paper to check to see if entire design has transferred. Do not attempt to remove entire design until it is completely transferred as it is nearly impossible to line up the design again. Note: transfers that have been used before will need a longer time to transfer. When transfers no longer have transfer ink remaining, bring them back to life by tracing over the design with an iron-on pencil.

5. Important: Transfer inks will not wash out of most fabrics. We assume no responsibility for any damage to fabrics caused by the transfer inks in this book. □

TOOTH FAIRY PILLOW - TRANSFER TOOTH POCKET SEPARATELY

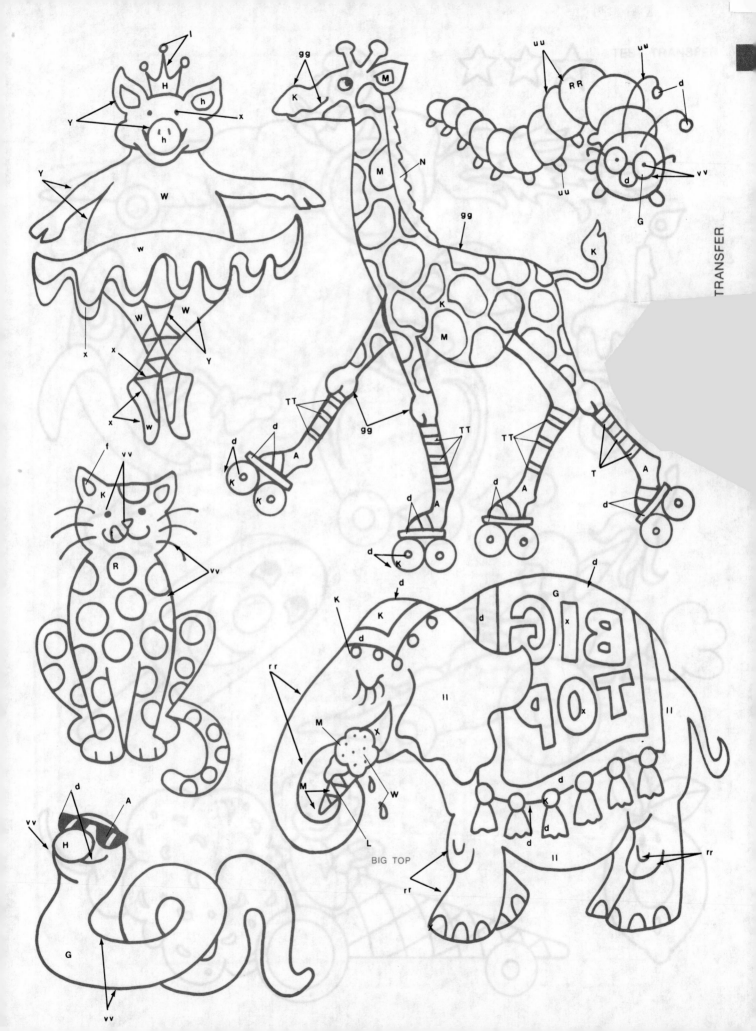

BIG TOP

BIG
TOP

TEST TRANSFER

TEST TRANSFER

TEST TRANSFER

WONDER KID

TOP DOG

YUM

PRINCESS

TEST TRANSFER

TEST TRANSFER

THE BEST !

TEST TRANSFER

TEST TRANSFER

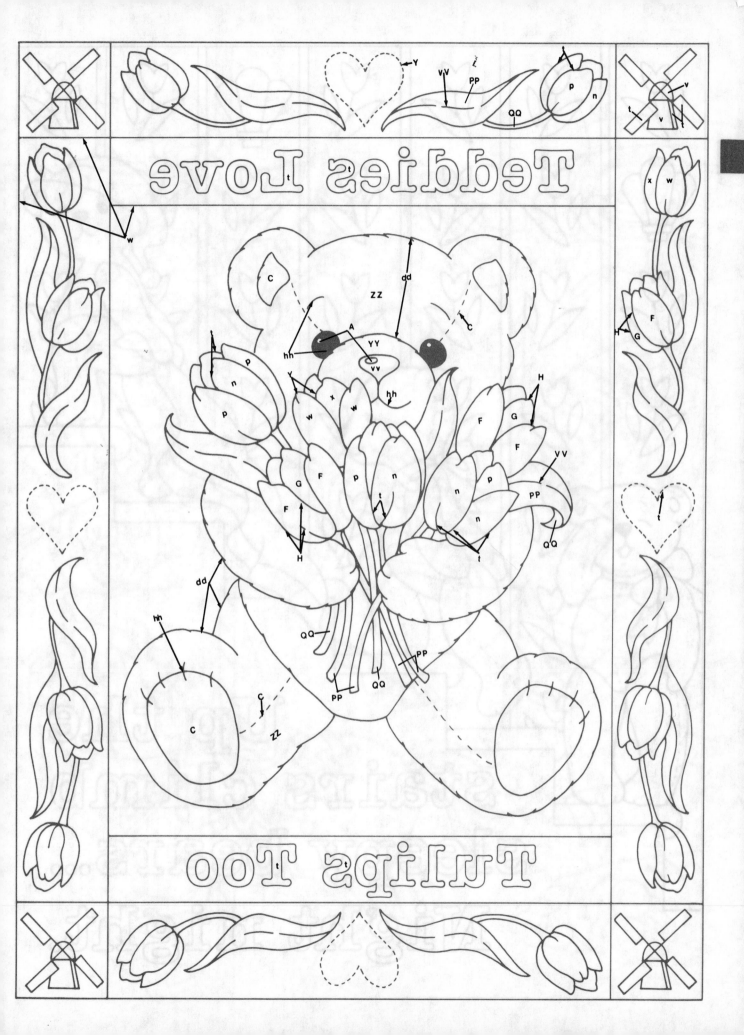

Up the
stairs climb
sleepy bears...
Night night.

Sew on Wednesday

Motion Thursday

Test Transfer

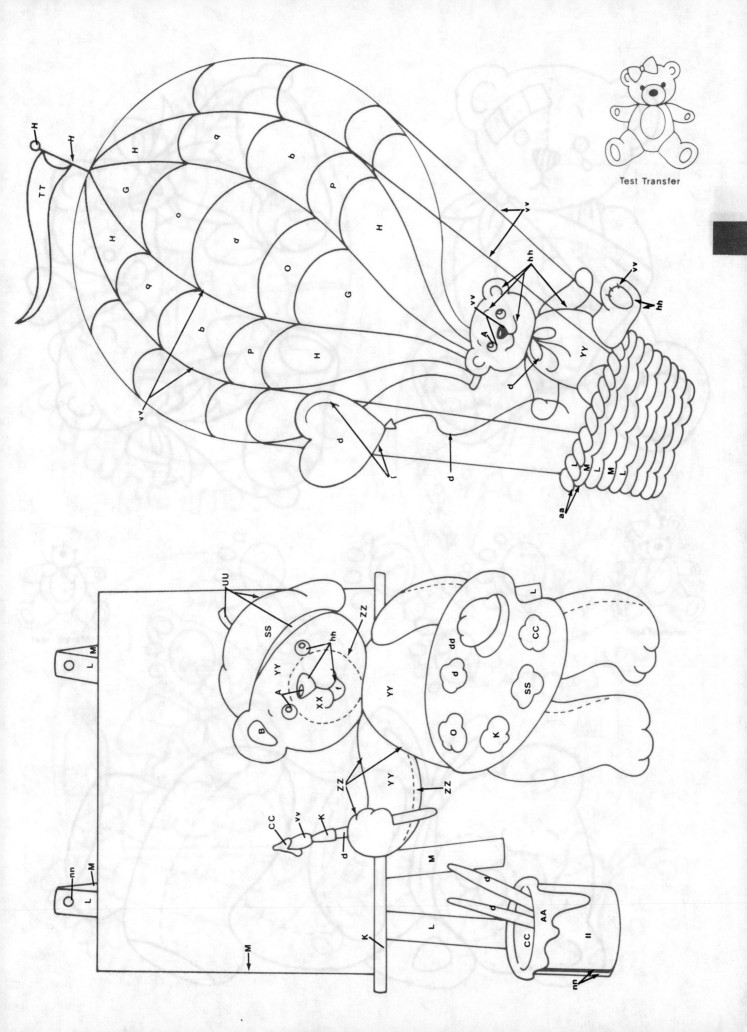

Test Transfer

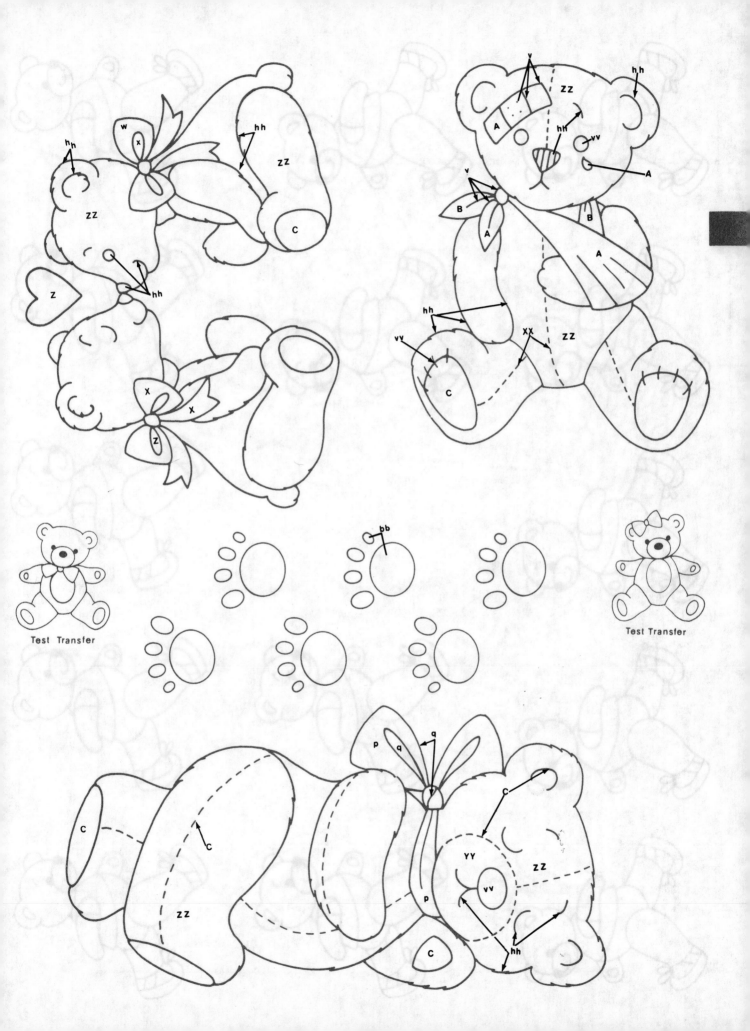

Test Transfer

Test Transfer

Test Transfer

Test Transfer

Test Transfer

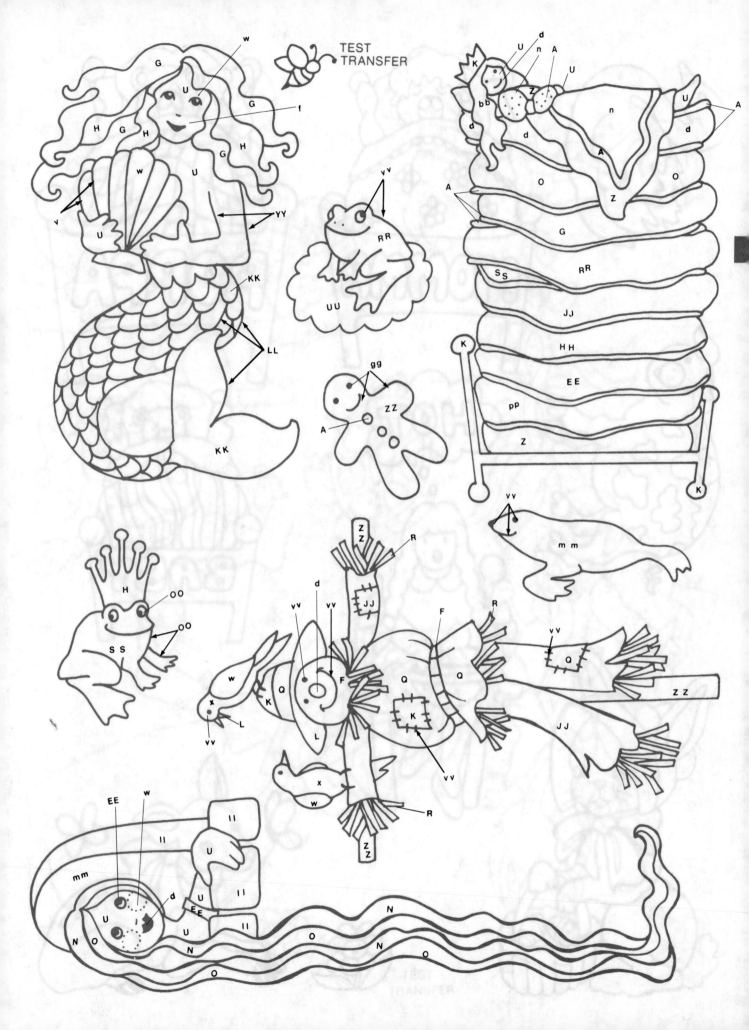

TEST TRANSFER

TEST
TRANSFER

TEST TRANSFER

TEST TRANSFER

TEST
TRANSFER

TEST TRANSFER

Test Transfer

Test Transfer

Test Transfer

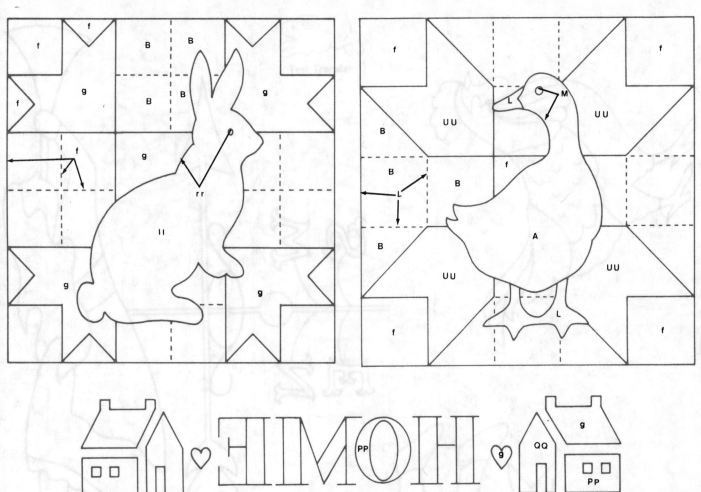

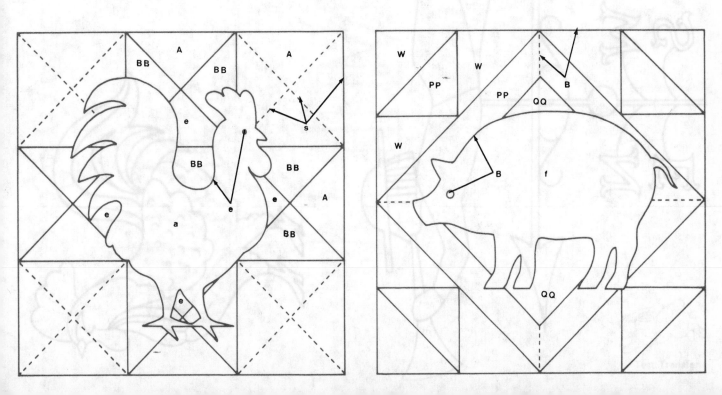

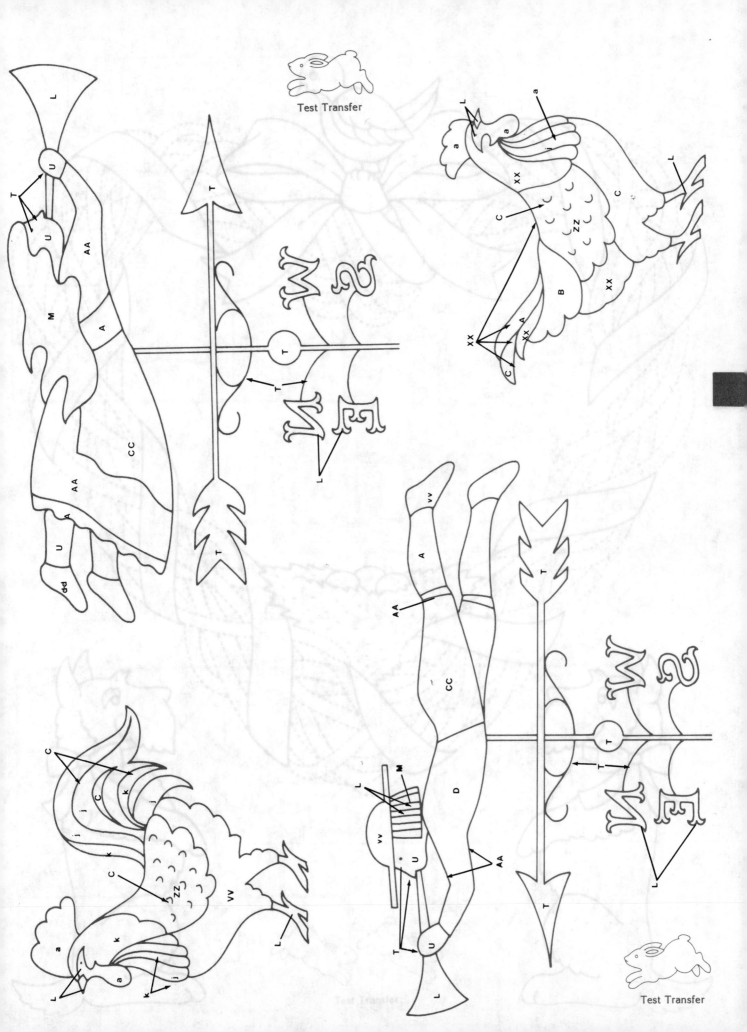

Test Transfer

Test Transfer

Test Transfer

Test Transfer

Test Transfer

Test Transfer

Test Transfer

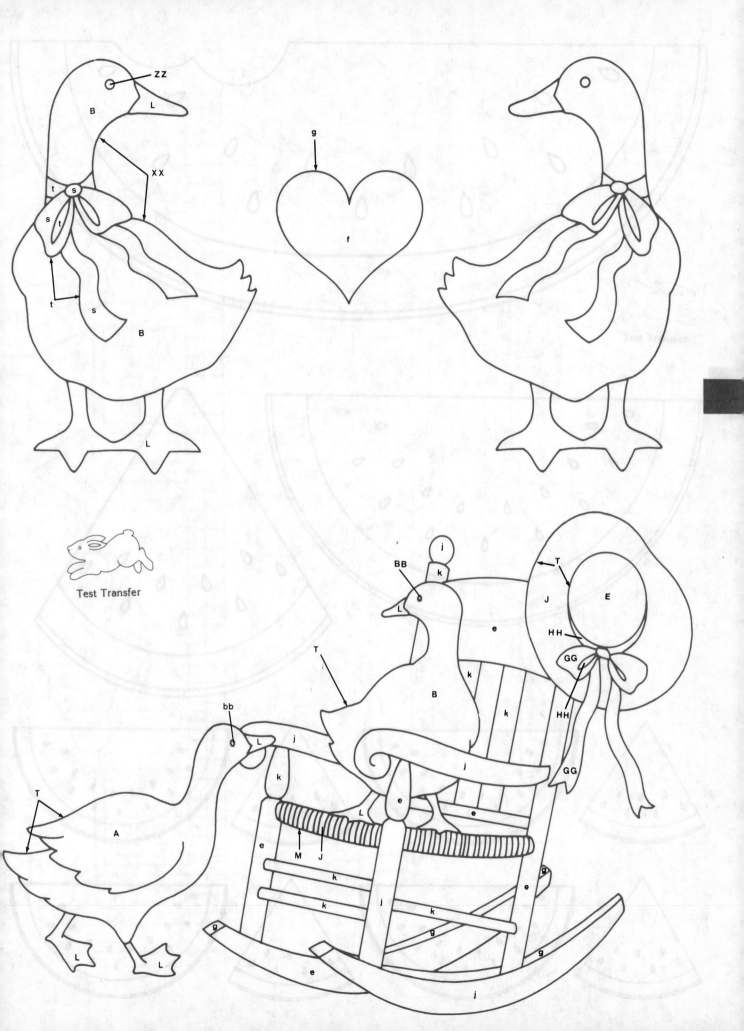

Test Transfer

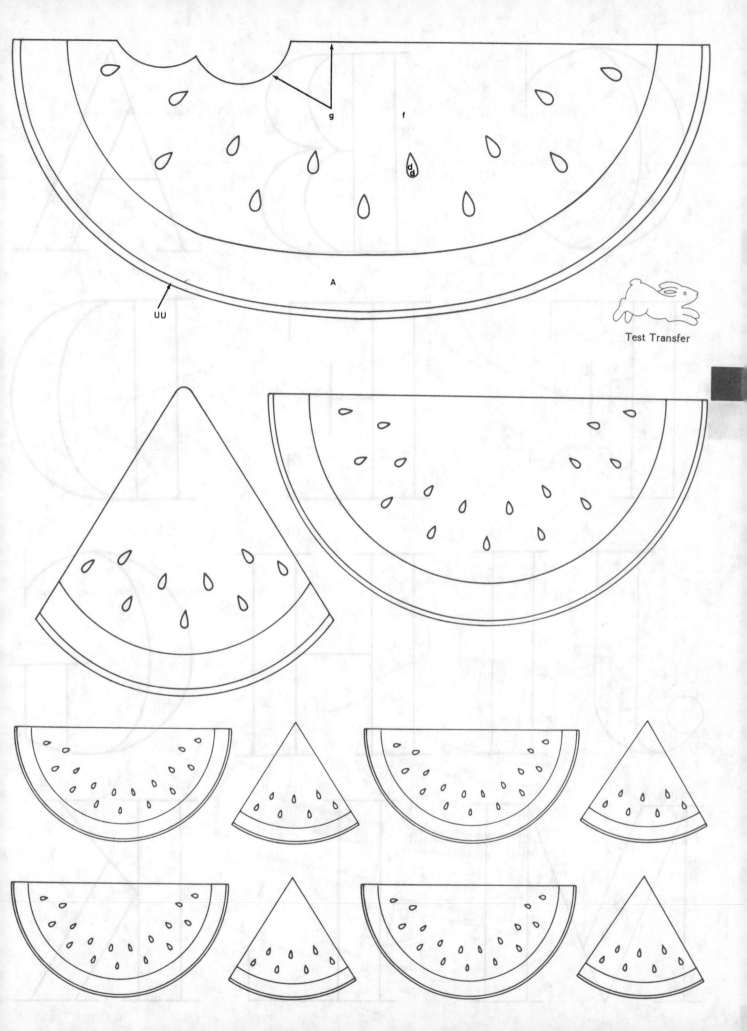

Test Transfer

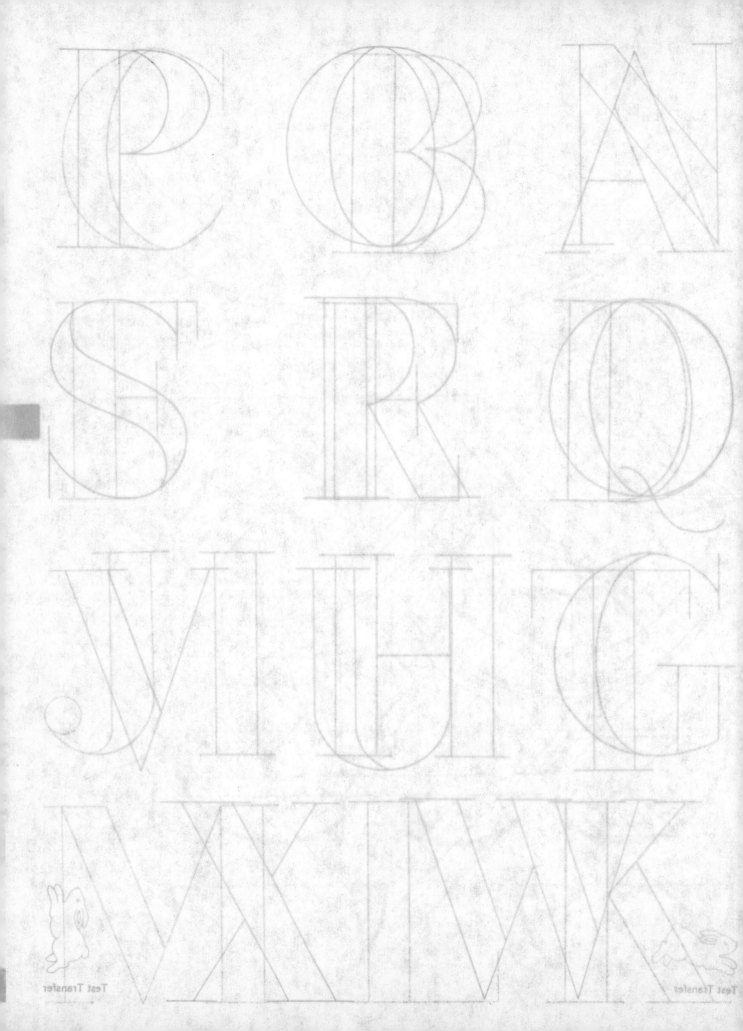

Test Transfer

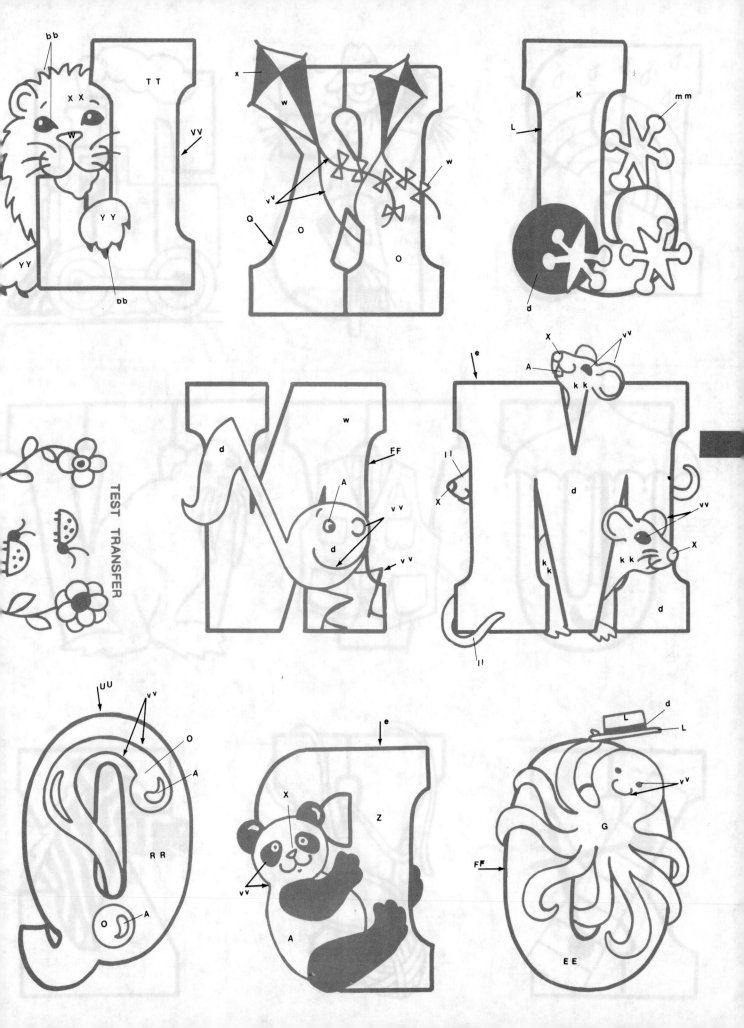

TEST TRANSFER

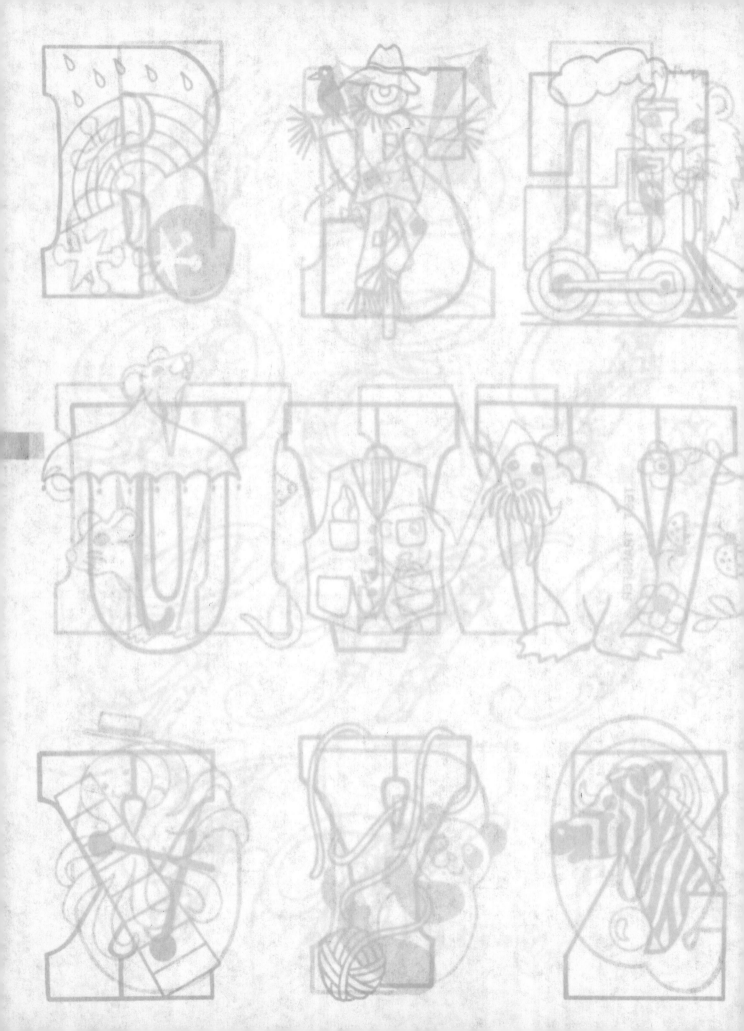

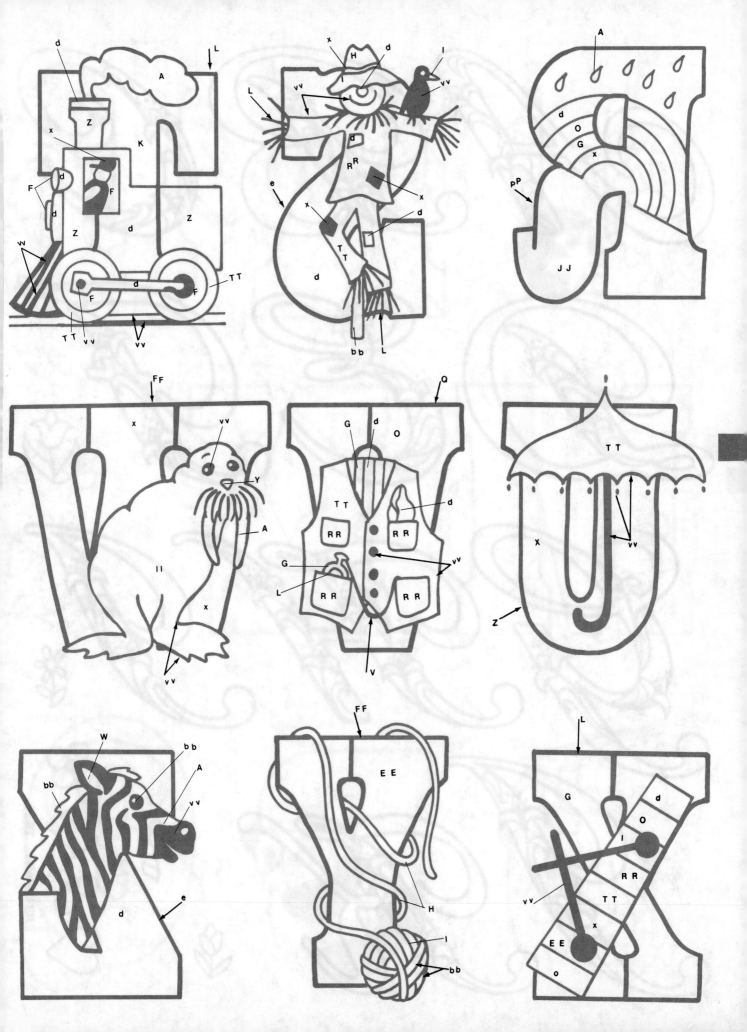

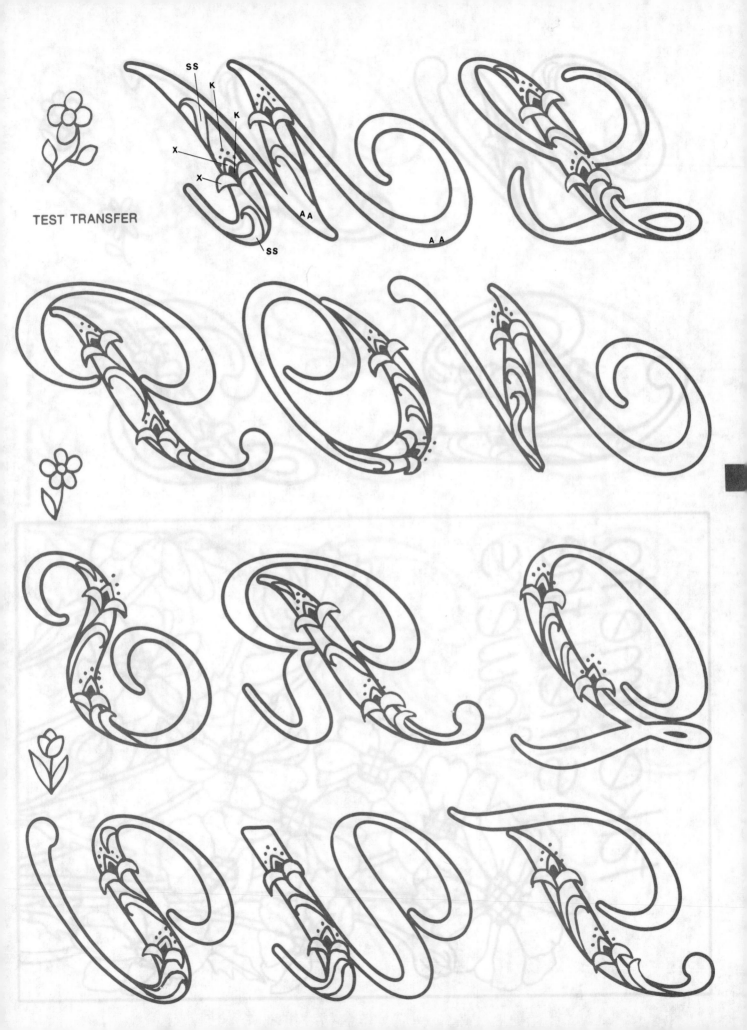

TEST TRANSFER

SS
K
K
X
X
SS
AA
AA

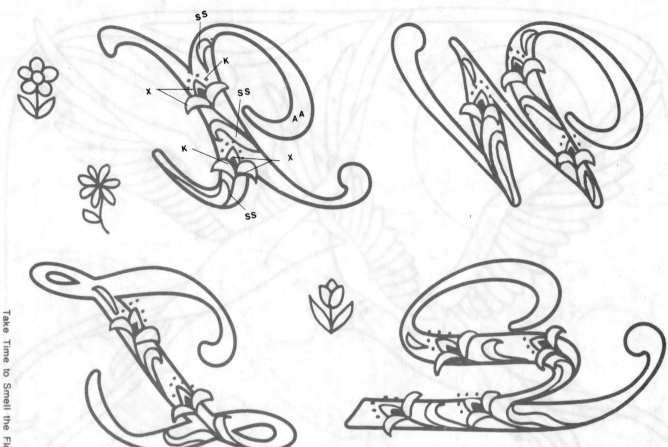

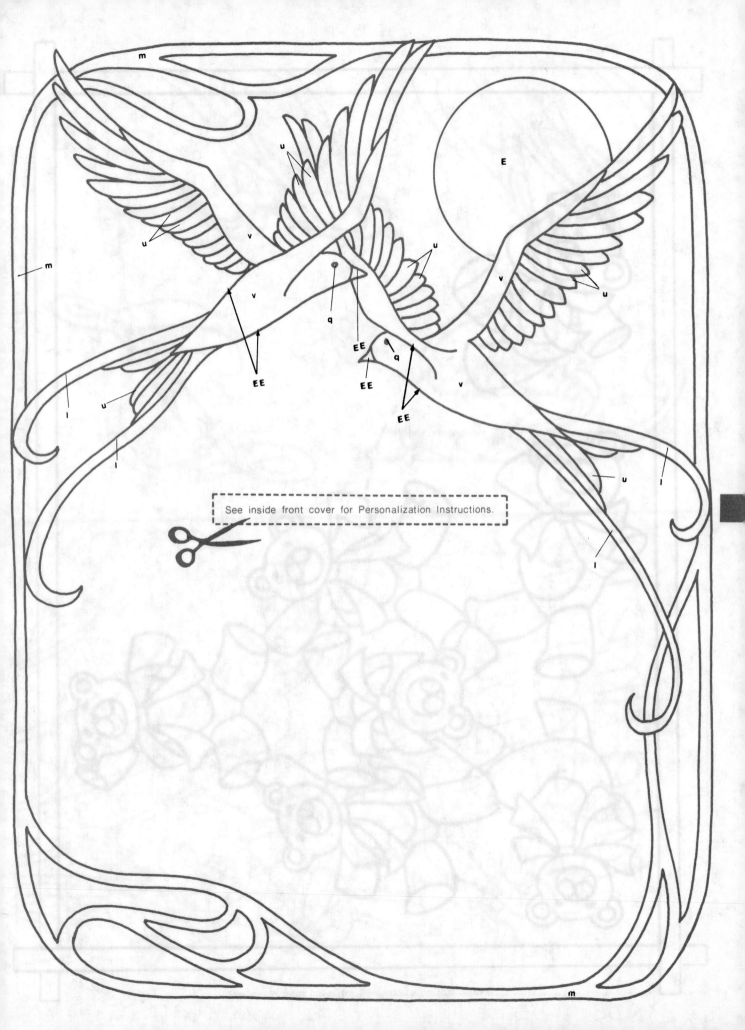

See inside front cover for Personalization Instructions.

See inside front cover for Personalization Instructions.

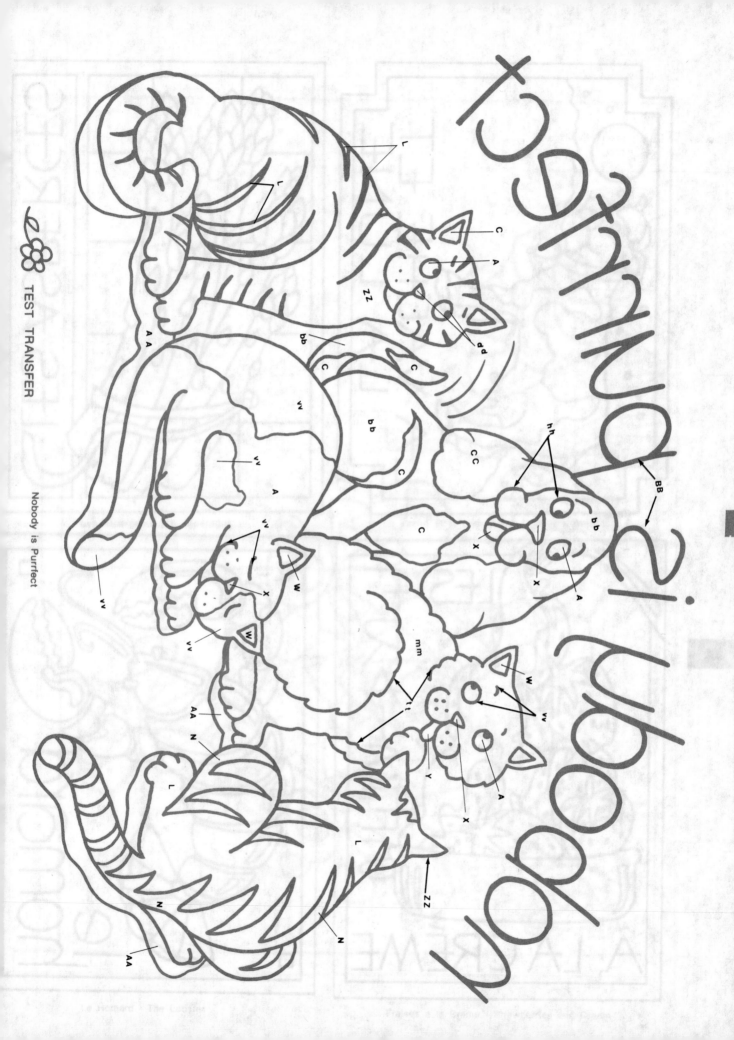

A LA CRÉME

LES ASPERGES

nomicrei

Fraises à la Crème - Strawberries and Cream

Le Homard - The Lobster

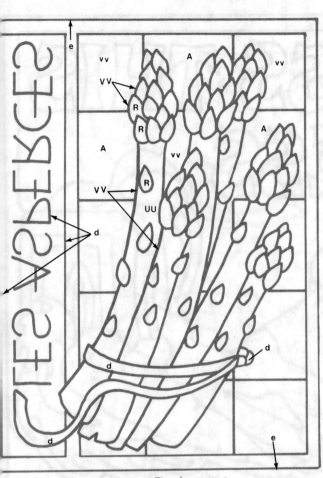

Les Asperges - The Asparagus

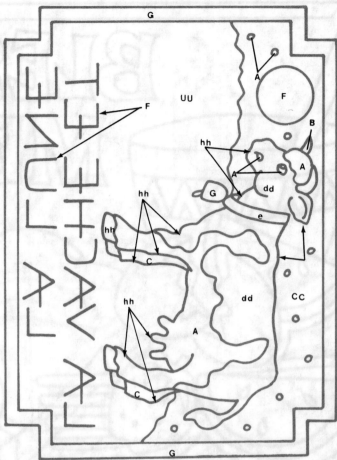

La Vache et la Lune - The Cow and the Moon

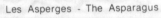

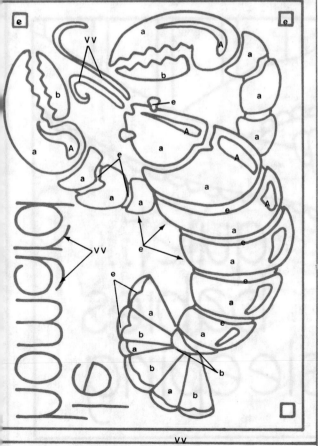

Le Homard - The Lobster

Fraises a la Creme - Strawberries and Cream

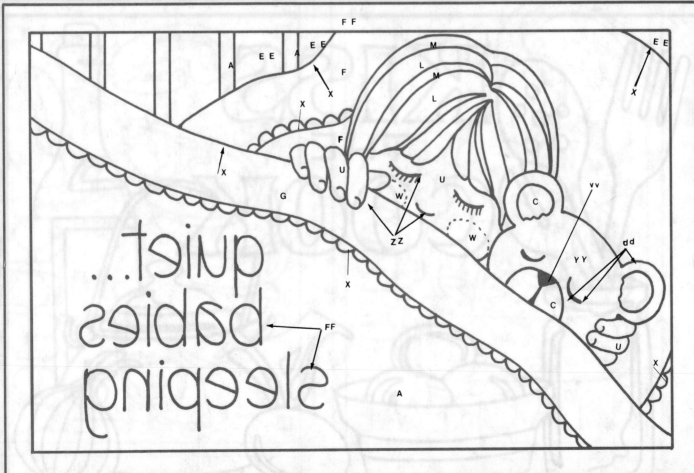

FRIENDSHIP SMOOTHES LIFE'S
UPS AND DOWNS.

Home IT'S NOT SO
EASY
BEING
SMALL

COOKIES

Home Is Where The Heart Is

TEST TRANSFER

MERRY CHRISTMAS

Merry Christmas

HAPPY NEW YEAR

1985

I LOVE YOU

BE MINE

GREEN IS BEAUTIFUL

1776

SHALOM-PEACE

SHALOM

PEACE

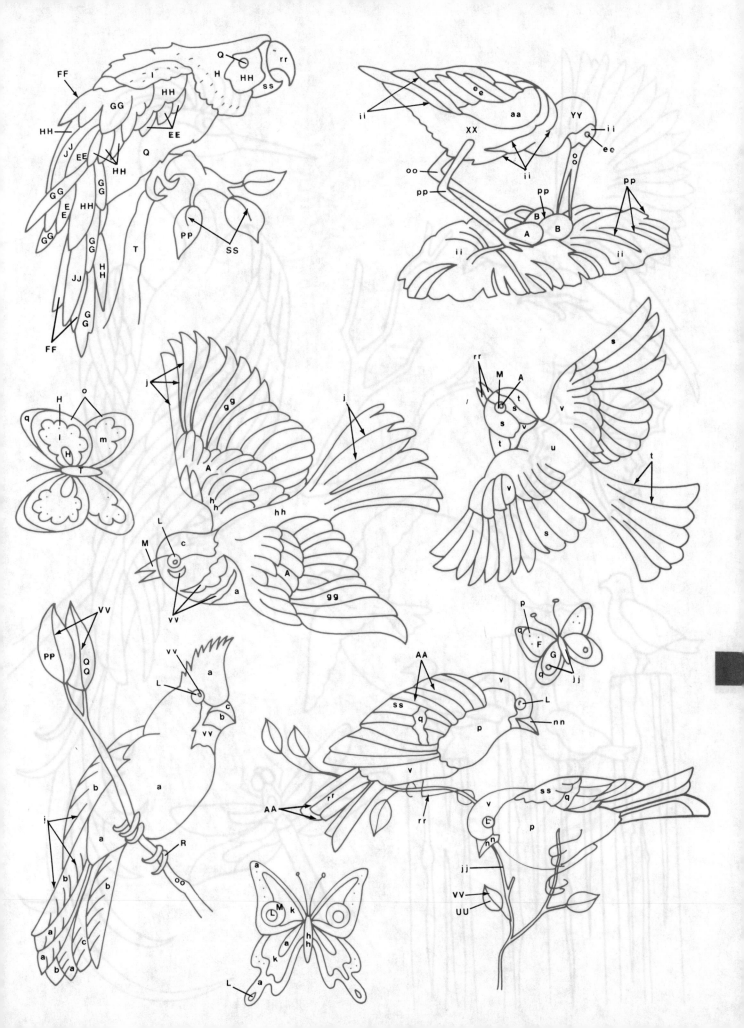

TEST TRANSFER

TEST TRANSFER

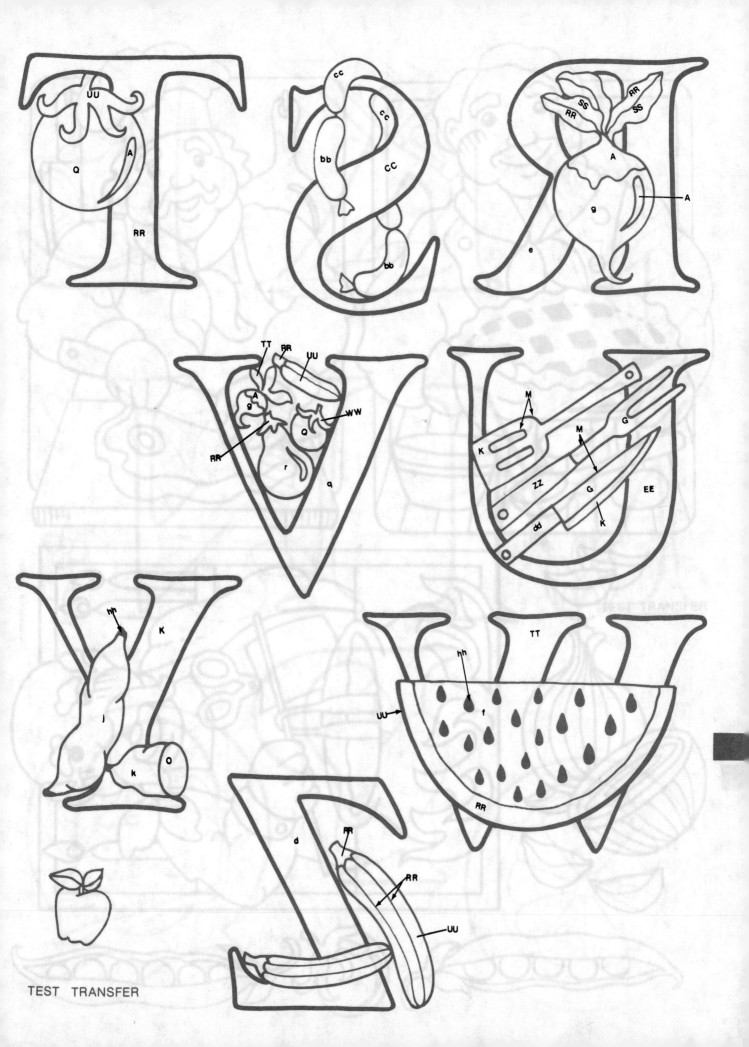

butcher

baker

candlestick maker

TEST TRANSFER

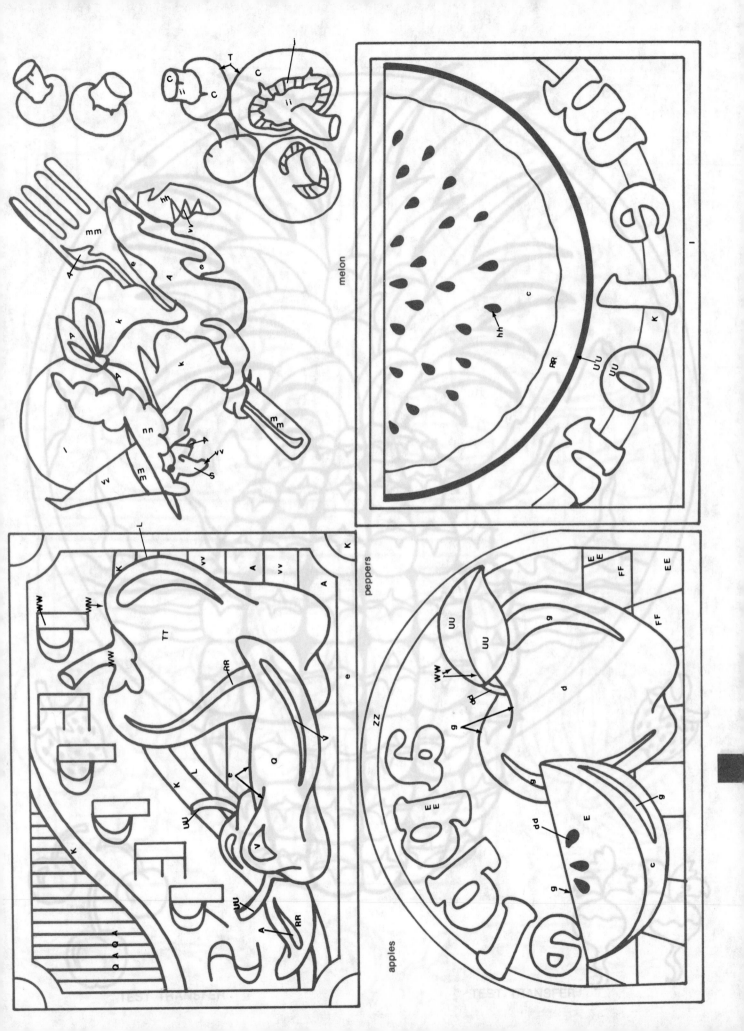

melon

peppers

apples

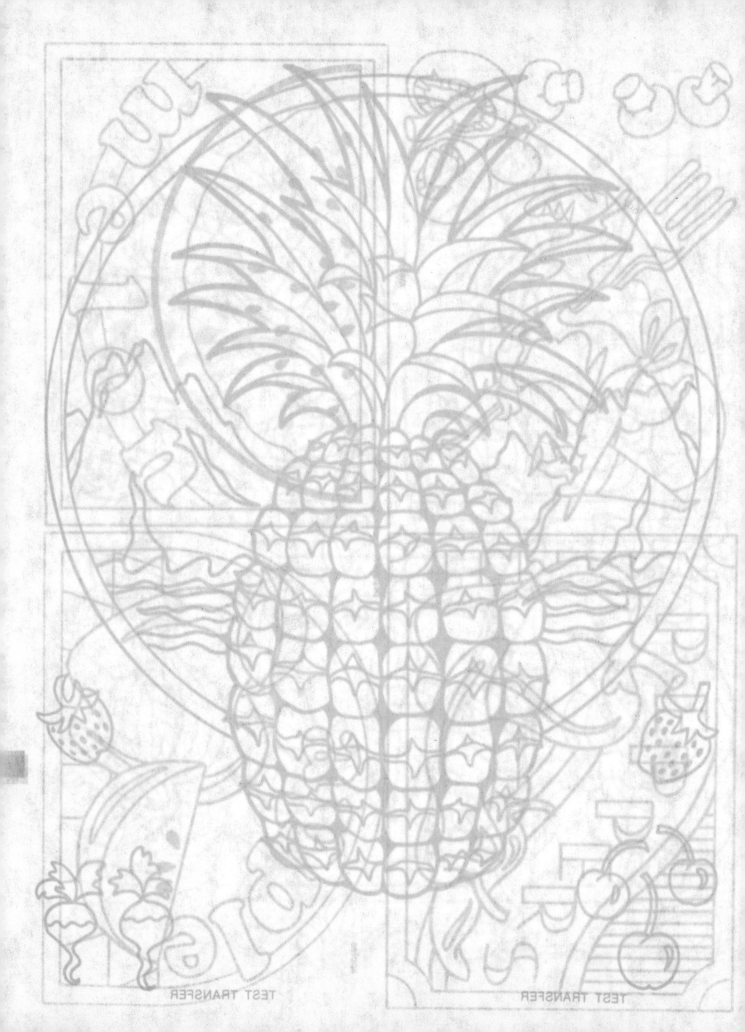

TEST TRANSFER

TEST TRANSFER

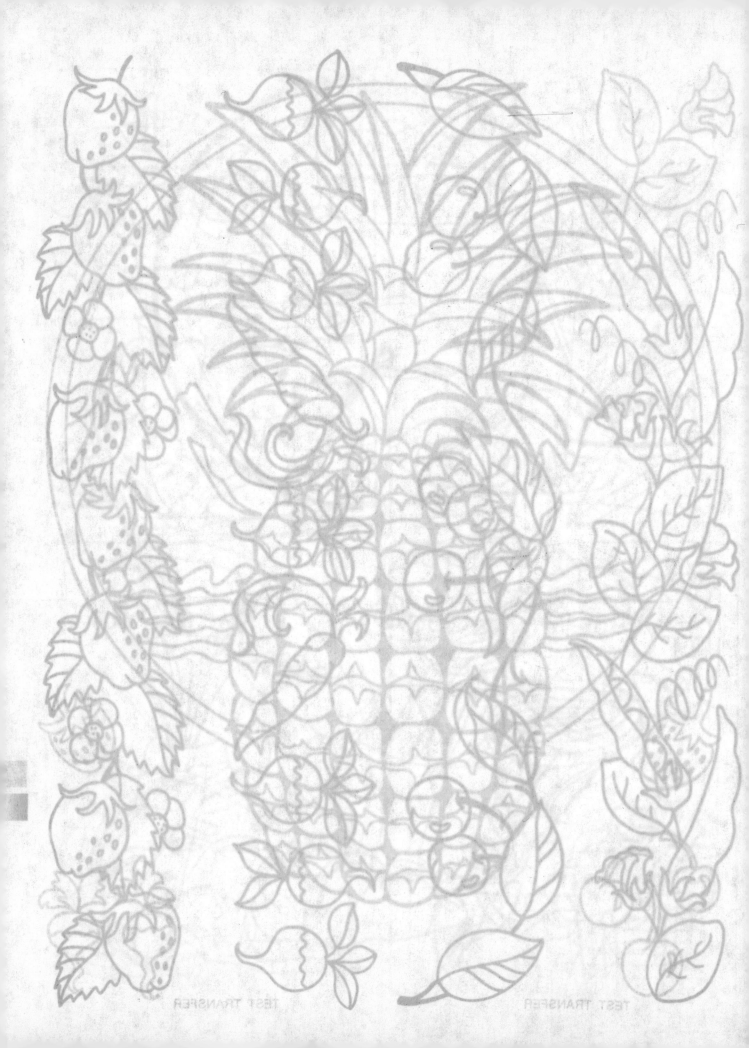

TEST TRANSFER

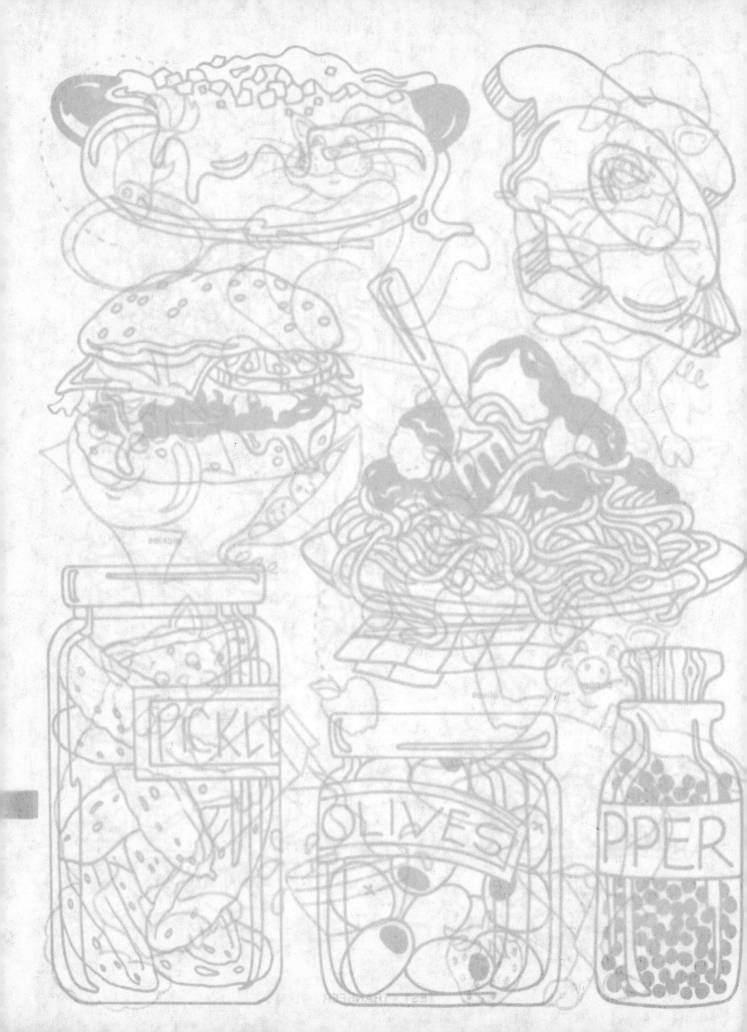

pickles

pepper

olives

January - Snow Drop

February - Violet

March - Primrose

April - Daisy

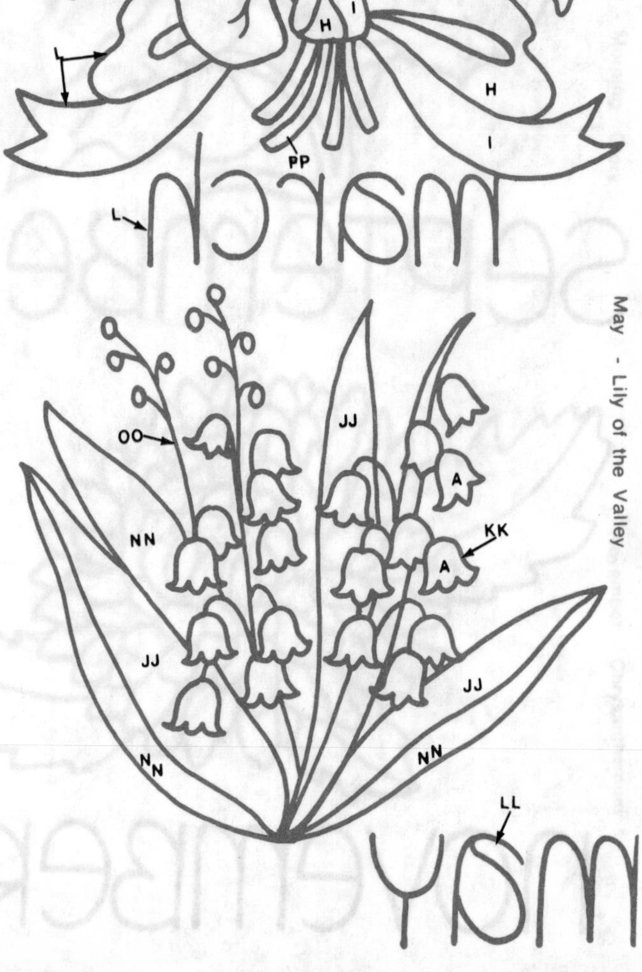

May - Lily of the Valley

June - Wild Rose

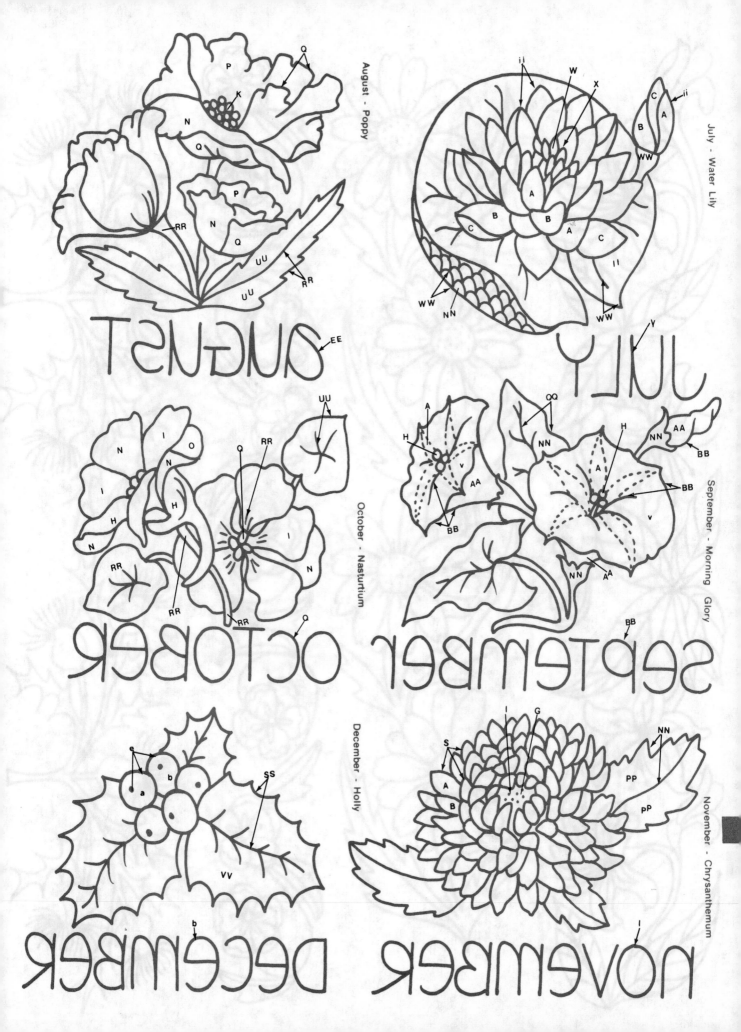

August - Poppy

July - Water Lily

October - Nasturtium

September - Morning Glory

December - Holly

November - Chrysanthemum

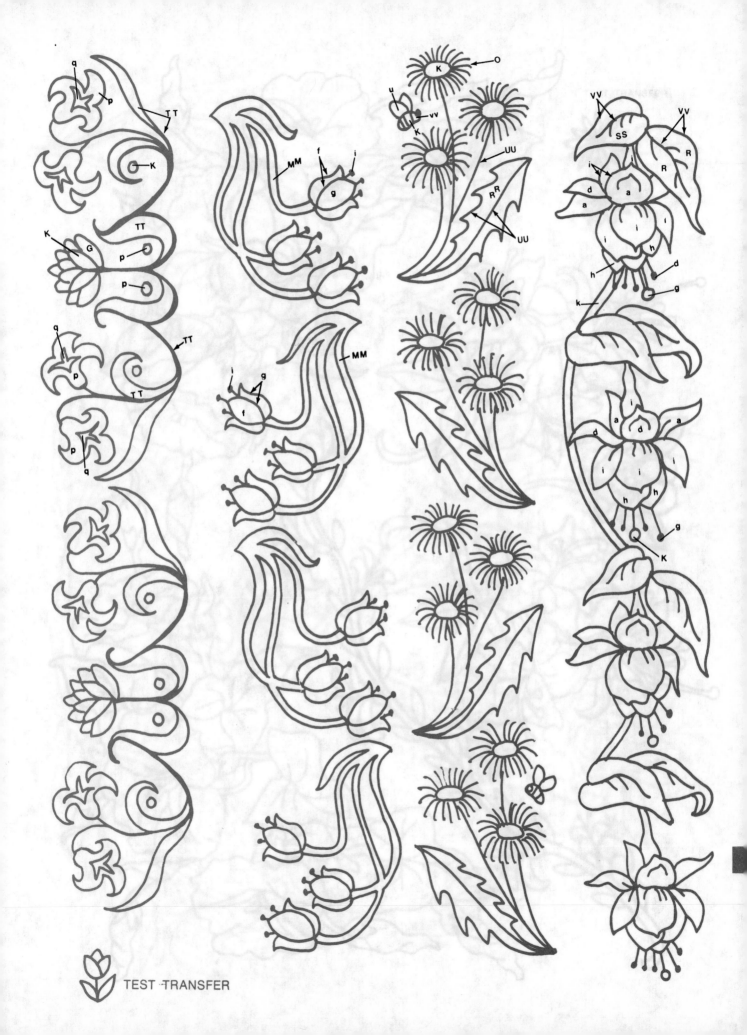

TEST TRANSFER

TEST TRANSFER

TEST TRANSFER

TEST TRANSFER

TEST TRANSFER

TEST TRANSFER

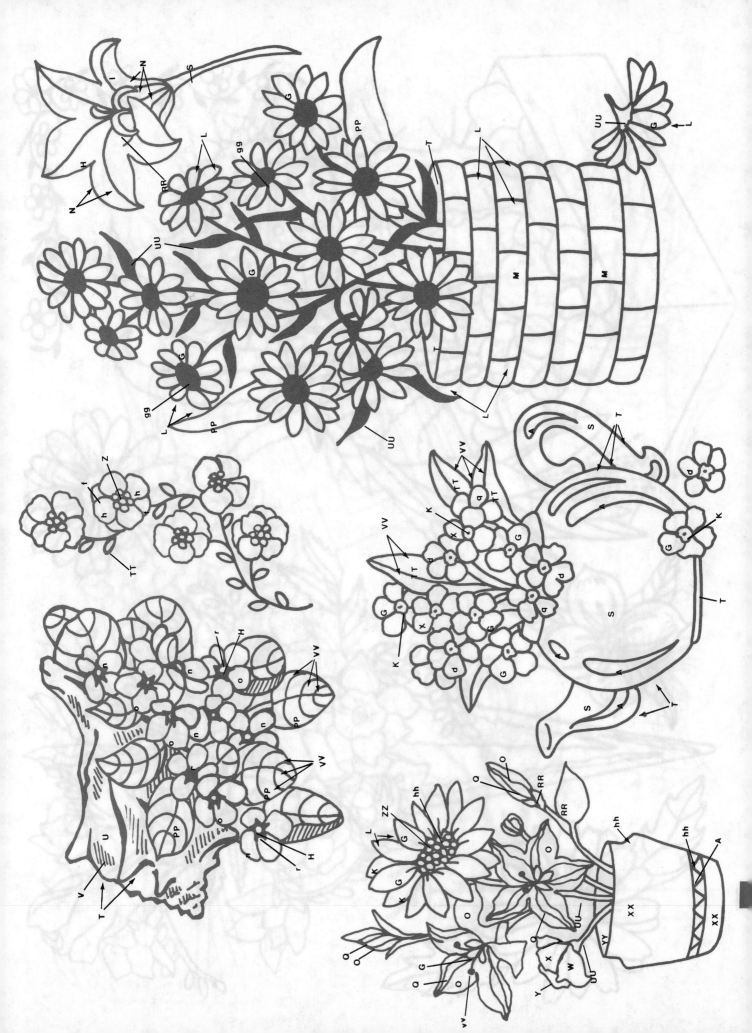

TEST TRANSFER

TEST TRANSFER

TEST
TRANSFER

TEST
TRANSFER

TEST
TRANSFER

TEST
TRANSFER

Quilting

Like so many needlecraft techniques, quilting is centuries old. This technique uses a simple running stitch which anchors a soft, lightweight filler between two layers of fabric. The stitches create a surface design texture.

Iron the transfer design on the upper fabric layer. Layer the three fabrics together, and then simply quilt over the design lines to create a unique item.

Count-less Cross-Stitch

Until you try it, you won't believe how beautiful the results are with this new cross stitch technique! There's no need to follow charts square-by-square—just "color in" areas with cross stitches as you go.

1. Start by ironing a transfer design directly onto No. 14 or 18 Aida evenweave fabric.

2. Using a dark color floss, cover all the design lines with a backstitch. Don't try to work your stitches exactly into the holes of the evenweave; rather, just follow the lines and let the stitches fall where they may.

3. After outlining, fill in with normal cross stitches using half stitches as they fit best near the outlines.

4. Finish the piece by sewing or framing as needed. You'll be amazed how beautifully the evenweave stitches work into the outlines and how fast Count-less Cross-Stitch® goes.

Stenciling

Unique and easy stencils can be made from the designs in THE BIG BOOK to create beautiful and lasting decorations on walls, furniture, floors, baskets and fabric. Use a single motif or repeat a single motif numerous times for a border design. Designs can also be combined to create larger composite motifs.

The transfers can be ironed directly or traced onto stencil paper or traced directly onto mylar, a another common stencil material.

Fabric Painting

Remember the satisfaction of those childhood hours spent coloring when the black-and-white page became a kaleidoscope of color? The same sense of satisfaction and accomplishment can once again become yours with a little fabric, a paint brush and acrylic paints or liquid embroidery pens. Loads of fun, what could be easier, or less expensive?

Simply iron the transfer directly onto the fabric and paint away.